❧ FEELING LIKE SAINTS

FEELING LIKE SAINTS

LOLLARD WRITINGS
AFTER WYCLIF

FIONA SOMERSET

CORNELL UNIVERSITY PRESS
Ithaca and London

First published 2014 by Cornell University Press

Printed in the United States of America

Library of Congress Cataloging-in-Publication Data

Somerset, Fiona, author.
    Feeling like saints : lollard writings after Wyclif / Fiona Somerset.
        pages cm
    Includes bibliographical references and index.
    ISBN 978-0-8014-5281-9 (cloth : alk. paper)
    1. Lollards—Sources. 2. England—Church history—1066–1485. 3. Wycliffe, John, –1384.
I. Title.
    BX4901.3.S66   2014
    284'.3—dc23   2013043186

Cornell University Press strives to use environmentally responsible suppliers and materials to the fullest extent possible in the publishing of its books. Such materials include vegetable-based, low-VOC inks and acid-free papers that are recycled, totally chlorine-free, or partly composed of nonwood fibers. For further information, visit our website at www.cornellpress.cornell.edu.

Cloth printing   10 9 8 7 6 5 4 3 2 1

❧ Contents

❧ ACKNOWLEDGMENTS

For my many interlocutors and readers over the course of the time I have been writing this book: I know how much I have learned from you, and from your published work. There is little room left over in a long book for footnotes. My first draft was replete with descriptions of your work, praise for your contributions to the field, and thanks for your generosity in conversation. Much of that is now gone, but I know my debts, and so do you.

I can at least acknowledge some of them here. First, to institutions. I am grateful to the Social Sciences and Humanities Research Council of Canada for the generous three-year research grant that allowed me to lay the groundwork for this book. Duke University supported me generously with research leaves and grants: I am especially grateful to Maureen Quilligan, Karla Holloway, Houston Baker, Priscilla Wald, Gregson Davis, and Srinivas Aravamudan for their support. A Faculty Book Manuscript Workshop grant from the Franklin Humanities Institute at Duke allowed me to present a full draft of the book to a range of colleagues outside my field: I thank Ian Baucom for administering this grant and chairing the session. The National Humanities Center provided me with a research leave in 2005–6 during which I was able to draft large parts of this book and finish two other books. I thank the marvellous staff and especially the librarians of the center, who brokered many extended interlibrary loans for me. I am grateful to my new colleagues at the University of Connecticut for welcoming me and helping me to negotiate my move without losing research momentum, and to Wayne Franklin for finding me summer research support in 2012. We may all be grateful for a subvention from UCONN's CLAS Book Support Award fund, which assisted with production costs and has reduced the price of the resulting book.

It is a pleasure to thank friends and colleagues, each named only once although some have worn many hats. Those who taught me: Jay Schleusener, Christina von Nolcken, Andy Galloway, Pete Wetherbee, Tom Hill, Anne Hudson, Norman Kretzmann. Collaborators: Nicholas Watson, Jill Havens, Derrick Pitard, Patrick Hornbeck, Steve Lahey. Editors of my work: Margaret

Aston, Colin Richmond, Renate Blumenfeld-Kosinski, Nancy Warren, Larry Scanlon, James Simpson, Helen Barr, Ann Hutchison, Mishtooni Bose, Amy Hollywood, Patricia Beckman, Alexandra Gillespie, Daniel Wakelin, Michael Van Dussen, Pavel Soukup, Caroline Palmer, Helen Spencer. Readers of drafts of this book, in whole or in part: Shannon McSheffrey, John Arnold, John Martin, Robert Swanson, Sarah McNamer, Rob Lutton, Dan Hobbins, Andrew Cole, Sarah Beckwith, Fred Biggs, Barbara Rosenwein. Fellows and helpers: Ralph Hanna, Margaret Connolly, Susan Einbinder, Liz Schirmer, Michael Kuczynski, Michael G. Sargent, Alastair Minnis, Louisa Burnham, Richard Firth Green, Suzanne Conklin Akbari, Wendy Scase, John Thompson, Ruth Nisse, Mary Dove, Henry Ansgar Kelly, Sabrina Corbellini, Maureen Jurkowski, Elisabeth Salter, Andrew Kraebel, Kathleen Kennedy, Matti Peikola, Kate Rudy, Nicole Rice, Amy Appleford, Robyn Malo, Simon Hunt, Vincent Gillespie, Kathryn Kerby-Fulton, Ryan Perry, Stephen Kelly, Margriet Hoogvliet, Ethan Knapp, Mike Johnston, Caroline Bruzelius, Mark Pegg, Lucie Doležalová, Rachel Koopmans, Clare Costley-King'oo, Ian Levy, Zach Stone, Fred Moten, Jehangir Malegam, William Reddy. Students, who are often readers and colleagues as well: Mary Raschko, Matt Irvin, Cord Whitaker, Jack Harding Bell, William Revere, Jim Knowles, David Watt, Heather Mitchell, Sarah McLaughlin, Leah Schwebel. Copyeditor extraordinaire: Michael Cornett.

At Cornell University Press, I thank Peter Potter for his editorial acumen and good advice, as well as Kitty Liu, Karen Hwa, Susan Barnett, and other production staff.

For permission to publish excerpts from manuscripts in their care I gladly acknowledge the Cambridge University Library and the Master and Fellows of Sidney Sussex College and Gonville and Caius College, Cambridge; Lambeth Palace Library; and in Oxford, the Bodleian Library as well as the Master and Fellows of Trinity College. My warm gratitude to the libraries and librarians who have facilitated my research on this book would take pages to detail.

No part of this book has been published before in similar form. However, some claims and some turns of phrase may repeat those made in introducing lollard writings to new audiences in *Wycliffite Spirituality* (*WS*), in a forthcoming article on textual transmission first presented at a comparative conference on religious controversy in Prague, and in a forthcoming contribution to conference proceedings from a comparative conference on fifteenth-century religion in Bochum: "Textual Transmission, Variance, and Religious Identity among Lollard Pastoralia," in *Religious Controversy in Europe, 1378–1536: Textual Transmission and Networks of Readership*, ed. Michael

Van Dussen and Pavel Soukup (Turnhout: Brepols, 2013), 71–104; "Lollards, Devotion, and Knowledge from an English Perspective," in *Die Devotio Moderna*, ed. Iris Kwiatkowski and Jörg Engelbrecht (Münster: Aschendorff, 2013), 141–55. I thank my collaborators, editors, and the audiences for this related work for helping me to hone the final form of the arguments presented here.

🍰 ABBREVIATIONS

Arnold	Thomas Arnold, ed., *Select English Works of Wyclif*, vol. 3 (Oxford, 1871)
BM	Adrian James McCarthy, ed., *Book to a Mother: An Edition with Commentary* (Salzburg: Institut für Anglistik und Amerikanistik, 1981)
CUL	Cambridge University Library
EA	Mary Dove, ed., *The Earliest Advocates of the English Bible: The Texts of the Medieval Debate* (Exeter: University of Exeter Press, 2010)
EETS	Early English Text Society
EV	Earlier Version
EWS	Pamela Gradon and Anne Hudson, eds., *English Wycliffite Sermons*, 5 vols. (Oxford: Clarendon Press, 1983–96)
FEB	Mary Dove, *The First English Bible: The Text and Context of the Wycliffite Versions* (Cambridge: Cambridge University Press, 2007)
FWD	Fiona Somerset, ed., *Four Wycliffite Dialogues*, EETS, o.s. 333 (Oxford: Oxford University Press, 2009)
H 2398	Commentary on the commandments within London, British Library, MS Harley 2398, fols. 73r–106r
HM 148	San Marino, CA, Huntington Library MS HM 148
IPMEP	R. E. Lewis, N. F. Blake, and A. S. G. Edwards, *Index of Printed Middle English Prose* (New York: Garland, 1985)
LALME	Angus McIntosh, M. L. Samuels, and Michael Benskin, *A Linguistic Atlas of Late Mediaeval English*, 4 vols (Aberdeen: Aberdeen University Press, 1985)
LP	Linguistic Profile, given in vol. 1 of *LALME* (see above)
LV	Later Version
Matthew	F. D. Matthew, ed., *The English Works of Wyclif*, rev. ed., EETS, o.s. 74 (London: Kegan Paul, Trench, Trübner, 1902)

MEBS	*Middle English Biblical Summary* in Oxford, Trinity College, MS 93
MED	Hans Kurath, Sherman M. Kuhn, and Robert E. Lewis, eds., *Middle English Dictionary*, 21 vols. (Ann Arbor: University of Michigan Press, 1952–2001); online edition at University of Michigan, http://quod.lib.umich.edu/m/med/
PL	J.-P. Migne, ed., *Patrologiae cursus completus, Series Latina*, 221 vols. (Paris, 1844–91)
PN Arnold I	Commentary on the Pater Noster printed in Arnold, 93–97
PN Arnold II	Commentary on the Pater Noster printed in Arnold, 98–110
PN Matthew	Commentary on the Pater Noster printed in Matthew, 197–202
PR	Anne Hudson, *The Premature Reformation: Wycliffite Texts and Lollard History* (Oxford: Oxford University Press, 1988)
RV1	Revised version 1 of Rolle's *English Psalter*
RV2	Revised version 2 of Rolle's *English Psalter*
RV3	Revised version 3 of Rolle's *English Psalter*
SEWW	Anne Hudson, ed., *Selections from English Wycliffite Writings* (Cambridge: Cambridge University Press, 1978)
SS74	Sermon cycle within Cambridge, Sidney Sussex College, MS 74, fols. 3r–142v
T 245	Ten commandments commentary found in TCD 245, Cambridge, MA, Harvard University, English 738, and York Minster, MS XVI.L.12
TCD 155	Dublin, Trinity College, MS 155
TCD 245	Dublin, Trinity College, MS 245
TWT	Anne Hudson, ed., *Two Wycliffite Texts: The Sermon of William Taylor 1406, The Testimony of William Thorpe 1407*, EETS, o.s. 301 (Oxford: Oxford University Press, 1993)
Visitation E	*Visitation of the Sick*, version E according to Robert Raymo, "Works of Religious and Philosophical Instruction," in *A Manual of the Writings in Middle English, 1050–1500*, vol. 7, edited by J. Burke Severs and Albert E. Hartung (New Haven: Connecticut Academy of Arts and Sciences, 1967), 2255–2378, 2467–2582

WC   Mishtooni Bose and J. Patrick Hornbeck II, eds., *Wycliffite Controversies* (Turnhout: Brepols, 2011)

WS   J. Patrick Hornbeck II, Stephen E. Lahey, and Fiona Somerset, eds. and trans., *Wycliffite Spirituality* (New York: Paulist Press, 2013)

❧ FEELING LIKE SAINTS

Introduction

This book is a study of lollardy, a religious movement associated with the Oxford heresiarch John Wyclif (ca. 1328–84). Maligned by contemporary chroniclers, condemned as heretical, then later celebrated as brave harbingers of the Reformation by protestant historiographers, Wyclif and his followers have been more noised about than read. Wyclif is said to have advocated and perhaps even participated in the translation of the bible into English, to have rejected or questioned the efficacy of the sacraments, especially the eucharist and confession, to have upheld a strictly determinist theory of predestination, and to have argued for the disendowment or abolition of religious orders and a restructuring of the ecclesiastical hierarchy.[1] Lollards, for their part, have been variously blamed or praised for upholding these views or for misunderstanding them, and for dissolving relatively quickly under persecution or persisting in their beliefs up until the 1530s.

Wyclif was a declared a heretic by Gregory XI in 1377, was again censured by the Blackfriars Council in 1382 after he had left Oxford in the previous year, and was posthumously condemned as a heresiarch, the founder of a new heresy, at the Council of Constance in 1415: each of these processes

---

1. For more on the conventional view of Wyclif's thought, see *WS*, 1–6.

produced a list of reported errors and heresies.[2] Wyclif's university followers were pursued in the 1380s, and many of them recanted; concern over
the spread of Wyclif's ideas also brought intensified attention to the pursuit
of heresy in England more generally. Records of the investigation of heresy
from diocese to diocese across the country for the fifteenth and sixteenth
centuries are incomplete but nevertheless reveal inconsistent but continuing
attention to its discovery across this period, with peaks of activity (or of the
preservation of its records) in the early decades of each century.[3] Careful
study of Wyclif's own writings in recent years has done much to sort out
how he developed and revised his views and to disentangle them from his
reputation.[4] However, this is the first book-length study of the lollard movement to do the same for lollards, that is, to investigate what we can know
about them based not on what others said about them but on what they
themselves wrote.

The corpus of extant manuscripts produced somewhere between roughly
1375 and 1530 and containing materials translated, composed, or adapted
by lollard writers is very large. After an initial phase of rapid and apparently highly coordinated production, lollard writings continued to be copied, recopied, adapted, and further developed in a wide range of manuscript
contexts, and for a variety of readers, across the fifteenth and early sixteenth
centuries. The handlist I have compiled includes close to five hundred manuscripts.[5] No religious movement persecuted as a heresy anywhere else in the
history of Christianity has left behind a textual record of anything like this
order of magnitude.[6] So it is rather surprising that no attempt has been made
to develop an intrinsic account of lollard belief and practice centered on the
movement's own writings, rather than on the extrinsic accounts of lollardy

---

2. For an introduction to Wyclif's life, successive condemnations, and later reputation, see
Stephen E. Lahey, *John Wyclif* (Oxford: Oxford University Press, 2009), 16–31.

3. For the methods and conduct of the inquisition in England, see Ian Forrest, *The Detection of
Heresy in Late Medieval England* (Oxford: Clarendon Press, 2005). On the beliefs of defendants, see
Patrick Hornbeck, *What Is a Lollard? Dissent and Belief in Late Medieval England* (Oxford: Oxford
University Press, 2010).

4. See among others Ian Christopher Levy, *Holy Scripture and the Quest for Authority at the End of
the Middle Ages* (Notre Dame, IN: University of Notre Dame Press, 2012); Levy, ed., *A Companion to
John Wyclif, Late Medieval Theologian* (Leiden: Brill, 2006); Lahey, *John Wyclif*; Anne Hudson, *Studies in
the Transmission of Wyclif's Writings* (Aldershot: Ashgate, 2008).

5. David Watt, and the Social Sciences and Humanities Research Council of Canada (who
funded his research assistantship as well as my research), helped a great deal with the initial compilation of this list. The newest handlist of the manuscripts of the biblical translation appears in *FEB*,
281–306.

6. On how later medieval heresies made use of books, see Peter Biller and Anne Hudson, eds.,
Heresy and Literacy, 1000–1530 (Cambridge: Cambridge University Press, 1994).

provided by heresy trial records, hostile chroniclers, and opponents of Wyclif and his followers.[7] It is as if we were to begin our research on Franciscans by reading antifraternal writings or base our study of Christianity on what Muslims affected by the Crusades have to say about Christians. How to define the corpus of lollard writings other than in the terms offered by extrinsic accounts is a question that presents some difficulties but not insuperable ones; it requires time and care, of a kind I will soon explain, but that is no reason not to make the effort.

This is not to say that the lollard corpus has been ignored. Most historians of late medieval religious culture in England now include lollard writings in their evidentiary base. However, even studies that devote sustained attention to lollard writings tend to use them to confirm or elaborate on what hostile sources tell them were the central tenets of lollard belief, not to question whether those hostile observers had it right. Where lollard writings do not confirm what the movement's opponents tell us that lollards said and thought and did, scholars usually conclude that what they are reading is not lollard after all, but more broadly reformist, part of an intermediary "grey area" between lollardy and orthodoxy, even "entirely orthodox."[8] Meanwhile, characteristics strongly prevalent among lollard writings have received surprisingly little attention, even characteristics that show Wyclif's direct influence and that reveal a considered intervention in late medieval

---

7. Fine studies that begin from the extrinsic accounts of lollard heresy have been completed: see John A. F. Thomson's *Later Lollards, 1414–1520* (Oxford: Oxford University Press, 1965), a survey of the heresy trial records; Hornbeck, *What Is a Lollard?*; and Forrest, *Detection of Heresy*. The foundational research and editing of lollard writings without which this book could not have been written also deserves high praise—especially for Margaret Aston and for Anne Hudson, whose *PR* provides a survey of lollard writings and the books in which they appear. Where Hudson seeks continuities between hostile accounts of lollardy and what lollards themselves wrote, I will privilege the evidence of lollard writings themselves, weighing extrinsic evidence more lightly, as explained more fully below.

8. The concept of the grey area is an important one, not least because it has encouraged scholars in the field to think past the black and white of "heresy" versus "orthodoxy": see, for example, Jill C. Havens, "Shading the Grey Area: Determining Heresy in Middle English Texts," in *Text and Controversy from Wyclif to Bale: Essays in Honour of Anne Hudson*, ed. Helen Barr and Ann M. Hutchison (Turnhout: Brepols, 2005), 337–52. However, it also reinforces these opposed poles as points of reference on a stable spectrum: any grey stands between a white and a black. Hornbeck, in contrast, foregrounds the importance of doctrinal variety and development (see esp. *What Is a Lollard?*, 10–22). But even he allows trial records and condemnations to set the agenda for his inquiry, with the result that his categories for variation sometimes obscure broader commonalities between the writings he surveys. For other efforts to rethink the opposed categories of "heresy" versus "orthodoxy" by looking beyond trial records to other documentary sources, see Shannon McSheffrey, "Heresy, Orthodoxy, and English Vernacular Religion, 1480–1525," *Past & Present* 186 (2005): 47–80; Robert Lutton, *Lollardy and Orthodox Religion in Pre-Reformation England* (Woodbridge: Boydell and Brewer, 2006); Maureen Jurkowski, "Lollardy and Social Status in East Anglia," *Speculum* 82 (2007): 120–52; Anne Hudson, "Who Is My Neighbour?," in *WC*, 79–96.

academic debates and their impact on the religious instruction of wider audiences. How these characteristics of lollard writings might contribute to new efforts to understand fifteenth-century religious culture on its own terms, rather than as a sort of hinge or intermezzo in larger narratives of the coming of the Reformation, the waning of the Middle Ages, or the birth of modernity, remains unexplored.[9] Nor have we yet taken advantage of the ways that the extensive overlaps with and mutual influence between lollard and mainstream writings might inform our understanding of late medieval English religious culture more generally, throwing into sharp relief the efforts some later writers made to distance themselves from this common ground.[10] Beyond England, we have not considered how these writings might throw new light on the intellectual and pastoral milieu of the theologian/reformer Jean Gerson, or the fortunes of the various new devout in communities and jurisdictions across the Low Countries and what is now western Germany, or the transmission of devotional as well as dissident English writings between England and Bohemia, or the extraordinary attention paid to Wyclif and Jan Hus at the Council of Constance.[11] I will not be pursuing these broader transnational comparisons in this book, where I have enough to do, but I hope to be opening the door to them.

Selective readings of lollard writings often attend only to their most polemical passages, or what is most heretical in the terms set by bishops seeking out deviant belief and practice, or what is most similar to later protestant views. These strategies emerge from the controversies that have beset the history of religion in England, amid which lollards are on the one hand presented as strident extremists of little lasting importance and, on the other, as

---

9. John Van Engen, "Multiple Options: The World of the Fifteenth-Century Church," *Church History* 77 (2008): 257–84.

10. A survey of late medieval English religious culture that signally misses the opportunity to consider overlaps and mutual influence between mainstream (for this author, "orthodox") and lollard writings is Eamon Duffy, *The Stripping of the Altars: Traditional Religion in England, c. 1400–1580*, 2nd ed. (New Haven, CT: Yale University Press, 2005). This second edition includes a "Preface to the Second Edition" justifying the author's decision to pay little attention to lollardy, xiii–xxxvii.

11. Some scholars of Wyclif have begun to consider his writings in a broader European context: see especially Michael Van Dussen, *From England to Bohemia: Heresy and Communication in the Later Middle Ages* (Cambridge: Cambridge University Press, 2012); Levy, *Holy Scripture and the Quest for Authority*, and Levy, "A Contextualised Wyclif: *Magister Sacrae Paginae*," in *WC*, 33–57; Kantik Ghosh, who also considers a few of the more academic Wycliffite writings, in "Wycliffite 'Affiliations': Some Intellectual-Historical Perspectives," in *WC*, 13–32; and Ghosh, "Logic and Lollardy," *Medium Aevum* 76 (2007): 251–67. See also Kathryn Kerby-Fulton, "Eciam Lollardi," in *Voices in Dialogue: Reading Women in the Middle Ages*, ed. Linda Olson and Kathryn Kerby-Fulton (Notre Dame, IN: University of Notre Dame Press, 2005), 261–78; Kerby-Fulton, *Books under Suspicion: Censorship and Tolerance of Revelatory Writing in Late Medieval England* (Notre Dame, IN: University of Notre Dame Press, 2006).

evidence that the key points of controversy in the English Reformation had been of long-standing concern. But these strategies may also emerge from an uncertainty, even among those eager to engage with the writings in question, about how we might identify what is lollard about them.[12] Only a handful of lollard works can be securely attached to specific writers or readers recorded in heresy trial proceedings. Only a few can be dated with any accuracy, and only because they refer unambiguously to events of historical record. While the Middle English dialects found in extant copies of lollard writings tell us something about where they circulated, this sort of evidence is more useful for linking texts with one another than it is for pinpointing where a given text was written.[13] So it is difficult to be sure where you are in the lollard corpus, and it is even harder to know where its edges are.

This uncertainty can be traced far and wide through scholarship on late medieval English religious writings. None of the following, for example, are distinguishing features of lollardy: advocacy or even production of biblical material in translation; specific doctrinal claims about the eucharist, the efficacy of confession, or indeed any of the sacraments; a specific attitude toward friars, monks, or the secular clergy; or certitude about one's own salvation or that of others. The first three vary within as well as beyond lollardy, while the fourth is affirmed (to my knowledge) by no one. Yet these criteria have commonly been deployed in attempting to assess whether a text is lollard or not—sometimes in genuine confusion, at other times in justification of a firm if perhaps not fully self-examined conviction. The results suggest that both those in search of reasons to discount the evidence of these texts and those genuinely curious about them are often not sure how they should go about investigating their affiliations with lollardy.

My method of investigating lollard affiliations is relatively simple to describe. I begin with what might seem an obvious and enabling assumption: that lollard writings are influenced by the writings of John Wyclif, often in ways that attention to questions asked in heresy trials and lists of condemned propositions may have obscured. I have based my understanding of the core characteristics of early lollard writings on translations of works

---

12. Several of the difficulties mentioned in what follows are also addressed in "The Problem of Sources," in *PR*, 9–32.

13. For a brief introduction to Middle English dialectal spelling, and to the complications of using the *LALME*, see Simon Horobin, "Mapping the Words," in *The Production of Books in England, 1350–1500*, ed. Alexandra Gillespie and Daniel Wakelin (Cambridge: Cambridge University Press, 2011), 59–78. See also Anne Hudson, ed., *Two Revisions of Rolle's English Psalter Commentary and the Related Canticles*, 2 vols. (of 3 projected, the last to be published as o.s. 343), EETS, o.s. 340–41 (Oxford: Oxford University Press, 2012–13), 1:lxxviii–lxxx.

by Wyclif and on writings that cite Wyclif's works heavily or claim him as an influence; here it is easiest to see what lollard writers took from Wyclif and how they adapted him. These works include the *Five Questions on Love*, the *Dialogue between Reson and Gabbyng*, the *Floretum*—a sort of Wycliffite encyclopedia of key topics—and its shorter version the *Rosarium*, and the *English Wycliffite Sermons*. The *Floretum*, *Rosarium*, and *English Wycliffite Sermons* are three of the six collaboratively produced and rapidly copied large-scale projects that Anne Hudson, among others, has associated with the early lollard movement and studied extensively in recent years; the others are the interpolated versions of Richard Rolle's *English Psalter*, which shares many core characteristics with the works already named, and the Wycliffite Bible and *Glossed Gospels*.[14] These last two works reveal lollard characteristics more indirectly, since they are respectively a translation of the whole bible and a set of verse-by-verse commentaries on the gospels compiled from patristic and mainstream sources. Nonetheless, the Wycliffite Bible and *Glossed Gospels* have developed and confirmed my understanding of what biblical passages and what authors lollard writers found most interesting, and the prologues and some further glosses attached to them in some manuscripts exhibit many core characteristics of lollard writings.[15]

Working outward from this core group of writings that we can link firmly with Wyclif's influence, I have proceeded more cautiously but found many other writings that exhibit strong similarities with the ones already described. Some of them are writings that appear in the small selection of manuscripts containing several strongly polemical works that were printed by Arnold and Matthew.[16] Some, such as the *Thirty-Seven Conclusions*, are extant in fewer copies than rapidly copied large-scale projects like the *English Wycliffite Sermons* but share many of their characteristics.[17] Some can be securely dated after 1400, some twenty to thirty years after Wyclif's death, but are nonetheless strongly similar to earlier writings that translate or cite

---

14. On these works and their production, see most recently Anne Hudson, "Five Problems in Wycliffite Texts and a Suggestion," *Medium Aevum* 80 (2011): 301–24. See also Henry Hargreaves, "Popularising Biblical Scholarship: The Role of the Wycliffite *Glossed Gospels*," in *The Bible and Medieval Culture*, ed. Willem Lourdaux and D. Verhelst (Louvain: Louvain University Press, 1979), 171–89; Christina von Nolcken, ed., *The Middle English Translation of the "Rosarium theologie": A Selection* (Heidenberg: Carol Winter Universitätsverlag, 1979); *EWS*; *FEB*; Hudson, *Two Revisions of Rolle's English Psalter Commentary*.

15. For critical editions of these prologues, see *EA*. Some discussion of glosses appears in *FEB*.

16. See the brief lists of manuscripts in Arnold, xiii–xv, and Matthew, vii–viii.

17. J. Forshall, ed., *Remonstrance against Romish Corruptions in the Church* (London, 1851): the title *Thirty-Seven Conclusions* is now preferred. A shorter, Latin version including the conclusions only is printed in H. F. B. Compston, ed., "The Thirty-Seven Conclusions of the Lollards," *English Historical Review* 26 (1911): 738–49.

Wyclif: these include the *Testimony of William Thorpe*, *Letter of Richard Wyche*, the sermon *Omnis plantacio*, and the *Tractatus de oblacione iugis sacrificii*. To help me in delineating what lollards shared with mainstream religion and where they departed from it, I have maintained a control group (so to speak) of writings that lollards responded to or adapted in their own writings but that show no signs of influence from lollardy in return—in most cases they pre-date it by at least a half century. These include Robert of Gretham's *Miroir*, Edmund of Abingdon's *Speculum ecclesie*, the *Lay Folks' Catechism*, Richard Rolle's *Form of Living* and *English Psalter*, the *Speculum Christiani*, the *Cloud of Unknowyng*, and the *Memoriale credencium*.

Proceeding on the basis of these principles has led me to conclusions that may surprise some readers. Rather than monotonously strident and hyper-intellectual, lollard writings vary widely in style and tone, employ a range of genres, and are often self-consciously well crafted. Rather than ignoring the pastoral needs of ordinary readers, lollard writers were often closely attentive to them. Rather than lacking in feeling and imagination, lollard writings can-not stop talking about them—indeed, showing their readers how to feel dif-ferently, and how to imagine their world otherwise, is at least as important to them as telling their readers what they need to know and to do. Rather than differing starkly in style, tone, and purpose from mainstream religious writ-ings, and sharing in none of their aspirations, lollard pastoral and devotional works are often not all that different from the mainstream works that they adapt or respond to in order to bring out their characteristic emphases. And rather than being especially doubtful instances of lollard writing, it is often the devotional and instructional writings whose lollardy has been most dis-puted or even denied, as for example the *Lanterne of Liȝt*, the *Lollard Sermons*, *The Two Ways*, or *Book to a Mother*, that most closely follow the concerns of those early lollard writings that draw heavily on Wyclif.

Still, there are also writings that follow the concerns of early lollard writ-ings less closely or even modify them, and these are no less worthy of at-tention. Tracing the sometimes more attenuated spread of Wyclif's ideas through miscellaneous volumes consisting mainly of instructional and de-votional writings can aid us in tracking the spread and influence of lollard thought and in analysing how readers responded to it. It is not at all easy to trace changes in lollard views over time or variations between regions given that lollard writings are so difficult to assign to a person or date or region. But it will become clear that there are topics where a range of views is ex-pressed, even if we cannot date or place them precisely, and others where there is very close consensus. Readers new to the field, rather than steeped in its controversies, may prefer to flip to the Conclusion for my summary account of the most characteristic emphases of lollard writings before they read further. The place to begin, however, is with the manuscripts in which lollard writings appear.

The Textual Culture of Lollard Writings

Among the nearly five hundred manuscripts containing lollard writings, about 250 contain all or part of the bible translation, about 50 are mainly biblical scholarship and commentary and summary of various kinds, about 50 are reference works, most in Latin, about 50 consist largely of sermons, around 50 are miscellaneous volumes focused on religious instruction or devotion, and around 40 contain polemical or controversial pieces, usually alongside pastoral or devotional works. This rough count serves only to give readers a sense of the proportional makeup of the corpus.[18] It cannot convey what readers familiar with manuscript culture will already be anticipating, to some degree, but what readers accustomed to modern printed books will not realize: how widely these books vary, even in cases where they are, or contain, copies of the same text.[19]

All manuscript books were written by hand, of course, a process that always introduces variation, if only the mechanical errors in copying, minor adjustments in syntax, substitutions of simple for difficult words, and spelling variations that are common in Middle English manuscripts more broadly. Texts were copied onto sheets of parchment (occasionally paper) that were then folded into quires and often assembled into larger booklets (a booklet is a unit within a book containing one or more quires) that might circulate independently and be used for further copying, then perhaps be bound together with others into books. The processes by which texts find their way into books, and the content and appearance of those books, vary more widely than readers of modern printed books might expect. Some writers of books were professional scribes: persons whose main business it was to write documents and books. They often copied books together, working simultaneously on different sections and checking one another's work. In this kind of textual culture, accuracy and consistency were highly valued. Books were often large, made with high-quality parchment, lavishly decorated, even illustrated: presentation copies, or books made lectern-size for public reading. However,

---

18. More detailed descriptive cataloguing will be the collaborative labor of years, eventually to be published online.

19. For an introduction to Middle English manuscript books, see further Kathryn Kerby-Fulton, Maidie Hilmo, and Linda Olson, *Opening Up Middle English Manuscripts: Literary and Visual Approaches* (Ithaca, NY: Cornell University Press, 2012).

while writing a book by hand demands time, materials, effort, and skill, it is an activity open to many other kinds of writer beyond the professional scribe—students, preachers, members of religious orders, merchants—who have many other kinds of purposes in making a book.[20]

So it is that books containing Middle English come in a wide array of sizes and shapes and formats, from tiny, cheap discolored parchment books with misshapen pages, no ruling, and minimal attention to layout and decoration, to closely written, highly abbreviated Latin volumes with a booklet of Middle English slipped in, to luxury hand-size volumes for personal devotion, to large assemblages of texts crammed together with little concern for aesthetic appeal. One person might copy materials into a single volume over a considerable period of time and, if a less practiced writer, may produce variations in handwriting that can be confused with the work of multiple scribes. Volumes might contain one text, or texts that are closely related in genre or theme, yet individuals or groups wishing to collect their disparate interests within the same covers might instead produce extraordinarily miscellaneous volumes, where for example recipes rub shoulders with prayers. Such miscellaneous volumes might instead, however, be the result of haphazard combining of booklets or accretions added in margins or on blank leaves over an extended period of time. Most importantly for an understanding of lollard textual culture, the contents of the texts themselves, as well as their writers, the formats of their books, and the ways those books were made, are more variable than print culture might lead us to expect. In some situations, for some kinds of texts, the copying errors and incidental variations normal in hand copying even by trained scribes are accompanied by more drastic and often more deliberate kinds of textual change.

The ways in which texts change when they are copied give us evidence of what we might call the textual culture in which they are circulated. Variance between texts can help us discover how writers and readers interacted, how and in what ways accuracy was valued, and what sorts of processes of composition, performance, recording, reception, adaptation, and intervention were involved in their creation. A number of recent studies closely attentive to the specific conditions of production and circulation in local textual cultures reveal to us the variety of ways that variance between texts, just as much as careful consistency in their reproduction, can provide evidence of deliberate,

---

20. For attention to writers of books other than professional scribes, see Jean-Pascal Pouzet, "Book Production outside Commercial Contexts," and Erik Kwakkel, "Commercial Organization and Economic Innovation," both in Gillespie and Wakelin, *Production of Books in England*, 212–38 and 173–91.

collaborative effort, of the forging and development of social bonds, rather than merely of careless inconsistency in copying.[21] Thus, Keith Busby shows that Chrétien's romances were copied with careful attention to preserving scansion, rhyme, the sense of the text, and the course of the narrative: a better term for the minor alterations in syntax or vocabulary that he finds among copies of would be "micro-variance." In the continuations of Chrétien's tales, in contrast, rivals and imitators give their creativity free play: stories are given new episodes and developed in different ways.[22] This and other examples suggest that variance is conditioned by, and can give us insight into, specific circumstances in the textual culture in which writings are produced. And thus, it is surely significant that while some of the rapidly produced collaborative texts of the early lollard movement exhibit extraordinary stability of text and consistency of production, of the kind Anne Hudson has described in the manuscripts of the *English Wycliffite Sermons*, most writings associated with lollardy exhibit textual instability and apparently purposive intervention to a very high degree.[23]

Until now, most attention to changes between copies of lollard writings has focused on trying to discern ideological motivations for them. The result is that some kinds of variation have been downplayed, while others have been played up. To be sure, it is important to know that some writers were strongly motivated to criticize friars, interpolating censure of friars into existing materials, while others disliked criticism of friars to the point of removing it as thoroughly as they could in their own copies of widely circulated lollard texts, whether by omitting it in copying or by scraping it out.[24] But antifraternalism is not a fault line that distinguishes lollardy from the mainstream, any more than are most kinds of anticlerical comment (see chap. 1, at n. 22). Equally, modifications to lollard and mainstream

---

21. For more comparison of case studies of textual cultures, see Fiona Somerset, "Textual Transmission, Variance, and Religious Identity among Lollard Pastoralia," in *Religious Controversy in Europe, 1378–1536: Textual Transmission and Networks of Readership*, ed. Michael Van Dussen and Pavel Soukup (Turnhout: Brepols, 2013), 71–104.

22. Keith Busby, "Variance and the Politics of Textual Criticism," in *Towards a Synthesis? Essays on the New Philology*, ed. Keith Busby (Amsterdam: Rodopi, 1993), 29–45.

23. Anne Hudson, "Middle English," in *Editing Medieval Texts: English, French, and Latin Written in England; Papers Given at the Twelfth Annual Conference on Editorial Problems, University of Toronto*, ed. A. G. Rigg (Toronto: University of Toronto Press, 1977), 34–57.

24. For the systematic interpolation of material critical of friars, see, e.g., Cambridge, Trinity College, MS B.14.50, as described in *FWD*, xvii–xxiii. For its removal, see, e.g., Anne Hudson, "The Expurgation of a Lollard Sermon-Cycle," repr. in *Lollards and Their Books* (London: Hambledon, 1985), esp. 203.

manuscripts produced by later censorship, as where "pope" or "purgatory" or "Mary" or "saint Thomas" (referring to Thomas Becket) is erased, are unlikely to reveal much to us about how lollard and mainstream writers differed from one another in the fourteenth and fifteenth centuries.[25] I will not pay much attention to later protestant modifications: they are part of the story of the historiography of lollardy, but that is a story that I want to tell elsewhere, not in this book. In this book I instead want to provide a more balanced and comprehensive account of the various forms of textual alteration that lollards and their contemporaries engaged in. I will be most interested in modifications that introduce, modify, or remove material that has to do with central lollard emphases, as I have come to understand them. This is where most of the energy and creativity in lollard variance is centered.

It may be helpful here to provide a brief survey of the kinds of variance one finds in lollard writings and of the terminology I have developed to account for them. I consider any piece of writing that appears in a manuscript that also contains one or more lollard writings to be *affiliated* with lollardy. I disregard cases where the binding or copying together that produced this affiliation occurred well after the 1530s—that is, in the seventeenth century or later; these may be useful to other kinds of research, but not to me.[26] But I include all writings with earlier (i.e., medieval) affiliations. This is not to say, however, that all items bound or copied together by medieval hands give evidence of one person's considered intention: not all affiliations are affiliations of sympathy. What now remains to us gathered in miscellaneous manuscripts is probably the end product of more dynamic processes of textual circulation, where copyists had access to unbound booklets, or loose sheets, or excerpted an item from within a longer work circulating whole or in pieces, or invented a short piece to fit in a small space. Some of these processes involve careful planning, others improvisation, while others may be the result of a forced choice from a very limited selection of available materials. Most revealing that a considered intention may have been at work are writings that appear together within the same booklet, in the same hand, or in the same format. But evidence of divided intentions can be useful as well, as for example when

---

25. There has been little analysis of this later censorship of English manuscripts. A preliminary study is Andrew Hughes, "Defacing Becket: Damaged Books for the Office," in *Hortus Troporum: Florilegium in Honorem Gunillae Iversen*, ed. Alexandre Andrée and Erika Kihlman (Stockholm: Stockholms Universitet, 2008), 162–75, with thanks to Rachel Koopmans for this reference.

26. For an example of critical work on later rebinding, see Jennifer Summit, *Memory's Library: Medieval Books in Early Modern England* (Chicago: University of Chicago Press, 2008), esp. chap. 4, 136–96.

a work was added by another hand at the end of a quire or, in contrast, erased or excised.[27]

Works that are affiliated with lollardy sometimes exhibit no significant variance from their copying tradition more generally, perhaps because they appealed to a lollard audience just as they were. However, it is common for mainstream works affiliated with lollardy to exhibit variance that cannot be attributed to copying errors or dialect translation or simplification. Sometimes lollard writers will interpolate polemical asides but leave the overall structure of the work unchanged. Sometimes they adjust a work more subtly, but also sometimes more thoroughly, to emphasize the topics they are most concerned to convey. And sometimes a lollard writer reworks his model throughout or departs from it part way to develop his topic in a new direction. I will refer to mainstream writings that have been thoroughly modified (whether subtly or more obviously, and whether through departure or reworking) as *lollard writings*, since in effect that is what they have become. I will refer to works that have been interpolated with obviously lollard content, but only in places, as *lollard-interpolated*. And I will refer to writings that have been adjusted subtly, but not in a systematic way, as *lollard-leaning* or *lollard-inflected*. It should be obvious that each of these descriptions is the result of an interpretative decision, and one where others (or I) may come to disagree. There is no litmus test for lollardy.

There was no litmus test for lollardy in the fourteenth and fifteenth centuries either. So it is that within predominantly mainstream manuscripts lollard texts are sometimes carefully expurgated to remove subtle emphases or more blatant declarations that reveal characteristically lollard concerns, but sometimes revised more carelessly or not at all. I will refer to copies where lollard content has been removed as *expurgated lollard writings*, except in cases where it is uncertain which the original version was, with the result that the direction of revision is unclear; in such cases, I will try to preserve that indeterminacy. Whichever direction it went, where revision has been careful and thorough, it can be very helpful in determining just where the edges

---

27. On materials circulated other than in book form, see Wendy Scase, "Imagining Alternatives to the Book: The Transmission of Political Poetry in Late Medieval England," in *Imagining the Book*, ed. Stephen Kelly and John J. Thompson (Turnhout: Brepols, 2005), 237–50. On the assembly of medieval English books, see Margaret Connolly, "Compiling the Book," in Gillespie and Wakelin, *Production of Books in England*, 129–49. On booklets, see J. Peter Gumbert, "Codicological Units: Towards a Terminology for the Stratigraphy of the Non-Homogenous Codex," *Segno e testo: International Journal of Manuscripts and Their Transmission* 2 (2004): 17–42; Ralph Hanna, "Booklets in Manuscripts: Further Considerations," rev. and repr. in *Pursuing History: Middle English Manuscripts and Their Texts* (Stanford, CA: Stanford University Press, 1996), 21–34.

of lollardy were. Still, at the same time, it seems obvious that not everybody could see those edges, or cared about them. Many readers seem to have been interested in the kinds of content that mainstream and lollard books shared, rather than in the bits that were ideologically loaded.

In addition to copying mainstream works unchanged or with alterations, lollard writers incorporate mainstream content within their own writings. In these cases, too, they commonly introduce variance. Anne Hudson and Mary Dove have drawn attention to how accurately and faithfully the Wycliffite Bible and the materials compiled into the *Glossed Gospels* seem to have been rendered. But in the course of making an argument, it is more common for lollard writers to modify quotations from patristic or more recent authors, interpolating explanatory phrases or adjusting their emphasis in order to bend the weight of authority they provide toward their own concerns. Perhaps more surprisingly, given the respect for the integrity of the biblical text that is often attributed to them, lollard writers also often interpolate or modify biblical quotations in order to tilt them in the direction of their desired interpretation. What is more, lollard writers modify not only their sources, but each other. Despite their admiration for Wyclif, they rarely render his writings word for word when they translate them, but rather adapt them freely. And in engaging with writings that already exhibit lollard concerns, writings with which they are probably broadly in agreement, they seemingly feel even more freedom: they excerpt and rework and modify them on the level not only of content but of form.

Taken together, all these kinds of evidence of variance in the lollard corpus can tell us a great deal about what happens in lollard writings as they spread—about the creativity inherent in their reception, as well as the tensions. They suggest to us a textual culture characterized not only by the threat of repression but by dynamic engagement. What is more, some lollard writings, and some heresy trial records too, offer corroborative evidence that lollard readers, as well as lollard writers, collaborated in producing and revising texts. The writer of the long sermon *Omnis plantacio* notes that he is leaving a written copy for his readers to peruse and asks them to report to him any faults or contrary arguments that they may find or hear in his absence; but this is only one of the most obvious of the many occasions (for another, see the Conclusion) on which lollard writings foster collaborative engagement between a writer and his readers in the collective endeavor of striving to live well.[28] Archbishop Henry Chichele's register records that

---

28. See *Omnis plantacio*, in Anne Hudson, ed., *The Works of a Lollard Preacher*, EETS, o.s. 317 (Oxford: Oxford University Press, 2001), 138/2939–139/2962. See also *PR*, 184–85.

John Claydon, in his trial for heresy in 1415, was said to have participated in the reading aloud and correction of the copy of the *Lanterne of Liȝt* that he had commissioned from a scribe;[29] and more generally, investigations in Norwich, Winchester, Coventry, and elsewhere reveal that lollards commonly gathered in small groups to read and discuss the books they owned or borrowed from others,[30] while evidence from London shows that lollards were participants in the book trade.[31] These examples are well known. But the variance found in the lollard corpus can tell us still more about how lollard writers worked together, and with their readers, to produce the lollard writings that remain to us.

There is one important consequence of lollards' widespread engagement in the collaborative production and ongoing revision of texts. The conceptual leap a scholar must make over and over again—from describing lollard texts to making claims about their nameless and faceless readers and writers—is not as vertiginous as it would be in a corpus more disengaged from its readers' and writers' aspirational practice of daily life. In their revisionist studies of reformist religion, Peter Lake and John Van Engen can each give names to the readers and writers of many works in their corpus and trace out their associations and the details of their lives.[32] However, while we can sketch out networks of association among persons named in heresy trials and even occasionally the owners of books, as recent work by Maureen Jurkowski and Anne Hudson has demonstrated, only very rarely can we name lollard writers.[33] The fact that most lollard writings cannot be linked with names and dates and places does not prevent us from talking about the nameless persons who wrote and read them, any more than it prevents us from using them as the basis of a revisionist study of their religion. It does, however, demand some comment on the terminology used to describe those persons. I have explained in detail how I use the word "lollard" to refer to texts: how do I apply it to people?

---

29. E. F. Jacob, ed., *The Register of Henry Chichele, Archbishop of Canterbury, 1414–1443*, 4 vols. (Oxford: Oxford University Press, 1938–47), 4:133–36. See also *PR*, 211–12.

30. See *PR*, 180–93; J. Patrick Hornbeck II, "*Wycklyffes Wycket* and Eucharistic Theology: Cases from Sixteenth-Century Winchester," in *WC*, 279–94.

31. *PR*, 206–7; Maureen Jurkowski, "Lollard Book Producers in London in 1414," in Barr and Hutchison, *Text and Controversy from Wyclif to Bale*, 201–26.

32. Peter Lake with Michael Questier, *The Antichrist's Lewd Hat: Protestants, Papists, and Players in Post-Reformation England* (New Haven, CT: Yale University Press, 2002); John Van Engen, *Sisters and Brothers of the Common Life: The Devotio Moderna and the World of the Later Middle Ages* (Philadelphia: University of Pennsylvania Press, 2008).

33. See most recently Maureen Jurkowski, "Lollard Networks," in *WC*, 261–78; Hudson, "Who Is My Neighbour?"

Who Are You Calling a Lollard?

One of my goals in this book is to move away from the entrenched debates that have often preoccupied the study of Wyclif and his followers. Still, even newcomers will need to know where the trenches are and what was at stake in digging them. The study of lollardy, as of Wyclif, has been beset with controversy ever since it was first associated with heresy, and all the more so after Wyclif was retrospectively named the Morning Star of the Reformation. Some readers will already be protesting that I have termed lollardy a "movement," for example, and will be wondering if I plan also to assert that the movement is a sect—I will not.[34] They will be alert to claims I might make about lollardy's centrality, importance, influence, duration, consistency in belief and practice, and cohesion, wanting to deny or minimize these in favor of the continuing importance of "orthodoxy" or of "traditional religion"—what I will more neutrally call mainstream Christianity.[35] They may be skeptical that it is possible to describe the characteristics of lollard writings independent of the points of doctrinal difference identified in heresy trials and condemnations. They will be especially sensitive, to a degree perhaps surprising for those new to the field, to my usage of the word "lollard," and curious about whether I plan to use "Wycliffite" as a synonym for it (I do, though sparingly).

As is often the case in a field undergoing rapid and contentious development, the conflict over the usage and scope of reference of the terms "Wycliffite" and "Lollard" or "lollard" in recent years is also a conflict over definitions. Until the late 1980s, scholars generally used "Wycliffite" to describe Wyclif's early university followers and "Lollard" to describe the lay dissenters, most of humble status, whose abjured beliefs are recorded in heresy trials.[36] In 1988 Anne Hudson proposed that "Wycliffite" and "Lollard" should instead be used as synonyms, since Wyclif's early academic followers and later lay followers were far more similar than many historians had supposed (*PR*, 2–4). This new usage was widely if not universally adopted: some scholars preferred one term to the other, others used both, but many seemed to agree that they were equivalent. This consensus has broken up

34. Margaret Aston, "Were the Lollards a Sect?," in *The Medieval Church: Universities, Heresy, and the Religious Life; Essays in Honor of Gordon Leff*, ed. Peter Biller and R. B. Dobson (Woodbridge: Boydell and Brewer, 1999), 163–92; J. I. Catto, "Fellows and Helpers: The Religious Identity of the Followers of Wyclif," in Biller and Dobson, *Medieval Church*, 141–62; *PR*, 168–73.
35. See Richard Rex's rather quixotic short book *The Lollards* (New York: Palgrave, 2002). The fullest description of "traditional religion" is in Duffy, *Stripping of the Altars*.
36. See, for example, Thomson, *Later Lollards*.

again recently, beginning around the turn of the century, with fresh questioning about the implications of the term "Lollard" or "lollard." Some have reasserted a version of the old distinction between Wycliffite academics and lay Lollards or lollardy.[37] Some, and I am among them, have worried that the capital *L* in Lollard, like the capital *P* now no longer used in research on English puritanism, asserts what ought instead to be investigated by implying that "Lollards" are a distinctive, cohesive social group. Using "lollard" adjectivally instead allows for a more flexible investigation of widely prevalent tendencies and emphases.[38]

The reader will have noted that my use of the word "lollard" is largely adjectival; where it is not, it derives from that adjectival usage. In my usage, a *lollard writer* is the writer (one or several) of a text that draws on Wyclif's thought or that shares many characteristics with other lollard writings that draw on Wyclif. A *lollard reader* is either the ideal reader projected by such a text, who reads it attentively and attempts to further its aims, or any other closely engaged reader who may in some respects resist the text's claims, perhaps even rewrite them, but remains in sympathy with their emphases. I include among lollard readers, often without explicitly distinguishing them, the wider penumbra of listeners who heard texts read aloud, whether they were able to read the texts for themselves or not. *Lollards* and *lollardy*, where I refer to them in this volume, are terms extrapolated from my understanding of lollard writers and readers. *Lollards*, then, are writers and readers engaged in a textual culture that collaboratively produced writings about reformed forms of life and that attempted to make them a way of life. The production and spread of the books themselves, as well as evidence from heresy trials, suggests that some did make this attempt: *lollardy* is the way of life they attempted to pursue.[39] The *lollard movement* is the collective engagement in this way of life that lollard writings exhort; their proliferation suggests that it was more than imaginary.

Yet none of these terms, when applied to persons, implies that lollard is a stable identity, nor that it applies in the same way to every reader or even every writer of lollard writings in ways that do not change over time.

---

37. See, e.g., Kantik Ghosh, "Wycliffism and Lollardy," in *The Cambridge History of Christianity*, vol. 4, *Christianity in Western Europe, c. 1100–c. 1500*, ed. Miri Rubin and Walter Simons (Cambridge: Cambridge University Press, 2009), 433–45.

38. For examples, see John Watts, "The Pressure of the Public on Later Medieval Politics," in *Political Culture in Late Medieval Britain*, ed. Linda Clark and Christine Carpenter (Woodbridge: Boydell, 2004), 159–80; Ian Forrest, "Lollardy and Late Medieval History," in *WC*, 121–34.

39. On how trial depositions support this account of lollardy, see J. Patrick Hornbeck II, "Wycliffite Spirituality in Heresy Trials: Personal Holiness and Spiritual Simplicity," in *WS*, 24–29.

Writers, as well as readers, might blow hot and cold. We cannot track these shifts with reference to the writings of a cluster of named individuals, as Peter Lake does so persuasively in *The Boxmaker's Revenge*.[40] Still, the distribution of incompletely expurgated or unexpurgated lollard writings across manuscripts with mainstream contents suggests that many persons read lollard writings or heard them read, often with enjoyment even if less than full engagement, and sometimes without knowing that they were lollard. And even while we remember that a heresy investigation might distort what its subjects might say about their beliefs, evidence that individuals might lose interest in lollardy, or abjure at trial and then later return, suggests that writers as well as readers may have passed in and out of close engagement with the lollard movement over the course of a lived life.

Still, there are also some scholars who avoid using the term "lollard" at all, out of skepticism that many lay defenders had any association whatever with the academic heresy with which it is associated, or in recognition that it is not the term used by either church officials or defendants in rural heresy trials, or in protest that the term is so ideologically loaded and various in its usages that it cannot be salvaged as a neutral term of description.[41] In my view, however, our usage of descriptive terms in the present still has much to learn from how "lollard" and its derivatives were deployed by fourteenth- and fifteenth-century writers. As far as we can tell from the written record, the term was employed largely by educated writers, in both English and Latin contexts, and largely to insult, or record insults, to themselves or to their peers; this educated usage is in itself is one reason not to reserve the word for describing rural lay dissenters. Sometimes, as for example in sermons and poetry that set themselves against what they describe as lollardy or lollards, "lollard" is little more than a synonym for "heretic." But at other times its meaning and application are deliberately brought into question, even as it is deployed. The term "lollard" appears at lyrically expressed, ideologically charged, rhetorically complicated moments—the moments where writers turn upon themselves, as well as their readers, their concern for the effects upon the community of any individual's attempt to live the best form of life.

Not all of the writings in which "lollard" is deployed exhibit the core characteristics of lollard writings, but all of them do seem to be aware that

---

40. Peter Lake, *The Boxmaker's Revenge: "Orthodoxy," "Heterodoxy," and the Politics of the Parish in Early Stuart London* (Stanford, CA: Stanford University Press, 2001).

41. See, for example, John Arnold, "The Materiality of Unbelief in Late Medieval England," in *The Unorthodox Imagination in Late Medieval Britain*, ed. Sophie Page (Manchester: Manchester University Press, 2010), 68–71; Hornbeck, *What Is a Lollard?*, 1–22; Andrew Cole, *Literature and Heresy in the Age of Chaucer* (Cambridge: Cambridge University Press, 2008), 72–74.

"lollard" is associated with arguments about how best to live in the world, and some refer to its association with controversy over doctrine. These usages of "lollard" are acutely self-aware and acutely concerned with the religious identity and consequent actions of writer as well as readers. Critical debate over the derivation, moment of origin, usage, and meaning of the noun "loller" or "lollare," and whether it was, or became, a synonym for "lollard," has not fully addressed this flexibility.[42] Arguments have usually hinged, it seems to me, on an understanding of lollard identity as a stable, even rigid, mode of being in the world. Either writers and readers are lollards, or they are not. If they are, they talk about lollers or lollards in order to assert that identity. If they are not, they mention lollers in order to dissociate themselves from and reject that identity. These alternatives are inadequate to the complexities of lived identity as we now understand them; they are also, it seems, inadequate to how these writers and their readers understood themselves.

When exactly people began talking about lollers we will probably never know; it seems unlikely that the written record preserves the first usage of a word used (so a variety of written sources report) in oral invective.[43] What is more crucial than pinpointing the moment of its coinage, though, is that the noun "loller," "lollard" as well, does not assign identity as much as it describes action. In all the talk of derivation of "lollard" from Latin "lolium" ("tares") or Dutch "lollaert" ("mutterer"), critics have overlooked the way medieval writers frequently link "loller" and even "lollard" with the activity of lolling. "Loll" is not a noun, but a verb—a verb that has received attention in passing in work on "lollares" in Piers Plowman, but whose importance

42. For the term's usage on the Continent, and speculations on its etymology, see D. Kurze, "Die festländischen Lollarden: Zur Geschichte der religiösen Bewegungen im ausgehenden Mittelalter," Archiv für Kulturgeschichte 47 (1965): 48–76. On satirical usages, see also Robert Lerner's chapter on Beghards and Beguines in The Heresy of the Free Spirit in the Later Middle Ages (Berkeley: University of California Press, 1972), 35–60, esp. 40–41. On its usage in England, see most influentially Wendy Scase, Piers Plowman and the New Anti-clericalism (Cambridge: Cambridge University Press, 1989), esp. 149–60; Wendy Scase, "'Heu! quanta desolatio Angliae praestatur': A Wycliffite Libel and the Naming of Heretics, Oxford 1382," in Lollards and Their Influence in Late Medieval England, ed. Fiona Somerset, Jill C. Havens, and Derrick G. Pitard (Woodbridge: Boydell, 2003), 19–36; Cole, Literature and Heresy, 25–71.

43. A sample of sources attesting or deploring that "lollard" or "loller" was, or might be, used as a verbal insult: W. W. Shirley, ed., Fasciculi Zizianorum Magistri Johannis Wyclif cum Tritico, Rolls Series 5 (London, 1858), 289; John Audelay's Marcolf and Solomon, lines 131–43, in John Audelay, Poems and Carols (Oxford, Bodleian Library MS Douce 302), ed. Susanna Fein, TEAMS Middle English Texts Series (Kalamazoo, MI: Medieval Institute Publications, 2009); and the Fyve Wyttes (see the Conclusion).

in any account of "lollare" activity has not yet fully registered.[44] A loller is someone who lolls, in all of that verb's range of senses. Writers' reflexive concern about what it might mean for a writer to be called a "loller" is often articulated through alliterative punning on the verb "loll" and hinges on conflicting assessments of the so-called loller's actions and their effects. The positive connotations of lolling—hanging on persistently to one's beliefs or virtuous practices, spending time in reflection, hanging back while others do wrong, hanging around rebuking the sins of others regardless of reprisal, imitating Christ's hanging from the cross—are counterbalanced by negative connotations: defying orders to amend one's ways, wasting time on dubious activities, refusing to do honest work, being suspended from one's social role for malfeasance, complaining about what you have not helped to fix.

The first recorded instance of "loll" in the *MED* appears in *Piers Plowman* A, not (like "loller") *Piers Plowman* C, where the term's deployment in some of what may have been the poem's final revisions has been the focus of most recent attention to its origins and usage. It is possible, then, though we cannot be certain, that both verb and noun were coined around the same time—even if *Piers Plowman* C claims an older usage for the verb, if not the noun.[45] But "loll" also gets linked with the perhaps older verbs "suspend" and "hang" and piggybacks on their similar ambiguity between virtuous and pejorative associations. For example, Wyclif puns deftly on "suspendere" in chapter 27 of his *Speculum ecclesie militantis*, also known as his *Dialogus*, probably written in the late 1370s (as Michael Wilks has noted).[46] Similarly, the undated vernacular Wycliffite *De officio pastorali*, derived from Wyclif's work of the same title, explains in closing that good curates should persist in preaching even despite being suspended from duty, and in this way imitate

---

44. Scase, for example, suggests, but without investigating further, that *Piers Plowman* C claims antiquity for the verb "lollen," rather than the noun "loller" (*Piers Plowman and the New Anticlericalism*, 151). Cole suggests that Wycliffites begin to expand the range of the noun "lollare" to include verbal and adjectival usages in the 1390s (*Literature and Heresy*, 33). However, this expansion should be dated at least a decade or two earlier, and it is not an innovation of lollard writers alone (even if they do have a special interest in it).

45. *Piers Plowman* C.9.214–18, in Derek Pearsall, ed., *Piers Plowman: A New Annotated Edition of the C-text* (Exeter: University of Exeter Press, 2008); and see previous note. Complications to developing a firm chronology include not only the limitations of the *MED*'s corpus, and the possibility that the word may have been widely used in oral invective before the A version was written, but the difficulty that most A manuscripts are late copies, none as early as this version's putative composition somewhere in the 1360s or 1370s.

46. John Wyclif, *Dialogus, sive Speculum ecclesie militantis*, ed. Alfred W. Pollard (London: Trübner, 1886), 57. See Michael Wilks, "Wyclif and the Great Persecution," repr. in *Wyclif: Political Ideas and Practice; Papers by Michael Wilks*, ed. Anne Hudson (Oxford: Oxbow Books, 2000), 187 n. 36.

Christ's suspension.[47] In repressive discourses, "loller" becomes a synonym for "heretic," and its polysemy is often flattened out. Reforming discourses, in contrast, whether lollard or not, strive to maintain the virtuous associations of lolling, as well as their associations with legitimate social complaint, and often deplore the word's pejoration into an insult or accusation.

One reason to continue using the word "lollard," then, is in order to be able to engage fully with its importance to writers who use it not to label what people ineluctably are, but to evaluate what people do and how their actions cause them to be viewed. Another is that even scholars in the present who are less rigid in their understanding of group and personal identity need, in my view, to revise their understanding of what mattered most to lollard writers and readers: what they tried to do, and where they most closely followed John Wyclif. It is the content of *lollard* belief and practice, rather than something broader or more nebulous such as *dissenting* or *reformist* thought, that I am seeking to redefine. My contention is that even amidst all Wyclif's notoriety and celebration, we have never quite understood how he mattered to writers in the following two centuries who drew on his thought to imagine their world otherwise, and who sometimes (not always) called themselves *lollers* or *lollards*. It is time to understand them better.

Few of the writings discussed here have been widely read, and indeed many remain unedited. For this reason, an argument by demonstration can only proceed hand in hand with extensive description, and often lengthy quotation. Readers unaccustomed to Middle English will find ample glossing of unfamiliar words; they may also want to consult the fully modernized versions of many of the texts discussed here in *Wycliffite Spirituality* (*WS*). Direct biblical quotation within quoted passages will be italicized, to aid readers in differentiating it from paraphrase and interpolation. As appropriate, underlining will draw readers' attention to a phrase within a quotation that will be discussed in detail, while bold font will highlight key terms repeated frequently across a larger work.[48]

---

47. "De officio pastorali," in Matthew, 405–57, on 456–57. The final chapters diverge from Wyclif's *Tractatus de officio pastorali* as edited by G. V. Lechler (Leipzig: Edelmann, 1853) from just one manuscript, so that the "suspendere" discussion does not also appear in this version of the Latin text. For the eighteen manuscripts now known, see W. R. Thomson, *The Latin Writings of John Wyclyf: An Annotated Catalog* (Toronto: Pontifical Institute of Mediaeval Studies, 1983), 95.

48. In quoting from unpublished manuscripts, I impose modern conventions of punctuation, word division, and capitalization, adopting, however, a minimalist approach to capitalization. I regularize *ff* to *f* except where I render it as capital *f* but maintain manuscript usage of *u/v* and *i/j*. Abbreviations are silently expanded in keeping with the text's dialect, with versions of the conventional abbreviation symbol for "Jesus" consistently rendered as "Iesu." Corrections are noted and followed unless obviously wrong. Emendations and variants in other manuscripts are presented in footnotes.

At times in the chapters that follow, I will build a case using many texts, tracing variance through lollard and mainstream versions or examining how lollard writers alter mainstream sources in order to make clear both the overlaps and the points of departure between lollard and mainstream writing. At other times, and sometimes through a whole chapter, I will examine a single text in more detail, in order to show how lollard writers integrated their key tenets into the compendious genres of vernacular pastoral instruction that seem to have become extraordinarily popular in fifteenth-century England. When I generalize about lollard writings in relation to a single example treated at length, I do so on the basis of more detailed discussions elsewhere in the book; I provide cross-references to help readers in drawing these connections, but I do not cite evidence or present arguments in full more than once. The conclusion of chapter 1, in particular, provides a preliminary account of characteristic emphases in lollard writings built from its analysis of a comprehensive lollard pastoral program, but pointing forward to topics developed further elsewhere; readers unfamiliar with the field may find the cross-references here especially useful in tracing their own paths through the book as a whole.

The argument of this book proceeds in three stages. Part 1 shows what lollard writers wanted their readers to do, tracing closely how their normative account of religious practice as an ethics of everyday life in the world differed from the mainstream. The texts surveyed here are largely pastoral writings: some polemical in aim, most largely focused on instructing their readers or deepening their engagement with fundamental teachings on the law of God and on prayer. Parts 2 and 3, on the other hand, focus on how lollard writers strove to make this alternative form of religious practice compelling for their readers. It is not obvious that the stringent daily demands of a form of living that might entail extraordinary personal risk should be appealing; I seek to understand why this was. Many of the works treated in parts 2 and 3 are also more ambitious, whether in scope or in style or in the nature of their

---

Biblical and some other references are inserted where relevant to my exposition, or updated from those provided in the manuscript, in a consistent format. However, I do not pretend to have traced every source, nor have I always consulted every extant copy: that kind of work awaits the critical edition of these texts. In quoting from published editions, I modify the presentation of spoken words and of biblical quotation to match my presentation of manuscript sources, introducing quotation marks, italics, bold font, and underlining as needed (see above). Similarly, I provide biblical references if supplied by the editor or if relevant to my argument, using the same parenthetical citation style as my own annotations. Changes of folio and indications of inserted words, too, are modified to my own format. However, I alter editors' expansions of abbreviations, word divisions, and capitalization of terms only when markedly inconsistent with modern editing practice, and indicate where punctuation is modified. Where I emend an editor's text, I justify the change in a footnote.

innovations, than the shorter works (though not the longer works) treated in part 1. Part 2 examines how lollard writers wanted their readers to feel, and how through exhorting their readers to model their feelings and actions on biblical narratives they encouraged them to feel like saints. While part 2 focuses more on individuals, albeit as members of groups, part 3 reverses this emphasis as it turns from narrative structures to metaphorical ones and from feeling to imagination; I show that metaphorical or allegorical redescription of the materials and institutions of the late medieval church is a central element in how lollard writings reimagine "Christ's religion" and redefine what it means to be a member of the "true church."

In the final chapter of part 3, and in the Conclusion, I demonstrate that my account of the lollard movement gives us more insightful ways to read texts whose ideological alignments have seemed especially puzzling to scholars. Rather than "reformist" or "orthodox" yet "tolerant" texts that demarcate the limits of lollardy, the *Book to a Mother* and *Fyve Wyttes* are very typical, indeed paradigmatic examples of lollard pastoral instruction, inflected throughout with characteristic lollard emphases and reflecting lollard spiritual and ethical ambitions. Much more work remains to be done on English religious writings extant in fifteenth-century manuscripts; in the end, I hope to have equipped readers to read works like these with greater subtlety and make decisions about their affiliations with lollardy for themselves.

✒ Part One

❧ CHAPTER 1

The Lollard Pastoral Program

Reform from Below

At some point in the 1390s, a parish priest in the West Midlands formulated a large ambition: to reconfigure traditional pastoral teaching so that it would reflect his new convictions and lead his own little flock toward salvation.[1] What he produced in pursuit of this goal has broad implications for our understanding of the lollard movement.[2] The written record of his efforts is a lengthy cycle of sermons (SS74) that throughout its length bears the marks of intended (or very thoroughly imagined) oral delivery, even if in its most complete and earliest extant copy it has been compiled into an anthology for devotional reading.[3] We can tell from the

---

1. My opening claim is a hypothesis that enables us plausibly to reconstruct a writer, audience, and occasion for this work and to place it in a context, rather than interpreting it as a free-floating expression of lollard views. We do not know who wrote this sermon cycle, or when, or for whom; neither the earliest extant copy in Cambridge, Sidney Sussex College, MS 74 (SS74), nor the later partial redactions in Oxford, Bodleian Library, MS Bodley 95 and Shrewsbury, Shrewsbury School, MS 3 tell us anything specific. *LALME* locates the dialects in which the SS74 sermons are copied to Worcestershire (LP 7591), Warwickshire (LP 677), and Northamptonshire (LP 705). For more details on the contents of the manuscript, its relationships with other manuscripts, and the contents of the sermon cycle, see Appendices A and B.

2. Christina von Nolcken has also used a lollard sermon cycle as a means toward a broader understanding of variations in style, tone, and purpose among lollard writings: see "An Unremarked Group of Wycliffite Sermons in Latin," *Modern Philology* 83 (1986): 233–49.

3. For the other contents of the manuscript, see Appendix A. Many of the sermons turn at points to address a listening audience in direct and personal terms, especially at the close of sections. See, for

results that the *SS74* sermon writer had close links with the group of early
Wycliffites who were engaged in producing the vast sermon cycle that would
become the *English Wycliffite Sermons* (*EWS*). He also had a wide-ranging
acquaintance with Wyclif's thought, as well as mainstream religious writing
more generally. But his aims in producing his own sermon cycle were both
narrower and broader than those of the *EWS* writers. Rather than 294 model
sermons in five sets to cover every liturgical occasion on which a sermon
might be required over the course of the whole year—54 sermons on the
Sunday gospels, 31 sermons on the gospel readings assigned for feast days for
general types of saints, such as apostles, evangelists, and martyrs, 37 sermons
on the gospels for feast days for specific saints, 120 sermons on the gospels
for weekdays that are not feast days, and 55 sermons on the Sunday epistle
readings—the *SS74* sermon writer aimed only to compile sermons for Sunday preaching across the year.[4] But on the other hand, rather than the *EWS*'s
tightly focused and usually polemical exposition of the assigned lection, in
most cases proceeding systematically through it section by section, in what
is sometimes called the "ancient" style, the *SS74* sermon writer aimed to
provide a comprehensive program of pastoral instruction, pitched throughout
toward characteristically lollard emphases and preoccupations and covering a
syllabus that includes but also exceeds the usual pastoral basics over the course
of the liturgical year. Thus, *SS74* is one lollard writer's fully realized version
of a distinctively lollard pastoral program. Both in its extensive similarities
with a broad range of more pastoral and devotionally oriented writings in
lollard manuscripts and in the more unusual aspects of its development of
key lollard themes, it will allow us in this chapter to lay the groundwork for
a newly broadened understanding of the audiences and purposes of lollard
writings and a newly sharpened picture of their central characteristics.

Each of the sermons in *SS74* combines a range of materials chosen to serve
the cycle's overall purposes.[5] It begins by quoting its thema, a verse taken from

example, *SS74*, fol. 94r. On various kinds of written records of sermons and their spoken delivery
to an audience, and for a lucid, brief introduction to written sermons more generally, see Siegfried
Wenzel, *Latin Sermon Collections from Later Medieval England* (Cambridge: Cambridge University
Press, 2005), 1–20.

4. For a general introduction to the contents and scope of the *English Wycliffite Sermons*, see *EWS*,
1:8–50; for a table of the 294 sermons (and explanation of the three missing from the Ferial set), see
EWS, 3:cxlix–clv. In the list given in the text, I paraphrase the names that liturgical scholars use for
each of these standard kinds of sermons so that nonspecialist readers will have a better understanding
of their occasions: the sets are (1) Dominical gospels, (2) Common of Saints, (3) Proper of Saints,
(4) Ferial gospels, and (5) Dominical epistles. For an introduction to preaching in medieval England
that explains the annual cycle of the liturgy, see H. Leith Spencer, *English Preaching in the Late Middle
Ages* (Oxford: Clarendon Press, 1993), 20–77.

5. For more details about the lections, topics, and contents of sermons in the cycle, see Appendix
B. Hudson collates the portions of the sermons drawn from *EWS* in her edition of the Sunday gospel

the Sunday epistle reading. Before pursuing that thema, it inserts a protheme, that is, an introductory exposition, often treating a different scriptural passage. Prothemes were often designed to develop a preacher's relationship with his audience in advance of the main thema and followed by an exhortation to prayer. In this sermon cycle, the prothemes are unusually lengthy and elaborate, and nearly all of them come from the same source: the *SS74* sermon writer inserts as his protheme the whole of the sermon on the gospel for that same Sunday from the *EWS*.[6] The *SS74* sermon writer seems to have approved the *EWS* Sunday gospel sermons' most fundamental overall assertion, reiterated in nearly every sermon: that Christ's religion is the best, and its adherents follow God's law, while many who make claims to religion, or even simply to be Christian, instead wrongly give precedence to rules or laws established only recently by men. He also seems to have endorsed the gospel sermons' more occasional development of other central lollard themes, such as what constitutes proper confession, what proper preaching consists in and how present practices undermine or hinder it, and the need to curb the clergy's excessive wealth and the practices that accumulate it. He appreciates, too, topics of more narrow academic interest that are treated only once or twice, such as the eucharist, God's absolute and ordained powers, and the modes of scriptural interpretation, for he does not tone down any of these. The *SS74* sermon writer's only significant modifications to each of the *EWS* gospel sermons are to add at its end a bridging passage, longer or shorter, that exhorts his readers to attend to what he sees as the sermon's central moral lesson, and sometimes (not often) to sharpen his *EWS* sermon's opening statement of the topic and content of the lection. Following his bridging exhortation and an invitation to prayer, the *SS74* sermon writer repeats and then pursues his own thema.

The *SS74* sermon writer's homiletic style in discussing his epistle thema differs markedly from that of the *EWS*. His preference is for "modern" rather than "ancient" exposition: he spins most of his discussion from a single verse, rather than a systematic exposition of all or most of the liturgical reading, and concatenates with this verse a range of biblical, patristic, and other quotations to undergird his argument. This means that his selection of the

---

sermons, *EWS*, 1; see also discussion on 115–23, 164. Helen L. Spencer traces the sermons' relationships with other extant sermon collections in "The Fortunes of a Lollard Sermon-Cycle in the Later Fourteenth Century," *Mediaeval Studies* 48 (1986): 352–96; and *English Preaching*, 298–311. Alan J. Fletcher identifies some textual relations and suggests that the sermons and indeed *SS74* as a whole are ideologically inconsistent: see "A Hive of Industry or a Hornets' Nest? MS Sidney Sussex 74 and Its Scribes," in *Late-Medieval Religious Texts and Their Transmission: Essays in Honour of A.I. Doyle*, ed. A. J. Minnis (Woodbridge: Boydell and Brewer, 1994), 131–55.

6. The two exceptions are sermons 7 and 8. For details, see Spencer, "Fortunes of a Lollard Sermon-Cycle," 353–54 and 360–65.

verse he places at the center of his exposition is crucial to his sermon's overall theme and development, rather than simply the starting point of what will be a longer selection. His choices of epistle themata are anything but accidental, as rapidly becomes clear; rather, they are carefully chosen to knit together his prothemes with his added material in a planned thematic sequence.[7] There are many signs of large-scale as well as local coherence, even if the cycle as a whole seems to have been written incrementally, perhaps in a series of concentrated bursts of work designed to address the liturgical demands of the parish year. The writer often structures his exposition by distinguishing the meanings or kinds of a given term: the six branches of pride, the three tokens of love, etc. While he agrees with the *EWS* writers' disdain for the common contemporary practice of incorporating exemplary stories in sermons, and like them he stringently avoids doing so, his prose style is more overtly rhetorical than theirs. He is fond of sequences of oppositions and of heavily alliterative flights of heightened style, and he often incorporates similitudes, or moralized comparisons with the natural world, to enliven his prose. After some discussion of his thema, finally, the writer adds a third section, usually of roughly the same length as the first and second. Here, he moves on to treat the next item in his overarching syllabus of pastoral instruction, stretching across the course of the cycle. This syllabus covers in turn the seven gifts of the Holy Spirit, the five wits, the seven works of mercy, the seven deadly sins, the commandments, then finally, an extended allegory of the city of the soul stretching across twenty sermons that canvasses the five wits (again), the seven virtues, the creed, and the sixteen conditions of charity.[8] The result has been described by Helen Spencer, in her comprehensive study of later medieval English sermons, as the most thoroughgoing experiment in integrating pastoral instruction into a sermon cycle in any medieval English manuscript.[9]

It will be readily apparent that the pastoral lists the *SS74* sermon writer uses to structure his teaching are in and of themselves anything but heterodox. Nor are they distinctively lollard, except in that the *SS74* sermon writer omits any systematic treatment of the seven sacraments while covering the rest of what was standardly covered in manuals of pastoral instruction

---

7. For example, the Pentecost sermon at the opening coincides with pastoral instruction on the gifts of the Holy Spirit, instruction that continues and knits together thematically with the following Trinity Sunday sermon and that is echoed in sermon 2's treatment of Apoc. 4:5's seven lamps as the seven spirits of God. The themata of sermons 4 and 5 treat in turn loving one another and being indifferent to the world's hate, in company with *EWS* prothemes on Dives and Lazarus and the wedding feast in Luke.

8. For more detail, see Appendix B.

9. Spencer, *English Preaching*, 220–22.

in depth.[10] Nor were many of the *SS74* sermon writer's sources and reference books lollard; this is obvious, even if few of them have yet been traced.
A work as vastly encyclopedic as *SS74* would of course in the textual culture
of late medieval English manuscripts be expected to draw extensively on a
range of contemporary sources, and even quote from them at length, without
acknowledgement. Smaller and larger units of text from a variety of older
and newer sources (older ones tend to be attributed, but not always) migrate
fluidly through a variety of manuscript contexts in this written culture, from
anthologies to florilegia to compilations, each potentially more or less tightly
organized and carefully ordered. Any collection of received wisdom will dip
into these materials, though some such collections will modify what they
gather more thoroughly and more consistently than others. Not only do a
wide range of later sermon collections (and probably other as yet untraced
writings as well) draw on *SS74*, but *SS74* itself clearly draws on previous
materials and on the kinds of reference works that preachers often used in
constructing sermons, such as distinction collections, indices, and penitential
manuals.[11]

Yet what is distinctive about lollard pastoral teaching, here and elsewhere,
is not that it strives to reinvent the enterprise of pastoral instruction from the
ground up or radically to alter its content. Lollards agreed with their contemporaries, broadly speaking, about what the fundamentals of lay pastoral
teaching should be. Nor is lollard pastoral teaching distinctive because it
seeks, always and everywhere, to smuggle in anticlerical complaint and heterodox doctrine of the kind bishops were seeking in their investigations of
heresy. While lollard writers do sometimes indulge in polemical asides, their
pastoral instruction is far more than a mere camouflage for the dissemination
of polemical claims. Instead, it presents a new and distinctive basis for thinking about church membership and religious practice.

Loving Together

Even if this cycle draws on a broad array of mainstream sources, there are several ways in which its author departs from convention to shift the emphasis

---

10. Other lollard pastoral manuals that omit the sacraments from systematic pastoral teaching
or merely list them briefly are the *Lanterne of Liȝt* (ed. Lilian M. Swinburn, EETS, o.s. 151 [London:
Kegan Paul, 1917]), and *Book to a Mother* (*BM*). For more detailed discussion of *Book to a Mother*,
see chap. 7. On indirect or metaphorical treatment of the sacraments in lollard writings, see below
and chap. 7.

11. F. N. M. Diekstra traces in detail the textual affiliations of *SS74*, one source used by the
Book for a Simple and Devout Woman (Groningen: Egbert Forsten, 1998). On reference works used in

of his pastoral instruction. Unlike every other copy of the *EWS* or of materials derived from them, this cycle begins at Pentecost, a key episode for lollard writers, who commonly derive their sense of special mission, even in the absence of institutional approval, from the model of the apostles and claim direct inspiration by the Holy Spirit.[12] While the opening pages of the manuscript are now missing, we can be fairly certain that it began with the *EWS* gospel sermon for Pentecost beginning from John 14:23, "If ony man loueth me, he schal kepe my word; and my fadir schal loue hym, and we schulen come to hym, and we schulen dwelle with hym." Dwelling together with God in love is the governing metaphor of the cycle as a whole, frequently reiterated at the conclusion of prothemes and completed sermons and developed at length across the extended architectural metaphor of its final twenty sermons. What remains of the end of *SS74*'s first sermon for Pentecost shows that the *SS74* sermon writer's added material on a protheme from the day's epistle reading similarly exhorts his audience to dwell together in love, this time on the basis of an exposition of Acts 2. Just as he dwelt in the apostles, the Holy Spirit will "dwelle in vs þorugh his grace oure lyfe for to reule to plese to hym in al oure myȝt þe while we here schule lyfe. And graunte vs whenne we heþen wende [depart from here] heuen blisse foreuer. Amen" (fol. 3). The writer's account of how the human community conforms its will to God's through love emphasizes mutuality through its rapid alternation of plural subject and singular object pronouns and the rather dizzying switches in focus they require: the Holy Spirit will dwell in *us* through *his* grace, to rule *our* life to please *him* in all *our* power while *we* here shall live. A relationship in which God rules our life so that we please him with all our might requires a human effort of will, of cleaving to God in love and maintaining virtue by keeping God's word, as well as grace.

This account of how to attain salvation is characteristic of lollard writings, and indeed of Wyclif's. Not long ago, lollards, like Wyclif, were thought to be strictly determinist predestinarians, convinced that God's selection of the recipients of salvific grace had already been made and could not be influenced

writing sermons, see M. Michèle Mulchahy, *"First the Bow is Bent in Study"* . . . *Dominican Education before 1350* (Toronto: Pontifical Institute of Mediaeval Studies, 1998), 400–552; Richard H. Rouse and Mary A. Rouse, *Preachers, Florilegia, and Sermons: Studies on the "Manipulus Florum" of Thomas of Ireland* (Toronto: Pontifical Institute of Mediaeval Studies, 1979), 3–42.

12. See, for example, *EWS*, sermon 53 and epistle sermon 29 in *EWS*, 1:464–68, 598–601, and the brief but pithy sermon for the vigil of Pentecost, no. 199 in *EWS*, 3:233–34. In addition to Acts 2, Luke 21:12–15 is important to lollard writers seeking to assert authorization through grace: see, for example, *Lollard Sermons*, no. 14, esp. 181/216–182/74; and the *Testimony of William Thorpe*, in *TWT*, 76/1706–77/1730.

by our actions. However, recent research has done much to advance our understanding of what had seemed simple categories.[13] In the context of a closer-grained and more fully contextualized understanding of later medieval views on salvation, it is clear that nearly all writers gave human effort a place alongside divine grace; what differs is how that effort is described. Similarly, most medieval people thought that God knew who would be saved in the future, since God was understood to know everything. But nearly all thinkers strove to explain how God's foreknowledge was compatible with human free will; very few were comfortable with the proposition that God both knew and had predetermined all human actions in advance. Wyclif certainly was not, and neither were lollard writers. Certainly Wyclif was condemned by his opponents for what were characterized as determinist views, and certainly both Wyclif and lollards use terms and metaphors in their polemical writings that at times might seem to imply a strict, predetermined separation between the predestined elect and those foreknown to be damned.[14] However, even in polemical contexts the account of salvation within which these terms are deployed is strongly voluntarist and focuses on human action. Wrong choices made by those who should know better are the focus of Wyclif's complaints about the clergy and his exhortations to others to reform them. Similarly, conversion from sin to virtuous action supported by a continuous effort of will is the focus of his exhortations to his readers. Uncertainty is the basis of all human judgment. We cannot know who will be damned and who will be saved, but a man's present actions allow us to guess at his eventual fate, and thus whether he deserves the social position he holds. We cannot know our own salvation either, but we can exert ourselves to conform our will to God's, in a constantly renewed effort bolstered by the proper disposition of the emotions and manifesting itself in action in accordance with truth. Wyclif's writings, and those of his followers, emphasize these two claims over and over again.[15]

---

13. For a newer characterization of William Langland's soteriology, see David Aers, *Salvation and Sin: Augustine, Langland, and Fourteenth-Century Theology* (Notre Dame, IN: University of Notre Dame Press, 2009). On Wyclif, see Ian C. Levy, "Grace and Freedom in the Soteriology of John Wyclif," *Traditio* 60 (2005): 279–337; and Stephen E. Lahey, *John Wyclif* (Oxford: Oxford University Press, 2009), chap. 6, 169–98. A broader historical survey with useful terminological distinctions and an attempt to track variation among Wycliffite soteriologies appear in Patrick Hornbeck, *What Is a Lollard? Dissent and Belief in Late Medieval England* (Oxford: Oxford University Press, 2010), 25–67.

14. On Wyclif's imagery, see Hornbeck, *What Is a Lollard?*, 32–33.

15. On guessing at whether others are saved, and hoping that we ourselves are, see "De blasphemia," in Arnold, 402–29, on 426; the *Dialogue between Reson and Gabbyng*, in *FWD*, 53/357–78; "The Church and Her Members," in Arnold, 338–65, on 344; the "Tractatus de Pseudo-Freris," in Matthew, 296–324, on 297; "Of Faith, Hope, and Charity," in Matthew, 347–55, on 350; "De officio

How to sustain or renew the effort of will required to maintain God dwelling within us: this is the *SS74* sermon writer's main concern throughout his sermon cycle. The third sermon in *SS74* concludes with a kind of defense of homiletics (rather than of poetry) where he explains how loving together results from the right sort of learning:

> Mony gladly wolen lurne to cunne [learn] sley3tes and wyles [tricks and wiles], songes, tales, and romances, enturledes [interludes] and pleyes and oþer mony suteltes [contrivances] þat nedeþ not to be lurned [need not be learned]. Bote to kunne þer Pater Noster, þer Aue Marie and þer crede, þe dedes of mercy and þe ten hestes, wiþ knowyng of þer fyue wittes, kepe þei not to kunne [they do not care to learn]. And so þe 3ifte of kunnyng þei turne to hire dampnacioun, and þerfore þei haten vchon oþer [each other] and louen not togedur. Bote God dwelleþ in vs 3ef [if] we louen togedur. Fle we þerfore þis false loue and leue we þis veyn cunnyng, þat we may kunne [learn to] louen him ouer al þing [above all things] in oure herte, þat we may dwelle whit [with] hym in loue in lyf þat euer schal laste. (fol. 7v)

The commonplace that is being recycled here is widely familiar, both in lollard contexts and elsewhere; pastoral writings frequently complain about the common preference for vain diversions, though it is more conventional to do so in a prologue. *SS74* will return to this theme repeatedly; the *EWS* had sounded it too, though less often. The readers or listeners of this cycle are exhorted to abandon the "veyn cunnyng" and "false loue" of those who prefer vain diversions. But knowing standard items of the pastoral syllabus should not be their final goal, even if these are listed as the alternative that false lovers do not care about. Pastoral learning is a means, not an end in itself; it produces in its recipients a disposition to love God above all things, and in this way to learn to "louen togedur." This is a communal activity, just as a wrestling bout or a play might be, not merely a private endeavor. While the cycle has become in this manuscript a compilation for private or perhaps group reading, even

---

pastorali," in Matthew, 408–57, on 422; *EWS*, sermon 199, 3:233–34, on 233; and the commentary on Psalm 87 from the longest, incomplete version of the interpolated versions of Rolle's *English Psalter*, especially the first verse, in *WS*, 229–41. Several of these passages are discussed in Fiona Somerset, *Clerical Discourse and Lay Audience in Late Medieval England* (Cambridge: Cambridge University Press, 1998), 204–8. On training the will toward God, see *The Two Ways* throughout; the *Dialogue between a Wise Man and a Fool* ("Cambridge Tract XII," in *EA*, 130–42), esp. the final exchange between Wise Man and Fool; and the last verse of Richard Rolle's psalter commentary (version RV3) on Psalm 87, all in *WS*, 164–82, 247–62, 240–41. For more detailed discussion of these examples and of lollard views on salvation, see chap. 4.

here the writer's frequent embedded addresses to a congregation—"fle we þerfore þis false loue and leue we þis veyn cunnyng"—gesture beyond any private reading to imaginary or actual implementation across a community. The community that loves together will dwell with God, and God will dwell in them.

"Louen togedur" is a frequently repeated injunction in this cycle, one that takes center stage in the six sermons on the gospel precepts and first commandment at its core but that is frequently treated elsewhere too, especially in the exhortations that the writer appends to the inserted *EWS* or in the closing sentences of his own sermons. As so often in religious writing that aspires toward personal and collective reform, the cycle's frequently articulated goal of mutual indwelling is the basis for an architectural allegory that allows the writer to move fluidly between individual and social concerns.[16] The writer first elaborates his theme of indwelling in explicitly architectural terms in sermon 6, where it is the hinge between the first, briefer discussion of the five wits in the cycle and the following list of the corporeal and spiritual works of mercy. His architectural theme finds its reprise in the final twenty sermons, through an extended allegory of the soul as city or castle that becomes the writer's central expository tool as he progresses toward a final, extended exposition of love. The twenty-eight sermons in between, treating the seven deadly sins and the commandments, are no less preoccupied with the personal and social implications of proper and improper love. These middle sermons are also the ones that were most heavily expurgated by later readers and that in their remaining parts are the most idiosyncratic in their pastoral exposition. While it is difficult to make firm conclusions on the basis of what is missing, especially when we cannot be sure whether it was excised before or after the English Reformation, the heavy expurgation of this section is to some extent matched by the nervous excerpting found in later fifteenth-century copies of these sermons and is certainly intriguing.[17] The sins, treated over thirteen sermons, are negative examples of improperly directed love and come in for widely varying attention depending on the *SS74* sermon writer's level of interest. His distrust of bodily pleasures in particular comes out in his detailed enumeration of the eleven kinds of lechery, the last and foulest sin that most draws man's love from God, across four sermons. The six kinds of sloth get two sermons, the three kinds of covetousness get one sermon each, while the rest of the sins are treated more

16. See Christiania Whitehead, *Castles of the Mind: A Study of Medieval Architectural Allegory* (Cardiff: University of Wales Press, 2003). For more on lollard uses of architectural allegory, see chap. 7.

17. For details, see Spencer, "Fortunes of a Lollard Sermon-Cycle," 377–96.

cursorily in a single sermon. Anger has been excised entirely by a later reader, as have the greater part of six of the protheme sermons in this section. After the sins come fifteen sermons on the commandments, of which sermons 21 through 26, as already mentioned, focus solely on the first commandment folded together with the gospel precepts. There seems to have been much here that offended later readers, for parts of each of sermons 20 through 27 have been removed.[18] The remaining nine commandments are treated in an idiosyncratic order that allows for a consecutive discussion of the writer's concerns about love of God and neighbour over the course of eight more sermons, but apparently sermons 28–34 included less that gave offense, for they remain intact.[19]

How to Tell the Truth

What, in the broadest sense, does this writer's selection and arrangement of material suggest? Plainly the writer of this cycle thought that the *EWS* on the Sunday gospels were a valuable tool for pastoral instruction at the parish level. But equally plainly, he thought that more was needed. His interest in the *EWS* challenges Eamon Duffy's assertion in his preface to the second edition of *The Stripping of the Altars*, justifying his decision not to include lollardy in his account of late medieval English religion, that the *EWS* provide a "sour diet" for parish Christians hungry for instruction.[20] But at the same time, the *SS74* sermon writer's augmentation of the *EWS* Sunday gospel cycle demonstrates that he felt there was more to lollard pastoral instruction than what the *EWS* on their own provide. In extending and developing the content of the *EWS* into fully realized parish instruction, the *SS74* sermon writer works harder to engage and entertain his audience than did the *EWS* writers. He focuses on instructing and improving his readers rather than condemning abuses (though he does include some polemic too, quite often). But his additions are not merely a sweetener, counteracting the sourness of the *EWS*. Rather, their devotional emphasis complements the *EWS*'s

---

18. Clearly later readers disliked something about the writer's central exposition of love. As for sermons 20 and 27, sermon 20 seems to have included a general introduction to the commandments that may have been problematic for similar reasons, while sermon 27 treated first the fourth (see following note) then the third commandment, honor the holy day, and seems to have discussed church feasts in a way that may have offended later protestant sensibilities.

19. The order of the commandments in sermons 27–34, following the Catholic numbering, is 4, 3, 2 over two sermons, 7, 5, 8, 6, 9, and 10.

20. Eamon Duffy, "Preface to the Second Edition," in *The Stripping of the Altars: Traditional Religion in England, c. 1400–1580*, 2nd ed. (New Haven, CT: Yale University Press, 2005), xxiv–xxviii.

repeated claims for the superiority of Christ's religion to that of the religious orders. These sermons flesh out what it would mean to practice Christ's religion; they demonstrate across their length that all moral conduct, all truth, begins and ends in the love that Christ enjoined.

A less charitable reading of SS74 might instead insist that haphazard conjunction rather than careful planning characterizes its compilation of materials and that what has been added is wholly or mostly "orthodox" rather than lollard. My brief summary of SS74 as a whole has suggested that there is more thematic unity and careful planning in the way this cycle is put together than anyone else has given it credit for, but what is lollard about its pastoral instruction? How, in particular, does the "modern" exposition of the epistle sermons and pastoral teaching complement, rather than merely dilute, the sinewy polemical tenacity of the "ancient" EWS gospel sermons?

In its compilation of polemical material with pastoral instruction this cycle enacts a kind of transaction between lollard modes: between telling the truth by complaining about abuses in the contemporary church, and telling the truth by providing the vital pastoral instruction that corrupt churchmen fail to convey. This combination of complaint and instruction is by no means new. Complaints about priestly inadequacy frequently accompany and often provide a rationale for the production of written pastoral teaching, as in mainstream examples such as Archbishop John Pecham's *Ignorantia sacerdotum* and its derivative the *Lay Folks' Catechism*, or the prologue to Robert of Gretham's *Miroir*.[21] Anticlerical or antifraternal complaints have a very extensive history too, far beyond lollardy, rooted in conflicts between orders and ranks among the secular and regular clergy but also amply distributed in vernacular writings.[22] Here too criticisms of the misprovision of pastoral instruction often play a part, especially in complaints against friars. However, in SS74, both sides of the truth telling have a characteristically lollard emphasis.

---

21. Pecham's *Ignorantia sacerdotum* is printed alongside the *Lay Folks' Catechism* in T. F. Simmons and H. E. Nolloth, eds., *The Lay Folks' Catechism*, EETS, o.s. 118 (London: K. Paul, Trench, Trübner, 1901). See also the prologue to the *Miroir*, in Thomas G. Duncan and Margaret Connolly, eds., *The Middle English "Mirror": Sermons from Advent to Sexagesima* (Heidelberg: Universitätsverlag, 2003), 3–23 (odd pages only).

22. As Siegfried Wenzel trenchantly explains, "Robert Lychlade's Oxford Sermon of 1395," *Traditio* 53 (1998): 228–29. See also Penn R Szittya, *The Antifraternal Tradition in Medieval Literature* (Princeton, NJ: Princeton University Press, 1986); Wendy Scase, *Piers Plowman and the New Anticlericalism* (Cambridge: Cambridge University Press, 1989); Andrew Jotischky, *The Carmelites and Antiquity: Mendicants and Their Pasts in the Later Middle Ages* (Oxford: Oxford University Press, 2002); G. Geltner, *The Making of Medieval Antifraternalism: Polemic, Violence, Deviance, and Remembrance* (Oxford: Oxford University Press, 2012).

What makes the polemic here lollard is relatively familiar: an insistence that the fundamental and only essential duty of the clergy is preaching and that any true priest preaches in his actions as well as his words; distrust of clerical wealth and exhortations to lay lords to redistribute church possessions for the good of the genuinely poor and reform the clergy toward simplicity; the claim that only the virtuous can own anything; above all assertions of the primacy of Christ's law or God's law over religious rules and human laws.[23] What characterizes lollard pastoral instruction is not yet as well understood, but I have already highlighted some key features here: an emphasis on love as a choice requiring sustained effort, an attendant insistence that love is a communal rather than a private endeavor, a strong predilection toward architectural metaphors of mutual indwelling as a means to modulate between concerns with self and community. Most characteristic of all is the distinctive way in which these two modes of truth telling, polemical and pastoral, are linked. Anyone who knows the truths of both right conduct and present failings must also declare them, regardless of the risk, despite persecution, even to death.[24] We will see other versions of this kind of lollard exhortation toward martyrdom across the course of this book.[25] The *SS74* sermon writer develops them with some rather surprising inflections. More than any other lollard work I have encountered, *SS74* encourages its audience to exercise prudence, to weigh circumstances and potential outcomes, when fulfilling the lollard moral imperative to tell the truth regardless of the consequences. For the most part, it also models this prudence itself: topics that lead more polemical lollard writings into extended diatribes are treated here more briefly or allusively. How this should lead us to characterize the lollardy of the sermons as a whole is a topic that will require extended investigation.

True Speech Makes Love: Truth and Prudence

As I have explained elsewhere, Wyclif and lollard writers ground their insistence on the obligation to speak truth in a legal theory of consent that had

---

23. See *PR* for a thorough account of lollard polemical tenets, although Hudson does not stress the primacy of God's law for lollards as heavily as I do. For more on God's law, see the introduction to *WS*, 8–12, and chap. 2 below.

24. For Wyclif's similar assertions, see Michael Wilks, "Wyclif and the Great Persecution," in *Wyclif: Political Ideas and Practice; Papers by Michael Wilks*, ed. Anne Hudson (Oxford: Oxbow Books, 2000), 179–203. For a broader perspective on Middle English authors, see Alastair Minnis, "Absent Glosses: A Crisis of Vernacular Commentary in Late-Medieval England?," *Essays in Medieval Studies* 20 (2003): 1–17. Postures of martyrdom are not unique to lollard writers in this period, but they are pervasive in their writings and integral to an ethical stance their writers urge readers to share, in a way not found elsewhere.

25. See chap. 2, chap. 4, chap. 5, chap. 7, Conclusion.

been extensively discussed among canonists since the late twelfth century.[26] The *SS74* sermon writer's discussion of this theory of consent is expansive, but it is complicated by its juxtaposition with his fullest presentation of his unusual restrictions on speaking the truth. It will be helpful to begin with a more typical example, from the short, polemical commentary on the commandments extant in a unique copy in Oxford, Bodleian Library, MS Bodley 789. Here, the relationship between true speech and martyrdom is perilously direct:

> As clerkis seyn, upon sixe maneris is þis consent doon, and men schulden wel knowe it. He consentit to þe yuel þat wirchiþ wiþ þerto [participates]; he þat defendiþ and conseiliþ þerto [advises]; he þat bi whos auctorite is þe yuel don; or he þat wiþdrawiþ his helpe or scharp repreuynge [does not help to prevent it or sharply reprove the sinner], whanne he miȝte don it [he is able to do this] and schulde bi Goddis lawe. And among alle synnes bi whiche þe feend bigiliþ [beguiles] men, noon is moore sutil þan such consent. And þerfore þe prophetis of þe olde lawe tolden men hire periles [the danger they were in], til þei suffriden deeþ; and in þis cause þe apostilis of Crist weren martrid, and we schulde, ȝif we weren trewe men. But cowardise and defaute of [fol. 115v] loue of God makiþ us sterte abac [step back], as traytours don.[27]

There are six ways in which a person or persons can be guilty of another's sin because they have consented to it: if they help in committing the sin, if they defend or advise it, if it is done by their authority, or if they do not help to stop it or speak out against it. These last two categories are the ones that most condemn passive onlookers who might want to claim they are simply not involved. Wyclif cites the six kinds of consent frequently in his writings, and lollard writings follow him. Both do so in order to emphasize the sixth kind of consent above all, insisting that any failure to speak the truth about another person's sin makes the person or persons who keep silent just as guilty of that sin as its perpetrator(s).[28] Whoever does not speak the truth, even if they may die as a result, is a traitor to God; whoever does speak the truth is a true successor to the prophets and apostles.

In *SS74*'s sermons, too, as in the passage from Bodley 789 just quoted, we find insistence on speaking truth, the peril of consenting to another's sin, and the suggestion that fear and insufficient or misdirected love may paralyze the speaker's will to resist that consent. However, the sermon cycle's writer

---

26. See *WS*, Introduction, 15–18.

27. Transcribed from Bodley 789, fol. 115r–v. The copy printed in Arnold, 87, contains errors.

28. See, for example, the *Dialogue between Jon and Richard*, in *FWD*, 30/990, and a long list of citations from Wyclif and lollard writings given in the notes, 990n on pp. 85–86.

develops these materials in a distinctive way. His most extended treatment of consent appears in the central discussion of love and the commandments at the sermon cycle's core, in sermon 21. (There are briefer expositions of how one might consent to another's sin scattered throughout the cycle, as well as some attention to the Augustinian idea that an individual consents to his own sin as soon as his will chooses to pursue it, even before he commits any other sinful act.)[29] In sermon 21, however, it almost seems as though the first authority quoted is urging the audience *not* to speak truth to sinners. The commentary that follows this quotation makes matters still more complicated when it urges that men do not always need to tell the truth. The writer may sound considerably more moderate here than is typical in lollard writings:

> Speke ȝe trouthe vche oon [each] wyth hys broþer. Bycause þat trewe speche and goode maketh loue among negheburs, and false speche and yuel speche maketh also wrathe, and moste of alle monnes lymes [a man's limbs] þe tunge maketh loue or wrathe. And þerfore in al þat we speke, to goode mon or to yuel, we schulden be war what we speke and bysyly kepe [busily guard] oure tunge. And þerfore sayde þe Prophete in þe sauter boke [Psalter], "*Posui ori meo custodiam cum consisteret peccator aduersum me.*" "*I putted kepyng to my mouthe* [guarded my mouth] *when þe synful schulde whitstonde* [withstand] *me.*" But when a mon schal speke, loke he speke [mind that he speak] þe trouthe.
>
> But ȝet men neden not alle tyme for to telle þe trouthe [do not always need to tell the truth], for þere as [where] hyt myȝte [might] do harme and profyte vnto noone [benefit no one], or elles þere as it myȝte do more harme þen [than] gode, þere vs owe to be war [we should be prudent] and holde oure tunge stylle. And when þat þou may plese God and profyte whit þi speche, þenne owe þe not to holde þe stylle [you should not keep silent] but sayth forthe [declare] þe trouthe.
>
> For if þou holde þe stylle and wult not speke þe trouthe for to helpe þin neghebure when þat he hath nede—for ȝifte or for preyer, for drede or for fleschely loue, for wrathe or for hate þat þou haste vnto [toward] hym—þou consentest to þat wronge þat þi[30] neghebure done, muche more þenne sunneth he [than one sins] þat speketh falsely in wyttenesse or moneste hys neghebure to harme [urges his neighbour to do harm] with lesynges [lies] or whit lyes and oþer false wordes. for þe lawe sayth "*Qui tacet consentire videtur.*"

29. Consent to one's own sin shows up in sermon 26. Briefer expositions on consent to another's sin appear in sermons 14, 31, 32, and 44.
30. þi] *prec. by canc.* me

And also sayth seynt Poule þus in hys Epystle. "*Qui talia agunt digni sunt morte non solum qui faciunt ea sed eciam qui concenciunt facientibus,*" þat is, "he þat holdeth hym stylle [remains silent] consenteth to þe dede [deed]" and "[not] *onely þey þat done suche thynges ben wurþi þe deth* [deserve to die], *but also þey þat consenten to hem þat done þese dedes.*" And þerfore speke 3e þe treuþe whenne þat it may profyte, and drede more God of [fol. 55r] heuene þen any erþely þing, and beþ war euer whit 3oure speche þat it myspaye not [does not displease] God. Bote speke 3e vche on [each one] treuþe whit his neyghbore. (fols. 54v–55r)

The quotations from canon law and from Romans 1:32 in the final two paragraphs here are the standard topoi in all late medieval discussions of consent, and they appear in the *Rosarium* in its discussion of consent as well.[31] Their development in the vernacular into a community ethic of truth and mutual responsibility is very typical of lollard writings, and very unusual outside of lollardy, even when it does not conclude with an exhortation toward the martyrdom that faces "trewe men."[32] However, while the *SS74* writer agrees that neither gifts nor prayers, fear nor fleshly love, wrath nor hate is a good enough excuse for staying silent, he does also, and very unusually, insist that in some circumstances true speech may do more harm than good, or no good at all. Lollard exhortations to speak truth are not normally accompanied by this level of qualification, so fully and imaginatively developed.[33]

To understand what is going on here, we need to attend to the kind of circumstances that the writer wishes his audience to consider. The writer's

---

31. See, for example, the Middle English *Rosarium*, Cambridge, Gonville and Caius College, MS 354/581, fol. 24r–v, s.v. "consentyng." "Qui tacet consentire videtur" is one of eighty-eight *Regulae juris*, or legal axioms, listed at the end of the *Liber Sextus*, now in the fifth book of the *Decretals*, VI 5.12.43. See *Decretales Bonifatii VIII* [Liber Sextus], in Emil Friedberg, ed., *Corpus iuris canonici*, vol. 2, *Decretalium collectiones* (Leipzig, 1881; repr. Graz: Akademisch Druck-u. Verlagsanstalt, 1959), cols. 929–1124. For the development of these theories in justifications of papal interdict, see Peter D. Clarke, *The Papal Interdict in the Thirteenth Century: A Question of Collective Guilt* (Oxford: Oxford University Press, 2007). On consent in the fourteenth and fifteenth centuries, see Philippe Buc, *L'ambiguïté du livre: Prince, pouvoir, et le peuple dans les commentaires de la Bible au moyen âge* (Paris: Beauchesne, 1994), 394–408. As Buc notes (394), later discussions of consent are often aligned with talk about correction. On fraternal correction, see Edwin D. Craun, *Ethics and Power in Medieval English Reformist Writing* (Cambridge: Cambridge University Press, 2010).

32. I know of only two treatments of consent in Middle English that concern themselves with this kind of community ethic but are *not* demonstrably lollard. One is in the *Memoriale credencium*, in which I see no lollard characteristics, but the work is affiliated with lollardy in that it appears in London, British Library, MS Harley 2398. The other is in the *Pore Caitif*, which similarly appears in manuscripts containing lollard writings: see, for example, Oxford, Bodleian Library, MS Bodley 938. For descriptions of each, see Appendix A. Much more needs to be said about the *Pore Caitif*'s lollard affiliations, but I will not treat them in this book.

33. This emphasis on tempering the truth of one's speech with prudence does appear in other lollard writings, however: see the Prologue to the *Testimony of William Thorpe*, 28/143–47.

foremost concern is prudence, even more than truth, but this is not a prudence focused on self-preservation. The harm the writer is worried about is not harm to the speaker of truth. Rather, he urges his audience to attend to how even the truth might produce wrath, and harm to one's neighbours and the community, as well as love. His exposition of the epistle reading and his subsequent pastoral instruction on how neighbours should "louen togedur" are closely integrated. Where speaking truth will please God and do good, no private interest may excuse the one who should speak from that obligation. Failing to speak truth in these circumstances is worse than speaking falsely. The only kind of true speech that should be curbed by prudence is the kind that does damage to love, rather than augmenting it.

The trick, of course, is to determine where loving prudence leaves off and where cowardice or malice begins. Perhaps this is why the *SS74* sermon writer discusses prudence at length on no less than five occasions and frequently mentions it elsewhere, telling his audience in sermon 41 that it is impossible to say too much on the topic.[34] In addressing hope, in contrast, he repeatedly refers his audience to a single discussion that seems to have been excised, for it is extant nowhere in the cycle as it stands.[35] Only love is more central than prudence to the *SS74* sermon writer's ethical scheme. The extended discussion of prudence in sermon 41 is preceded by four previous discussions in the writer's expositions of epistle themata: in sermon 5 on "Sobrii estote et vigilate" (1 Pet. 5:8), in sermon 21 on "Loquimini ueritatem vnusquisque cum proximo suo" (Eph. 4:25) as just quoted; in sermon 22 on "Videte fratres quomodo caute ambuletis" (Eph. 5:15), and in sermon 36 on "Nolite esse prudentes sed cum omnibus hominibus pacem habentes" (Rom. 12:16, 18).

The writer distinguishes self-interested from virtuous prudence in sermon 36, where he compares his thema with 1 Peter 4:7, "estote prudentes et vigilate," closely similar of course to the thema of sermon 5 from 1 Peter 5:8. Should we be prudent, as 1 Peter 4:7 and 1 Peter 5:8 recommend, or should we avoid prudence, as Romans 12:16, 18 urges? Both, the *SS74* sermon writer says, for prudence may be turned to good or evil:

> *Wole ȝe not be slye* [prudent], *bote hauynge pees* [maintain peace] *whit alle men.* Poule semeþ meruelouse in hise wordes seyinge [Paul's words are

---

34. "Sum what haue Y spoken of prudence herbyfore. Bote men may not speke to muche [too much] to make men to be war" (fol. 110r).

35. The *SS74* sermon writer promises a lengthy treatment of hope elsewhere in sermons 6, 29, and 50. Perhaps he refers to a separate work on hope, perhaps a missing section of the sermon cycle; in either case, the contrast with his frequent discussions of prudence, or love for that matter, is quite striking.

hard to credit]. For in anoþer place he byddeþ [bids] þat ȝe schal be slye: "*Estote prudentes et vigilate.*" And here, he seiþ wole ȝe not be slye. Lord, what meneþ þis sleiȝte [prudence]? Þis sleiȝte or þis prudence is warnesse byfore [foresight], þe wuche [which] may be turned boþe to good and yuele. Mony men ben prudent to do an yuele dede for anoþer, or falsely to excusen hem whit sutel peynted [ornamented] wordes, þat [so that] þei þat heren hem speke schulen ȝeue [give] trust vnto hem. And suche kunne glaueren [know how to deceive] and glosen [speak falsely] whit þer feire speche, til þat þei han geten hire wille of þat þat þei desyren [got what they desire], or for to ȝeuen a man þe wurse [give a man the worse end of the deal] whit feire plesynge wordes. And ȝef any harme schal falle, losse, or disese, warly [prudently] þei wolen voyden hit [dispel it] and putten hit to [visit it upon] anoþer. And herfore spekeþ þis apostel þuse wordes in his pistel, "*Nolite esse prudentes apud vosmetipsos nulli malum pro malo reddentes.*" "*Nule ȝe* [Do not wish to be] *be prudent anentes* [concerning] *ȝoure selue alone ȝeldynge vnto noun on yuele* [giving nobody one evil] *for anoþer.*" For þou schuldest noht loke al only þyn oune auauntage [attend only to your own advantage], bote also þe auauntage of þi neigbore. For þou art holden [required] to loue þi neiȝbore as þi selfe. (fol. 95r)

Love is what distinguishes good prudence from bad. If we love our neighbour, we look to his advantage as well as our own and, if need be, more. Without love, we harm ourselves as well as others, even as we may think we are acting out of self-interest.

But the ability to distinguish good prudence from bad depends not only on the right kind of love but on the right kind of knowledge. In sermon 41 the writer distinguishes the "worldly warnesse" that protects people from present perils such as sharp dealing and the threat of physical harm, as opposed to the sort of wise foresight about perils in the future that is available to those who have sought and benefitted from proper instruction:

Men han worldly warnesse [prudence], and bisily þei vsen hit in alle maner chaffaryng [business] þat falleþ to [pertains to] þe world, þat noun [none] schal bygylen [beguile] hem for ouȝt [fol. 110v] þat þei can [all they can do]. And also man kan [is canny] be way of [as concerns] bodyly harm. Þis warnes of þis world helpeþ bote for a tyme. Bote he is a wise man þat can be war byfore of periles þat ben to come. And þat preueþ Salamon where he þus seiþ: "*Cor prudentis possidebit scienciam et auris sapiencium querit doctrinam*" (Prov. 18:15). "*Þe herte of þe*

war man schal kepe wisdam and eere of wise men schal sechen aftur techyng."
For whenne hit comeþ to "hadde y wiste" [if only I had known] þenne
is al to [too] late. And þerfore God biddeþ we schal be war as eddres
[snakes] and also þerwhit [also] simple as doufes [doves].

Þe eddur condicioun [nature of the snake] is þat whenne men ben
abouten to scharme hure [when men intend to charm her] scheo haþ
þis condicioun [she behaves in this way]. Scheo leith hire on eere [lays
one ear] to þe erthe, and stoppes þe toþer [other] whit hure [her] tayl,
for ȝef scheo herkene [listens] not hise wordes hit schal noht auayle
[succeed]. And in þe hote somer scheo casteþ hure olde skyn and
þenne scheo is clene and feir to þe syȝte; and whenne scheo schal consceyue [conceive], by kynde [according to her nature] scheo casteþ out
hire venym. Þis is gret warnesse of a wilde worm. Þus schulde mon be
warer [more prudently] reulyd by resoun. Þe deuel is aboute to charme
mon to synne whit his sleyteful [deceitful] speche and his false lore.
Bote þenk þenne þat þou schalt be erþe, þou ne wost [know] neuer hou
soone. And ȝef þou assente to his sawe [agree with his teaching] þenne
artou combred [then you are burdened]. And þerfore herkene not þat
counseil þat þe fend techeþ, and stoppe þin oþer eere whit þi taile þat
is muynde [memory] of þi deth. For in what plyȝt [plight] deth fyn-
deþ þe, so þou schalt be demed [judged]. And þerfore war þe wel whit
rychesse [be wary about gaining riches] and *putte þyn herte to prudence.*
Noli laborare ut diteris sed prudencie tue pone modum (Prov. 23:4). *Prouide-*
bam dominum in conspectu meo semper etc. (Ps. 15:8). *Euermore* warly *haue*
God in þi syȝt. In somer, þat is, wile [while] þou hast tyme to do boþe
good and yuel, sleue of [slough off] þin olde hame [skin] of synne þat
makeþ þi soule so foule, whit sorwe and hard penaunce by lore of holy
chirche. And þenne þi soule wil be semely in þe syȝte of God. And
spitte out þi venym, ȝef þou wolt consceyue þorw grace of þe Holy Gost
holy lyf and vertues þorw þe wuche þou may be wurchiped in heuen
for euermore. (fol. 110r–v)

If only those who have been properly taught can distinguish good advice
from bad, this passage is a kind of tour de force of proper teaching, based on
a common homiletic topos and using the writer's heightened style. He begins
with alliterative, metrical, gnomic quasi-verse that quotes direct speech: "Þe
herte of þe war man schal kepe wisdam and eere of wise men schal sechen
aftur techyng. For whenne hit comeþ to 'hadde y wiste' þenne is al to late."
He grounds his claim in paraphrased biblical quotation, of Matthew 10:16,
where Christ warns his disciples to be wise as serpents and simple as doves.

He then gives a natural-historical exposition of the passage he has just paraphrased, again markedly alliterative, in the form of a similitude of the kind
he often favors. This he bills as a description of the adder's "condicioun,"
or nature. The adder's self-inflicted deafness, as in Psalm 57:4–5, is a commonplace.[36] But here the comparison does more, however conventionally the
SS74 sermon writer begins, in that it explains in detail how an individual
person can avoid sin through the prudent exercise of reason, foresight, will,
memory, and at the very least figurative hearing and sight: ruled by reason,
thinking ahead to his end, refusing assent to the devil's teaching, remembering death to avoid hearing the devil, keeping God in his sight. What is
more, the *SS74* sermon writer continues his similitude to describe the adder's
shedding of skin and spitting out of venom, treating them (though not very
specifically) as analogues for penance. The result is a very full guide to how
prudence may guide a person in the cultivation of individual virtue, in what
is presented here at least as a relatively autonomous form of care of the self.
While this passage's attention in closing to a penitential process involving
sorrow for sin, penance according to holy church's teaching, and even oral
confession ("spitte out þi venym") is by no means as incongruous with lollard religious life as some readers might anticipate (on this see further below),
nonetheless even in discussing confession there is no explicit reference to
reliance on others in the individual's progress toward salvation.

More common in this cycle, however, is a broadening of this focus on
personal virtue as an individual pursuit to consider the social effects of each
person's actions: we need to be true not only to ourselves, as we have already
seen the writer emphasize, but to each other. Speaking the truth as we should
also depends on having the right kind of fear and avoiding the wrong kinds
of fear. In sermon 38, the writer discusses in detail six kinds of fear human
beings feel, of which only the sixth is correctly disposed toward God. As in
sermon 21 and in the discussion of consent in Bodley 789, social as much
as individual virtue requires the proper disposition of emotions in order

---

36. See, for example, *EWS*, sermon 64: "An heddre [adder] haþ þis wyt [good sense]; whan
chermerys [charmers] comen to taken hym, þe ton [one] of his erys [ears] he clappiþ to [fixes on]
þe erþe, and wiþ ende of his tayl he stoppuþ þe toþur [other]; and so Godys children, whon þei be
temptyde to synne, þei þenkon [think] mekely how freel þei ben [frail they are] made of erþe, and wiþ
greet þowt [thought] of þer deþ þat schal come, þei wyte not whonne [know not when], and dreede
of þer iugement leste þei ben demed [condemned] to helle, þei stoppon þer oþur eere and kepon hem
[keep themselves] wel fro synne. And þus han þei prudence þat God haþ 3ouun [given] to serpentis"
(2:52/120–53/128). See also *BM*, 121/9–14. In Rolle's *English Psalter*, in contrast, the adder stops its
ears against God's word rather than against the devil's; Richard Rolle, *The Psalter, or Psalms of David
and Certain Canticles, with a Translation and Exposition in English by Richard Rolle of Hampole*, ed. and
trans. H. R. Bramley (Oxford, 1884), 205.

to make prudent choices. The second kind of fear, "monnes drede," is a social sin, one that "al to muche is vsed [is all too common], whenne mon leueþ [omits] to seie þe treuþe for drede of monnes wratþe, to plese þerwhit almy3ty God and also helpe his nei3bore; bote flatere folk in hire synne and consente vnto hem" (fol. 102r). Like the other four kinds of incorrect dread, "monnes drede" is thus a failure of righteousness and also of love for God and neighbour. The way it is articulated here as a moral obligation—to speak the truth regardless of the human anger it may provoke, and so never fail in helping one's neighbour and pleasing God—is clearly related to more extensive discussions of consent and prudence elsewhere in the cycle. Recall that incorrectly motivated fear and love were among the reasons mentioned for not speaking out in sermon 21 and that both were also mentioned in the commentary in Bodley 789: this is a closely knit, mutually referential discussion where emotions and will are subjected to sustained attention.

Sermon 24 addresses in more detail the consequences for the community of flattering folk in their sin, this time in a chillingly perceptive account of the social consequences of false love. Recall that sermon 24 is in the midst of the sermons on the first commandment that have been especially heavily excised: only the end of this sermon's pastoral section remains, and the accounts of two further kinds of love discussed in the following two sermons, feigned and true, have similarly been removed. The *SS74* sermon writer explains that prudence in recognizing false love is important because it is so prevalent: "For false loue is þer muchel vsed in þis world and þerfore where hit nede [it is needful] þat men weren war þerof." He goes on to define false love and explain its operations:

> Þis false loue is fleschly loue, as [as when] man loueþ man in synne [a man sinfully loves a man], as a lechour doþ anoþer [a lecher loves another], or elles a þef [thief] a þef. As lete [if one leaves] men ligge [lie] in lecherie in pruyde or in glutonye, in wraþþe, slouþe or enuye, or elles in curside couetise. Þou schalt fynde men ynowe [enough men] to excuse alle þuse [these], boþe þe fadur and þe modur, þe sibbe [relative] and þe fremde [stranger]. 3ef he be a lechour, þei seien it is bote 3ouþehod [his youth] and a likynge [pleasant] þing a man for to pleye hym. Wolde God, þei sei, þat no man dude worse. 3ef he be a proud man þei sayen it is bote honeste [honesty] and acordeþ to his state [fitting to his status] suche for to be. 3ef he synne in glutonye þei callen hit good felachip [fellowship], and gret menske [honor] and monhede [manliness] it is for al his kyn. 3ef þat he be wrathful to berien hit longe in herte [inclined to nurse a grudge] and sone [quickly] to taken

veniaunce þei callen hit lordlynesse and seien he were ful semely [fit-
ting] lordchipe to haue. ʒef þat þei synne in slouþe [sloth] þei say þat þei
may bygynne al in good tyme God for to serue: ʒung seynt old deuele,
þis is þer prouerbe. Whanne þou art waxen an old man and myʒt no
more synne, þenne turne vnto God, and take now þi tyme. Enuye is
cald bote riʒtwisnesse [only righteousness] for to hate þin enemy, elles
myʒten þei soone [otherwise they might soon] þe say, leten alle men
ouergon hem [let all men overcome them]. Coueitise þei calle wisdam,
a man to helpen hym selue [helping oneself]. Be hit false, be hit wrong,
þei callen hit wel geten [well gotten]. And þus marieth [marries] þe
deuel here hire seuen douʒteres by counseil [advice] of anticrist, þat is
þe deueles bawstot [bawd]. And þis is þe false loue þat þis world vseth,
and alle suche han þe malisoun [curse] of God þat is in heuen, where
he seiþ on þis wyse by Isaie þe prophete: "*Ve qui dicitis bonum malum et
malum bonum, ponentes tenbras lucem et lucen tenebras.*" "*Who be vnto ʒou
[Woe to you] þat seien yuele is good and good is yuel, puttyng* [calling] *lyʒte
derkenesse and derkenesse lyʒt, and þat callen swetnesse bittur and bitturnesse
swete.*" And so doun al suche folk þat þus excusen synne. For *ʒef ʒe lyuen
aftur ʒoure flech* [according to the flesh], soþely [truly] *ʒe schulen dye* [die].
Si secundum carnem vixeritis [fol. 64v] *moriemini.* And þerfore suche ben
noʒt ʒoure frendes bote ʒoure fulle foes. And þis maner of loue schul-
destou [you should] not loue þi neyʒbore; for þis loue, as I seie, is only
flechly loue. And þerfore I praie God þat ʒoure charite be waxinge
more in cunnyng [grow wiser]. (fol. 64r–v)

As the *SS74* sermon writer catalogues how society commonly excuses common failings, he may seem temporarily to embrace a kind of moral relativism,
where sin might be a matter of perspective. However, his subsequent quotation of Isaiah counteracts this impression. All members of a society might not
agree on what should be called wisdom and righteousness, what covetousness
and envy. But there is no real possibility for disagreement on sense perceptions: light and darkness, bitter and sweet are readily distinguishable, just as
are good and evil. In order for a person to have the discernment necessary
for the proper exercise of prudence, proper instruction is needed, so that their
"charite" may be "waxinge more in cunnyng." But the grounding for that
"cunnyng," or knowledge, is secure, based in sensory perceptions, and available to anyone who trusts the evidence of their senses. The same linkage of
sense perception and the work of conscience also appears in the polemical
treatise *Of Dominion* (Matthew, 291/1–18).

Confession True and False

The unusual emphases I have been tracing across the *SS74* sermon cycle thus far, on mutual responsibility rather than autonomy, yet also on individual discretion in assessing the worth of community values and the truth of teaching, nonetheless emerge from much that is conventional. More sharply distinctive is this sermon cycle's treatment of confession, a topic that emerges repeatedly as part of the writer's broader general interest in forms of true and false speech and their effects on individuals and communities. Properly speaking, of course, confession is a type of speech that is involved in a sacrament, rather than simply being equivalent to the sacrament of penance, and sacramental confession is only a subtype of confessional speech more broadly (more on this in a moment). Nonetheless, the *SS74* sermon writer's references to confession to a priest in the course of some of his discussions of confession are this sermon cycle's only extended treatment of any of the sacraments. Lollard views on confession have presented themselves as a worry or source of confusion in a wide range of critical writings that attempt to assess the ideological affiliations of later medieval English writings. What is more, the discussions of confession in *SS74* in particular have been described as inconsistent.[37] It will be useful to take the time to propose a new understanding of what seems to be a common locus of perceived doctrinal waffling.

The following description of confession has seemed doctrinally suspect to previous readers: it comes after sermon 49's discussion of the eleventh and twelfth articles of the creed, the communion of saints and remission of sins, and addresses in more detail the question of who is able to forgive sin and how human beings might be able to help one another toward salvation. The passage that has drawn attention is underlined. But what is most centrally at stake in the broader surrounding discussion is not confession but a conflict over what constitutes absolution. In this conflict, only one doctrinal position is voiced. "Oure byleue" is that God mercifully forgives the sins of those who regret them and amend their lives; this view is supported by Ambrose, Augustine, and even canon law.[38] "Þe world," on the other hand, prefers to rely on priestly absolution regardless of the sinner's intentions, in a collusion

---

37. Fletcher assesses the underlined quotation from sermon 49 as "outspoken heresy," and the underlined section of sermon 33 as "faultless orthodoxy." He concedes that the discrepancy may be the result not of "unprocessed orthodoxy," but rather of unresolved "infighting within the sect." Fletcher, "Hive of Industry," 131–32 and esp. n. 2.

38. A later mainstream compilation, Oxford, Bodleian Library, MS e Musaeo 180, overtly contradicts the implications of the quotations from Augustine and Ambrose, then interpolates instruction on the eucharist. See Spencer, *English Preaching*, 315.

between sinful laymen and covetous priests who fail to point out to them that human absolutions in return for money are worth nothing unless accompanied by some real change of heart:

> *Remissionem peccatum.* In forȝeuenesse [forgiveness] of synne schulen we byleue also [we should also believe], þat we schulen [shall] haue forȝeuenesse holly [completely] of al oure synne of [from] hym þat is domesman [judge] ȝef we forþinke [repent] oure synne and amenden vs [make amends] in oure lyfe as Goddes lawe vs techeþ, whitouten suche indulgences as men now buggen [buy]. For God selleþ not his mercy as men buyen indulgence whit oþur absoluciouns sold for worldly wynnynge [profit]. For seynt Ambrose seiþ, and is writen [it is written] in þe lawe, *"verbum dei dimittit peccata etc. Ille solus dimittit peccata qui solus pro peccatis nostris mortuus est."* "Hee only forȝeueþ synne [Only he forgives sin] þat suffrede deth for oure synne." And also seiþ seynt Austyn, and is in þe lawe, *"Nemo tollit peccata mundi nisi solus Christus qui est agnus tollens peccata mundi."* "No man doþ awey synne no bote [except] only Crist þe wuche is lomb doynge awey [the lamb taking away] þe synnes of þe world." And þerefore seiþ God hymself, by Ezechiel þe prophete, *"In quacumque hora peccator conuersus fuerit et ingemuerit vita viuet et non morietur."* *"In what* [whatever] *houre þe synful mon is turned fro his synne and* sorweþ [is sorrowful] *whitinne in his herte, he schal lyue and noȝt dye."* And so forȝeuenesse of synne only to God longeþ [belongs only to God], and of [from] hym we byleuen of synne to haue forȝeuenesse.
>
> Mony lewede folk wene it sufficeþ vnto hem [is sufficient for them] whenne he haþ spoken whit þe prest and payed a schrift peny [confession-penny] and leyd his hond on his hed and seiþ he assoilleþ [absolves] hym, for to pay a trental and synge hit hymself [for pay for singing mass for the dead], or vche Friday to offre [for offerings each Friday] to ymages in þer chirche, or elles to ȝeue a pound of waxe to þe hye auter [high altar], or elles pay a porcioun [sum of money] to þe poure [poor] freres, and þe man turneþ aȝeyn [returns] to his olde lyfe. Þis schrift desceyueþ men, for it is not tauȝt hem, and mony for þer wynnyng [their own profit] wolen þus assoyle [absolve] folke. Bote þou schalt neuer be forȝeuen bote only of [except by] God þorw trewe contricioun and wille no more to trespace. [fol. 130v] And þerfore seiþ Ambrose þus vpon Luke: *"Non inuenio quid dixit Peter, inuenio quod fleuerit, lacrimas eius lego, confessionem sacerdoti non lego."* "I fynde not what Petre seide whenne þat he hade trespaced; wel [certainly] Y fynde þat he wepte bitturly þerfore. His teres y rede [I read of his tears], bote not

his schrift to a prest." And þus sorwe of monnes herte doþ awey his synne whit forȝeuenesse of God þat knoweþ þat sorwe. And þus oure byleue ouercomeþ þe world. (fol. 130r–v)

Only God can forgive sin, and only contrition and a "wille no more to trespace" is required for this forgiveness: "þou schalt neuer be forȝeuen bote only of God þorw trewe contricioun and wille no more to trespace." Speaking with a priest and paying him money is not sufficient, whatever "lewede folk" may think. But oral confession in and of itself is not decried as harmful; the problem is only that it can be deceptive when administered by those motivated by profit, especially when "lewede folk" misunderstand its role. Those "lewede folk" need to be taught the truth so that they may arrive at true contrition.

Consider now sermon 33's account, not in the pastoral exposition but at the beginning of the exposition of the epistle thema "Confesse ȝe to þe lord and clepeþ in his name." Here the act of confession is the focus, rather than the forgiveness of sin, and the writer is at pains to isolate and distinguish true confession, a subspecies of the true speech *SS74* as a whole values so highly, from the many kinds of false confession he also describes. Even so, he focuses on the confession of sin, rather than the broadest range of kinds of confession he might incorporate. The quotation previously labelled as "orthodox" is underlined:

Confessioun is a medicyne gostely [spiritual medicine] for monnes soule, bote vche on [each one] þat confesseþ is not hool [made whole] þerby. Trewe confessioun and false boþe þuse ben vsed [are both practiced]. Judas confesside and þerwhit was ful sory [was very sorry when he did] and for al þis schrift ȝet he is dampned. And mony confessen hem on scorn [scornfully] and tellen hire yuele dedes, and mony confesse þe treuþe and wolen hem not amende. And mony confesse þe soþe [truth] bote not er [before] þei schulen dye, as þeues and false men whenne dom [judgment] is ȝeuen on hem, and þat is more for drede þen for any sorwe. Mony confessen þe synne þat þei han doun and wolen do, as lechoures and comyn wymmen [prostitutes] and suche mony moo, þe wuche purposen hem byforen yuele for to do [premeditate their sins]. And somme confessen þe treuþe for mony yuele purpos [for evil purposes]. Somme to be preised for þei lakken [because they disparage] hemself, and somme tellen oþer mennes defautes [faults] and leten þer oune be [neglect to tell their own]. Þey tellen hit for an yuel ende [with evil intent] albeit it be [even though it is] soth. Somme confessen hemself coleredly [gloss over] of somme of

hire dedes and excusen hem [excuse themselves] of somme, albeit þei
be gulty, and somme huyden for schame þe fouleste þerof [the foulest ones]. And mony suche false confessiones þer ben, moo þen I can
rehersen, of þe wuche mony men foule [foully] ben disceyued, for
fro hym þat al knoweþ may no þing be hud [hidden], to whomsoeuer
we confesse dedes þat we han doun. Þe forзeuenesse stondeþ only in
[comes only from] God. And þerfore, as I seide, confesseþ to hym whit
schame and sore forþinkyng [fol. 88r] whitinne in þin herte and whit
ful purpose neuer to synne more, and þenne knowelache whit þi mouþe
and whit penaunce doyng, for whitouten verrey sorwe is þi schrift noht
[nothing]. [A long string of corroborative quotations from St Bernard follows; here is the peroration of the epistle sermon after another
repetition of the thema:] <u>Trewe confessioun oweþ to be hasty, naked,
and hool</u> [complete]<u>, whit hertely forþinkynge</u> [wholehearted repen-
tance]<u> whit good auysement</u> [consideration]<u>, and whit ful purpose</u> [the
intention]<u> neuer more for to synne, bote schamed þerof, whit meke
schewyng to a prest of good lyf þat con boþe leuse and bynde</u> [is able
to loose and to bind]. For of twey bodyly leches [two physicians] a seek
[sick] man schulde raþer chese [choose] hym þat wol leye [lay down]
his lyf for his to helen [heal] hym þen anoþer þat wol not bote ley [will
not do more than lay] a plaster to hym and take largely þerfore [take a
large fee for it], profite what it may. And þus by trewe confessioun we
clepen in Godes name and зef we þus continue [persevere in this] we
schulen be saued þerby. (fols. 87v–88r)

In the catalogue of many kinds of false confession given here, the writer
focuses on the faults of those confessing, rather than their lack of knowledge
and who is to blame for it, or even their collusion with others in a false community consenting together in sin. His examples highlight the contrast with
the ensuing account of true confession and draw in too a wider-ranging
contrast with other kinds of true speech and action. But near the end of this
passage, where he concludes, just before the quotations from St Bernard that
I omit, with "as I seide, confesseþ to hym whit schame and sore forþinkyng,"
his "as I seide" refers not to the negative account he has just developed, nor
forward to the underlined passage, but two sermons back, to his treatment
of prayer in an exposition of "The lord is nigh" in sermon 31, where he
described confession to God alone:

God is nyз [near] to alle þat clepeþ [call] hym inwardely in treuþe.
Mony clepen God outwardly bote not inwardely . . . and þerfore seiþ
oure lord þus in þe gospel. "*Non omnis qui dicit mihi domine domine*

intrabit in regnum celorum etc." "*Into þe kyndom of heuene schal not vche*
[each] *mon entre þat saiþ lord lord only whit þer mouthe bote he þat dooþ my*
fadres wille wuche þat [who] *is in heuene.*" He þis schal soþely [truly] entre
into heuenly kyngdam. And God is ny3 to alle þo [all those] þat clepen
hym on þis wyse [way]. For suche clepen inwardly whit loue to plese
God whit trewe forþinkynge whitinneforth [inward repentance] of
hire [their] wykede dedes. And at þis clepynge, he is ny3 [nigh] whit
mercy to amenden vs. (fol. 82v)

This description of confession to God alone in prayer is the kind of confession of sins that lollards typically valued most highly. Nevertheless, in sermon 33, while listing the conditions of true confession, the *SS74* sermon
writer twice mentions oral confession, first urging his audience to "knowelache whit þi mouþe," and then, after a long string of quotations, suggesting
"meke schewyng to a prest of good lyf þat con boþe leuse and bynde." As with
the prudent adder's spitting of its venom, but more explicitly, the *SS74* sermon
writer endorses oral confession here, and even to a priest, rather than simply
in prayer aloud. This is the kind of statement that critics have had most difficulty in reconciling with their understanding of lollard views on confession.

However, the difference between these passages lies not in their description of essentials but in their context and occasion. It is not that the writer is
inconsistent but that he tolerates a wider range of statements on this doctrinal issue than post-Reformation readers looking for proto-protestants might
expect. In the context of a complaint about corrupt confessors, the observation that only God can confess sins and only confession to God is strictly
necessary carries the writer's fullest conviction. When discussing prayer, the
SS74 sermon writer assures his readers of the efficacy of confession inwardly
to God alone, if accompanied by the proper disposition in the sinner. In an
exposition of false as opposed to true confession, however, where every kind
of false confession involves speaking (or failing to speak) before a larger or
smaller audience, the *SS74* sermon writer develops his contrasting account
of true confession to the fullest by including spoken confession to a human
audience, specifically a priest, in his account of the kinds of true speech. It is
crucial, though, that not any priest will do; it must be "a prest of good lyf þat
con boþe leuse and bynde." This is a qualified, rather than an unconditional,
recommendation, approving only the kind of priest who would lay down his
life for his sheep: "þat wol leye his lyf for his to helen hym." (Notice that it is
the priests's valuing of love over death, his willingness to imitate Christ's passion through martyrdom, that serves to illustrate his virtue.) Oral confession
is not necessary, but where a reliable confessor is available, it can be helpful.

Only God can forgive sin, however, as all three passages affirm. This assertion might seem incompatible with the admission that there are priests of good life who can loose and bind. Indeed this is a controversial stipulation, unique to the version of this sermon in *SS74*; the two later redactions instead specify that the priest should be one's parish priest (in Bodley 95) or (an addition in Shrewsbury School 3 only) another if the parish priest gives leave.[39] The "prest of good lyf þat con boþe leuse and bynde" seems incompatible both with orthodoxy and with the lollardy of protestant imaginings. On the one hand, it limits the efficacy of the priest's absolution—though not of the sacrament, if properly performed by the sinner—to cases where the priest passes muster with God, while on the other it affirms the efficacy of the sacrament (though only where God forgives as well). Yet qualified statements about oral confession of just this kind are common among lollard writings.

Considering first the power to loose and bind, *EWS* 19, used in *SS74* as the protheme to sermon 21, gives a detailed explanation of the limited sense in which priests can indeed loose and bind, as "vikerys [vicars] of Godys wylle," in the context of a broader discussion of how men can and should forgive trespasses done to them, if not the sin itself.[40] Turning to consider what kind of priest will suffice, a similar stipulation to that found in *SS74* appears, for example, in the Wycliffite reference work the *Rosarium*, whose broader distinction between confession of faith, confession of love, and confession of sin spans a wider range of kinds of true speech. Even confession of sin in the narrow sense covered by the sacrament of penance comes in two kinds:

> Sacramentale confession is double, þat is to sey, mentale and vocale. Mentale is a wilful sorow of hert for vnriȝtly [wrongly] done synnes with purpose of confessyng and makyng asethe [amends] in fourme of þe gospele [as the gospel requires]. Sacramentale confession after Austyn is bi wiche a hidyng sekenes [that by which a hidden ill] for hope of forgeffenes [forgiveness] is oponed. Confession sacramentale vocale is a lawful schewyng of syne to a conable preste kunnyng for to [appropriate priest who knows how to] bende and louse [bind and loose], for hope of forgifnes and iustificacioun. [A string of quoted authorities is omitted here.] He þat wilt confesse his synnes, þat he fynde grace, seke he [let him seek] a kunyng prest for to bynde and to louse, þat not wen he is reckeles aboute hymself he be reckelessed or despised

39. Spencer, *English Preaching*, 272–73.
40. *EWS*, 1:298/48–299/82, quotation from 299/66.

of Hym þat mercifully moueþ, and after þat boþe falle noȝt into þe dike. (Cambridge, Gonville and Caius College, MS 354/581, fol. 23r)

The only difference between the two is the grounds of the priest's qualifications: good life in *SS74*, knowhow in the *Rosarium*. Yet these are two interrelated essentials, as the polemical work "Of Confession" explains while it is positioning oral confession to a priest in a wider frame (as in the *Rosarium*) within which its importance is reduced:

> Two virtues ben in mannes soule by whyche a man shuld be rewled: hoolynesse in mannes wille, and good kunnyng in his witt . . . hoolynes goþe before [precedes] and kunnyng sueþ [follows] in worþinesse; for lyue a man hooly lyf, and kunnynge inow [enough] wil folow aftur. To make hoolynesse in men is confession nedful; and þerfor shuld hooly churche witt [know] sumwhat of confession. Confession generaly [in general] is knowlechinge [acknowledging, declaring] made wiþ wille; and sum confession is made wiþoute synne, and sum is knowlechynge of synne; and boþe þise two ben goode in man. . . . Confessioun þat man makiþ of synne is made of man [by a man] in two maners. And sum confessioun is made to man, and þat may be on many maneres; ouþer opynly [publicly] and generaly, as men confesseden in þe oolde lawe, or priuely [privately] and rownyngly [in a whisper], as men confessen nowe a daies. Whenne a man is constreyned by bodily peyne to telle his gilte, he confesseþ not; but confession mut be wilful, or ellis it is not medeful [meritorious] to man.[41]

Not only torture but a wide range of sources of human corruption render oral confession invalid, as the discussion continues; this treatise has almost nothing good to say, throughout its length, about what the sacrament of penance has become in the late medieval church. However, even this writer preserves the possibility that confession to a qualified priest might do some good, if there were any such priest: "men of conscience wolen not telle here þus her synne to prestis, for þei seyne þat no prest is able, but oonly Crist, to here þus shriftes [confessions]; and if eny diffame [defame] hem or pursue hem by þis lawe, þei baden shewe hem [ask them to show them] an able prest to here þus synnes of hem, and þei wol bleþely shryue hem þus [happily confess in this way], and ellis [otherwise] not, as þis lawe techiþ" (Matthew, 337/23–28). This writer's concession that confession to other humans might not always be worthless is a pessimistic version of the same stipulation found

---

41. "Of Confession," in Matthew, 327–45, here 327/1–3, 17–328/4.

in the *Rosarium* and in *SS74*. The variation between them is not doctrinal but a matter of religious practice. Lollard writers do not reject oral confession outright (as often claimed), and they do not even reject the possibility that priests might participate in absolution. All they reject is the claim that confession to a priest is necessary for the forgiveness of sins.

But even if oral confession to a priest is not strictly necessary, plainly a number of lollard writers felt that many parishioners would benefit from the opportunity to confess to a properly qualified priest. They may even, in some cases, have been that priest. The eighth and ninth articles of the exhaustive, highly legalistic *Thirty-Seven Conclusions* explain that confession to God with proper contrition and the reso.ve to continue in virtue is "nedful," confession to a faithful priest in good life who can bind and loose is merely "spedful [beneficial]," while on the other hand confession to an unfaithful priest who is "contrarie to Jesu Crist" is perilous. The "Sixteen Points on which the Bishops accuse Lollards," a set of clear and careful qualifications of lollard positions responding to sixteen positions imputed to "men whiche þei clepen [call] lollardis" by bishops, likewise tells us that "very [true] contricioun is þe essencial parte of penance, and confecioun of mouþe is þe accidental parte. But naþeles confession of hert done to þe hiʒe prest [high priest] Crist is as nedeful as contricioun."[42] Even the lollard manifesto the *Twelve Conclusions* focuses on deploring the social effects of the assertion that oral confession and absolution from a priest is necessary to salvation but does not deny that confession might be beneficial (see *SEWW*, 27/114–28/134).

What is more, even mainstream religious writings concede that in extreme circumstances where no other kind of confession is possible, a confession to God alone, with true contrition and the will to sin no more, may be an acceptable substitute.[43] The declarative affirmation sought by Chichele's bishops in the 1430s when examining parishioners for lollardy, "whether it is necessary for the soul's salvation to confess to a priest," does not give a good description of the complexities of either mainstream or lollard belief. Indeed,

---

42. H. F. B. Compston, ed., "The Thirty-Seven Conclusions of the Lollards," *English Historical Review* 26 (1911): 743; *SEWW*, 21/77–80.

43. The lollard treatise on the sacraments in Bodley 938 makes just this point: see fol. 267v, where readers are assured that any layperson may "here a mannes schrifte or a wommans in tyme of nede." For a description of the manuscript, see Appendix A. Jean Gerson, at the opening of his discussion of preparation for death in part 3 of his immensely popular *Opusculum tripartitum*, assures his readers that every truly contrite sinner may be saved at the point of death. This work was widely circulated in Latin; part 3 was translated into English ca. 1410 as the *Boke of the Craft of Dying* (see Robert Raymo, "Works of Religious and Philosophical Instruction," in A *Manual of the Writings in Middle English, 1050–1500*, vol. 7, edited by Albert E. Hartung [New Haven: Connecticut Academy of Arts and Sciences, 1986], 2361–64).

the version of this question in the more carefully qualified second list in Bishop Thomas Polton's register, "whether it is necessary to the salvation of an adult sinner having the capacity to confess according to ecclesiastical form that s/he should confess according to that form," indicates some awareness of the complexity of the issues and the various possibilities for equivocation in responding.[44] Where the *SS74* sermon cycle might sound theologically uneven or inconsistent, we should consider whether the issue is not rather that we are reading a bit too much like Chichele's bishops, or like later protestants on the hunt for pre-Reformation precedents for their own claims.

Reform from Below

The pastoral lollardy of *SS74* differs from what we find in late fourteenth- and early fifteenth-century polemical writings that have often been thought of as providing an epitome of lollard belief and that have been most widely read in the present day. Works such as the *Twelve Conclusions* (nailed on the doors of Westminster and St Paul's in 1395) and the more lengthy *Thirty-Seven Conclusions* (circulated in a Latin version and a longer English version, also in the early years of lollardy) address themselves to the ruling class and most especially secular lords. They are singlemindedly and declaratively polemical: their platform for reform most signally involves urging lords to seize the clergy's excessive wealth and remove clerics from secular offices of all kinds. Insofar as they address mainstream religious practices, it is chiefly to denounce their abuses and deny their efficacy. In contrast, the reforming program of *SS74* and of a wide range of more pastorally oriented lollard writings, many of them very lengthy and unprinted, is articulated rather differently. They are far more closely engaged with mainstream religious culture. Indeed, their production, copying, and readership create difficulties of definition and identification, since they were often produced out of mainstream sources and genres to which they were also sometimes reassimilated, as they circulated among other lay reading populations or even within religious

---

44. "Item an sit necessarium ad salutem anime confiteri sacerdoti" (list 1, article 6); "An sit necessarium ad salutem peccatori adulto habenti facultatem confitendi ecclesiastice quod ecclesiastice confiteatur" (list 2, article 5); my translations. Quoted from Anne Hudson, "The Examination of Lollards," repr. in *Lollards and Their Books* (London: Hambledon, 1985), 133 and 135. The two lists of questions to be used in examining heretics, the first generated by jurists and the second by theologians, are a version of the questions developed out of discussions in the Canterbury convocation of 1428 (July and November) in response to Chichele's concern to improve the detection and examination of possible heretics.

houses. They address ordinary parishioners, as well as the rather more well-heeled reading public who were the main audience for mainstream religious manuscripts, rather than the ruling elite. And their polemical convictions and positions on key tenets of lollard belief, while no less forthrightly expressed, are diffused among a great deal of practical, positive instruction that aims to build up beliefs and practices rather than to tear them down—often on a rather different foundation and in a different form than those familiar in the mainstream, often one derived from Wyclif, but rarely one that was identified as heretical. Lollard writings of a more pastoral or devotional bent, like *SS74*, are, however, no less committed to reform than are polemical writings addressed to the ruling class. In fact one might argue that they are more committed to reform than are polemical writings and less prone to be distracted by abuse of their opponents or by posturing—by the envy and pride that *SS74* insists are destructive of community.

The reform from below that *SS74*'s sermons attempt to instill in their audience does not merely appeal to individuals to turn from sin to virtue, nor merely exhort the community to forge strong horizontal bonds of love and mutual practical support, though it does both of these, at every turn. These sermons and other writings like them also hope that a converted third estate might convert in turn their priests, their bishops, and their lords. The least intrusive way in which it is suggested that this might occur is by example. Servants should obey their lords, not only if they are good and Christian, but also if they are faithless tyrants (1 Pet. 2:18). However, the example of good living that servants provide might convert their sinning lords; this is a hope that the *Schort Reule of Lif* articulates, for example.[45] While many lollard writings quote 1 Peter and urge obedience to superiors regardless of their virtue, however, a good number advocate for more discriminating or resistant forms of obedience. As parishioners are taught what they should expect from their priest, they are also encouraged to avoid priests who do not measure up.[46] As they are taught to be critical of the church as it is, they are also encouraged to reform it.

Consider, for example, this description of the church as it is and the church as it should be, drawn from *SS74*'s exposition of the tenth article of the creed:

> And so vs oweþ [we ought] to byleue in Crist and in his membres
> þat alle whit [with] charite schule [shall] come togedur and be one

---

45. See the new edition published as an appendix in Mary Raschko, "Common Ground for Contrasting Ideologies: The Texts and Contexts of *A Schort Reule of Lif*," *Viator* 40 (2009): 410/74–77.

46. In addition to discussions of confession that stipulate what kind of priest should be sought (see above, nn. 40–41), the *City of Saints* in Oxford, Bodleian Library, MS Laud Misc. 23 states explicitly that reform must come from the commons (*WS*, 276–90, here 288/5–6).

in heuen, as on [one] God and one wille and one loue in alle, and þis
schal laste for euermore in ioy whitouten ende. Bot þat þat [that which]
men clepen holy chirche is often ful fer þerfro [very far from that],
bote [but] synagoge of Sathanas þat gretly is to sorwe [a cause of great
sorrow]. Þei þat schulden gouerne holy chirche aftur Iesu Crist, þei
forsaken Cristis reule and reulen hem [govern themselves] aftur luste.
And ȝet [still] þei seyen þei ben reulares [rulers] to lede þe flok [flock]
to heuen, bote al by a wrong wey þat is not Iesu Crist. For he is wey
and he is lyfe as hymself seiþ, "*Ego sum via veritas et vita.*" Bote Crist
was poure [poor] and þei ben riche, he meke [meek] þei proude, he
dispised and þei wurshiped, he pursued [persecuted] and þei pursewe,
he fastide and þey fare wel [eat well], he seruede and þei aren seruyd, he
knelede and men knelen to hem, he preiede and þei curse, he prechede
and þei holden hem stille, he had hise preche and þei forfende [forbid
(preaching)], he forȝaf [forgave] and þei punische, he bad pees [asked
for peace] and þei bydden sle [order killing], he wepte and þei laughe,
he fedde þe pepul and halpe [helped] his flok, þei robben and dispoylen,
he suffrede colde þei sitte ful [very] warme, he oon cote [had one
coat] and þei han twenty, he whit [kept company with] poure and þei
whit lordes, he in hulles [hills] and þei in halles, he bar þe crosse [bore
the cross] þei beren þe purse [carry the purse], he forsok wurchipes
[avoided honors] and þei take [take them], he sauede [saved] and þei
dampne, he tastede eysel [vinegar] and þei piement [spiced wine], he
corouned [crowned] whit þornes and þei whit perles, he bouȝte and þei
sellen, he stey vppe [rose up] and þei wenden [go] doun, he wente to
heuene and þei to helle. Þus is þis chirche chaungyd þat pyte is to here
[in a way that is pitiable to hear]. God forbede [forbid] we schulden
byleue in suche maner chirche [a church of this kind], bote mende [fol.
128v] we [let us reform] into betur þat we han wrouȝt amysse [what
we have made amiss]. (fol. 128r–v)

Helen Spencer has noted that the version of this passage in Bodley 95 is even
more expansive in its description of abuses than that given here: it seems
likely that *SS74*'s writer is drawing on another polemical source.[47] The key
point here, though, is that he urges his audience not to believe in the kind of
church where these kinds of manifest contradictions of Christ's example take
place, but rather to "mende we into betur," "amend ourselves into a better

---

47. Spencer, "Fortunes of a Lollard Sermon-Cycle," 384–86. See also Fletcher, "Hive of Industry," 132 n. 3.

one." This communal resolve upon reform, and refusal of belief to a corrupt church, does not appear in Bodley 95, even if its version voices more complaints; instead, Bodley 95 exhorts personal reform in more conventionally individualistic terms: "God forbede it þat we schuld lyue in suche a maner, but amend we vs to better þat we haue done amysse."[48]

But what might relatively ordinary people do, faced with the need to reform not just themselves but their society as a whole? Rarely, lollard writings do make practical suggestions. *EWS* 31, incorporated into *SS74*'s sermon 33 where the *SS74* writer's protheme exposition discusses true and false confession at length, explains that Christians should occasionally withhold their obedience from men when it conflicts with obedience to God:

> [H]erfore men schulden lernen obedience to aȝenstonden [defiant obedience]. Whan any creature of God biddeþ þe [orders you to] do contrarie to þat þat [the opposite of what] þi prelat [prelate] byddeþ þe do by expresse signes, and God by his creature biddeþ þe do þe contrarye, þanne þow schuldest aȝenstonden [defy] þi prelat in þis, and obesche to [obey] God in what signe þat he vseþ. (*EWS* 1:354/96–101)

While this sermon confines its recommended resistence to an example of wrongful commands from a high-ranking member of the institutional church, the implications are obviously far broader. In sermon 44, the writer of *SS74* develops those implications in their broadest possible scope, yet with the hopeful, constructive impulse that is so broadly typical of his writing. Rather than urging disobedience, he exhorts meekness, calling on the whole of society alike to employ this virtue in all their dealings:

> [B]eþ folewares [followers] of God as hise derrest chidren and kepeþ þuse [these] þre degrees of mekenesse as I seide, to lowen hym [humble himself] to his souereigne, his neigbore, and his sugette [subject], for Crist þe kyngus sone of heuene tauȝte vs þis hymselue and seynt Poule biddeþ hit [requires it] where he þus seiþ, "*Obedite prepositis vestris non tantum bonis et modestis sed eciam discolis.*" Þus oweþ vs alle to do [should we all do] by þe reule of God.
>
> Firste oure souereynes to reule hem [should govern themselves] aftur [by] Godes lawe; or elles [otherwise] bygynne þei to breken þis degre [breach the requirements of their rank] as þei þat folewen Lucifer þat no souereigne wolden haue. Hou schulde þei reulen oþer wele þat

48. Quoted and compared in Spencer, "Fortunes of a Lollard Sermon-Cycle," 384–85, here 385/13–14.

han no reule hemself? Popes, emperoures, and kynges schulden reulen hem aftur Crist vchon [each one] in his degree þat he is clepid inne [in the status to which he has been called]. And vche lower [each person of lower rank] meke hym [should humble himself] to his souereigne. Þus reulyd [If the world were ruled in this way], þis wolde make pees bytwene kynges and kynges, bytwene lordes and comunes [commoners], hosebondes and wyues, and so schulde al þe pepul lyue in loue and pees. And þis tauȝte Crist whenne he suffrede for vs and seide *"Pater non sicud ego volo sed sicud tu."*

Þe toþer mekenesse schulde be bytwene euene and euene [equals], as vche [each] mon to his neyghebore whitouten any enuye, vche on to suffre of oþer [each to bear with the other] whitouten veniaunce takyng [vengefulness], þe wyseste to be mekeste and moste seruiȝable [eager to serve], as Crist ȝaf [gave] vs ensaumple in his oune persone, waschynge [washing] hise disciples feet seyinge on þis wyse [speaking in this way]. *"Exemplum dedi vobis sicut et ego feci ita et vos faciatis."* "I haue ȝeuen ȝow [given you] *now ensaumple þat so as Y haue do so do ȝe* [As I have done, so do you], etc." Whoso [whoever] is moste [greatest] among ȝow, Y wol þat he meke hym þus [humble himself in this way]. For þe disciple oweþ not to be more þen [should not be greater than] þe maistre. And þus we ben alle breþeren, be we riche or poure, þat lyuen as Cristis children and reulen vs þus by mekenesse. And whoso moste mekeþ hym moste schal ben in heuen.

A man to lowen hym [fol. 119r] to his lasse [For a man to humble himself to his inferior] is þe þridde degre. Noht to dispise poure men, ny [nor] be to cruel to his seruauntes, ny his meyne [household], ny to hem þat han mysdoun [mistreated] hym. And preie for hem, as God techeþ, þat ben enemyes to þe. For Crist biddeþ þus hymself in þe gospel *"Orate pro persequentibus et calumpniantibus vos."* And here schulden lordes and riche men taken hede to hemselue, to be meke and merciful to bonde men and hire [their] tenauntes, al be hit [even if] þei ben in þis lyue lower þen þei. For Crist bouȝte [redeemed] vs alle and maade vs alle free. Crist ȝaf ensaumple þus for to meken vs whenne he suffrede þe curside Jewes to buffeten hym and scorgen hym and to spitte in his face and coroune [crown] hym whit þornes and aftur nayle hym on þe cros bytwene twey þeues [two thieves], þat whit a word of his mouþ myȝthe [could] haue struyed [destroyed] hem alle. And preiede for hem to his fadur, seyinge on þis wyse *"Pater dimitte eis quia nesciunt quid faciunt." "Fadur forȝeue* [forgive] *hem for þei wyten not* [do not know] *what þei doun."* And so beþ þus folewars of Crist as his derrest children. (fols. 118v–119r)

Not only churchmen but all of society must imitate Christ, and every member of society may be judged by Christ's standard. Even if this claim has revolutionary implications, this is not, of course, a call to revolution. It begins, reassuringly perhaps to some, with the usual quotation from 1 Peter (not Paul) that bad lords must be obeyed as well as good ones. But as it proceeds, it presents an unusual take on political thought for a parish sermon, some of which draws directly on Wyclif's *De civili dominio*.[49] In asserting that lords who cannot rule themselves are not fit to rule, in describing how equals should humble themselves to serve one another, in giving a detailed description of the sins lords should avoid in dealings with their inferiors, in asserting that Christ made us all free, it seemingly has most to tell its primary audience about how lords should behave and least to say about the conduct of the members of its primary audience themselves.

For lollard writers, far more urgently and insistently than the general mass of late medieval Christians, love is a choice, and a stark choice with dire consequences. Love is an act of will in tandem with properly disposed emotions, one that requires constant renewal, that is difficult to maintain, that places extraordinary burdens on the individual Christian, but also that permits (even requires) extraordinary freedoms. These freedoms might include sharply criticizing not only one's inferiors and one's peers but one's social superiors, and refusing to obey orders when they require one to commit sin. Lollard writers often soft-pedal some of the more radical implications of their commitment to truth. Even (or perhaps I should say especially) in polemical writings overtly or covertly addressed to secular lords and gentry, for example, the topic of how a secular lord should respond to corruption and greed in the church emerges far more often than that of how servants might refuse obedience to a sinful lord. However, in pastoral writings, especially when they are overtly addressed to audiences including persons of lower status, it is far less clear what specific application these exhortations toward truth might find and more clear that their consequences are far-reaching.

The Lollard Pastoral Program

Admittedly, these radical implications are not developed explicitly in what remains to us of the prudent work of this sermon writer. Anne Hudson's "provisional characterization" of these sermons as "the work of a Lollard

---

49. For details on how and where Wyclif asserted claims much like the ones that follow, see A. S. McGrade, "Somersaulting Sovereignty: A Note on Reciprocal Lordship and Servitude in Wyclif," in *The Church and Sovereignty c. 590–1918: Essays in Honor of Michael Wilks*, ed. Diana Wood (Oxford: Basil Blackwell, 1991), 261–78; and Lahey, *John Wyclif*, 199–221.

sympathizer, though not on the extreme wing of the movement" similarly emphasizes their restraint but attributes their mutedness to the ideological standpoint of their writer (*EWS*, 1:123). I argue, instead, that this writer's style of truth telling may reflect not the extent and degree to which he identifies with lollardy, but rather the occasion and audience for his sermons. Just as he urges his listeners to attend to circumstances as they fulfill the ethical imperative to speak truth, prudently assessing how their speech might contribute to or detract from loving together in Christ, so he does himself. All variation within lollardy need not be attributed, as it sometimes is by scholars less kindly disposed toward the movement, to inconsistency, lukewarm belief, or failure of commitment. Both persons and books may identify to varying degrees in different times and places with lollardy, but equally, they may exhibit variation even when their lollard views remain the same.[50] A lollard writer might say rather different things in his sermons than he might say in a jointly written manifesto nailed on the doors of Westminster and St Paul's, for example, even without having experienced any change of heart.[51]

We might regard *SS74* as a blurry, incompletely preserved snapshot of one context and occasion for the delivery of lollard pastoral teaching. It represents neither the beginning nor the end of the materials it compiles, some of which passed in and out of lollard identity in their varying redactions and interpolations. And they are not even all still there, in the manuscript as it stands.[52] But it provides, nonetheless, a remarkably coherent and fully realized picture of what lollard preachers, and pastoral writers, most wanted to communicate. This summary will provide a reference point for subsequent chapters, in which its features will be developed in more detail.

Lollard pastoral teaching did not reject the sacraments outright, as some scholars have claimed and as some trial evidence seems to suggest. But it did diminish the mainstream emphasis on the role of the institutional church in administering them. Rather than being treated systematically, sacraments tend to emerge piecemeal within larger discussions, and they are often developed metaphorically or within a broader definition encompassing more than the institutional sacrament, in ways that emphasize the individual Christian's relationship with God rather than doctrinal instruction in the sacrament's "correct" performance (see chap. 3, chap. 4, chap. 7, Conclusion). More

---

50. See Fiona Somerset, "Afterword," in *WC*, 319–33; Hornbeck, *What Is a Lollard?*, 18–22.

51. In surveying the extant oeuvre of Stephen Denison, Peter Lake makes a similar point about how changing audiences and generic expectations may produce differences of emphasis and purpose rather than of doctrine: see *The Boxmaker's Revenge: "Orthodoxy," "Heterodoxy," and the Politics of the Parish in Early Stuart London* (Stanford, CA: Stanford University Press, 2001), 11–52.

52. On where material has been excised, see Appendix B.

polemical lollard works often focus on abuses in the institutional administra-
tion of the sacraments and even to some extent in religious practice. But they
only rarely suggest that the sacrament should instead be avoided altogether.
Generally, the focus of their exhortations toward reform is an insistence
that priests should instead devote the bulk of their energy to preaching,
teaching, and living in accordance with the instruction they provide (see
chap. 3, at n. 34).

Many lollard pastoral and devotional writings develop their accounts of
how to establish and maintain proper love toward God in sometimes quite
technical accounts of moral psychology; they are interested in the disposition of the emotions and their ordering, the proper work of the informed
will, how conscience should operate, what can be known with certainty, and
what must remain an arena for doubt and therefore for either hypothesis or
faith.[53] Some parts of this account, such as descriptions of emotions in terms
of virtues or vices or the linking of (but not the strong emphasis on) words,
works, and will, are common more broadly in a wide range of pastoral writings. Others, such as descriptions of guessing in the face of doubt or debates
about consent, are relatively new to vernacular readers and rarely discussed
elsewhere in Middle English pastoralia, even though they were topics of
widespread and lively discussion in academic contexts.[54]

Neither the lollard insistence on doubt about one's own and others' salvation nor the lollard insistence that every member of every parish should be
properly taught is consistent with the strict, determinist predestinarian beliefs
often imputed to lollard writers.[55] Wyclif's views on this topic closely resemble those of lollards, for all that he and they use terms like "foreknown"
or "elect." However, as we will see later, lollard writings typically confine
membership in the church to "those that shall be saved," even if they do not
know who in the end these people will be, and this phrase appears frequently
in their writings.[56]

Proper love toward God and man requires truth, and truth requires fidel-
ity to oneself and to others, as much as conformity with states of affairs in

---

53. For discussions of the emotions, the senses, or the mind's faculties, see esp. chap. 6, and also
chap. 2, chap. 4, chap. 5, chap. 7, and the Conclusion. On doubt, see the following note.

54. On consent, see the detailed explanation given above, but also chap. 2, chap. 4, chap. 5,
n. 62, chap. 6, and chap. 7. On uncertainty or doubt, see esp. chap. 4 at n. 57, but also above at n. 15,
and the Conclusion.

55. See above at n. 15, and also chap. 4 at n. 53.

56. See chap. 4, and WS, 18–20. There are, of course, other favored terms lollard writers use to
describe their community, such as the "little flock" (see chap. 6) or "true people" or "true men" (see
e.g. chap. 2). On lollard self-description, see further Matti Peikola, Congregation of the Elect: Patterns
of Self-Fashioning in English Lollard Writings (Turku: University of Turku, 2000).

the world. Truth requires consistency, in words, works, and will and even in feeling. The moral imperative to speak and act in ways that promote truth, even to the point of martyrdom, is frequently articulated, and truth in words and actions is often linked with a stringent account of how we may consent not only to our own sins, even when we commit them only in our hearts rather than in deed, but even to the sins of others as well.[57] Emphasis on consent as a feature of social as well as individual life is, as well, a feature of the lollard emphasis on will.

Except in that they usually avoid listing or explaining the sacraments of the institutional church, and are often critical of current religious practice when they do so, lollards agree with their mainstream contemporaries about what the content of pastoral instruction should be, as in what is popularly known as Pecham's syllabus: these are the articles of faith (whether twelve as in the creed or fourteen as in Pecham's list), the ten commandments and two gospel precepts, the seven deadly sins, and the seven virtues (three theological and four cardinal, and sometimes also seven virtues that oppose the seven sins).[58] Lollards agree with their mainstream contemporaries, too, on the prayers it is most important for laypeople to learn: the Pater Noster, Ave Maria, and creed. The relative emphasis that they give to the elements of this instruction differs, however, and in fairly consistent ways. Creative reworking, and often reordering, of traditional catechetical lists and materials is common in lollard writings, as is prolonged amplification of topics considered especially important and associative rather than sequential development of topics in order to bring out lollard emphases and integrate their exposition into the thought process of a larger whole.[59] The most common and most expansive topic of lollard amplification is the commandments, or "God's law," as will be explained further in the next chapter.

---

57. On truth and martyrdom, see n. 25 and the cross-references given there. On consent, see n. 54.

58. On literature of religious instruction in England, see E. A. Jones, "Literature of Religious Instruction," in A *Companion to Medieval English Literature and Culture, c.1350–c.1500*, ed. Peter Brown (Malden, MA: Blackwell, 2007), at *Blackwell Reference Online*, http://www.blackwellreference.com/public/book.html?id=g9780631219736_9780631219736 (accessed June 11, 2012). On lollard writings and the sacraments, see above, chap. 7, and the Conclusion.

59. In addition to the examples of reworking the treatment of the commandments given above and in chap. 2, see chap. 3, chap. 6, chap. 7, the Conclusion, and Fiona Somerset, "Textual Transmission, Variance, and Religious Identity among Lollard Pastoralia," in *Religious Controversy in Europe, 1378–1536: Textual Transmission and Networks of Readership*, ed. Michael Van Dussen and Pavel Soukup (Turnhout: Brepols, 2013), 71–104.

❧ CHAPTER 2

God's Law

Loving, Learning, and Teaching

Near the end of the final chapter of the *General Prologue* to the Wycliffite Bible, as the writer's defense of biblical translation comes to an end, he expresses his hopes for the effect that English translation might have upon the people of England. Until now they have been deprived of access to scripture, whether because of the negligence of the clergy or their own sinfulness. Now, he hopes this may change: "[May] God for his merci amende [rectify] þese yuele [evil] causis and make oure puple to haue and kunne [know] and kepe treuli hooli writ to liyf and deþ."[1] Having and knowing and keeping, truly, and even unto death: this is a familiar concatenation of terms in lollard writings, as we will soon see. But most typically what readers are exhorted to have and know and keep in lollard writings is not holy writ, as here, but "God's law."

"God's law," or its rather less common alternate "Christ's law," is one of lollard writers' most favored terms and most common points of reference.[2]

---

1. The *General Prologue* is edited by Dove under the title "The Prologue to the Wycliffite Bible" in *EA*, 3–85. For this quotation, see *EA*, 84/2945–46.

2. Although not listed among common lollard locutions in Anne Hudson's article "A Lollard Sect Vocabulary?," repr. in *Lollards and Their Books* (London: Hambledon, 1985), 165–80, terms or circumlocutions such as "law of God" occur, for example, four times in the *Lanterne of Liȝt*, fifteen times in the *Apology for Lollard Doctrines*, twice in the *EWS* (which, however, cite Christ or God tout court very frequently), and in items 1, 4, 7, 8, 9, 10, 17, 21, 22, 23, 26, and 28 in Matthew. Mainstream

What do they mean by it? Most broadly, as the Prologue writers' substitution of "hooly writ" for the more common "God's law" would suggest, God's law *is* holy writ. More precisely, it is the moral instruction contained in the bible. But even while the bible's translators obviously attach importance to making the whole of the bible accessible, this need not mean that the *General Prologue* writer, or any lollard writers, envisage that every lay reader will read the whole of the translated bible.[3] As he made very clear in the first chapter of his prologue, and as he reiterates in chapters 12 and 13, the *General Prologue* writer follows Augustine, and Wyclif, in the conviction that the bible's truth is easily accessible in the most "open," that is, the most clearly expressed, of its parts, not only through comprehension of the whole.[4] "Open" is a keyword that lollard writers often use in referring to the bible's meaning, as others have noted.[5] The part of the bible in which its moral instruction is most "open" is "God's commandments" or "hestis": they are the epitome of biblical truth, and all truths about moral conduct may be derived from their exposition. So it is that no lollard work of religious instruction or devotion with any sort of scope is complete without an extended exposition of the commandments. Where a work treats a variety of subjects, the section on the commandments is typically the longest by far: consider, for example, *SS74*, the *Lanterne of Liʒt*, and John Clanvowe's *The Two Ways*.[6] (By contrast

---

writings, too, use the term, but without making an explicit contrast with human laws or dismissing them as inferior. These statistics were culled from Frances McSparran, ed., *Middle English Compendium*, University of Michigan, at http://quod.lib.umich.edu/m/mec/, but readers will find it easy to confirm these findings in other works.

3. Mary Dove, "The Lollards' Threefold Biblical Agenda," in *WC*, 211–26, suggests the *General Prologue* writer hopes readers will read the whole bible. She has some warrant, for the author has just been strongly advocating translation of the bible as a whole. However, see chap. 5.

4. *EA*, 5/78–82, 65/2264–75, both citing Augustine's sermon 350 in praise of charity; and 70/2419–30, citing Augustine, *De doctrina Christiana*, book 2, chaps. 6 and 7. On Wyclif's understanding of the senses of scripture, see *De veritate sacre scripture*, ed. Rudolph Buddenseig, 3 vols., Wyclif Society (London: Trübner, 1905–7), 1:119–25, where, however, Wyclif cites John Duns Scotus and refers to what is literal (*literalis*) rather than what is open (121/18–122/6). Wyclif cites Augustine on scripture's explicit and implicit meanings in his *Trialogus cum supplemento trialogi*, ed. Gotthard Lechler (Oxford: Clarendon Press, 1869), 240. For an introductory discussion of Wyclif's hermeneutical principles and their intellectual underpinnings, see Ian C. Levy, "Holy Scripture and the Quest for Authority among Three Late Medieval Masters," *Journal of Ecclesiastical History* 61 (2010): 40–68, and see also Levy, *Holy Scripture and the Quest for Authority at the End of the Middle Ages* (Notre Dame, IN: University of Notre Dame Press, 2012).

5. See Kantik Ghosh, *The Wycliffite Heresy: Authority and the Interpretation of Texts* (Cambridge: Cambridge University Press, 2002), passim (see entry in General Index, 296); and among others, Rita Copeland, "Rhetoric and the Politics of the Literal Sense in Medieval Literary Theory: Aquinas, Wyclif, and the Lollards," in *Interpretation: Medieval and Modern*, ed. Piero Boitani and Anna Torti (Woodbridge: Brewer, 1978), 19–20; Andrew Cole, "Chaucer's English Lesson," *Speculum* 77 (2002): 1146–48.

6. For *SS74*, see chap. 1. On the disproportionate or otherwise unconventional treatment of the commandments in the *Lanterne of Liʒt* and other works, see *WS*, 9–10.

the commandments are treated more proportionally in mainstream works such as Robert Mannyng's *Handlyng Sinne*, the *Memoriale credencium*, and the *Speculum Christiani*.) Even pastoral or devotional pieces that are ostensibly on another topic are reworked, in lollard hands, so that they recur constantly to the commandments, where comparable mainstream works develop different or more varied themes.[7]

What, then, are the commandments of God's law? The commandments or "hestis" are not only the decalogue or ten commandments as given in Exodus 20:1–17 and Deuteronomy 5:4–20, but also Christ's two gospel precepts to love God above all things and your neighbour as yourself (Matt. 22:37–39; see also Mark 12:29–31; Luke 10:27) and Paul's subsumption of all the commandments into love (Rom. 13:10; cf. Gal. 5:14). That the gospel precepts, Paul's injunction to love, or the decalogue could be interpreted as different expressions of the same law had become in the later Middle Ages a commonplace of exposition. The first three commandments of the decalogue were considered to address love of God, while the remaining seven addressed love of neighbour. (Lollard writers, like all of their contemporaries, used what is now called the "Catholic" rather than the later "Protestant" numbering.)[8] Christ and Paul themselves emphasize equivalences between their versions of the commandments and the decalogue of the Hebrew Bible, though not in the schema later exegetes developed, and lollard writers frequently cite these biblical passages as well. As the *Dialogue between a Wise Man and a Fool* explains them,

[W]ite þou [know] wel þat þese ten hestis ben closed in [contained within] tweyne [two], þat is, in *loue* to *God aboue al þinge* and to *þi neiȝbore as to þiself* (Matt. 22:37–39, Mark 12:30–31, Luke 10:27). And Crist seiþ þat *in þese tweyne loues ben closed al þe lawe and þe profetis* (Matt. 22:40). And, be witnesse of Poul, *he þat loueþ* parfiȝtly [perfectly] *haþ fulfilled þe*

---

7. See, for example, *WS*, 9–10; and Fiona Somerset, "Textual Transmission, Variance, and Religious Identity among Lollard Pastoralia," in *Religious Controversy in Europe, 1378–1536: Textual Transmission and Networks of Readership*, ed. Michael Van Dussen and Pavel Soukup (Turnhout: Brepols, 2013), 71–104. See also, for example, the various versions of *Pride, Wrath, and Envy*, a loosely organized and highly variable text that blends basic instruction with polemical content, text F.21 in P.S. Jolliffe, *A Check-list of Middle English Prose Writings of Spiritual Guidance* (Toronto: Pontifical Institute of Mediaeval Studies, 1974). On *Pride, Wrath, and Envy*, see also Margaret Connolly, "Preaching by Numbers: The 'Seven Gifts of the Holy Ghost' in Late Middle English Sermons and Works of Religious Instruction," in *Preaching the Word in Manuscript and Print in Late Medieval England: Essays in Honour of Susan Powell*, ed. Martha W. Driver and Veronica O'Mara (Turnhout: Brepols, 2013), 83–100.

8. On versions of the commandments, see John Bossy, "Moral Arithmetic: Seven Sins into Ten Commandments," in *Conscience and Casuistry in Early Modern Europe*, ed. Edmund Leites (Cambridge: Cambridge University Press, 1988), 214–34.

lawe (Rom. 13:8–10, cf. Gal. 5:14). For whoso [whoever] loueþ God aboue al þingis, he wol not breke his comaundementis. And he þat loueþ his neiȝtbore [neighbour] as himself wole do noþinge to his neiȝtbore but [except] as he wolde his neiȝtbore dede [did] to him.[9]

Whoever loves perfectly will also follow the law, for all of the law comes to nothing more than love. But there is a tension here, one that the biblical exposition of the commandments itself addresses, that is registered in the interpolation of "parfiȝtly" into the *Wise Man and a Fool*'s quotation from Romans, and that the very large volume of commentary the commandments generated across the medieval period as a whole only intensifies.

Commentary on the commandments, we should remember, was produced in Latin as well as in French and English, for a wide range of different kinds of audiences. At their simplest, commentaries may take the form of short verses designed, it seems, only to impart the most rudimentary knowledge yet also to commit that knowledge to memory.[10] At their most complex, commentaries build on the conviction that the commandments epitomize all the truth of the bible to develop extraordinarily wide-ranging and learned expositions of the teaching the commandments are said to contain within them. Even if the commandments can be said to contain the whole of the law, even if that law can be epitomized in a single word, they also require exposition. Rather than being the product of love alone, the capacity to follow the law—any law—is more usually seen as the product of prolonged study of that law, or at least of rudimentary teaching about its key precepts, and of some process of external guidance and adjudication.[11] How, then, can loving on its own, even loving perfectly, fulfill the law?

Many lollard writings address this tension between loving, learning, and teaching. The *Five Questions on Love*, for example, asserts that "a man may wite [know] bi himsilf wher [whether] he þenkiþ [thinks] on Goddis lawe and loveþ it and kepiþ it, and þanne Crist seiþ þat he loveþ God" (consolidating here Wyclif's use of John 14:23–24, Ps. 1:1–2, 1 John 4:8, Matt. 19:17, and 1 John 5:3 in the *De amore*).[12] You may know by yourself that you love, by thinking and loving and doing. Wyclif in his *De amore*, on the other hand, places more emphasis on the learning process, quoting John 14:21 to claim

---

9. Edited as "Cambridge Tract XII," in *EA*, 138/298–303; punctuation modified.

10. On versified instruction, see Elisabeth Salter, *Popular Reading in English, c. 1400–1600* (Manchester: Manchester University Press, 2012).

11. For a forceful statement of this double bind, see chap. 3 of "On the Seven Deadly Sins," about pride in knowledge, in Arnold, 122–23.

12. Arnold, 184/4–5, and see *WS*, 163/19–21.

that "the most effective means of realizing the love of God in this life is in one's careful study of God's law."[13] Rather than loving God by loving his law, in Wyclif's version you love God by *learning* his law. Even so, this learning is portrayed as a self-directed process, with no mention of a teacher. Many lollard writers seem to agree: even where they include biblical quotations that seem to suggest no learning is necessary in order to love, they do so in the context of providing the means for extended study. For example, the commentary on the commandments in London, British Library, MS Harley 2398 assures its readers on the basis of John 14:23 that "Crist seiþ þat what [whatever] man loueþ him wel schal kepe his word, þat is his byddyng."[14] Yet this claim appears in the midst of a lengthy work in which commentary on the commandments becomes extraordinarily expansive, a means toward instruction in biblical exegesis and even moral theology. And even while many writings strongly encourage self-directed learning, many do also place great emphasis on the obligations of teaching and correction that members of the community should fulfill toward one another: they complain about the lack of proper preaching and pastoral direction by priests, and they stress that every person is obligated to teach others the commandments, in words as well as by example.[15] Thus, the assertion that an ordinary person may know whether he loves God as he should is not necessarily an anti-intellectual one, even if it often appears alongside criticism of oversophisticated clerics who fail in love of God even as they devote themselves to learning (and these are widespread, of course, rather than specific to lollardy). Instead, we might read it as one of several ways that lollard writers seek to reimagine what a community united by love and governed by law might look like, and how its members might behave.

13. "[P]reparacio ad dileccionem Dei pro statu vie potissime stat in isto, quod homo diligencius studeat legem Dei": John Wyclif, *De amore sive ad quinque quaestiones*, in Wyclif, *Opera minora*, ed. J. Loserth, Wyclif Society (London: C. K. Paul, 1913), 8–10, at 8/22–24. Translation drawn from *WS*, 85/37–86/1.

14. Judith Jefferson, ed., "An Edition of the Ten Commandments Commentary in BL Harley 2398, and the Related Version in Trinity College Dublin 245, York Minster XVI.L.12 and Harvard English 738 Together with Discussion of Related Commentaries," 2 vols. (PhD diss., University of Bristol, 1995), 2:2/5–6; subsequent citations are parenthetical and by volume, page, and line numbers. This chapter owes a heavy debt to this as yet unpublished dissertation, which lucidly describes the relationships between a large cluster of related commandments commentaries in a way that supersedes all previous work and is likely to remain definitive for the foreseeable future. I use Jefferson's numbering of the commentary versions throughout this book; she modifies those of C. A. Martin, ed., "Edinburgh University Library Manuscript 93: An Annotated Edition of Selected Devotional Treatises with a Survey of Parallel Versions," 2 vols. (PhD diss., University of Edinburgh, 1978).

15. See, for example, the highly variable treatise on the seven works of mercy discussed and edited in Somerset, "Textual Transmission."

Lollard writers explain how God's law might order and govern a community by means of a cluster of favorite biblical quotations, cited repeatedly.[16] Many of these are clumped together in the most densely biblically allusive prologue in any commandments commentary in Middle English, that in CUL Nn.4.12. CUL Nn.4.12's prologue begins, like the many other widely varying forms of this prologue that share these opening sentences, with Matthew 19:17:

> Alle maner of men schulde holde Goddes heestes, for wiþouten holdynge of hem may no man be saued. And so þe gospelle telliþ how oon [someone] axed Crist what he schulde do for to come to heuene. And Crist badde him *ȝif þat he wolde entre into blisse, þat he schulde kepe þe comaundementes of God.* (fol. 3r)

After these shared opening sentences CUL Nn.4.12 diverges from the "standard version" of this prologue that most scholars label as "orthodox" in order to pile up after them several more biblical quotations that we will examine shortly.[17] But even this opening leads off in a lollard direction. The negative emphasis at the end of the first sentence here, "wiþouten holdynge of hem may no man be saued," was clearly regarded as innocuous by the mainstream revisers and compilers who adapted and copied this prologue. Yet this negative emphasis is unusually important to lollards, and they develop it in characteristic ways.

It is important to lollard writers that Matthew 19:17, "if you will enter into life, keep the commandments," should stand alone, as the basis for moral conduct for every Christian. They do not go on to quote Christ's second response, the one that most inspired St. Francis: "If you will be perfect, go sell what you have, and give to the poor" (Matt. 19:21). For many medieval Christians, Christ's first exchange with the young man establishes a minimum common standard, however important its content, one that is complemented by "counsels of perfection" that impose greater commitments and higher standards on members of religious orders, and one that requires supplementation and expansion through subsequent human legislation. For lollard writers, in contrast, Christ and the young man's first

---

16. For lollard use of these quotations, see in addition to the following example the *Dialogue between a Wise Man and a Fool*, the *City of Saints*, and the *Five Questions on Love*, the last three all modernized in *WS*.

17. CUL Nn.4.12's commentary is Jefferson's DVII (Discursive Version 7): this copy shares its prologue in full with two other copies of DVII, and also the two copies of DRI (Discursive/Rhetorical Version 1) and the single copy of DRIII. See Jefferson, "An Edition of the Ten Commandments Commentary," 1:cxxxi–cxxxvi (list of manuscripts of versions), clxxxi–clxxxiv (description of DVII), cxci–cxciv (description of DRI and DRIII).

exchange is the basis of all moral conduct for every Christian. They do attach value to poverty, but they discuss this topic separately and without developing a special standard of poverty for adherents to religious rules. If keeping the commandments is what any Christian must do to be saved, then God's law is all that any Christian needs. Any further rules imposed by the institutional church are at best superfluous, an obfuscatory distraction from the truth, while in the worst case they conflict with truth and prevent their adherents from following the commandments. The rules of religious orders, like canon law, are more likely to lead their adherents astray than to help them achieve greater sanctity. Prelates and priests need not be obeyed unless their directives accord with God's law. No person is a Christian unless they keep Christ's commandments. And once even the most ordinary of persons has been properly instructed in those commandments (although what instruction "open truth" requires is often difficult to explain), they are well qualified to decide for themselves how well rules and persons conform to the truth.

These conclusions were too radical to escape notice, even if the affirmative convictions that underlie them had largely been ignored, and so it is that they begin to appear in inquisitional contexts. The trial of Richard Wyche before Bishop Walter Skirlaw of Durham early in the first decade of the fifteenth century turns—in his written account of it, at any rate—on the terms of an oath requiring him to affirm his obedience to the laws of the church as set out in canon law and the question of whether these laws are the law of God.[18] The lists of standard questions for defendants that seem to have been developed in convocation in 1428 and are preserved in Polton's register address these themes repeatedly, for example in questions that ask whether decreta, decretals, or papal constitutions, synodal or provincial, should be kept; whether "mali [evil persons]" are part of the catholic church; and whether someone entering a private religion is thereby enabled better to observe the commandments.[19] Similarly, Margery Baxter in Norwich in 1428 asserts

---

18. The Latin version of Richard Wyche's letter recounting his trial is extant in a single copy in Prague; it seems clear that it has been recopied by a Bohemian scribe unfamiliar with English names and probably translated from English. It is printed in F. D. Matthew, ed., "The Trial of Richard Wyche," *English Historical Review* 5 (1890): 530–44, and will be cited by page and line number. A translation into modern English together with helpful introductory commentary appears in Christopher G. Bradley, ed. and trans., "The Letter of Richard Wyche: An Interrogation Narrative," *PMLA* 127 (2012): 626–42. I thank Chris for sharing his work with me in advance of publication and for much useful discussion. For the oath Wyche was required to swear, see 531/19–22, or the more elaborate restatement of its terms on 535/7–12. Wyche makes it clear that he believes the law of the church is God's law, rather than canon law, at 534/27–28.

19. These are in list 1, articles 33 and 40, and in list 2, article 16, respectively. See Anne Hudson, "The Examination of Lollards," repr. in *Lollards and Their Books*, 134–35.

that no person who does not keep the commandments is a Christian.[20] In setting himself against the idea that God's law is sufficient as a moral law, in his *Repressor*, Reginald Pecock correctly isolates one important basis for lollard dissent.[21]

In lollard writings focused more on pastoral instruction than on polemical assertion, the lollard emphasis that the commandments are the basis of moral conduct is developed by providing readers with means of discerning whether they and others are living by God's law. These means of discernment are usually biblical, most typically a cluster of quotations from the gospel and first epistle of John. Here is what follows in the commentary in CUL Nn.4.12, for example:

> Almiȝty God seiþ in his lawe in þis wise [way], in þe firste epistel of Ion, þe secounde chapitur: "*Whoso seiþ þat he loueþ me and kepiþ not myn heestes, he is a lier and treuthe is nouȝte in hym*." And as God seiþ, "þe feend is fader of alle lesinges." Þerfore, leste we bicome þe feendes childeren thorouȝ lesynges [lies] in Goddes heestes, know we sadli [let us consistently affirm] Goddes ten heestes and holde we hem [let us hold to them] bisily at al oure miȝte [with all our might], as trwe men to Iesu Crist. (fol. 3r)

The devil's children lie by not keeping the commandments, while men true to Jesus Christ, still in peril of becoming the devil's children, know and keep them with all their might. While it is relatively lightly belabored here, this is a version of the usual lollard demarcation between the true church, holding only those who keep the commandments, and false liars outside.[22]

This cluster of Johannine quotations is most fully developed in *The Two Ways* to provide a fuller description of the behaviour of members of the true church:

> Crist, þat may not lyen [lie], seiþ þus, "*Who þat loueþ me schal keepe my woordes and my commaundementȝ, and my fadir shal louen hym, and we*

---

20. Norman Tanner, ed., *Heresy Trials in the Diocese of Norwich, 1428–31*, Camden Fourth Series 20 (London: Royal Historical Society, 1977), 41–51, esp 42.

21. The first error of the lollards that needs to be refuted in the *Repressor*, and at great length, is that the bible can serve as a basis for moral law. See Reginald Pecock, *The Repressor of Overmuch Blaming of the Clergy*, ed. Churchill Babington, 2 vols. (London, 1860), 8–92. See also Kirsty Campbell, *The Call to Read: Reginald Pecock's Books and Textual Communities* (Notre Dame, IN: University of Notre Dame Press, 2010), chap. 6, 181–216.

22. This opposition between true church and false church is most fully developed in Lilian M. Swinburn, ed., *Lanterne of Liȝt*, EETS, o.s. 151 (London: Kegan Paul, 1917), chaps. 6–10 and 13, 22–76, 127–37.

shullen commen to hym and maake oure dwellynge with hym. And who that
loueþ not me keepeþ not my woordis" (John 14:23–24). Also Crist seiþ
þus, *"He þat hath myne commaundementȝ and keepeth hem, þat is he þat*
loueth me" (John 14:21). And Seynt Iohn seiþ, *"In þat we witen* [know]
þat we knowen God ȝef þat we keepen hise commandementȝ. And who seith
þat he knoweþ God and keepeþ not hise comaundementȝ, he is a lyere [liar]
and treuth is not in hym" (1 John 2:3–4). And also he seith, *"Loue we not*
[let us not love] *with woord ne with toonge, but with deede and with treuth"*
(1 John 3:18).[23]

Having, knowing, and keeping the commandments, with truth, in actions
as well as in words. This is a compelling simplification of what might have
seemed a very complicated set of instructions for the Christian community,
as those instructions are presented not only across the extent of the bible but
in canon law and local ecclesiastical legislation and religious rules and all the
customs and practices of the late medieval church in England. While at this
point this description has not voiced any opposition to those other laws and
rules and practices (often dismissed as superfluous in more polemical lollard
writings), it nonetheless clearly aims to revise its readers' understanding of
what rules should govern their conduct, from the ground up.

What these instructions for the Christian community require may be simple to convey, but it is also a tall order. Other lollard writings (although not
the CUL Nn.4.12 prologue) make it even taller by insisting that thoughts,
intentions, and impulses, as well as actions, must conform with God's law, and
quoting Psalm 1:2 in support: "in lege Domini voluntas eius et in lege eius
meditabitur die ac nocte," "his will is in the law of the Lord, and on his law
he shall meditate day and night."[24] Against the stringent difficulty of these
requirements they counterpose the reassurance offered as CUL Nn.4.12
continues:

And wite þou wel [know well] þat oure lord haþ not beden [asked]
vs to do bot þat [anything except what] we may wel kepe (cf. 1 Cor.

23. John Clanvowe, *The Two Ways*, in *The Works of John Clanvowe*, ed. V. J. Scattergood (Cambridge: Brewer, 1967), 79/835–47, with biblical citations added. For other lollard quotations of
these passages, see, for example, the commandments commentary in Harley 2398, and the *Dialogue
between a Wise Man and a Fool*, edited as "Cambridge Tract XII" in *EA*, 130–42 and modernized in
WS, 247–62.

24. See, e.g., Wyclif, *De amore*, question 3, 8/22–28, and more allusively in its translation, the
Five Questions, questions 3 and 4 (Arnold, 184/2–5); Swinburn, *Lanterne of Liȝt*, 62/12–63/8. See
also the *Rosarium*'s entry on "lex," in Christina von Nolcken, ed., *The Middle English Translation of
the "Rosarium theologie": A Selection* (Heidenberg: Carol Winter Universitätsverlag, 1979), 74/14–16.

10:13), ȝif we do oure bisynesse [make an effort]. For elles [otherwise] it hadde ben [would have been] aȝens resone [unreasonable] to haue bounden men vp peyne [on pain] of her [their] dampnacioun to haue kep his heestes. And in oure goode God may noon vnresone [nothing unreasonable] be, by ony maner [fol. 3v] weie [in any way]. And God seiþ in þe gospelle of Matheu, in þe elleueþ chapitur, to alle maner of folke, "*my ȝok* [yoke] *is swete and my charge* [burden] *is liȝt*" (Matt. 11:30). And seynt Ion þe euangelyst [evangelist] seiþ in þe first epistel þe fyueþ chapitur, "*þe charge* [command] *of God is to kepe his heestes and þei ben not greuouse neiþer heuy*" (1 John 5:3). (fol. 3r–v)

To these three biblical reassurances other commentators add the not altogether comforting point, drawn from James 2:10, that just as anyone who breaks any of the commandments breaks them all, so anyone who succeeds in keeping any one of them keeps them all.[25] Any one of them can be interpreted as referring to all sin, as the commentary on the commandments in Harley 2398 does for the first commandment or the *Dialogue between a Wise Man and a Fool* for the fifth. Thus, keeping any one commandment (although in these terms it does not sound easy!) allows a person to avoid all sin.

To sum up how lollard writers differ, often subtly, from the mainstream in their teaching on the commandments: Lollard writers place unusually heavy emphasis on the commandments, equating them with God's law, God's will, God's word, and with the moral teaching of the bible as a whole. They insist (though this is not unusual) on the negative consequences of not keeping the commandments. From this common ground with the mainstream they develop a distinctive understanding of the community governed by God's law as well as the obligations of its members. They separate unfaithful from true Christians and assert that only the second constitute the true church of those who shall be saved. They maintain that the commandments alone are sufficient for salvation, without the superfluous rules imposed by canon and other law or by custom (except where those rules are in their view consistent with the commandments).[26] They denounce clergy and groups within the church who they claim do not keep the commandments as they should, often because they obey those superfluous rules instead.[27] They describe means of self-examination that grant the individual Christian unusual

---

25. See, e.g., the *Dialogue between a Friar and a Secular*, in *FWD*, 37/201–38/212.

26. See, e.g., the *Thirty-Seven Conclusions*, article 17: J. Forshall, ed., *Remonstrance against Romish Corruptions in the Church* (London, 1851), 44/15–47/16; and Arnold, 90, 222, 364.

27. See, e.g., Arnold, 392.

autonomy and capacity for self-discernment, but at the same time they insist that members of the community should take responsibility not only for themselves, but for one another. Suggesting that every Christian must have and know and keep the commandments, with an unwavering will, in their deeds as well as with their words, clearly imposes a standard very difficult to maintain. So lollard writers offer biblically grounded reassurances that salvation is indeed attainable and that God does not impose unreasonable burdens on humanity. Reassurances against despair are of course widespread in pastoral writings of all kinds, but in place of the talk of God's mercy and grace that these writings would more usually deploy (and that lollard writers use elsewhere) here the emphasis, despite the difficulty of what is being asked, is on God's reasonableness and on the ease and pleasure involved in doing as he commands.

Chapter 1 developed a set of claims about what the lollard pastoral program might look like, in both its overlaps and its differences with mainstream religion, by means of a case study. Here in chapter 2, my synthetic account of the lollard community united by love and governed by God's law comes first, not last. In what follows, I engage with commentaries on the commandments across their full extent, as formal systems each of which attempts to find a balance amid the tensions involved in the lollard attempt to center the religious life of a community on the commandments—love versus learning, self-discernment versus correction of others, difficult versus easy, certitude versus despair, sufficiency versus inadequacy, all truth in few words versus few words that somehow encapsulate all truth. I examine, first, all of the extant freestanding exegeses of the gospel precepts in Middle English and, second, the single copy of the longest and most compendious of all lollard commentaries on the commandments, one of hundreds of closely and distantly related examples. If they have been discussed at all, the commentaries I treat in this chapter have provoked disagreement, doubt, or confusion among scholars aiming to describe their relationship with lollard thought. What I hope to illustrate here is a means of reading texts of this kind. Each new example of late medieval English religious writing we read may corroborate what we already suppose is true of lollard writings, might serve as a counterexample, might challenge our working model, but will certainly refine it and give it greater depth and subtlety. By this point of course, after many drafts and much thought, this chapter is inevitably an exposition of what I have already decided about the texts it examines. But it remains, nonetheless, what it was when I first traced the path it now follows, in a process punctuated by excitement, tedious enumeration, inspiration, bafflement, and triumph: an investigation.

Commentaries on the Gospel Precepts

Given the importance that lollard writers attach to exposition of the gospel precepts, we would expect them to show interest in providing commentary on this standard catechetical item. What is rather startling is that *all* of the extant, catalogued freestanding commentaries on the gospel precepts are lollard, lollard-leaning, or closely related to lollard versions.[28] Commentary A is unique and unprinted; it appears in Bodley 938, a manuscript containing several other lollard writings.[29] Commentary B was printed from University College 97 by Horstmann; it appears also in Harley 2385, Westminster School 3, Douce 246, and Laud Misc. 210.[30] Each of these manuscripts contains other writings associated with lollardy.[31] Commentary C appears in two widely divergent versions in TCD 155 and HM 148 and was recently edited by Ralph Hanna, who draws attention to the TCD 155 copy's deployment of lollard discourse.[32] None of these commentaries is overtly polemical

---

28. I exclude here, because they treat the gospel precepts only in passing, both Rolle's *The Commandment* (in C. Horstmann, ed., *Yorkshire Writers: Richard Rolle of Hampole, an English Father of the Church and His Followers*, 2 vols. [London, 1895–96], 1:61–71), and the short, lollard-leaning *Seven Commandments of the New Testament*, a unique copy in Oxford, University College, MS 97, fol. 93v. The "Eight Points of Charity" consists mainly of commentary on the gospel precepts; it has no apparent lollard leanings but is nonetheless lollard affiliated, for Manchester, John Rylands Library, MS English 85 contains other lollard writings. For an edition of this text, see Margaret Connolly, "The 'Eight Points of Charity,' in John Rylands University Library MS English 85," in *"And gladly wolde he lerne and gladly teche": Essays on Medieval English Presented to Professor Matsuji Tajima on His Sixtieth Birthday*, ed. Y. Iyeiri and M. Connolly (Tokyo: Kaibunsha, 2002), 195–215.

29. Bodley 938, fols. 58r–59v; G.25 in Jolliffe, *Check-list*. See Appendix A. Described in Ralph Hanna, *The English Manuscripts of Richard Rolle: A Descriptive Catalogue* (Exeter: University of Exeter Press, 2010), 142–44.

30. Horstmann, *Yorkshire Writers*, 2:454–55; G.26 in Jolliffe, *Check-list*. Full call numbers of the manuscripts abbreviated in the text are Oxford, University College, MS 97; London, British Library, MS Harley 2385; London, Westminster School, MS 3; Oxford, Bodleian Library, MS Douce 246; and Oxford, Bodleian Library, MS Laud Misc. 210. I will quote from Douce 246.

31. Harley 2385's first booklet contains a Pater Noster commentary, a polemical Pater Noster commentary printed as *Seven Heresies of Friars*, an Ave Maria commentary, the commentary on the gospel precepts under discussion here, and "Faith, Hope, and Charity." Items 3 and 4 are ascribed to Wyclif by the scribe, while item 2 cites him. All but the commentary on the gospel precepts were printed by Arnold, 93–97, 441–46, 111–13; or Matthew, 346–55. The rest of this manuscript is in Latin. On Westminster School 3, see Hanna, *English Manuscripts of Richard Rolle*, 113–16; the manuscript also includes the *Schort Reule of Lif* among other lollard items. Douce 246 is an English Book of Hours that draws its translation of the Psalms from the Wycliffite Bible: for more details, see Kathleen Kennedy, "Reintroducing the English Books of Hours, or 'English Primers'" (forthcoming). The manuscript also contains a commandments commentary (Jefferson's DIV) and a table listing the six manners of consent (on which see chap. 1). Laud Misc. 210 is described in Hanna, *English Manuscripts of Richard Rolle*, 160–62; the commentary on the precepts directly follows *Book to a Mother*.

32. *Diliges Dominum*, in *Richard Rolle: Uncollected Prose and Verse, with Related Northern Texts*, ed. Ralph Hanna, EETS, o.s. 329 (Oxford: Oxford University Press, 2007), 58–82 (even pages are the Dublin version, odd pages the Huntington version). For Hanna's comments on the text's association with lollardy, see lxvii. Henceforth cited by page and line numbers.

at any point. However, all but one of them, the shorter version of C in HM 148, exhibit just the sorts of lollard emphases in discussing the commandments that we have already been tracing. The contrast between the longest of them by far, the version of C in TCD 155, with the non-lollard version of C in HM 148 is especially striking.

It seems rather odd that only one version of one of these freestanding texts has no lollard characteristics: surely lollard writers do not hold a monopoly on interest in the gospel precepts. Granted, many mainstream works of pastoral instruction include discussion of the gospel precepts within a more comprehensive whole, often subsuming them into a discussion of the decalogue. But the interest in extracting the precepts for separate attention seems to be predominantly a lollard one. It is not always easy, of course, to make a firm decision, in any given manuscript compilation, about what is or is not a "freestanding" work. Certainly we have some evidence about whether those involved in producing the book perceived it that way, on the basis of whether it is marked out as a distinct item by means of an enlarged initial capital, a title, an explicit, a running title, or other similar devices, in a way that is consistent with other such markings in the same manuscript or booklet. Yet manuscript books or even booklets are not always consistent across their length, and copyists make mistakes. So do enumerative bibliographers, particularly when they are dealing with large numbers of similar short pieces: there may well be other (more or less indisputably "freestanding") commentaries on the gospel precepts not yet described. Still, what may be visible here is a tendency by lollard writers to excerpt the gospel precepts for separate discussion as a way of foregrounding how the lollard understanding of love differs from that of the mainstream. This wish to foreground what is distinctive about the lollard understanding of love is also, in a different way, the enterprise of Wyclif's *De amore* and its vernacular translation the *Five Questions* in their responses to Rolle's *Form of Living*.[33] The resemblances between *De amore* and the *Five Questions* and the commentaries on love to be discussed here are in fact surprisingly extensive. But what the commentaries on the precepts seem especially concerned to develop from this lollard account of love is an account of the mutual obligations of Christian community, rather than the individual Christian's obligation to remain steadfast in truth even to the point of martyrdom.

The changes the writer of TCD 155's commentary has made to the material he shares in common with the HM 148 commentary allow us greatly

---

33. For more on the *De amore* and *Five Questions*, see Fiona Somerset, "Wycliffite Spirituality," in *Text and Controversy from Wyclif to Bale: Essays in Honour of Anne Hudson*, ed. Helen Barr and Ann M. Hutchison (Turnhout: Brepols, 2005), 375–86; *WS*, 84–87, 162–64; and see also the brief discussion in chap. 4.

to augment Ralph Hanna's observations about the TCD 155 commentary's lollard characteristics. (The writer does not seem to have worked directly from HM 148, but it does seem reasonable to suppose that the version he was adapting was similar to HM 148's: the shorter version is more tightly structured, and the manuscript in which the longer version appears includes four other works that have been extensively modified from their more standard versions.)[34] The TCD 155 *Diliges Dominum* text is over twice the length of the one in HM 148; it is more similar to HM 148's version over its first half but interpolates and diverges significantly in its second half, expanding the material it shares with HM 148 in order to incorporate an extended exposition of the second precept that combines it with a detailed treatment of the bodily and spiritual works of mercy in order to explain not only what Christians should feel but what they should do for one another.[35] The second, early fifteenth-century booklet in HM 148, on the other hand, seems to have been compiled by someone interested in collecting the works of Rolle and other similar writings. The closely related dialects of its scribes have been mapped by the *Linguistic Atlas* to the northern Yorkshire/Lancashire border.[36] The bulk of it is filled by an uninterpolated copy of Rolle's *English Psalter*, preceded by its prologue and followed by Rolle's commentary on the Old Testament Canticles and Magnificat. A different scribe has added on Rolle's *The Commandment*, the shorter version of the *Diliges Dominum* text that is our focus, and a series of other, more miscellaneous items not by Rolle.[37]

In their opening expositions of "Þou [you] schalt loue þi [your] lord God with al þi hert, with al þy soule, with al þi þout [thought]" (TCD 155, 58/1–2), both versions incorporate some faculty psychology in order to explain how each of these aspects of the soul can best love God. But only TCD 155 elaborates at length on the concept of conscience. Good conscience is "a trewe vnderstandyng and consentynge to Goddis lawe": it must be grounded

---

34. In TCD 155, Rolle's *Ego dormio* is supplied with different lyrics, Rolle's *Form of Living* is excerpted, Rolle's *Oleum effusum* is paraphrased, and the final item, the "Speculum huius vitae," is a version of the *Prick of Conscience*. The manuscript also includes a copy of Thomas Wimbledon's sermon *Redde racionem* and some shorter prayers and excerpts at the ends of booklets. For these and further details, see Hanna, *English Manuscripts of Richard Rolle*, 51–53.

35. In Hanna's edition in Rolle, *Uncollected Prose and Verse*, HM 148 gives 52 of 202 lines to the second gospel precept, and 16 lines to the works of mercy; TCD 155 gives 222 lines to the works of mercy, and 17 to introducing the second gospel precept before embarking on their exposition, for a total of 239 of 431 lines of text. For a similar conflation of works of mercy teaching with teaching of the commandments, see Somerset, "Textual Transmission."

36. *LALME*, LP 454, 406, 404.

37. For a detailed description, see Hanna, *English Manuscripts of Richard Rolle*, 196–98.

in holy writ, and it must accord with God's law and God's will.[38] Consent to God's law is assured if someone conforms his will to God's. His will remains steadfast in truth if nothing in this world can sway him from "ry3t [right] entent and gode conscience" and if he gives public witness: if he "noþing hyde in schewyng [showing] of trewþe" (TCD 155, 58/21–23). None of this is in HM 148. Similar insistence that loving God consists of true understanding, conformity of will, and public testimony to the truth is also, however, found in *De amore* and the *Five Questions*, as well as far more broadly among lollard writings.[39]

TCD 155 further develops its emphasis on intention as well as action in its greatly extended exposition of the second gospel precept. Here, the writer explains what intentions toward one another should knit together the Christian community. In explaining what it is to love one's neighbour the writer juxaposes Luke 10:27 with Matthew 7:12, "alle þing þat 3e [you] <u>wolden</u> þat men duden [did] to 3ow [you], doo 3ee [you] to hem for þis is þe lawe and þat [what] þe prophetes seyden," 70/200–202). This emphasis on what anyone might wish for their own personal welfare, and might by means of this exhortation be led to intend toward others, is biblical, but in his exposition the writer draws yet more attention to intention by incorporating the vocabulary of social consent whose implications we examined in more detail in chapter 1: "ne doo [do not do] <u>ne consente to</u> noon harme ne yuel to hym oþerwyse than <u>þou woldes</u> þat he dude to þe" (70/197–98).[40] Members of the community must not only treat others as they want to be treated but do all they can to ensure that others do likewise. Although he gives the bodily works only a brief survey, in his explanation of feeding the hungry he again pauses to emphasize the disposition and culpability of the will. If you want to help your neighbour when he is hungry and you cannot, then God "wole [will] rewarde þe for þi gode wille, for þat is the princypal þing þat God takeþ hede [heed] too." But good will is not enough if action is also a possibility: if you are able to help your hungry neighbour and fail to do so, then you are the cause of his difficulty, even his killer (72/215–16, 216–19).

In the exposition of the spiritual works in TCD 155, too, the proper disposition of the will in forming a community of mutual obligation is given prominent attention. Each of the spiritual works depends on and develops

---

38. See 58/25–26 for the quotation, and for the appositions that make these claims equivalent, 60/35–36, 38, 42.

39. See, e.g., the *Letter of Richard Wyche*'s final exhortations to its readers (Matthew, "Trial of Richard Wyche," 541/30–542/1, 542/27–543/19); the prologue to the *Testimony of William Thorpe*, in *TWT*, 24/1–29/159; and chap. 11 of Swinburn, *Lanterne of Li3t*, 76–80, among many other examples.

40. On the lollard emphasis on consent, see chap. 1.

mutual good will. Rather than presenting the spiritual works as predominantly the work of the clergy, as is common in mainstream writings,[41] TCD 155 asserts an even greater universal obligation for the spiritual works than for the bodily ones: "þer byn [there are] seuen werkes of mercy gostly þat man is holden [required] to doo after hys conyng [knowledge] and hys my3t. And alle maner men, pore and riche, byn holden to doo þes 3if [if] þey wolen be saued" (72/235–37).[42] All members of the community must dwell together in love, and all must correct and if necessary exclude those who fail in this obligation. The emphasis on the disposition of will probably goes some way toward explaining the idiosyncratic order in which the spiritual works are treated, in both versions, even if there is very little by way of any kind of explanation for this reordering in HM 148.[43] In contrast to the more common order "teach, counsel, chastise, comfort, forgive, suffer, pray," this discussion gives "forgive, chastise, pray, teach, counsel, comfort, suffer."[44] Discussing forgiveness first allows the writer to equate ill will with murder, just as he did in his exposition of the bodily works: whoever hates his brother kills him in his heart, and so anyone who does not forgive those who have wronged him is just as culpable as if he had killed them (72/235–45). Placing chastisement of sinners second allows him further development of the topic of social consent, complete with its usual biblical grounding. Not only those who do wicked deeds but those who consent to them are worthy of death (Rom. 1:32), while sinners who will not abandon their sin should be shunned (2 Thes. 3:6) (74/275–79).

The basis for these difficult decisions is the "treuþe [truth] of Holy-chirche." TCD 155 greatly extends HM 148's paraphrase of Gregory the

---

41. The widely distributed *Lay Folks' Catechism* asks that everyone should perform the spiritual works but requires teaching only of those who have the necessary learning, for example. See T. F. Simmons and H. E. Nolloth, *The Lay Folks' Catechism*, EETS, o.s. 118 (London: K. Paul, Trench, Trübner, 1901), 74/364–76/379, even pages only. On greater emphasis of the bodily works of mercy in writings for the laity, see also P. H. Cullum, "'Yf lak of charyte be not ower hynderawnce': Margery Kempe, Lynn, and the Practice of the Spiritual and Bodily Works of Mercy," in *A Companion to the Book of Margery Kempe*, ed. John H. Arnold and Katherine J. Lewis (Cambridge: Brewer, 2004), 177–93.

42. Notice the similar emphasis in the expanded copy of the *Lay Folks' Catechism* in London, Lambeth Palace Library, MS 408, as printed in Simmons and Nolloth, *Lay Folks' Catechism*, 77/1153–63. On versions of the *Lay Folks' Catechism* and their lollard interpolations, see Anne Hudson, "A New Look at the *Lay Folk's Catechism*," *Viator* 16 (1985): 243–58; and Hudson, "The *Lay Folk's Catechism*: A Postscript," *Viator* 18 (1988): 307–9.

43. HM 148 has no quotation of Matt. 12:7, no mention of consent, no emphasis on human will. The only work of mercy that it explains at all is the first bodily work, and there it does allow for good intentions: "if he be hungre, if þou may, fede hym; and if þou haue noght warof to help hym in his nede, ande if þou wallde do if þou myght, Gode haldes it as don" (73/171–73).

44. On the usual ordering and makeup of the list of works of spiritual mercy, and on variation from it, see Cullum, "'Yf lak of charyte be not ower hynderawnce.'"

Great's (actually Columba's) claim that God's chosen desire this wisdom. Only TCD 155 goes on to specify that that "treuþe" is "tauȝt and gronded in holy writee" and that all that is not grounded in belief is sin.[45] Whoever would be saved must hold to true faith: here the writer is quoting the Athanasian Creed, but with a difference, since he substitutes "true faith" for "catholicam fidem" and is building on his own definition of "trouþe" as grounded in holy writ (62/88–91). The quotation from Matthew that follows is also tendentiously translated: "for þat Crist wold þat alle men were sadde [constant] in þe byleue, he seiþ hymselfe in þe gospel, "*Super hanc petram, id est super stabilem fidem, edificabo ecclesiam meam,*" þat is, "*I schal bulde my chirche on* stable feiþe" (62/94–97). The translation substitutes the writer's interpolation of "stable faith" as a gloss on "this rock" to produce an interpretation: the rock on which the church is built is not punningly Peter (justifying the succession of the popes as leaders of the institutional church) but stable faith. As the writer goes on to explain, stable faith is nothing more than for men to believe truly as God's law teaches them, for God has granted the bliss of heaven to those who keep his commandments (62/98–100). But every man who wilfully does a deadly sin should be called "þe fendes [fiend's] man and noȝt [not] Cristes man"; in the act of sinning he excludes himself from the Christian community (64/113–16). The cumulative effect of this extended exposition is to develop a biblically grounded exposition of the "truth of holy church" as what God' law, God's will, God's commandments, or holy writ shows to be true rather than what the institutional church explains is the truth. "My church" becomes not the institutional church but the church of those who would be saved and follow the commandments in order to attain that goal.

The other two commentaries on the two gospel precepts, while considerably shorter, similarly deploy faculty psychology to insist on the importance of witnessing to truth publicly, of knowing for oneself what the truth is, and of helping others as well as oneself. They do not, as a devotional work that draws on faculty psychology more typically might, urge an inwardly focused cultivation of the self.[46] Commentary B concludes its discussion of what it means to love God with all one's understanding by strongly emphasizing each Christian's obligation to destroy sin in others as well as himself and to teach the commandments as well as keeping them: "for þis vnderstondynge of þi

45. 62/79–83, and contrast with 63/43–46 in the HM 148 version.

46. Consider, for example, the *Cloud of Unknowyng*'s emphasis on inwardness, especially in its most sustained engagement with faculty psychology in the account of the inward wits in chaps. 63–66; for more on this text, see chap. 6.

[your] God þou most fle [must flee] and destroye synne boþe in þe [yourself] and in oþere men vp [to the limit of] þi power and wytte [understanding], and kepe and teche þe commaundementȝ of God, and mayntene riȝtewisnes [righteousness] and gode [good] lyuynge and very [true] pees and charite."[47] Similarly, in explaining how to love God with all one's strength the writer urges readers to "mayntene truþe of Goddes lawe vp al þi power, connynge [knowledge], and grete desire of riȝtewisnes."[48] Truth is God's law; God's law is the commandments; all must know and declare them. Commentary A extends this emphasis on public witnessing yet further, to anticipate the possible scorn, and even suffering, that his readers may need to withstand and urge them to defend God and his will without fear of the consequences:

> Also, þou louest God wiþ al þi power and alle þi myȝtis [faculties] when þou art redy for þe loue of God to suffre repreef, myssaiynge [slander], pouerte [poverty], nede. Myȝti and glad [Able and willing] to do penaunce for þi synnes and for þe brennynge [burning] loue þat þou felist in þi soule to putte þi body [put forth your body] to suffre for God and for his lawe. Dredyng no man to answere [Fearing to answer no man] for þi lord God when þou herist [you hear] him dispised or his wille vndon [not done]. And þus mayst þu knowe [you may know] when þou louest God, as I haue seid before. (Bodley 938, fol. 59v)

Just this kind of exhortation toward suffering for God's law is where the *Five Questions* concludes; and just as in the *Five Questions*, the writer also assures his readers that they can know for themselves, based on their own behaviour, whether they love God as they should (see above, n. 12). With this capacity for self-knowledge also comes responsibility. In commentary A's very full account of the mutual obligations that accompany love of neighbour, each Christian is responsible not only for doing for his neighbour "þe seuen werkis of mercy when þat he haþ nede" but also "for to wite besily [pay careful attention to] wher [whether] he haþ nede or noon [not]" (fol. 59v). And at the conclusion, every man is responsible for keeping the two commandments "after [according to] his kunnynge [knowledge] and his myȝt [capacity]," but "ȝif he be v[n]kunnynge [if he is not knowledgable] hym oweþ for to [he is required to] lerne Goddis lawe" (fol. 59v). In contrast with more minimal suggestions elsewhere that loving God allows one to fulfil his law, but in

---

47. Douce 246, fol. 104r. Cf. Horstmann, *Yorkshire Writers*, 2:454/9–13.
48. Douce 246, fol. 105r. Two copies, this one and University College 97, specify that the truth is that of God's law, while two others, Harley 2385 and Laud Misc. 210, do not. I have not examined Westminster School 3.

collusion with every lollard insistence that every Christian must teach God's law—and, implicitly, with every commentary that provides instruction—here understanding God's law requires attentive study, while fulfilling it requires careful attention to one's neighbour's needs as well as one's own.

Commentary on the Decalogue

If freestanding commentaries on the two gospel precepts are surprisingly rare in medieval English manuscripts, commentaries on the ten command-ments are everywhere, sometimes two or three of them in a single manu-script. Judith Jefferson has done much to clarify relations between these commentaries, tracing and describing the variations and complex possible lines of influence between no less than sixty copies of what she identifies as twenty-seven versions.[49] But there are yet more outliers, in yet more manu-scripts. There are freestanding prose commentaries unrelated to the very large cluster of mutually related texts that Jefferson was investigating, such as the one in Laud Misc. 210.[50] There are sermons or series of sermons devot-ing themselves to exposition of the commandments for most or part of their length, as for example some of the SS74 sermons discussed in the previous chapter, sermons 18 to 22 in London, British Library, MS Royal 18.B.xxiii, or the sermons in Dublin, Trinity College, MS 241 and Cambridge, St John's College, MS G.22.[51] There is Dives and Pauper, a vast early fifteenth-century dialogue between a rich layman and a poor mendicant preacher that com-ments on each of the commandments in exhaustive detail.[52] And there are commentaries embedded within larger works of pastoral instruction; Jeffer-son does include the Pore Caitif as edited by Brady in her discussion because it is a relative of the freestanding commentaries she surveys, but there are

---

49. I will quote by page and line number from Jefferson's parallel-text edition of Harley 2398's very long commentary and of its closest relative, the shorter commentary found in TCD 245, York Minster XVI.L.12, and Harvard English 738 in "An Edition of the Ten Commandments Com-mentary." I rely on her thorough research on relations between the versions; while she may yet modify her conclusions before publication, the ones that are germane to my argument I have been able to verify for myself.

50. Fols. 147v–156v. For yet more freestanding verse and prose versions, see Robert Raymo, "Works of Religious and Philosophical Instruction," in A Manual of the Writings in Middle English, 1050–1500, vol. 7, ed. Albert E. Hartung (New Haven: Connecticut Academy of Arts and Sciences, 1986), 2255–2378, 2467–2582, on 2284–89.

51. See chap. 1; W. O. Ross, ed., Middle English Sermons, EETS. o.s. 209 (London: Oxford Uni-versity Press, 1960), 103–33; and H. Leith Spencer, English Preaching in the Late Middle Ages (Oxford: Clarendon Press, 1993), 224–27.

52. Priscilla H. Barnum, ed., Dives and Pauper, 2 vols. (vol. 1 in 2 parts), EETS, o.s. 275, 280, 323 (London: Oxford University Press, 1976–2004).

many others.[53] The extent of mutual influence in this larger sphere has yet to be charted.

One difficulty in identifying lollard writings within this sphere is that of the sheer mass of material that needs sifting. Another is the extraordinarily pervasive extent of mutual influence: the incipit of a commentary elsewhere copied with a strong lollard slant may be followed by a far more squarely mainstream commentary, whether as the result of expurgation of the present copy or interpolation of the first. But on the other hand, a commentary that contains much characteristic lollard statement, even polemic, may in some contexts have been recopied for its instructional value by and for those less attuned to its lollard characteristics. We need to be aware that there is a difference between motivated intervention in an existing commentary tradition and the perhaps less clearly motivated reproduction of such interventions, even if we cannot always clearly distinguish one from the other. Further, while some commentaries are intermittently interpolated and others are thoroughly revised, we cannot always be sure whether one of these processes may have occurred in the copy we are reading or in a previous copy; the extent to which one version varies from others is not always an index to the lollardy of either its scribe or its manuscript.[54] And more intermittent intervention need not suggest lesser interest in lollard ideas on the part of the writer; reasons to intervene less drastically might include the perceived intrinsic value or conformity with lollard ideas of the original being adapted. Still, the distinction is a useful one; the difference is usefully illustrated by the contrast between the commandments commentary in Laud Misc. 23, where fitful, even if frequent, revisions are found, and the thorough revision across the very lengthy commentary in Harley 2398 that will occupy most of the rest of this chapter.

Harley 2398's commentary (*H 2398*) is perhaps the longest freestanding commentary on the commandments anywhere in extant Middle English writings after *Dives and Pauper*. In contrast with the most proximate extant sources that it incorporates, combines, and adapts, it is reworked and interpolated throughout its length. It quotes at length in translation from a variety of Latin sources, older and more recent. It seamlessly incorporates material

---

53. The *Pore Caitif* is Jefferson's DVI (see "An Edition of the Ten Commandments Commentary," 1:cxxxiv and clxxix–clxxxi), but she does not trace the variation between copies of its commandments commentary in detail.

54. For thoughtful consideration of the interpretative issues raised by layers of revision and recopying, see Mary Raschko, "Common Ground for Contrasting Ideologies: The Texts and Contexts of *A Schort Reule of Lif*," *Viator* 40 (2009): 387–410; Jefferson, "An Edition of the Ten Commandments Commentary," vol. 1, passim.

from at least three other vernacular texts, two of them extant in the same manuscript.[55] And it draws extensively on Wyclif's *De mandatis divinis*. This pedigree is all the more intriguing when we realize that some of what this writer draws from Wyclif is what some of *H 2398*'s recent readers have presented as evidence that the work is not lollard. Closely examining *H 2398* offers us the opportunity to reconfigure our understanding of what lollardy derived from Wyclif.

H 2398 stands at a kind of compendious nexus of late medieval English commandments commentary. Two of the many related commentaries that Jefferson describes are the most familiar to modern readers because they are the two that have been printed in EETS editions: these are what she calls DI, also known as the "standard version" or "Standard Orthodox Commentary" because it is the most common of the related versions, and DII, also called the "Wycliffite version"; *H 2398* is related to each of these.[56] DI was printed by Francis in his edition of the *Book of Vices and Virtues*, from the copy incorporated into that text in the Simeon manuscript (London, British Library, Additional MS 22283).[57] However, there is variation and adaptation among the twenty other known copies of this "standard version," some of it clearly anticlerical or suggesting lollard preoccupations.[58] Here and there across the whole of its length, the "standard version" corresponds closely in wording with sections of the commentary on the decalogue that Wyclif incorporated, at the request (so he reports) of a devout layman, into ten of his collected sermons on the Sunday gospels.[59] Wyclif too drew on an extensive tradition of commentary on the commandments, of course; some of these overlaps may be incidental. Still, the extent of the similarities, and the topics they cover, should provoke further analysis of this commentary and the variation between its versions (although I will not pursue this topic here). They suggest that another name for DI than the "Standard Orthodox Commentary"

---

55. For details of how *H 2398* incorporates material from *Visitation E* and *Of Wedded Men and Wifis*, see below, nn. 64 and 77. For a full list of the contents of the manuscript, see Appendix A. *Visitation E* is on fols. 156r–160v, directly followed by *Of Wedded Men and Wifis* on fols. 160v–166v.

56. The "standard version" is *IPMEP* 48; the "Wycliffite version" is *IPMEP* 49. However these entries need revision in light of Jefferson's thesis.

57. Appendix I in W. Nelson Francis, ed., *The Book of Vices and Virtues*, EETS, o.s. 217 (London: Oxford University Press, 1942), 316–33.

58. On this variation, see Jefferson, "An Edition of the Ten Commandments Commentary," 1:cxliii–cxliv.

59. "Circa istum sermonem et novem sequentes (ut mandatus sum a quodam devoto layco) propono compendiose dicere sentenciam mandatorum": John Wyclif, *Sermones*, ed. Johannes Loserth, 4 vols., Wyclif Society (London: Trübner, 1887–90):1:89/22–24. Jefferson first noted these correspondences ("An Edition of the Ten Commandments Commentary," 1:cxli); my interpretation of them differs.

might be more apposite. *H 2398* incorporates and further augments extensive excerpts from DI throughout, although it seems likely that it drew not, or not only, on a copy like that printed from the Simeon manuscript by Francis but on a version with more polemical content such as that in Leeds, University Library, MS Brotherton 501 (Jefferson, 1:cxlv–cxlvi).

The commentary Jefferson labels DII, a shorter and more polemical commentary extant in one copy in Bodley 789 and printed by Arnold, was perhaps not the ideal version to serve, by virtue of its early printed availability, as the paradigmatic Wycliffite commentary on the decalogue. DII seems to be an abbreviated redaction, with a few additions, of the material found in *H 2398* and its closest relative, the version Jefferson edits from TCD 245, also found in Cambridge, MA, Harvard University, MS English 738 and York Minster, MS XVI.L.12 (Jefferson, 1:clxi–clxxii). The commentary found in the Dublin, Harvard, and York manuscripts (*T 245*) might have been the best choice for early printing, for it appears to have taken its prologue from DI, then departed from that text to produce an extended lollard commentary on the commandments that shares little content with DI, though it seems to have influenced several of the other related versions in addition to DII, including some copies of the *Pore Caitif*. *H 2398* and DII share many common passages; they have more in common than does *T 245* with DII, suggesting that the version abbreviated by the writer of DII may have looked more like *H 2398* than like *T 245*. *H 2398* seems to have been developed from a version of *T 245*, its main source, though it is half again as long thanks to all the other material it incorporates, and it removes some of the passages critical of friars.[60]

I choose *H 2398*, rather than *T 245*, as the basis of my discussion of lollard ten commandments commentaries here because in my view it is, among extant copies at any rate, the apogee of lollard compendiousness in commentary on the commandments. Jefferson's view, instead, is that its writer "took an unorthodox commentary and added orthodox material," that the copy in Harley 2398 has been watered down by its additions (1:cxlviii). In Jefferson's view the commentary she edits from *T 245* is the version most thoughtfully revised to reflect lollard concerns throughout its length, while DII's redaction of *T 245* makes DII more extreme by removing what is less polemical, and several other related commentaries include lollard content less

---

60. Again, these are Jefferson's conclusions, in the previously cited discussions of DI, DII, and DVI (*Pore Caitif*). Jefferson notes the removal of criticism of friars and points to evidence that friars were among Wyclif's early followers, suggesting that the author may have been a friar. This is certainly possible, but a more tempered position on friars than Wyclif's own seems to have been relatively common among writers, copyists, and readers of Wycliffite writings.

systematically.[61] Jefferson is a sensitive and careful reader of lollard writings; my disagreement here is not so much with analysis of the relationships between these versions, or even her interpretation of those relationships, as with the way of thinking about the relationship between lollardy and orthodoxy that is its basis. The very extensive material added to *H 2398* can be labelled "orthodox" if our definition of "orthodox" encompasses "any material that is not strongly polemical in familiar lollard ways, or that is not among the topics most famously included in heresy trials." But when defined in this way, "orthodox" is not a useful antonym to "lollard," for much that is "lollard" is also "orthodox"—even much that Wyclif wrote is "orthodox" in this sense. Instead of assigning to orthodoxy whatever is not polemical and whatever was not a topic of examination in lollard trials, we would do well to draw on the lollard commentaries themselves in order to build up our account of how lollards wanted to instruct readers in God's law. Among extant commentaries, *H 2398* is the one that gives readers the most extended instruction and draws on the widest range of sources in order to do so.

The sources of *H 2398*'s augmentations certainly do not attenuate its relationship with other lollard writings. The writer draws very extensively on Wyclif's most fully developed engagement with the commandments in his *De mandatis*, a work frequently quoted in the lollard compendia the *Floretum* and *Rosarium* and fundamental to Wyclif's pastoral project as developed in the vernacular writings.[62] The writer also draws on the *Floretum* and *Rosarium* themselves, independently, as well as the sources Wyclif used for his *De mandatis*; we can imagine, perhaps, an attentive reader of these works turning to what they cite and delving deeper. And he incorporates excerpts from vernacular writings that circulate among predominantly lollard materials in other manuscripts, though whether he does so because these works too were lollard, or because lollard writers and readers liked them, or because both works draw on another previous work remains uncertain. Rather than seeking "heresy" in these added materials, we will consider what themes they allow the writer to pursue and how the commentary that results may confirm or complicate the understanding of lollard commentary on the commandments that we have developed thus far.

H 2398's prologue provides a good example of the writer's methods of augmentation and a useful point of departure. We have already examined

---

61. For lucid exposition of the textual tradition as a whole, see Jefferson, "An Edition of the Ten Commandments Commentary," 1:xxxiii–cxciv.

62. On the centrality of *De mandatis* to Wyclif's pastoral project, see Stephen E. Lahey, "John Wyclif: Spiritual and Devotional Guide?" in *WS*, 30–39, esp. 34–38.

CUL Nn.4.12's densely biblical adaptation of the commandments commentary prologue in DI, the "standard version," as well as several other
related commentaries. *H 2398* develops this same prologue more fully than
any other version, incorporating the whole of what appears in DI and DII
and adding substantially to the material *H 2398* shares with *T 245*. In the
quotation of the opening to *H 2398*'s prologue that follows, all of the first
paragraph is shared with DII, DI, and *T 245*, while the second and third paragraphs are shared with DI and *T 245*. Parts of what follows from the fourth
paragraph onward are shared with *T 245* only; the material in *H 2398* that
augments *T 245* is underlined, so that it may easily be distinguished, while
substantive variants in *T 245* are recorded in footnotes.[63] In the eighth (pen-
ultimate) paragraph, which is drawn from the *Visitation of the Sick* version
E (*Visitation E*) and has no analogue in *T 245*, variants are instead from the
copy of *Visitation E* in University College 97.[64]

> Alle maner men scholde holde Godes byddynges, for wiþoute holdy-
> ing of hem may no man beo saued. And so þe Gospel telleþ how on
> [someone] axede Crist what he scholde do for to come to heuene.
> And Crist bad him, if he wolde entre into blysse, þat he scholde kepe
> þe comaundementӡ of God.
>
> And þes kepeþ Jewes [Jews keep these], as alle sectes scholde. For alle we
> scholde beo [we should all be] Cristene men and treweliche serue God, but
> þis may we nouӡt [not] do bot if [unless] we kepe þes commaundementӡ.
>
> O Lord, if a kyng byt a þyng beo keped [gave a binding order] to alle
> hys lyge [liege] men vp peyne of [on pain of] here [their] lyf, how by-
> syliche [attentively] wolde þey kepe þis commaundement. Bot byleue
> techeþ ous [us] þat God is more lord þan eny erþeliche [earthly] man
> may beo in þis world; and wel we wyteþ [know] þat, as a lord ys more
> [greater] in himself, so scholde his byddyng beo more ykeped [kept]
> and yworscheped [honored].[65] Bot who woteþ not [does not know] þat

---

63. There is also some minor variation, e.g., þe/þis, and/for, among the copies of TCD 245 and
between TCD 245 and Harley 2398, but it will not be important to our purposes here.

64. Raymo, "Works of Religious and Philosophical Instruction," describes six versions of the
Visitation of the Sick, listing this one as version E, the most popular. The *IPMEP* instead lists it as version B. See also Jolliffe, *Check-list*, L.5b. The copy of *Visitation E* in University College 97 is printed
in Horstmann, *Yorkshire Writers*, 2:449–53. Minor variation in syntax between *H 2398* and this copy
is not recorded in the variants I give below. Both of the substantive variants may be the result of copying errors, but even so, they produce a different sense. The excerpted borrowing was first noticed
by Amy Appleford, who discusses it in the first chapter of her forthcoming book, *Learning to Die in
London, 1380–1540*. My thanks to Amy for helpful discussion.

65. more ykeped and yworscheped] kunned, kept, and worshipid TCD 245

God ne scholde beo [should be] most loued? And Crist seiþ þat what [whatever] man loueþ him wel schal kepe his word, þat is his byddyng.

And if þou seye that scharploker [more sharply] ben kynges byddynges [the king's commands] execut [put into practice] and more scharp censures beþ put on men þat brekeþ hem þan for brekyng of Godes byddynges (for who techeþ or sueþ [follows] þe commaundementʒ of God?), O þenke wyslyche [consider wisely] þe witt [understanding] of þe Lord, how þat he wolde [wishes] þat frelyche [freely] his commaundementʒ were ykept [kept], for bot [unless] þey beo wel[66] [are well] ykept þe mede [merit] is aweye [gone].

And wyte þou wele [know well] þat he haþ ybede þe [bid you] vpon grete peyne ʼto kepe þes commaundementz, þat is vpon peyneʼ[67] of dampnacioun in helle. And he may nouʒt [not] forgete[68] or fayle for to ʒyue [give] it to whomeuere þat kepeþ nouʒt his hestes þat he byddeþ.[69] Ne no þyng may bowe him fro his purpos, for it were expresse [would be expressly] aʒen [against] his owne word þat ys yrad [read] yn þe holy gospel, whare he seyþ himself [fol. 73r] þat he schal ʒeue [give] treweliche to eueryche [each] man ryʒt [just] as he haþ deserued. And oure beleue [belief] witnesseþ [attests to] þe same; for as he wole ous lyue [wishes us to live] in hope to haue heuene[70] blysse, so he wole þat we triste [wants us to be confident] þat alle men schal beo dampned þat kepeþ nouʒt his commaundementz, syþ þey beþ pure lyʒte [such a light burden].

Bot þis grete lord, syþ [since] he is ful of mercy, haþ ʒeue ous [given us] tyme to kepe hem for tyme [term] of oure lyf, and speciallyche [especially] in oure ende, if we schulle beo sauf [saved]; for al onelyche [only] he is saued of [by] God þat in tyme of his deþ is founde in his seruyce [found to be serving him].

And wyte þou wel þat it is lytel ynow [little enough] to kepe continuuelliche [continually] his hestes to make a goed ende. For seynt Austyn seyþ þat oure laste day is to ous vnknowe [unknown to us], for [so that] we scholde spende wel alle oþer dayes. And we schold haue yn oure mynde [keep in mind] þat alle we schulleþ [we will all] passe þurgh þe ʒate [through the gate] of deþe; for seynt Austyn seyþ þat alle

---

66. wel] wilfully TCD 245
67. *marg. corr.*
68. forgete] forgete þis peyne TCD 245
69. byddeþ] biddiþ. Ne freris ne preieres may bowe him fro þis purpos. TCD 245
70. heuene] his TCD 245

men þat lyueþ on eorþe in þe day of dome [on judgment day] schal deye bodylyche [undergo bodily death], and whanne Crist schal aly3te [Christ descends] to deme [in judgment] þay schal sodeynliche [suddenly] aryse a3eyn [again]. For Seynt Bernard `seiþ´[71] "It ys certeyn þat þou schalt deye, bot is is vncerteyn whanne, oþer [or] how, oþer where, for oueral [everywhere] deþ abydeþ þe [awaits you], bot, and [if] þou beo [are] wyse, þou schalt abyde [await] him." Þerfore, þe wyse man warneþ þe and seyþ, "*Haue mynde* [be mindful], *for deþ schal nou3t tarye* [delay]." And he ne 3eueþ nou3t [does not give] þis conseille [this advice] onlyche [only] for oolde men and feble and syke [sick], bot also for 3oonge [young] men and boolde and stronge.

For euerych [every] day a man ney3eþ [draws nearer] to his deþ nere [nearer] and nere; for þe more a man in his lyf wexeþ [grows] in dayes and 3eres [years], þe more he vnwexeþ [diminishes], for, as seyntes seggeþ [say], þe furste day in the weke þat[72] a man is ybore ys þe furste day of his deþ, for eueryche day he is deyng [dying] whyle he is in þis lyf. And þerfore seyþ þe Gospel, "*Awake, for þou wost neuere* [never know] *whiche oure* [at which time] *God is to come*, wheþer in þy 3onge [young] age, oþer in þy myddel age, oþer in þy laste dayes, or pryue-liche [privately], oþer openlyche." And þerfore loke þou beo [mind that you are] alwey bysy in his seruyse [service] and þenne, what tyme euer [whenever] he come, þou mayst beo to him[73] redy [ready for him]. For it is semeliche [seemly] þat þe seruaunt abyde [await] þe lord, and nou3t [not] þe lord his seruant. And namelyche [especially] whanne gret hast ys [there is great haste], he is worþy blame [blameworthy] þat is þenne vnredy [unprepared]; bot gretter hast no man redeþ of [may advise] þan schal beo in comynge of Crist.

And þus þou mayst wel yknowe þat it is lytel ynow to kepe con-tinuelliche Godes hestes to make a goed ende. Þy gostlyche enemys, and specialliche þe fendes [fiends], beoþ faste aboute [all around you] to tempte þe in þe oure [hour] of deeþ [death]. Bot syþ [since] God may nou3t bydde [ask] bot skylful þyng and ly3t [anything not reason-able and easy], wete we wel [let us know well] þat we may[74] [are able to] kepe þes ten commaundementz. For as he þat brekeþ oon offendeþ

---

71. *suplin. corr.*

72. weke þat] whiche *Visitation E*

73. bysy in his seruyse and þenne, what tyme euer he come, þou mayst beo to him] om. *Visita-tion E*

74. may] may ay TCD 245

in alle, so he þat kepeþ wel oon kepeþ hem [them] alle. (Jefferson, 2:1/1–6/7, punctuation and paragraphing modified)

As we saw in examining the three opening sentences common to the bulk of the related commentaries at the start of this chapter, the text's opening example implicitly sets itself against forms of Christian community that depart from the truth. Elsewhere, lollard writers develop this argument more openly by asserting that the commandments alone are sufficient as a moral law for the church and guide toward salvation, while human laws are at best a distraction and at worst contradict the law given by God. DI and *H 2398* and *T 245* develop this implied point when they add that all sects should keep the commandments; the implication is that not only some individuals but some groups who have separated themselves from Christianity do not do so, while even Jews do. The implied targets might include religious orders, but also any law created by the institutional church on earth that imposes additional and potentially conflicting requirements, beyond keeping the commandments, for membership in the true church.

The analogy to service to a king that follows appears only in DI, *T 245*, and *H 2398*, among all Middle English prologues to commandments commentaries; it is most fully developed in *H 2398*, which extends it even into the material it shares with *Visitation E* by incorporating there another reference to service (see n. 73). Analogies between earthly and heavenly service are by no means uncommon, of course.[75] But as it is deployed here, this analogy provides grounding for a lollard exposition of the commandments in two ways. First, it leaves no space for service to any ecclesiastical institution: either one is serving an earthly lord, or one is serving God. Second, it appeals to what its readers know well: what belief teaches, for who does not know this? Through these appeals to readers' own resources it asks them to draw on their common sense and lived experience in making the decision to place service to God very firmly above any form of service to an earthly lord. In doing so it implicitly asserts that every Christian is capable of loving God and keeping his commandments on the basis of this common knowledge.

---

75. These are surveyed broadly in a dissertation by Jim Knowles, "Love, Labor, Liturgy: Languages of Service in Late Medieval England" (PhD diss., Duke University, 2009). There are many partial echoes of the analogy between service to Christ and service to a king in battle, perhaps most notably in the Middle English *Arma Christi* poem discussed by R. H. Robbins, "The 'Arma Christi' Rolls," *Modern Language Review* 34 (1939): 415–21. Many draw on Eph. 6:11–13, of course. Strikingly similar comparisons between service to Christ and service to a king in battle are developed in the "Sermon of Dead Men," in Gloria Cigman, ed., *Lollard Sermons*, EETS, o.s. 294 (Oxford: Oxford University Press, 1989), 207–40, on 216/328–220/482.

H 2398 and *T 245* go on to emphasize that people should keep the commandments by their own choice, willfully, even while those commandments are not being properly taught, or kept, by others. This emphasis on will and this complaint (however muted) about problems in Christian teaching and observance are characteristic of lollard writing about the commandments, as we have seen. So are the biblically based emphases that follow: that the commandments are easy and reasonable, that we have time (even if we can never know how much is left) to restore ourselves to God's service, and that we break all the commandments by breaking one, but keep all by keeping one. What appears here provides a basis and justification for dissent, rejection of church authority, insistence that every Christian can know and love and direct his or her will toward God, and even (potentially) placing one's own conscience above allegiance to a secular ruler. *H 2398* removes *T 245*'s mildly acerbic point that neither friars nor prayers can turn God from his purpose (see n. 69) but adds in place of that comment, and in what follows, greater stringency and greater emphasis on personal responsibility. God would be going against his own word if he were to mitigate his punishment of those who go against his commandments. And in the interpolated passage that spans paragraphs seven and eight, a miniature exposition of the claim that "it is lytel ynow to kepe continuuelliche his hestes to make a goed ende," daily mindful attentiveness to one's end and busyness in God's service is the responsibility of every Christian, rather than only those who know they are close to death.

H 2398's prologue continues beyond what has been quoted here, augmenting *T 245* to become two and a half times its length and the longest prologue to a decalogue commentary in Middle English. The writer quotes the whole of the commandments in translation, then goes on to give explicit directions on how the following commentary can be used to help readers gain "ryȝt [right] vnderstondyng" of them—directions of a kind not found in any other commandments commentary prologue. He then expresses his hopes for the effects of this instruction: that it will make not just priests but "lordes, ladyes and oþer gentyles [gentlefolk], boþe of men and wommen," or later, "alle men," responsible for knowing, holding, and teaching the commandments through both word and action, as a help to "alle trewe Cristene peple, þat is Holy Churche."[76] In closing *H 2398* then converges with *T 245*, and also with DI, to explain how the ten commandments correspond with the two gospel precepts and Paul's one injunction of love. *H 2398* and

---

76. Jefferson, "An Edition of the Ten Commandments Commentary," 2:9/3–19. This resembles the discussion of teaching children in *Of Wedded Men and Wifis*. See next note.

T 245's prologues conclude by urging once again how easy and beneficial it is to keep the commandments and how thinking about the commandments can help men to withstand the impulses that might cause them harm: within this final peroration *H 2398* alone intersperses yet one more quotation from Augustine and one more exhortation toward careful study.

Thus, *H 2398*'s prologue articulates its writer's extraordinary ambition, even greater than that of *T 245*: that his expansive augmentation of the genre of commandments commentary might, when carefully studied, re-form the whole of the church as he defines it by giving ordinary people the "ry3t vnderstondyng" to direct their own spiritual lives. As his commentary continues, these ambitions are most fully developed in his commentary on the first commandment, which is almost five times longer than *T 245*'s and by far his longest sustained effort. More typically, his commentaries on single commandments are fifty lines or so longer than *T 245*'s in Jefferson's typescript edition, or in three cases slightly shorter because he has omitted material critical of friars. The exception is the fourth commandment, just under twice the length of *T 245*'s, largely because he has incorporated the fourth chapter from *Of Wedded Men and Wifis* (like *Visitation E*, also found in Harley 2398) whose concerns chime with the prologue's: on how parents are obligated to teach their children, and especially to instruct them in the commandments, so that they may be saved.[77]

H 2398's treatment of the first commandment has also been where he has seemed to some critics most "orthodox." I mean to show instead that his augmentations of his commentary on the first commandment are Wycliffite—how could they not be, since they are largely drawn from Wyclif?—and what is more, that they are broadly typical of lollard writings. The writer of *H 2398*, like Wyclif himself, is certainly more interested in the ways images can be used well than many lollards seem to have been, especially later in the movement's history. Still, demonstrating the possible benefits of images is far from his main point. Instead, the impetus behind his additions here, as with his additions in the prologue and across the whole of his commentary, seems to be the writer's conviction, and wish to show, that every Christian can learn how to direct his own spiritual life through careful study and practical implementation of the commandments.

The *H 2398* commentator gives us a painstakingly consecutive exposition of the words of the first commandment, phrase by phrase, in the style

---

77. Jefferson, "An Edition of the Ten Commandments Commentary," 2:91/2–94/9; cf. Arnold, 195/12–197/24. The first sentence of the version in *H 2398* is modified to smooth the join, but the rest follows *Of Wedded Men and Wifis* very closely. See also n. 55 above.

associated with an "ancient" sermon or homily rather than a "modern" or "academic" sermon. This is also, of course, the expository style of the *English Wycliffite Sermons*. He sets the tone at the outset: "ar [before] we passe any forther here in þis commaundement, þou mayst aske a questioun why Crist in Godes lawe ys ycleped [called] by þes two names, "Lord" and "oure God," and for what cause [reason] þys name "Lord" is ynemmed byfore [named first]?" (Jefferson, 2:14/4–7, punctuation modified). The submerged dialogue between anticipated questions and the expositor's answers is not one that this commentary will maintain throughout. But the writer will continue to demonstrate just this kind of close attention to the words of the text he is explaining and just this kind of emphasis of his role as the educator of a curious, inquiring reader eager for knowledge as a means toward deepening love of God. He develops his expositions figurally so as to pursue this theme, as when "Egypt" means "derkenesses" and "out of Egypt" means "out of derknesse of ignorance and vncunnynge [ignorance] to knowe þynges þat my3te [might] him helpe" (16/10–11). He expatiates on the proper way to serve God (or return to serving God) rather than serving sin, with the proper disposition of the emotions of love and fear. He explains that children who have achieved discretion should be taught to love God and keep his commandments by means of biblical instruction, a theme that the fourth commandment's commentary will return to at length. Like *T 245*, he develops the injunction not to love "alien gods" into an exposition of the first commandment's all-encompassing scope. Any sin breaks the first commandment: those who think they keep this commandment need to recognize that whatever a man loves more than God, he makes into his god, so that in fact they live contrary to the first commandment in many ways.

The *H 2398* commentator's emphasis on teaching discernment to his readers remains prominent throughout his exposition. Like *T 245*, he emphasizes that the commandments are a tool for self-knowledge: "þes ten commaundement3 beþ as ten myrours þat men may se [see] hemself þerinne, wheþer þey plese God or no" (Jefferson, 2:21/7–8). He gives expansive quotations from patristic authors—Augustine, pseudo-Chrysostom, Bernard—as well as from the bible. He provides a conspectus of sin as misdirected love, by means of the trio of the world, the flesh, and the devil from 1 John 2:16. This quotation is a common lollard expository tool, but almost as common elsewhere; what is distinctive about this commentator's development of the theme is that it is explicitly a means toward self-discernment for ordinary Christians, through the recognition that they love another thing more than God. "God byddeþ þe [bids you] loue him ouer [above] alle þyng. Bot eche man and womman loueþ þat þyng more þan God for þe whiche þyng, whateuer it

be, þay brekeþ Godes heste. And þus þay mowe yknowe [may know] þat hy
[they] loueþ nouȝt God ouer alle þyng" (Jefferson, 2:23/12–24/1, punctuation modified). *T 245* shares the first sentence here with *H 2398*, but only
H 2398 goes on carefully to define misdirected love in relation to the commandments and to explain how sinners may discover their error.

The *H 2398* commentator takes a sharply different direction than does
T 245 when he turns his attention squarely upon images and their value:
it is here that some critics have felt that he diverges most sharply from lollardy and toward "orthodoxy."[78] *T 245* opened the topic with "But here
moeuen clerkis [clerks ask the question] wheþer ymagis ben leueful [lawful],
and it semeþ nay," where *H 2398* introduces the opinion that images are
forbidden only in order to refute it: "Here by þis commaundement sume
men paraunter [perhaps] weneþ [suppose] þat it beo forbode [is forbidden]
to make eny ymages; bot of this spekeþ þe noble clerk Bede" (Jefferson,
2:30/*T 245* lines 12–13 and *H 2398* lines B7–8, respectively). Supposing that
H 2398's writer is working with some version of *T 245*, his main source,
at his elbow, it is clear that he has chosen to modify that text's approach
to images heavily. Where both texts converge again, after *H 2398*'s quotation from Bede (32/ *T 245* line 1, *H 2398* line 18), *T 245*'s conclusions
about the possible benefits in using images are far more cynical: "in þes
synnes traueilen [suffer] many folk, boþe lerid [learned] and lewed [un-
educated] . . . so þat me þinkiþ [it seems to me], saaf [in want of] betere
iugement, þat it were more profijt [would be a greater benefit] vnto Hooli
Chirche þat alle þes ymagis weren left [abandoned], as God bad þe Iewes"
(Jefferson, 2:33/4–9). Given the poor judgment this writer sees displayed all
around him, in his view holy church will be best served by returning to the
rules God established for the Jews. For *H 2398*, in contrast, the benefits of
images are too great for them to be abandoned. But before we conclude that
he is diverging from lollardy, let us note that the authoritative argument that
he quotes in favor of images comes from Wyclif. Images are beneficial when
they are used "to lyȝte [light up] and haunte [arouse] and to styrye [excite]
oþer meue [move] þe soules of goede [good] Cristene folke forte [so that
they] þe more bysyloker [busily] and deuouteloker [devoutly] worschepe

---

78. For Jefferson's measured discussion, see "An Edition of the Ten Commandments Commentary," 1:cv–cix. G. R. Owst, who was well aware of the close links between lollard and mainstream
views, saw this section as an excellent example of orthodox homiletic writing: see *Literature and Pulpit
in Medieval England*, 2nd ed. (Oxford: Basil Blackwell, 1961), 143 (following a long quotation on
141–43). Margaret Aston suggested that this section might be evasive, deliberately so, and given its
context within a predominantly lollard exposition, a sign of "infighting" within lollardy: see *England's
Iconoclasts*, vol. 1, *Laws Against Images* (Oxford: Clarendon Press, 1988), 116–19, esp. 119.

her [their] God" (Jefferson, 2:33/1–4). Like the lengthy quotation from Bede's "On the Temple of Solomon" that precedes it, this quotation derives from Wyclif's *De mandatis divinis*. This quotation is also incorporated in the early Wycliffite reference works the *Floretum* and *Rosarium*, and the Middle English *Rosarium*; clearly it was a description of the utility of images that appealed to lollard compilers.[79]

To "ly3te" and "haunte" and to "styrye" or "meue": these are strongly emotive terms, and while the recipients of their effects are souls, the terms themselves make analogies to more material, somatic processes. This way of describing what images do is far more than merely an equivalent to Gregory's often quoted claim that images are the books of the laity, though *H 2398* will soon quote that one too, again drawing it from Wyclif's *De mandatis*, where it directly preceded Wyclif's own more emotive formulation.[80] For Wyclif, and for the writer of *H 2398*, images when properly used stir the emotions, motivate the will, persist in the memory, enlighten the mind, and ease the proper disposition of the soul toward God. When badly used, they can cause people to err from the truth of faith by worshipping them as if they were God.[81] The solution, however, is not to get rid of images but to teach discernment in their use. So it is that *H 2398* has already devoted considerable attention to superstitious customs and now goes on to quote Gregory, Robert Holcot, Augustine, pseudo-Bernard's *Tractatus de interiori domo*, pseudo-Chrysostom, and pseudo-Clement, greatly exceeding the terms of Wyclif's account as he does so but very evidently making use of, yet also augmenting, the resources provided in the *Rosarium*, in order to provide perhaps the most carefully balanced and certainly the lengthiest explanation of how images should be used anywhere in extant lollard writings.

Why does this lollard writer have so much to say about images, when many lollards rejected them in such strong terms? The tempered account that he draws from the *Rosarium*, but then extends yet further, provides some clues. As we have already seen in its development of "confession" in chapter 1, the *Rosarium* often chooses to address a contentious topic by taking a step back from what is controversial about it in order to place it in a wider frame, where the position eventually taken on the controversy will appear in a stronger light. So it is that for the *Rosarium*, an image can be understood in three ways.

---

79. Jefferson herself lays out these relationships: "An Edition of the Ten Commandments Commentary," 2:177–79.

80. Jefferson, "An Edition of the Ten Commandments Commentary," 2:35/2–17; John Wyclif, *De mandatis divinis*, ed. J. Loserth and F. D. Matthew (London: Kegan Paul, 1922), 156/1–14.

81. Wyclif, *De mandatis divinis*, 156/17–18; cf. Jefferson, "An Edition of the Ten Commandments Commentary," 2:33/4–6.

Within the Trinity Christ is God's image, yet equal to him. Man is an image of God, yet not equal to him. And a painted image resembles its subject, yet imperfectly. It is the image of God in man that *H 2398*'s commentator fixes upon and develops into a means of pursuing his ongoing concern to train his readers in self-discernment. He quotes pseudo-Bernard at great length in order to show readers how attempting to reform the image of God within their souls will restore them to the right sort of love of God, and he quotes pseudo-Chrysostom and pseudo-Clement to show that this reformed image is required to engage in charitable action in the world. A true image is like its maker. Similarly, a true disciple follows his master by performing the works of mercy, by this means restoring and maintaining the image of God in other men. *H 2398*'s exposition converges here with what we found in the freestanding lollard commentaries on the gospel precepts; he shares with those commentaries an interest in urging readers toward both thoughtful introspection and social action, as well as their tendency to come at these topics by discussing faculty psychology and the seven works of mercy.

Now, finally, *H 2398* comes round to more polemical, and perhaps more familiar, lollard territory: he asserts that it is better to worship God in the true, meek, poor man who is his living image, by serving that man, than to focus on images that are human artifacts.[82] But in my view the delay is not because the writer is being ambiguous or evasive, as Aston has suggested (see n. 78). Nor do I think this writer's strong concern to foreground the positive value of images is necessarily a sign of infighting among lollards, as she also suggests, though certainly this writer is carefully differentiating his own position from that of his main source, and perhaps from that of other lollards who develop these claims about living images as well. Variation is not always the product of corrosively divisive dispute; sometimes it reveals the energetic development of varying convictions. *H 2398*'s convictions come through clearly here as he explains his quotation:

> Seynt Clement axeþ [asks], "What worschep of [honor to] God," he seyþ, "ys it to renne [run] aboute by stonyn [stone] and treyn [wooden] ymages and to worschepe vayne ymages and wiþoute soules as godes [gods] and dyspyse [despise] oþer sette man at nou3t [consider worthless a man], in whom ys þe verray [true] ymage of God?" But þis ys

---

82. For a survey of ways in which this position emerges in lollard trial documents, see J. Patrick Hornbeck II, "Records of Heresy Trials," in *WS*, 45–52. For similar claims in other lollard writings, see J. H. Todd, ed., *Apology for Lollard Doctrines*, Camden Society (London, 1842), 88/28–89/11; von Nolcken, *Middle English Translation of the "Rosarium theologie,"* 98/23–99/29; "Images and Pilgrimages," in *SEWW*, 83/15–21, 84/59–85/100; *Twelve Conclusions*, in *SEWW*, 27/97–101.

not yseyde [said] for þat [so that] eny man schold despyse ymages of
holy seyntes and sette hem at nouȝt, bot for þey scholde trewelyche
worschepe God in þe trewe, meke, poure [poor] man, þat ys a quyke
[living] ymage of God, seruynge him, as y tolde byfore, and nouȝt suffre him [not allowing him to] be naked and cold, hungry and þyrsty
[thirsty] and in oþer dysayses [in other distress], and cloþe, vysyte [visit]
and fede [feed] dede [dead] ymages þat neyþer [neither] þyrsteþ ne
hungreþ ne feleþ no coldnesse, neyþer suffreþ dysaise [distress]. For
þey mowe [may] nouȝt fele, ne see, ne heere, ne speke, ne loke [look],
ne helpe eny man of eny desayse [distress], as þe holy prophetes wyt-
nesseþ. And so who þat trusteþ on hem, worschepynge [fol. 84r] hem
wiþ worschepe þat onlyche [only] parteyneþ [belongs] to God, he
makeþ to him [makes for himself] false and alyene [alien] godes and
brekeþ þe commaundement of God. (Jefferson, 2:40/14–41/8)

The misdirection of resources involved in ministering to images what is
needed by people in need is a waste of time as well as money. But it seems
that despising images is also a waste of time, especially when reflection upon
images may help us in recognizing the likeness between the needy and ourselves. Lengthy explanation of the distinction between worship appropriate
to God as opposed to the worship appropriate to statues seems also to strike
the writer as a waste of time, for he does not indulge in this common digression here.[83] Instead he provides what may be the most thoroughly developed
working out of the potential tension between loving, learning, and teaching
anywhere in extant lollard writings.

Like other lollard writers who quote or excerpt Augustine's remarks on
memory, reason, and will in *De Trinitate* or else the pseudo-Bernard work *Trac-*
tatus de interiori domo, *H 2398*'s commentator seems to think that by teaching
people about the image of God within themselves—something their external
and internal senses have the capacity to perceive and recognize for themselves, and also see reflected in others—he can also teach them the discernment they need to follow the commandments by behaving lovingly toward
God, themselves, and others. He can give them a set of principles for making
decisions that may contradict what their secular or spiritual leaders may tell
them. What he offers in his commentary on the first commandment, as
well as in his interventions and elaborations across his commandments commentary as a whole, is a training for the conscience, accompanied by a range

---

83. For a contrasting case in which this distinction is carefully explained, see *Twelve Conclusions*,
in *SEWW*, 27/101–4.

of opportunities to consider both the individual and social implications of choices presented to the human will for its consent or refusal.[84]

The investigation undertaken in this chapter has taught us to see *H 2398*'s discussion of images as a crucial locus where the writer's instructional aims are fully explained, rather than a dilution of or digression from his articulation of lollard views as these have previously been understood. Here all the writer's emphasis on darkness as opposed to light, on knowing and understanding, on the commandments as mirrors for the self, comes into focus. Here all his inserted references to individual and social consent fall into their proper place. For this writer, commentary phrase by phrase on the first commandment has allowed him to help his readers to learn to see the right images rather than the wrong ones, to bend their wills toward what is worth achieving, and to keep that image always in mind. This emphasis continues through his exposition of the rest of the first commandment. When explaining how God is the spouse of the soul, "A strange louere gelouse [strong, jealous lover]" (41/11), for example, he claims that spiritual adultery occurs when created things come into the inmost chamber of the heart where only God belongs, and presents its products as proud bastard children. These children are uneasily poised between being metaphorical children, sins themselves, and the poorly educated children reared by the sinful in contrast with the "lausom [lawful] and gostlyche children" of good meek men (44/8–9). This passage echoes the section of *Of Wedded Men and Wifis* on parents' obligation properly to teach their children that this commentator interpolates into his exposition of the fourth commandment, and also his briefer exposition of the same topic in his prologue.[85] We are accountable for the wasteful or self-destructive impulses we nurture in the house of the heart by consenting to them, in very much the same way that we are accountable for wasting resources on material products that do nobody any good, for indulging and supporting the sinful rather than correcting them, and for depriving the needy.

These emphases on gaining self-knowledge and knowledge of God through study of the commandments are not entirely absent from *T 245*, of course. If they were, the *H 2398* commentator might not have found the common version that lies behind both these commentaries appealing. *H 2398*'s writer removes (or does not add) some of the polemical passages

---

84. Here I would like to acknowledge the helpful influence of Will Revere, whose dissertation research on late medieval English writings on conscience has been illuminating for me during the writing of this book.

85. See also *Book to a Mother*'s development of a similarly metaphorical description of sins as children, *BM*, 132/14–133/12; and see chap. 7.

found in *T 245*. But this is not because he is less lollard than the writer of *T 245*, though it is certainly likely that he is less motivated to criticize friars. Rather, the difference is that where *T 245* uses the commandments to demonstrate how various social groups, especially the clergy, are sinful, *H 2398* uses them to train his readers to become agents of reform themselves, on the basis of their own powers of discernment. If the commentaries on the gospel precepts present us with an unusually fully developed account of how their writers understood the mutual obligations within a community governed by God's law, then *H 2398* may give us lollardy's fullest description of the demands this ethics of community place upon the self.

 CHAPTER 3

Lollard Prayer

Religious Practice and Everyday Life

How did lollards pray? Until recently, there was little interest in this question. Yet the historical study of religion asks different questions now than it did in the past. Sharpened interest in religious practice has produced attentive studies of local variations in worship, sacramental practices, saints' cults, the uses of written prayers, and so on. These have added depth and subtlety to our understanding of medieval religion and its role in the daily life of ordinary lay folk as well as of members of religious or elite groups.[1] But studies of this kind, especially those focused on England, have often valued tradition and community; they have rarely been interested in documenting the practices of religious movements they perceive as heretical.[2]

---

1. Eamon Duffy's *Stripping of the Altars: Traditional Religion in England, c. 1400–1580*, 2nd ed. (New Haven, CT: Yale University Press, 2005) reimagines later medieval English religion from the point of view of lay practice. For a helpful brief overview of developments in the study of "lived religion" since the 1970s, see John H. Arnold, *Belief and Unbelief in Europe* (London: Hodder, 2005; repr. New York: Bloomsbury, 2010), 7–15. Arnold is in part responding to John Van Engen, "The Christian Middle Ages as a Historiographical Problem," *American Historical Review* 91 (1986): 519–52.

2. Mark Gregory Pegg, *The Corruption of Angels: The Great Inquisition of 1245–1246* (Princeton, NJ: Princeton University Press, 2001), is an exception, yet he focuses on lived experience and religious practice precisely to argue that the "heresy" of the defendants he writes about was in the eyes of their beholders. Shannon McSheffrey, "Heresy, Orthodoxy, and English Vernacular Religion, 1480–1525," *Past & Present* 186 (2005): 47–80, attends to the vernacular devotional practices of later heresy defendants. Robert Lutton traces evidence of religious practices shared and overlapping between

Conversely, most of the emphasis in the study of heresies until recently has been doctrinal: in question was which beliefs made members of the group into heretics, and the documents that could answer that question were inquisitorial records or heresy condemnations. Where the actions of heretics drew attention as well as their beliefs, it was because they were seen as strikingly distinctive or even threatening by their contemporaries and recorded in heresy proceedings or else in chronicle accounts.

Sometimes these hostile reports of heretical practice take the form of atrocity stories, designed to shock, as when the group of heretics near Soissons described by Guibert of Nogent in his *Monodies* are said to engage in infant sacrifice, or when Richard Waytestathe and William Smith near Leicester were reported by Henry Knighton in his *Chronicle* to have used a statue of Saint Katherine as firewood to cook their cabbage; Knighton even includes a poem recounting the event.[3] On a wider range of occasions, the actions of those being investigated for heresy were recorded because they were considered evidence of potential heresy. The evidence that was sought out draws to some extent on long-established types or patterns of behaviour, influentially laid out, for example, in the first three Canons of the Fourth Lateran Council, which briefly define what constitutes orthodox belief, condemn and describe punishments for heretics who contravene these beliefs as well as their helpers and supporters, seek to curb unauthorized preaching, and require bishops and archbishops to inquire through their dioceses in search of persons who hold secret assemblies or in other ways differ from the norm in their life and habits.[4] These were questions that were still being asked in fifteenth-century English inquisitions into heresy and kinds of behaviour that were still recorded in the depositions of witnesses.[5] More informative,

---

conformist and dissenting persons and groups: see especially *Lollardy and Orthodox Religion in Pre-Reformation England* (Woodbridge: Boydell and Brewer, 2006); and "'Love this Name that Is IHC': Vernacular Prayers, Hymns, and Lyrics to the Holy Name of Jesus in Pre-Reformation England," in *Vernacularity in England and Wales, c. 1300–1550*, ed. Elisabeth Salter and Helen Wicker (Turnhout: Brepols, 2011), 119–45. On how research on lollardy might contribute to wider trends in the study of late medieval history, see Ian Forrest, "Lollardy and Late Medieval History," in *WC*, 121–34.

3. Guibert of Nogent, *Monodies*, bk. 3, chap. 17, in *Monodies and On the Relics of Saints*, trans. Joseph McAlhany and Jay Rubenstein (London: Penguin, 2011), 168–71; *Knighton's Chronicle*, ed. and trans. G. H. Martin (Oxford: Clarendon Press, 1995), 294–98.

4. These canons summarize, affirm, and extend the range of previous legislation; the opening statement of faith is recycled at the beginning of the *Decretals*. See Norman Tanner, ed. and trans., *Decrees of the Ecumenical Councils*, 2 vols. (London: Sheed and Ward; Washington, DC: Georgetown University Press, 1990), 1:230–35.

5. John H. Arnold first drew attention to the use of inquisitorial discourse in English heresy trials: "Lollard Trials and Inquisitorial Discourse," in *Fourteenth Century England II*, ed. Chris Given-Wilson (Woodbridge: Boydell, 2002), 81–94. Ian Forrest, *The Detection of Heresy in Late Medieval*

perhaps, are the occasions where actions are recorded in heresy investigations because they have come, over time, to be seen to characterize the behaviours of a specific group. So it is that considerable attention has been given to secret meetings of lollard groups that were called schools or conventicles, meetings for the purpose of reading books, and the ownership, exchange, and concealment of books.[6] While some kinds of behavior were sought out from the beginning because they corresponded with what continental investigations into heresy had sought out from the late twelfth century onward, the terminology and the questions used in England to investigate how people helped and learned from so-called heretics also developed over time, in response to both the development of local legislation and the behaviour of the persons it sought to control.[7]

Thus, hostile reports about how suspected heretics behaved may not correspond closely, if at all, with what people we might want to call "lollards" actually did. (We will not assume that all persons investigated for heresy in documentary records or described as "lollards" or "heretics" in narrative accounts were what I myself might call "lollards": on debate over the usage of "lollard," "Lollard," and "Wycliffite," see the Introduction.) Even where trial records and chronicles do give us information about what the people *they* call lollards or heretics actually did, they still provide only a very partial account of how these people practiced their religion, how that practice mattered to them, and how much it separated them from their neighbours, if at all. Did these people attend mass, for example? Defendants were often questioned about their failure to fast as required and to abstain from labor, in part perhaps because these were noticeable as well as conventional infractions.[8] But most seem to have gone to church, and to have participated in the sacraments, in ways that rarely distinguished them sharply from their neighbours. How did they pray at mass? Did they pray differently when they were alone, or meeting in a like-minded group? One reason why these questions have attracted little attention is that hostile sources give us little evidence that would allow us to pursue them: the prayer of so-called lollards or heretics did not

---

England (Oxford: Clarendon Press, 2005), details how English clergy from the 1380s onward assimilated and adapted previous legislation and legal practice in order to develop means of investigating heresy in England. J. Patrick Hornbeck II explains how English heresy trials can be used to uncover evidence of belief and practice: "Records of Heresy Trials," in *WS*, 45–52.

6. See especially Anne Hudson, *Lollards and Their Books* (London: Hambledon, 1985); and *PR*, chap. 4, 174–227.

7. In addition to Forrest, *Detection of Heresy*, see *PR*, 175–80; Fiona Somerset, "Censorship," in *The Production of Books in Britain, 1350–1500*, ed. Alexandra Gillespie and Daniel Wakelin (Cambridge: Cambridge University Press, 2011), 239–58.

8. Hudson canvasses the evidence in *PR*, 147–51.

draw much attention, whether in heresy trials or condemnations or chronicle accounts.[9] Perhaps we can assume that for the most part, to all outward appearances at any rate, lollards prayed more or less as their neighbours did.

However, the evidence gathered in heresy trials does suggest that persons we might want to call lollards also gathered to read and discuss books in ways that may have formed an adjunct to mainstream religious worship and that surely informed their participation in that worship. They probably also read these books individually or in smaller household groups. Even if their prayer was not outwardly distinctive, we might still inquire whether it was inwardly distinctive and in what ways it may have been informed by the books they read. Extant books containing lollard writings and prayers and instruction on prayer point toward the same conclusion as the hostile evidence: lollard prayer was in many ways similar to mainstream prayer. Manuscripts containing lollard writings also contain mainstream prayers and instructions on prayer, polemical lollard writings about prayer draw on mainstream sources without changing them beyond recognition, and lollard and mainstream prayer commentaries overlap significantly. However, the extensive overlaps between mainstream and lollard writings on prayer do not merely obscure what was distinctive about lollard prayer. They also reveal it.[10]

In this chapter I will show that lollard writings about prayer attach distinctive meanings to prayer as an activity and to the words that should be prayed, even as they draw very extensively on the common ground they share with the mainstream tradition. How widely the lollard writings on prayer I select for discussion were read, and by whom, and how they influenced the religious practice of ordinary people, some of whom may also have been investigated for heresy, remains of course uncertain. However, in closing I will present an example of a heresy trial defendant whose views about prayer do seem to have been influenced by his reading of material that may not have been itself heterodox but may have been made accessible to him by lollard writers and

---

9. Suspects were in a very few cases questioned about whether they knew, had copies of, and had taught their children the Pater Noster, Ave Maria, and creed in English. However, as McSheffrey points out, these prayers were readily available by this point in orthodox printed books, so their use cannot in and of itself have been evidence of heresy ("Heresy, Orthodoxy, and English Vernacular Religion," 52–61). Lutton cites Archbishop William Warham's 1511 investigation of persons strolling outside, or sitting still, during the procession in church. Yet it is difficult to know what these actions meant to the defendants or to the community, especially since it seems likely that such behaviour was common, and not necessarily a reflection of dissident belief, in Kent as elsewhere, then as now (*Lollardy and Orthodox Religion*, 1–4).

10. In addition to Lutton, "'Love this Name that Is IHC,'" two previous articles have traced evidence of lollardy in prayer commentaries: Matti Peikola, "'And after all, myn Aue-Maria almost to the ende': *Pierce the Ploughman's Crede* and Lollard Expositions of the Ave Maria," *English Studies* 81 (2000): 273–92; and Anna Lewis, "Textual Borrowings, Theological Mobility, and the Lollard Pater Noster Commentary," *Philological Quarterly* 88 (2009): 1–23.

book producers and within a lollard reading circle. The relationship between writings about prayer and the meanings ordinary people attached to prayer are not completely unrecoverable and deserve further investigation.

Writing about Prayer: An Overview

Lollard writing about prayer draws deeply upon extensive discussion of the topic in all three of England's languages. A preliminary overview of the written sources will be helpful. Many of the most influential sources date from the thirteenth century, when a widespread movement of pastoral reform and an impulse toward systematized knowledge produced William Peyrault (Peraldus)'s *Summae virtutum ac vitiorum*, Laurent d'Orleans's *Somme le Roi*, Edmund of Abingdon's *Speculum ecclesie*, Robert Grosseteste's *Templum Domini*, Richard of Wetheringsett's *Summa qui bene presunt*, and Thomas Aquinas's *Catena aurea*, among other works. But lollards of course draw more deeply on the Christian tradition too, citing Augustine, Cassian, Cyprian, and pseudo-Chrysostom among others. Discussions of prayer in these works and authors were available to later medieval English readers in translations as well as in their original languages, and in compendia, florilegia, redactions, excerpts, and reference works as well as in versions of the whole text. The conversation continued up through the sixteenth century and beyond; it is worth recalling that heresy prosecutions in which vernacular prayer was an item of questioning, those by Bishops John Hales in 1486 and John Stafford in 1520 in Coventry and Lichfield and by Bishop John Longland in Buckinghamshire in the 1520s, were something of an anomaly, even among heresy trials and most certainly in the broader picture (see n. 9). That laypeople should know their prayers in the vernacular as well as in Latin, and that they should ponder the meaning of what they were saying, was widely encouraged, certainly not only by lollard commentators.

To this end, a wide range of Middle English works recommending modes of meditation and prayer, and giving translations of and commentaries upon the Pater Noster, Ave Maria, and creed, proliferated throughout the fourteenth and fifteenth centuries. They did so far beyond the bounds of what is known as Pecham's syllabus, for Pecham's syllabus itself did not include instruction in the Pater Noster, Ave Maria, and creed, even though these prayers, and particularly the Pater Noster, were the accepted foundation of religious literacy.[11] Books of Hours, also known as Primers because they

---

11. E. A. Jones, "Literature of Religious Instruction," in *A Companion to Medieval English Literature and Culture, c. 1350–c. 1500*, ed. Peter Brown (Malden, MA: Blackwell, 2007), online at *Blackwell Reference Online*, http://www.blackwellreference.com/public/book.html?id=g9780631219736_ 9780631219736; and see his annotated bibliography.

were used in basic instruction, included prayers in English and rubrics about how to engage in prayer alongside material in Latin.[12] Prayer books or rolls similarly provide rubrics giving instruction on prayer as well as a wide variety of written prayers in English, not only the foundational prayers that were the most frequent subject of commentary.[13] That these other written forms of vernacular prayer were widely valued and commonly used is obvious: they appear far and wide in miscellaneous instructional and devotional collections, are commonly copied into leftover space and at the end of longer discursive texts in manuscripts, and are extant in widely varying forms.[14] Written sermons contain instruction on prayer, suggesting that this was a topic in oral preaching.[15] Pastoral and devotional miscellanies include both devotional works that guide their readers in meditation and prayer and commentaries on the words of standard prayers that guide them in understanding their meaning.[16] Commentaries on the Pater Noster in particular could become the occasion for meditative, mystical, or theological reflection that did far more than provide an exposition of the meaning of the scriptural words. John Lydgate's longer Pater Noster commentary may be parodying this trend when, in a long praeterition, he tells us that he does *not* plan to discuss the four gospel writers, the four rivers of paradise, Ezekiel's four spears, the four elements, the four seasons, the four complexions of sun and moon, the four winds, or the four cardinal virtues.[17]

Given that vernacular instruction in prayer was widely available, the following brief survey covers highlights only, with special attention to works quoted or interpolated by lollard writers or affiliated with lollard writings. The final chapter of the *Contemplations of the Dread and Love of God* describes

12. Nigel Morgan, "Books for the Liturgy and Private Prayer," in *The Cambridge History of the Book in Britain*, vol. 2, *1100–1400*, ed. Nigel Morgan and Rodney M. Thomson (Cambridge: Cambridge University Press, 2008), 306–16, and on the term "Primer," 308.

13. Morgan, "Books for the Liturgy," 314–16.

14. R. H. Robbins has done the foundational research here: see especially "Private Prayers in Middle English Verse," *Studies in Philology* 36 (1939): 466–75; "Popular Prayers in Middle English Verse," *Modern Philology* 36 (1939): 337–50; and "Levation Prayers in Middle English Verse," *Modern Philology* 40 (1942–43): 131–46.

15. H. Leith Spencer, *English Preaching in the Late Middle Ages* (Oxford: Clarendon Press, 1993), 211–27.

16. For overviews, see P. S. Jolliffe, *A Check-list of Middle English Prose Writings of Spiritual Guidance* (Toronto: Pontifical Institute of Mediaeval Studies, 1974), class M, 53–54, 126–30; and Robert Raymo, "Works of Religious and Philosophical Instruction," in *A Manual of the Writings in Middle English, 1050–1500*, vol. 7, ed. Albert E. Hartung (New Haven: Connecticut Academy of Arts and Sciences, 1986), passim.

17. John Lydgate, "An Exposition of the *Pater Noster*," in *The Minor Poems of John Lydgate*, ed. H. N. MacCracken, EETS, e.s. 107 (London: Kegan Paul, Trench, Trübner, 1911), 61/41–62/80.

how one should dispose oneself to prayer through meditation on the passion; this chapter was frequently excerpted, and some copies are in lollard manuscripts.[18] There are no less than three independent Middle English redactions of Peraldus's discussion of hindrances to prayer in his *Summae virtutum ac vitiorum*, which itself circulated in a variety of redacted Latin versions. Two of the Middle English versions of Peraldus on hindrances to prayer, those within the *Holy Boke Gratia Dei* and a commentary on the Pater Noster, the *Pater Noster of Richard Ermyte*, apparently derived from another Middle English version of the same material. This independent version, the *Twelve Lettings of Prayer*, appears in lollard manuscript contexts, as indeed does the *Pater Noster of Richard Ermyte*.[19] Laurent's *Somme le Roi* contains commentary on prayer which appears in at least four of its Middle English derivatives: the *Book of Vices and Virtues*, the *Aȝenbyt of Inwit*, the very popular *Speculum vitae* (a massive catechetical poem that takes the form of a compendious commentary on the Pater Noster's seven petitions and incorporates in its encyclopedic train every other significant catechetical list of seven—the sins, the virtues, the gifts of the Holy Spirit, etc.), and the *Speculum vitae*'s prose derivative, the *Myrour to Lewde Men and Wymmen*.[20] The *Speculum vitae*'s matching up of the Pater Noster with other groups of seven has a long history in religious instruction, one that is also disseminated in other media. There is a chart laying out schemes of seven that can be related to the Pater Noster in the Vernon manuscript (Oxford, Bodleian Library, MS Eng. poet. a.1). Malvern Priory reportedly had a stained glass window in the form of an exposition of

---

18. See Margaret Connolly, "Mapping Manuscripts and Readers of *Contemplations of the Dread and Love of God*," in *Design and Distribution of Late Medieval Manuscripts in England*, ed. Margaret Connolly and Linne R. Mooney (York: University of York Press, 2008), 261–78, especially the timeline of manuscripts on 277–78 listing sixteen extant manuscripts containing all or part of this so-called AB chapter, among them Harley 2398, Glasgow, University Library, MS Hunter 520, Laud Misc. 23, and Bodley 789—all manuscripts containing lollard writings. Indeed, the earliest manuscript listed containing any part of the *Contemplations* is Harley 2398 (contents listed in Appendix A).

19. F. G. A. M. Aarts, ed., *Þe Pater Noster of Richard Ermyte* (The Hague: Nijhoff, 1967); the lollard-affiliated copies are in Westminster School 3 and Sidney Sussex 74. On the *Twelve Lettings*, see F. N. M. Diekstra, "The *XII Lettyngis of Prayer*, Peraldus's *Summae virtutum ac vitiorum*, and the Relation between *Þe Holy Boke Gratia Dei*, *Þe Pater Noster of Richard Ermyte*, and *Book for a Simple and Devout Woman*," *English Studies* 80 (1999): 106–45. There are extensive close textual overlaps between the *Holy Boke Gratia Dei*, the *Pater Noster of Richard Ermyte*, the *Book for a Simple and Devout Woman*, the *Lollard Sermons*, and *SS74*, perhaps resulting from a common source now lost. See F. N. M. Diekstra, ed., *Book for a Simple and Devout Woman* (Groningen: Egbert Forsten, 1998), 316, 320–25, and 46–66.

20. On these relationships, see Ralph Hanna's introduction to *Speculum Vitae: A Reading Edition*, 2 vols., EETS, o.s. 331–32 (Oxford: Oxford University Press, 2008). See also Venetia Nelson, ed., *Myrour to Lewde Men and Wymmen: A Prose Version of the Speculum Vitae*, Middle English Texts (Heidelberg: Carl Winter, 1981).

the Pater Noster. A hanging with a similar expository scheme was reportedly displayed in York Minster and maintained by the town's Pater Noster guild. This guild was founded to take charge of staging performances of a Pater Noster pageant in seven short plays, known to have been staged in York from at least the late fourteenth until the late sixteenth century; similar plays were also staged in Beverly and Lincoln.[21]

Returning to extant textual sources, most versions of Edmund of Abingdon's *Speculum ecclesie* include in their discussion of the second grade of contemplation a commentary on the Pater Noster. The *Speculum ecclesie* is extant in a wide range of versions in Latin, Anglo-Norman, and English translation, and while it was originally designed for a religious audience, it plainly reached a wider lay audience in the late fourteenth and fifteenth centuries and indeed was circulated even more widely in excerpted form.[22] At least one copy of the *Speculum ecclesie*, that in Oxford, Bodleian Library, MS Bodley 416, has been subtly modified for lollard readers, and the excerpted version of Edmund's Pater Noster commentary in Harley 2398 has extensive interpolations, as we will see.[23] While the appeal of the *Speculum ecclesie* to lollard readers was rather surprising to Anne Hudson some twenty years ago, the field as a whole has now developed a clearer sense of why Edmund's idiosyncratic combination of advice for those seeking to live in religious perfection, commentary on pastoral basics, and affective devotion might have been appealing to lollards as well as to a wide range of mainstream readers with no intention of joining a religious order.[24] Works that

---

21. Avril Henry, "'The pater noster in a table ypeynted' and Some Other Presentations of Doctrine in the Vernon Manuscript," in *Studies in the Vernon Manuscript*, ed. Derek Pearsall (Cambridge: Brewer, 1990), 89–113; Vincent Gillespie, "Thy Will be Done: *Piers Plowman* and the *Paternoster*," in *Late-Medieval Religious Texts and Their Transmission: Essays in Honour of A.I. Doyle*, ed. A. J. Minnis, York Manuscripts Conferences, Proceedings 3 (Cambridge: Brewer, 1994), 95–119; Sue Powell, "Pastoralia and the Lost York Plays of the Creed and Paternoster," *European Medieval Drama* 8 (2004): 35–50.

22. The Lincoln Thornton copy of the *Speculum ecclesie*, from Lincoln Cathedral, MS A.1.17, is printed in C. Horstmann, ed., *Yorkshire Writers: Richard Rolle of Hampole, an English Father of the Church and His Followers*, 2 vols. (London, 1895–96), 1:219–40; and in George G. Perry, ed., *Religious Pieces in Prose and Verse*, EETS, o.s. 26, 3rd ed. (London: K. Paul, Trench, Trübner, 1914), 15–47. I will also draw on unpublished work by Jennifer Arch (see n. 49). An edition of the Latin is Edmund of Abingdon, *Speculum religiosorum and Speculum ecclesie*, ed. Helen P. Forshaw, Auctores Britannici Medii Aevi 3 (Oxford: Oxford University Press, 1973).

23. On these modifications, see Nicholas Watson, "Middle English Versions and Audiences of Edmund of Abingdon's *Speculum Religiosorum*," in *Texts and Traditions of Medieval Pastoral Care: Essays in Honour of Bella Millett*, ed. Cate Gunn and Catherine Innes-Parker (Woodbridge: York Medieval Press, 2009), 115–31.

24. *PR*, 425. But see Hudson, "Who Is My Neighbour?," in *WC*, 79–96.

similarly attempt to provide a "form of living" that includes some discussion of prayer, whether they were adapted from materials originally intended for religious or written with devout laypersons in mind, include the many adaptations of *Ancrene Wisse* (also known as the *Ancren Riwle*), Walter Hilton's *On Mixed Life*, a set of "Instructions for a Devout and Literate Layman," and the lollard *Schort Reule of Lif.*[25] In addition to the commentary on the Pater Noster already mentioned, the *Pater Noster of Richard Ermyte*, there are three freestanding lollard commentaries on the Pater Noster, two of them extant in several copies, printed in Arnold and Matthew (*PN Arnold I, PN Arnold II*, and *PN Matthew*), as well as a lollard polemical commentary on the Pater Noster's seven petitions known as the *Seven Heresies of Friars.*[26] Other extant Pater Noster commentaries include another short meditative commentary ascribed to Rolle, several anonymous commentaries in both prose and verse, and commentaries incorporated within a variety of longer works including the fourteenth-century *Pore Caitif* and *Cursor Mundi* and the fifteenth-century *Jacob's Well* and *Memoriale credencium.*[27] Known fifteenth-century writers who produced commentary on the Pater Noster include John Audelay, John Lydgate (who wrote two), Reginald Pecock, and Nicholas Love, whose *Mirror of the Blessed Life of Jesus Christ* interpolates into the Latin text's account of the Sermon on the Mount a curiously skittish exposition of the Pater Noster that seems concerned to distinguish itself from even

---

25. On the textual tradition of *Ancrene Wisse*, see Bella Millett, ed., *Ancrene Wisse*, 2 vols., EETS o.s. 325–26 (Oxford: Oxford University Press, 2005–6), 1:xi–xlv. See also Walter Hilton, *On Mixed Life*, in Horstmann, *Yorkshire Writers*, 1:264–92; W. A. Pantin, "Instructions for a Devout and Literate Layman," in *Medieval Learning and Literature: Essays Presented to Richard William Hunt*, ed. J. J. G. Alexander and M. T. Gibson (Oxford: Clarendon Press, 1976), 398–422; Mary Raschko, "Common Ground for Contrasting Ideologies: The Texts and Contexts of *A Schort Reule of Lif*," *Viator* 40 (2009): 387–410. On lay forms of living, see also Nicole R. Rice, *Lay Piety and Religious Discipline in Middle English Literature* (Cambridge: Cambridge University Press, 2008).

26. See Arnold, 93–97 (in CUL Dd.12.39; TCD 245; London, British Library, Additional MS 17013; Harley 2385; London, Lambeth Palace Library, MS 408; Bodley 789; Paris, Bibliothèque Ste. Geneviève, MS 3390; York Minster XVI.L.12); Arnold, 98–110 (in Cambridge, Trinity College, MS B.14.38; CUL Nn.4.12; Harley 2398; Manchester, John Rylands Library, MS English 85; Manchester, John Rylands Library, MS English 90; Norwich, Castle Museum, MS 158.926.4g.3; Bodley 938; Princeton, NJ, University Library, Taylor MS 16, Matthew, 197–202 (in Cambridge, Corpus Christi College, MS 296); Arnold, 441–46 (in TCD 245; Harley 2385; Oxford, Bodleian Library, MS Douce 274; York Minster XVI.L.12).

27. For overviews of these works, see Valerie M. Lagorio and Michael Sargent, "English Mystical Writings," in *A Manual of the Writings in Middle English, 1050–1500*, vol. 9, ed. Albert E. Hartung (New Haven: Connecticut Academy of Arts and Sciences, 1993), 3135–36; Raymo, "Works of Religious and Philosophical Instruction," 2276–78, 2262, 2268.

the aspects of lollard discussion of prayer that lollards most unproblematically shared with the mainstream.[28]

Prayer as a Way of Life

Rather than beginning from the substantial overlaps between lollard and mainstream views on prayer in less obtrusively polarized writings, we will start from where lollard views are most noticeably distinctive, in order to discover where and how they depart from their common sources. We begin with *De precationibus sacris*, an undated short polemical lollard treatise on prayer that is at least equally as concerned as Nicholas Love to draw strict boundaries around what constitutes proper prayer. In *De precationibus sacris* the writer is concerned first to establish that prayer most broadly should be a way of life. Christian men can follow the Pauline injunction to "pray without ceasing" not in fact through prayer by mouth at all, but through charity:

> Seynt Poul biddiþ [asks] Cristene men preie [to pray] wiþoute cessynge [ceasing], or lettynge [stopping]. And þis is understonden of preiere of charite, and not of preiere of mannis voys [voice], as Seynt Austyn declariþ [explains] wel; for ellis [otherwise] myȝtte no man [no man could] fulfille þis heste [command], to preie evermore [always]. For as longe as a man lyveþ just lif, kepynge Goddis hestis and charite, so longe he preieþ wel whatevere he do; and whoeere lyveþ best, he preieþ best.[29]

As the citation of Augustine indicates, the idea that prayer without ceasing should take the form of living in charity is not unprecedented. However, comparing this writer's use of the idea with that of one of his possible sources helps to highlight what is unusual about this treatment of it.

The writer of *De precationibus sacris* is certainly drawing on Augustine's commentary on 1 Thessalonians 15:17 in chapter 9 of his Letter 130, to Proba.[30] Augustine's commentary may, in addition, come to him at one

---

28. John Audelay, *Poems and Carols (Oxford, Bodleian Library MS Douce 302)*, ed. Susanna Fein, TEAMS Middle English Texts Series (Kalamazoo, MI: Medieval Institute Publications, 2009), 216–18; Lydgate, "An Exposition of the Pater Noster," and see n. 17. Reginald Pecock reports that he gives an exposition of the Pater Noster in the seventh treatise of the *Reule of Crysten Religioun*, no longer extant; see Kirsty Campbell, *The Call to Read: Reginald Pecock's Books and Textual Communities* (Notre Dame, IN: University of Notre Dame Press, 2010), 111; Nicholas Love, *The Mirror of the Blessed Life of Jesus Christ: Full Critical Edition*, ed. Michael G. Sargent (Exeter: University of Exeter Press, 2005), 83/13–86/4.

29. Arnold, 219–29, quotation on 219/4–10. Subsequent citations are parenthetical and by page and line numbers.

30. See Augustine, *Epistola CXXX*, in *PL* 33, cols. 494–507.

further remove: through the discussion of hindrances to prayer in Peraldus's *Summa virtutum*, or else from one of the Middle English translations of this discussion, such as that in the *Twelve Lettyngis of Prayer*. Regardless of whether the writer of *De precationibus sacris* follows Peraldus or a derivative work, or whether he makes this change himself, he focuses all his attention on Augustine's explanation of how "pius affectus" ("pious feeling") is itself a form of prayer. He does not remark on Augustine's accompanying explanation of how even as we pray without ceasing through maintaining this continual desire in faith, hope, and charity, so we should also frequently pray using words.[31] Here is how Peraldus similarly emphasizes that prayer without ceasing not only requires but even consists in the right sort of feeling:

> Item oratio sic describitur: Oratio est pius mentis affectus in Deum directus. Iste affectus desiderium est. Vnde super illud prime Thessalonie vltim. Sine intermissione orate. Dicit glos. Ipsum desiderium bonum oratio est: et si continua est desiderium si continue est oratio. Pietas, a qua pius est affectus, quae est oratio, est theosebia, siue cultus deo debitus qui comprehendit fidem, spem, et charitatem. Vnde augustinus de orando Deo ad Probam: Ipsa, fide, spe, et charitate continuato desiderio semper oramus.[32]

> [Again, prayer is described in this way. Prayer is a pious feeling in the mind directed toward God. That feeling is desire. And thus, 1 Thessalonians at the end, "pray without ceasing." The *Glossa Ordinaria* says that the desire in question is good prayer, and if the desire is continual, so is the prayer. Piety, from which a feeling is made pious, and thus a prayer, is "theosebia" or the worship we owe to God, and holds within it faith, hope, and charity. That is why Augustine in his letter to Proba about prayer to God says "Let us pray always in continual desire, with that same faith, hope, and charity."]

Like the writer of *De precationibus sacris*, Peraldus cites Augustine in order to emphasize that a "pius affectus" can itself be a prayer. He does not

---

31. "In ipsa ergo fide et spe et charitate continuato desiderio semper oramus. Sed ideo per certa intervalla horarum et temporum etiam verbis rogamus Deum, ut illis rerum signis nos ipsos admoneamus, quantumque in hoc desiderio profecerimus nobis ipsis innotescamus, et ad hoc augendum nos ipsos acrius excitemus" (*PL* 33, col. 501) ("We *pray always*, therefore, with continual desire in that same faith and hope and charity. But we also address God in words periodically, at specific times, so that by these signs of things we may alert ourselves to how we are progressing in this desire, and stir ourselves to increase it the more ardently").

32. Quoted from the parallel-text reproduction of Peraldus and an edition of the *Twelve Lettings*, in Diekstra, "The *XII Lettyngis of Prayer*," 143.

also rehearse Augustine's advice that Christians should frequently pray using words.

The redactor who excerpted and translated Peraldus's discussion of hindrances to prayer to produce the Middle English *Twelve Lettyngis of Prayer* shifts the emphasis yet further. He quotes Augustine in his explanation of how prayer requires, and even consists in, clean living:

> But here take hede that prayer stont most in [consists most of all in] clene lyuyng, that [so that] the prayer with the mouth accorde with the dede. And so contynu, and thow shalt take. Therefore Chryst seyth in the xviii chaptre of Luke: "*Hit behoueth to* [you should] *prey euer* [always] *and sese nat* [not cease]." Austyn seyth: "As long as thow hast holy desyre and lyuest aftyr [according to] Goddis lawe in charyte, thow prayest euer well. And yef thow lyue in glotony eyther [or] in other gret synnes, how many euer [however many] praysyngis thy tung sowneth [utters], thy lyfe blasphemeth, that ys, scornyth and despyseth God."[33]

Like *De precationibus sacris*, this text shifts the emphasis from desire, and even from faith, hope, and charity as abstract virtues, to action, the practice of those virtues. In the *Twelve Lettyngis*, "prayer stont most <u>in clene lyuyng</u>" (rather than in "pius affectus"). And the rendering of the quotation from Augustine does not merely name the virtues but focuses on their implementation: "<u>Ipsa fide, spe, et charitate</u> continuato desiderio semper oramus" becomes "As long as thow hast holy desyre <u>and lyuest aftyr Goddis lawe in charyte</u>, thow prayest euer well." Notice that virtues are implemented here through living in God's law, one of several hints that the *Twelve Lettyngis* itself is inflected with lollard concerns. Similarly, the *De precationibus sacris* explains what "preiere of charite" means not by naming virtues but by describing a way of life: "as longe as a man lyueþ just lif, kepynge Goddis hestis and charite, so longe he preieþ wel whatevere he do; and whoeere lyveþ best, he preieþ best." Keeping God's law in charity is the best form of prayer.

The competitive tone of *De precationibus sacris* as it informs readers that "whoeere lyveþ best, he preieþ best" and its subsequent use of this conclusion to condemn priests who do not live spiritually, persevere in right living, and preach to the people are predictable and indeed stereotypical strategies of polemical lollard writing.[34] However, not much attention has been paid

---

33. Diekstra, "The *XII Lettyngis of Prayer*," 143; punctuation modified.

34. See also John Wyclif, *Sermones*, ed. Johann Loserth, 4 vols., Wyclif Society (London: Trübner, 1887–90), 1:251/38–40: "Cum autem factum sit Deo accepcius quam est sonus, patet quod oracio qua Deus placatur debet magis constare in iusticia operis quam in verbis" ("Since deeds are more

to the lollard emphasis that prayer consists chiefly in the practice of rightful living, as opposed to that of oral (or even silent) recitation, or even correctly disposed and properly directed emotions. Having the right emotions is an essential component of rightful living as lollard writers describe it: as we will discover in much more detail in chapters 4 and 5, virtue comes from acting with the right sort of feeling.[35] So it is that the discussion of petitionary prayer in *De precationibus sacris* does not promise salutary effects from calling on the name of Jesus according to the form of words that follows, as a rubric instructing the reader of a book of prayers on how to use a prayer to the Holy Name, or more implicitly the words of such a prayer, more conventionally might.[36] Instead it explains what intentions, emotions, and virtues the person asking in the name of Jesus ought to have:

> [W]e axen [ask] in þe name of Jesus whanne we axen þing [for something] nedeful or profitable for savynge of mennis soulis, so [provided] þat we axen þis devoutly, of [with] gret desir, and wittily [wisely], or mekely and lastyngly [persistently], bi [by means of] saad [constant] feiþ, riʒtful [rightful] hope, and lastynge charite. And whatevere we axen þus, we schullen have of þe Fadir of hevene. (220/21–26)

The notion that all proper prayer should be virtuously disposed and should ask for the right things is conventional and again may draw on Augustine's Letter 130, to Proba, or one of its many derivatives. However, the prayer described in this passage is not a prayer accomplished through repeating certain words but a prayer accomplished in and through the practice of the three theological virtues, "bi saad feiþ, riʒtful hope, and lastynge charite," even before that prayer might also issue in spoken words. Where written prayers, and instructions for praying them, often suggest that saying their words produces greater virtue as well as other spiritual benefits and incites the correct emotions, for the writer of *De precationibus sacris*, virtuous living and properly disposed feelings are instead prerequisites for any benefit that might be obtained through saying words.

---

pleasing to God than sounds, it is clear that works, rather than words, of justice are the prayer that pleases God more").

35. See especially chap. 4, my discussion of the RV3 commentary on Psalm 86.

36. See, for example, the opening rubric in Urbana-Champaign, University of Illinois Rare Book and Manuscript Library, MS 80, which promises that its prayers are meedful, speedful, and profitable to every man and woman who can read and will excite, stir, and induce them to virtue while teaching them to know, love and dread God, both more and better, and be more busy to avoid sin and cultivate virtue so as to save their souls (fol. 1r). I thank Sara Weisweaver for bringing this manuscript to my attention. Consider also the petitionary prayers in the large Latin and English Book of Hours in Oxford, University College, MS 179, or the prayers in CUL Ii.6.43. On Holy Name prayers, see Lutton, "'Love this Name that is IHC.'"

This emphasis on prayer as a way of life is also consonant with the unusual emphasis on the practice of active, daily life in the lollard form of living known as *A Schort Reule of Lif*. The *Schort Reule* prescribes a daily round of meditation and prayer for all members of the three estates of priests, lords, and labourers. It tendentiously imitates mainstream adaptations of the "form of living" for lay readers—works for the laity that exhort them toward a way of life that would allow them to aspire to perfection as if they were members of a religious order living under a rule—but pointedly excludes religious orders, and even all other statuses within the church apart from parish priests, from its version of Christian community.[37] In the *Schort Reule*'s model, in contrast with most vernacular forms of living, oral prayer is markedly de-emphasized in proportion to exemplary living and teaching.

The general injunctions to all with which the work begins recommend a morning and evening routine of meditation, reflection, prayer in thanks to God for his mercy and goodness, and petitionary prayer for grace to continue in right action. Other forms of living, ranging from early works for religious to mainstream adaptations of the genre for laypeople, often devote a similar kind of attention to explaining how reflection and prayer should be incorporated into the daily routine, and indeed, Books of Hours and anthologies of prayers that provide materials for daily prayer by laypeople could be seen as implicitly engaged in the same sort of enterprise.[38] But where a mainstream form of living tends to focus on describing specific words and actions or specifying what prayers ought to accompany what daily routines, the *Schort Reule*'s recommended reflections issue forth, both morning and evening, in a resolve to serve God and teach others to do the same:

> First whanne þou risist [rise] or fulli wakist [awake], þenk on [think about] þe goodnesse of God: hou for his owne goodnesse and noon oþer nede [not out of any need] he made al þing of nouȝt, boþe aungelis and men and alle oþere creaturis goode in þer kynde.
>
> Þe secunde tyme [second], þenk on þe grete passioun and wilful [willing] deþ þat Crist suffrid for mankynde. Whanne no man myȝte make satisfaccioun for þe gilt of Adam and Eue and oþere moo [others

---

37. For much more on how lollards adapt religious rules, see chap. 7.

38. For contrasting examples emphasizing specific actions and the words of prayer, see Millett, *Ancrene Wisse*, part 1; Arne Zettersten, ed., *The English Text of the Ancrene Riwle: Edited from Magdalene College, Cambridge MS. Pepys 2498*, EETS, o.s. 274 (London: Oxford University Press, 1976), part 1; Hilton, *On Mixed Life*, in Horstmann, *Yorkshire Writers*, 1:283–84 (on prayers upon waking) and 289–90 (on how spoken prayers and reading the psalter are a more certain means toward devotion than meditation); and Pantin, "Instructions for a Devout and Literate Layman," esp. 398–400, 420–22.

as well], ne none [and no] aungelis owen [should] ne my3ten [could] make aseeþ [atone] þerfore [for that], þanne Crist of his endeles charite suffride so gret passioun and peyneful deþ þat no creature my3te suffre so moche.

And þenk þe þridde tyme hou God haþ saued þee fro deþ and oþere myscheues [mishaps] and suffrid [allowed] manye þousandis [thousands of others] to be lost þat ny3t [night]: summe in water, summe in fier [fire], summe in sodeyn [sudden] deþ, and summe to be dampned wiþouten ende. And for þese goodnessis and merci, þanke þi God of al þin herte. And preie him to 3eue [give] þee grace to spende in þat dai and eueremore alle þe my3tis [powers] of þi soule as [for instance] mynde, resoun, wit, wil, and alle þe my3tis of þi bodi as strengþe, beute [beauty], and þi fyue wittis in his seruise and his wrshipe. And in no þing forfete a3ens [act against] his comaundementis, but redi [be ready] to perfoorme werkis of merci and to 3eue good ensaumple of holi lif boþe in word and in dede to alle men aboute. . . .

And in þe ende of þe dai, þenk hou þou hast offendid God, and hou moche and hou ofte. And þerof [for that] haue enteer [full] sorwe and amende it whil þou mai [make amends when you can]. And þenk hou manye God haþ suffrid pershe [allowed to perish] manye weies þat dai, and summe to be dampned wiþouten ende, and hou graciousli he haþ saued þee, not for þi desert [because you deserved it] but for [out of] his owne merci and goodnesse. And þerfore þank him wiþ al þin herte and preie him of grace to dwelle and ende in his trewe and clene [pure] seruise and verri [true] charite and to teche oþere men þe same doyng [way of acting].[39]

The reader's recommended round of daily meditation spans salvation history, from the most general to the particular: God made everything; Christ died to redeem humanity; God has preserved the reader from death and possible damnation over the previous day or night. This emphasis on the many who have died and been damned may sound especially lollard, and perhaps even sanctimoniously so. However, a more elaborate list of unfortunates, who have suffered the same possible fates listed in the same order, appears in the versions of the thirteenth-century *Speculum ecclesie*.[40] More characteristically

---

39. Raschko, "Common Ground for Contrasting Ideologies," 408/3–19, 408/34–409/40.

40. See, e.g., the version in the Lincoln Thornton MS, Lincoln Cathedral, MS A.1.17, printed in Horstmann, *Yorkshire Writers*, 1:221/26–30: "þare-for [therefore], whene þou ryses of þi bedde at morne, or at mydnyghte, thynke als-tite [right away] how many thowsand mene and womene ere perischede [have perished] in body or in saule þat nyghte. Some in fyre, some in oþer manere, als in

lollard in emphasis, as the Introduction and chapter 2 have taught us to recognize, is the way the *Schort Reule* stipulates what readers must do: they should keep the commandments, perform the works of mercy, live in charity, and teach others to do the same in both word and deed.

How to act rightly in the world is explained in more detail in the *Schort Reule*'s intervening description of how readers should behave during the day. Readers should be well occupied at all times; they should dispose themselves toward right action through moderate habits and through properly disposed emotions: fear, love, desire, and thoughts of hell's pain and heaven's joys. They should teach others to do the same. As the *Schort Reule* continues with specific instructions for each of the three estates, the writer explains how through their rightful dealings with superiors, equals, and inferiors each person should spur others toward similar virtue—the same kind of emphasis on mutual responsibility, operating upwards as well as downwards in the social hierarchy, that was also evident in the *SS74* sermons and in lollard writings on the commandments (see chapter 1, chapter 2). In marked contrast to the daily routine of withdrawal for prayer at intervals across the course of the day recommended, for example, in Books of Hours, such prayer as is recommended here during the day will happen in the press of daily affairs, rather than at a remove from them, and may indeed take the form of action rather than words.

Still, even if lollards do place unusual emphasis on prayer by deeds rather than prayer by words, it seems fairly clear that lollards did pray using words as well. The *Schort Reule of Lif* fully describes the correct mental disposition and process of daily prayer, even if it does not specify what words should be said. And lollard texts do discuss the words that should be prayed, even if they are always careful to emphasize that those words must be accompanied by the right feelings and by right living and teaching or preaching.[41] Where lollard works discuss prayer by words, they typically emphasize the central importance of the Pater Noster; less often, they might discuss other prayers such as the Ave Maria, the creed, the Psalms, or the Canticles. Conversely, it is common rather than unusual for Pater Noster commentaries more broadly to serve as the occasion for a more general discussion of the best way to pray. This is no accident, since Christ teaches his apostles the Pater Noster in response to their

---

water or one lande. Some robbide, woundide, slayne, dede sodanly [suddenly] with-owttyne [without] sacramentis and fallyne in-till [fallen into] dampnacione ay-lastande [everlasting]." Expansions of abbreviations are modified.

41. In addition to the commentaries discussed below, see the commentary on the last verse of Psalm 86, in chap. 4.

question about how they should pray (Luke 11:1–4) and to show them how to pray better than hypocrites (Matt. 6:5–13). Commentaries on the Pater Noster tend to address these passages in addition to the words of the prayer itself and in ways that self-consciously respond not only to Christ's treatment of them in the bible but to each other.

The Pater Noster: The Best Prayer

Writers of vernacular commentaries on the Pater Noster were well aware that they were participating in a widespread initiative aimed at readers of the vernacular. However, even if scholarship on vernacular literature for the instruction of the laity has not often reminded us of this broader context, writers of these commentaries were also drawing on a deeper well. They themselves were familiar with a very extensive tradition of commentary on the Pater Noster in Latin, none of it explicitly aimed at lay readers, though sometimes with the edification of the faithful at large as its final aim. Bloomfield's index of incipits to Latin commentaries on the Pater Noster, for example, lists 1,261 items, many of them extant in a large number of copies.[42]

The dissemination of translations and compilations in French available in England is also extensive, though not yet as comprehensively studied, nor of course accessible to as many readers as works in English, even if French translations often facilitated English translations.[43] Þe Pater Noster of Richard Ermyte comments that female religious such as the "dere sistir" that is its addressee, no less than male religious highly competent in Latin, desire to read the Pater Noster with a deeper understanding that will enhance their affective engagement while praying.[44] However, this suggestion that expositions of the Pater Noster might be inaccessible to lay readers is unusual, perhaps because there are so many of them in English in late medieval manuscripts. The quirks in Lydgate's exposition, or as we will see in Pecock's or in Love's, just as much as the distinctive features of lollard commentaries, only become visible on extensive acquaintance with the cultural conversation these various commentaries draw upon and further develop.[45] It can be easy for a reader to miss these

---

42. "Incipits of Works on the Pater Noster," in Morton W. Bloomfield et al., eds., *Incipits of Latin Works on the Virtues and Vices, 1100–1500 AD* (Cambridge, MA: Medieval Academy, 1979), 567–686.

43. For some preliminary assays and surveys of specific topics, see section III of Jocelyn Wogan-Browne et al., eds., *Language and Culture in Medieval Britain: The French of England, c. 1100–c. 1500* (Woodbridge: York Medieval Press, 2009), 235–358.

44. Aarts, *Pater Noster of Richard Ermyte*, 3/5–20.

45. A comprehensive study of the relationships between Pater Noster commentaries available in England, like the one Jefferson has produced for commandments commentaries, would be very helpful, but this chapter is not the place for it; my comments here will be more impressionistic.

features, as indeed some compilers and copyists of fifteenth-century miscellanies in search of a Pater Noster commentary surely did when they included a lollard copy, and as some modern commentators have in claiming that one or another lollard commentary "contains nothing specifically Wycliffite," is "largely orthodox," or "contains no clearly identifiable Wyclifite ideas."[46]

De precationibus sacris discusses the Pater Noster only briefly but draws on many of the most important resources for this topic available to lollard commentators and their mainstream contemporaries in England:

> Crist tauȝte and comaundid us to preie þe Pater Noster, þat is best and liȝttest [easiest] and most siker [certain] preiere of alle. For þat conteyneþ [contains] al nedful þing, and profitable for body and soule, and noon error ne singularite aȝenst [against] Goddis wille; and Jesus Crist made it, and comaundid it in schorte wordis, for [so that] men schulden not ben hevy [reluctant] ne werie [weary] to seie it, ne combrid [burdened] to lerne it. And herfore Seynt [*sic*] blameþ men þat leven [abandon] þis Pater-Noster, tauȝt and comaunded of God, and chesen [choose] singuler [private] preieris maade of [by] synful men. (221/6–14)

By no means do all commentaries on the Pater Noster, but a great many of them, begin by asserting that the Pater Noster is the best of prayers and listing the attributes in which it excels; usually three, although sometimes two or four, are listed. The qualities listed vary widely, in Latin as well as in translation, to a perhaps surprising extent in such a widely distributed expository method. Where *De precationibus sacris* lists "best," "liȝttest," and "most siker," for example, all three of the lollard commentaries that have been printed give authority, subtlety, and profit as their trio; only one other commentary, embedded in sermon 9 in London, British Library, MS Royal 18.B.xxiii, a fifteenth-century compilation that includes material from *SS74* as well as other sermons in its manuscript, uses exactly the same list.[47]

46. These quotations are drawn respectively from James Simpson, *The Index of Middle English Prose, Handlist VII: A Handlist of Manuscripts Containing Middle English Prose in Parisian Libraries* (Cambridge: Brewer, 1989), 24; Gillespie, "Thy Will be Done," 100 n. 21; A. L. Kellogg and Ernest W. Talbert, "The Wycliffite Pater Noster and Ten Commandments, with Special Reference to English Mss. 85 and 90 in the John Rylands Library," *Bulletin of the John Rylands Library* 42 (1960): 355.

47. Anna Lewis, "Textual Borrowings," 6–7, notices the same list in the Royal 18.B.xxiii sermon, edited in W. O. Ross, ed., *Middle English Sermons*, EETS, o.s. 209 (London: Oxford University Press, 1960). Innocent III's very widely distributed commentary gave authority, brevity, sufficiency, and fecundity as the attributes of the Pater Noster, and there are a number of other Latin commentaries that follow him with similar lists (Bloomfield et al., *Incipits*, 602–3, 624, 653, 679–80, etc.). Edmund's *Speculum ecclesie* gives dignity and profit, while *Þe Pater Noster of Richard Ermyte* lists dignity, worthiness, and price.

While the adjectival lists diverge, the brief or longer expositions that they inaugurate converge around a small set of key points, as here in *De precationibus sacris*, though with crucially differing emphases.[48] Christ made the Pater Noster. It contains all that is necessary, but no error, and nothing against God's will; in some commentaries this may develop into criticism of other prayers, and of incorrect ways of praying, drawn from the surrounding discussion of hypocrisy and hypocritical prayer in Matthew 6. The Pater Noster is brief; some Latin commentaries comment that its brevity makes it easier to repeat many times (seemingly unconcerned by Matt. 6:7's strictures on repetition), while generally English commentaries instead suggest that its brevity makes it easy to learn and leaves no room for excuses about not being able to do so. The Pater Noster brings profit to both body and soul for those who pray it properly; some commentaries seize this occasion to describe how their content may facilitate this correctly oriented prayer, while others go on to discuss proper prayer, or condemn improper prayer, in more depth.

De precationibus sacris touches most of these key points even in its very brief exposition here. Although this has not previously been recognized, it also, in the final sentence just quoted, draws on the *Speculum ecclesie*. "Seynt [*sic*] blameþ men þat leven þis Pater-Noster, tauȝt and comaunded of God, and chesen singuler preieris maade of synful men" sounds thoroughly lollard in its condemnation of those who neglect the Pater Noster God asked men to pray. One might even speculate that the unnamed "seynt" here is Wyclif in disguise, as it often is in lollard writings. Instead it is Edmund of Abingdon at the end of the *Speculum ecclesie*'s commentary on the Pater Noster:

> I blame hem þat leten [abandon] þe preiere þat God himself made and tauȝt, and takeþ hem to orisouns [prayers] of a symple seint, þouȝ [even if] þei fynde hit write [should find them written]. For oure lord seiþ in þe gospel, "whanne ȝe preieþ, ne preie ȝe not [pray not] wiþ many wordis, but seie ȝe þus [say this]. 'Pater noster et cetera.'" (Bodley 416, fol. 128v)[49]

Here Edmund, like many other writers, follows Matthew 6 by criticizing improper prayer just before developing his account of the best sort of prayer. *PN Matthew*, too, draws on Edmund, though more allusively, as it

---

48. Anna Lewis, "Textual Borrowings," 5, also notes this convergence.

49. There is no published critical edition of the *Speculum ecclesie*, nor do I present one here; instead, I will quote transcriptions from specific manuscripts and note any especially interesting variants. I have benefitted greatly in my work on this text from the generosity of Jennifer Arch, who is preparing an edition and has shared her findings with me. The Thornton MS (Lincoln Cathedral, MS A.1.17) has "sinful," but all other copies I have seen have "simple."

concludes: "lord, hou moche ben þei [they are] to blame þat bisien hem aboute [busy themselves with] preieris maade of synful men and leuen [leave] þis pater noster þat is best and most hesy [easy] of alle, and comprehendiþ [includes] alle goodis for body and soule" (202/8–12). In context Edmund's critique is carefully qualified, more so than in its use by the lollards who quote him. He began by saying that he does not blame Augustine, Gregory, and many other saints who have prayed "aftur here affecciouns [following their desire]" (Bodley 416, fol. 128v). Yet he is also more sharply critical than *De precationibus sacris* or *PN Matthew* of "curiouse [oversophisticated]" prayers in verse that seduce hundreds of thousands away from the prayer that pleases God most (fol. 128r); here Edmund's disdain for formal elaboration is reminiscent of Duffy's version of lollardy.

Edmund may be drawing in turn on Augustine's more detailed explanation, in his Letter 130, to Proba, chapter 12, of how any other words used in prayer at best repeat the Pater Noster's succinct formulations while running the risk of generating a superfluity of words and, at worst, ask what should not be asked.[50] Chapter 12 of Augustine's letter was incorporated into both the *Glossa ordinaria* and the *Catena aurea* in commentary on Matthew 6 and so was widely known. It is, in and of itself, a condensed commentary on each petition of the Pater Noster in turn and a widely influential one. Indeed the final paragraph of *PN Arnold I* translates the whole chapter closely, truncating a few of its quotations but otherwise leaving it unchanged.

This lollard rendition is worth quoting in its entirety:

[W]hatevere oþir [other] wordis þe desire of him þat praieþ [the one praying] fourmeþ in bifore-goynge [forms beforehand], þat it be cleer [to make it clear], oþir addiþ afterwarde, þat it encreesce [to increase it], we seie noon oþir þinge þan þat [except what] is conteyned in þe praier of þis Lord, ȝif we praien riȝtli and covenabli [appropriately]. For whanne a man seiþ, "*be þow glorified in alle folkis as þow ert glorified in us*" (2 Thess. 3:1), what oþer þing seiþ he þan þat, "*Þi name be halwid?*" And whanne a man seiþ, "*Lord, schewe þi face to us, and we schulle be saaf*" (Ps. 79:20), what oþer þinge seiþ he þan þat, "*Þi rewme* [kingdom] *come?*" Whanne a man seiþ, "*Lord, dresse* [direct] *my steppis up* [according to] *þi spechis* [words]" (Ps. 118:133), what oþir þing seiþ he þan, "*Þi wille be doun?*" Whanne a man seiþ, "*Lord, ȝif* [give] *not povert ne richessis to me*" (Prov. 30:8), what oþer þing seiþ he þan þis, "*ʒif us today oure eche daies* [daily] *breed?*" Whanne a man seiþ, "*Lord, have mynde of* [remember] *David and of al his myldnesse*" (Ps. 131:1), and, "*ʒif* [if] *I have ʒolden* [given] *yvelis to hem þat ʒolden yvelis to me, falle I voyde* [may I fall away empty] *from myn enemyes*" (Ps. 7:5), what oþer þing seiþ he þan þis, "*Forʒive to us oure dettis, as we forʒyven to oure dettoures?*" Whanne a man seiþ, "*Lord, do awey fro me* [deliver me from] *þe coveitise of þe wombe* [greed]" (Ecclus. 23:6), what oþir þing saiþ he þan þis, "*Leed us not into temptacioun?*" Whanne a man seiþ, "*My God, delyvere me fro myn enemyes*" (Ps. 58:2), what oþir þin saiþ he þan þis, "*Delyvere us from yvel?*" And ʒif þou rennest aboute bi [go over] alle þe wordis of holy praieris, þou schalt fynde noþing whiche is not conteyned in þis praier of þe Lord. Whoevere seiþ a þing þat may not perteyne to þis prayer of þe gospel, he praieþ bodili and unjustli and unleeffulli [unlawfully] as me þenkiþ [it seems to me]. Whanne a man saieþ in his praier, "Lord, multiplie myn richesses, and encreese myn honouris," and seiþ þis, havynge þe coveitise of hem, and not purposynge [intending] þe profit of hem to men, to be bettir to God ward [to direct them better toward God], I gesse þat he may not fynde it in þe Lordis praier. Þerfore be it schame [it is shameful] to aske þo þingis, whiche is not leefful [lawful] to coveyte [desire]. If a man schameþ not [is not ashamed] of þis, but coveytise overcomeþ him, þis is askid, þat he delyvere fro þis yvel of coveytise, to whom we seyn, "*Delyvere us from yvel.*" (96/23–97/30, punctuation modified)

This lollard writer is perhaps fascinated by Augustine's emphasis on the desire of the person praying, as much as the words that may clarify and amplify that desire. Augustine's exposition is a miniature guide to proper prayer, showing its reader how to assess words formed or added by desire that might excite their feelings in turn, but more than that, showing them how to assess and reform both their own desires and those of others. What makes the prayer "Lord, multiplie myn richesses, and encreese myn honouris" carnal, unjust, and unlawful is not the words themselves, even if they are the only example Augustine gives that is not drawn from the bible. While unpromising, they might be intended metaphorically and for the good of the community. Instead, as Augustine is careful to specify, the problem is that the speaker "seiþ þis, havynge þe coveitise of hem, and not purposynge þe profit of hem to men, to be bettir to God ward." Prayer accompanied by covetous and selfish desires cannot succeed.

Indeed, while the content of the Pater Noster is ideally suited for proper prayer, even its words, or those of prayers compatible with it, can be blameworthy for those saying them in the wrong way. The lollard *De precationibus sacris* devotes several pages to the sins of the clergy and to emphasizing that while a sinful priest can perform the sacraments, though to his own harm, he cannot pray meritoriously, for no prayer uttered in sin can succeed (Arnold, 222–29). The lollard *Dialogue between a Friar and a Secular*, on the other hand, concludes that a sinful man can pray to God meritoriously, and in that very act acquire grace, if he prays with penitent intent.[51] While these delineations of sin are unusual, and might be used to support a rejection of the sacraments that neither writer does actually express, there is no disagreement on the basic point that sinful prayer is not meritorious—a point that is by no means unorthodox. The sinfulness of the person praying is in fact the first of the twelve hindrances to prayer so influentially discussed by Peraldus.[52]

Augustine's exposition of the Pater Noster and brief guide to prayer in chapter 12 of his Letter 130, to Proba, can also be taken as a pithy commentary on the practice of commentary. After all, the words of any exposition of the Pater Noster, as much as any spontaneous effusion or written script for prayer, are designed to form, properly direct, and augment desire even as they also impart information. The *Pater Noster of Richard Ermyte* addresses these goals quite explicitly in its opening, as we have already seen, where it explains to the female religious it anticipates as its first audience how it aims to help her to "hertily [in your heart] undirstonde þat [what] þou preiest with mouþ. And for noþing ellis [for no other reason] but onely for to kyndil [kindle] þi loue to hym and more lerne to loue hym, to whom þou þi preier makist."[53] *PN Arnold II* similarly suggests that the Pater Noster's marvellous capacity to convey in so few words an inexhaustible fount of learning, beyond the scope of human telling, should incite its readers' love and praise:

> [I]n . . . so schort a prayer is conteyned so muche wyt [wisdom] þat no tonge of man may telle it al here in erþe. And syþþe [since] a craft of gret sotilte [subtlety] is muche y-preysed of worldlyche [praised by worldly] men, muche more scholde þis sotylle gospel, þis worþy prayer, be loued and preysed of Cristes dere chyldren. (100/5–10)

Here "wyt" is what inspires love and praise, and should do so more than worldly "sotilte," while in the *Pater Noster of Richard Ermyte* love precedes and

---

51. *FWD*, 37/188–98.
52. Diekstra, "The *XII Lettyngis of Prayer*," 131, gives the first hindrance to prayer as explained by Peraldus and his Middle English derivatives in parallel columns.
53. Aarts, *Pater Noster of Richard Ermyte*, 3/17–19.

is given far greater stress than learning. However, both commentaries balance cognitive and emotional outcomes against one another.

We might inquire, though, exactly how *PN Arnold II* proposes to form and augment its readers' love and learning, particularly if its words might multiply endlessly without ever explaining the Pater Noster's "wyt." Like *PN Arnold I* and *PN Matthew*, this commentary does not comment overtly on its mediatory role as an aid to Christ's children in informing and deepening their love, or make any recommendations on how it might be read or used. On this point, Edmund's *Speculum ecclesie* is once again influential. The lollard commentaries printed in Arnold and Matthew do not quote Edmund's remarks, at the end of his discussion of the Pater Noster, about how he anticipates that his commentary will influence his readers. But the *Speculum vitae* picks them up and imports them into its adaptation of Laurent's *Somme le Roi*, as does the *Myrour*, with the result that they are widely available in the copies of these Middle English works.[54] And we can see how lollard writers in particular responded to Edmund's description of the relationship between commentary and prayer in two interpolated copies of Edmund's Pater Noster commentary found in lollard manuscripts: the copy of the full *Speculum ecclesie* in Bodley 416, and the excerpted and interpolated Pater Noster commentary in Harley 2398. Each modifies its version of the passage in significant ways.

I quote the passage that follows from Bodley 416's version of Edmund's commentary on the Pater Noster. Additions and elaborations in the interpolated version in Harley 2398 are listed in footnotes, while Bodley 416's most significant divergences from the rest of the Middle English versions are underlined. In general, compared with other Middle English versions, Bodley 416's is a lean, spare rendition that resists any temptation to elaborate and excises the concluding passage that Harley 2398 interpolates and expands. Yet the two versions share a preoccupation with the inward experience of prayer.

> And ne undurstonde not [do not get the idea that] þou shalt seie [should say] wiþ þi mouþ[55] al þat ich here haue write. But sei onliche [only] þe naked wordis [words of the prayer themselves],[56] and þenk [think] in þine [your] herte of þat oþer [the other part] þat here is write,[57] upon euerich word bi himself [word by word]. And take non hede to [don't

---

54. See Hanna, *Speculum Vitae*, 1:112/3303–113/3336; Nelson, *Myrour to Lewde Men and Wymmen*, 102/1–14.

55. wiþ þi mouþ] word by word

56. wordis] lettre by mouþe

57. of þat oþer þat here is write] on þat I haue expouned

concern yourself with] multeplien[58] many pater nostres. For bettur is to seien on [one] alone, wiþ[59] deuocioun and undurstondinge,[60] þan a þousand wiþoute undurstondinge.[61] For seint Poul seiþ þus openlich [openly]: "Ich hadde leuere [would rather] to seien fiue wordis in myn herte deuoutliche þan fiue þousand <u>wiþ my mouþ</u>[62] wiþouten undur-stondinge." [fol. 131v] And <u>þerfore</u>[63] þou shalt do þin offis [service (see n. 69)] <u>in þin herte,</u>[64] <u>deuoutlich.</u> And so seiþ þe prophet: "Singeþ wislich [wisely]."[65] To synge wislich is þat [what] men seien wiþ mouþ, seie also wiþ herte.[66] For ʿ ʒifʾ[67] [if] þi bodi be in þe quer [choir] and þi lippes in þe sauter [psalter], and þin herte in þe stret [street] or in þe market, wrecchedlich artow [you are] þanne [then] departed [di-vided].[68] (fol. 131 r–v)

Edmund explains here that readers are not expected to recite aloud the whole of the extended Pater Noster commentary that precedes this recommenda-tion, just as it is written out in full in the *Speculum ecclesie*. Rather, they should pray "þe naked wordis" of the prayer itself with their mouths, while using the commentary as a tool for intensive meditation upon the text's meaning: "þenk in þine herte . . . upon euerich word bi himself." The commentary enables "deuocioun and undurstondinge" by providing an expansive if not exhaustive guide to the meaning concealed beneath the surface of the Pater Noster's deceptively simple wording. Saying the prayer once with properly directed and meaningful devotion is better than saying it a thousand times without.

Where Bodley 416 has "<u>þerfore</u> þou shalt do þin offis <u>in þin herte, deu-outlich,</u>" other versions have stopped talking about praying the Pater Noster altogether. In place of Bodley 416's "þerfore," they introduce a comparison with "in the same maner" and go on to describe the performance of the divine office, spoken and sung, as part of a choir (or at the very least, in

---

58. *adds* ofte þe Pater Noster or to seye

59. wiþ] wiþ a (I emend Bodley 416 here)

60. deuocioun and undurstondinge] vnderstondyng in goed entent and deuocioun

61. *adds* and deuocioun

62. wiþ my mouþ] *added.* (According to Jennifer Arch, no other Middle English copy specifies in this way, but at least one Anglo-Norman version does.)

63. And þerefore] In þe same maner

64. in þin herte] in þe churche

65. Singeþ wislich] seye ʒe þe psalme wysly, þat is, synge þou and seye vers of psalmes wysly

66. þat men seien wiþ mouþ, seie also wiþ herte] to vnderstonde wysly in herte þat þat a man seyþ by mouþe

67. *insert from marg.*

68. Harley 2398 continues: see next quotation.

church).[69] Bodley 416's "þerfore" instead makes "in þin herte, deuoutlich" into an extended exposition of the quotation from Paul that all other copies had used to conclude their discussion of the Pater Noster. In addition to extending discussion of that quotation, Bodley 416 augments the quotation itself, interpolating into it "wiþ my mouþ." The end result of Bodley 416's modifications is sharply to divide prayer in the heart from prayer with the mouth, to value prayer in the heart far more highly, and to make prayer in the heart the place where a reader can "do þin offis"—an injunction, now newly shorn of its liturgical referent, that might now apply to any sort of religious duty.[70] In this pared-down version, to sing wisely is to say with your heart what "men say" with their mouths. Prayer is in the heart, for Bodley 416's writer, and should conform to the properly expounded meaning of what others say, even when the reader does not say them orally at all. These alterations are in keeping with changes carefully executed across this version as a whole that, as Nicholas Watson has shown, remove references to religious institutions, shift the emphasis away from the ecclesiastical hierarchy to society as a whole, and focus the reader's attention upon his or her own feelings and intentions.[71]

For the most part, the version of this passage in the Harley 2398 copy provides amplifications rather than parings and alterations. But this copy too stresses devotion and intention (notice the increased emphasis at nn. 60–61, for example) and gives one of the longest versions of the conclusion, omitted entirely by Bodley 416, explaining the results of prayer. I begin just before Bodley 416 leaves off, with Harley 2398's extended description of the divided self, followed by its final exhortation, in which I underline the more unusual components:

> For yf þy body is in þe quer þy lyppes in þe sauter and þyn herte in þe chepyng [market] þou art most wrecchedly departyd in þy self and

---

69. All copies contrast body in the choir, lips in the psalter, and heart in the market in their equivalent to Bodley 416's final sentence here, regardless of their alterations to the sentence under discussion; this may have been a common saying or verse tag. It appears, as well, in the *Lanterne of Liȝt*'s discussion of prayer (Lilian M. Swinburn, ed., *Lanterne of Liȝt*, EETS, o.s. 151 [London: Kegan Paul, 1917], 50/34–51/3). For Bodley 416's "in þin herte, deuoutlich," Vernon (Oxford, Bodleian Library, MS. Eng. poet. a.1) and Lincoln Thornton (Lincoln Cathedral, MS A.1.17) have "in the choir," Oxford, Bodleian Library, MS Douce 25 and Harley 2398 have "in church," and Aberystwyth, National Library of Wales, Peniarth MS 395D has "with hert"—the closest and chosen, like Bodley 416's version, to emphasize desire over location but without the same level of systematic, deliberate change across the whole passage. Harley 2398's version of the topos appears in full in the next quotation.
70. See *MED*, s.v. "office," n.; "don office" can mean to perform one's duty (3 [b]) or to perform divine service or mass (5 [a]).
71. Watson, "Middle English Versions."

þou art nouȝt graciously herd of God. And for our lord Iesu Crist
seyþ in þe gospel, "*Seke ȝe first þe reume* [kingdom] *of God and alle þese
þynge schulleþ be cast to ȝow*, þat is, to how many þynges ȝe haue nede of
temporal goed, hy [they] schulleþ be ȝyue [given] to ȝow [you] wiþoute
axyng." Þerfore þou schalt wyte [know] what þou schalt haue in þe ioye
of heuene. Amen.

The conclusion of this section explaining the Pater Noster varies widely
as different translators and copyists labor to explain its point in different
ways. However, Harley 2398 is unique in its impulse to explain that the
dividedness of the body described in this common topos is also a division
of the self, one that results in not being heard by God. The translation and
paraphrase of Matthew 6:33 in the Vulgate that follows this explanation is
decidedly unusual, especially in the context of a commentary on prayer. Like
the Wycliffite Bible, the writer gives "all these things shall be cast to you" for
"omnia haec adicientur vobis," where most versions of the *Speculum ecclesie*
instead paraphrase to assure readers, more straightforwardly, that God will
give them what they need. But this writer also adds that seeking God's kingdom will lead readers to receive what they truly need without even asking
for it, again an unusual move in commentary on prayer and one that exceeds
the terms of what other versions offer in their paraphrases of the quotation.

Harley 2398's version is also unique (though this may simply be an error)
in subsuming what in complete versions of the text is usually an introduction
to the following description of the bodily and spiritual gifts of heaven into a
conclusion to the promise it has just made. The effect is that its concluding
sentence rounds out its promise that temporal necessities will be provided
with an accompanying reassurance about the joy of heaven. In place of
instruction in properly disposed oral prayer, Harley 2398's version leaves us
with an exhortation to live with the whole heart fixed upon attaining the
heavenly kingdom and in this way receive what is needed in this life and the
next, even without any petitionary prayer whatsoever.

We have been surveying the very extensive overlaps between lollard and
mainstream commentary on prayer as well as the smaller but significant divergences. We have learned that both lollard and mainstream writers use the
Pater Noster as a focus for heightened devotion, but also instruction, for
both lay and clerical audiences. We have also learned that mainstream and
lollard writers alike seize opportunities to discuss the proper way to pray,
both in commentary on the Pater Noster and on other occasions, in terms
that criticize contemporary practice and even specific groups. This is not to
say that the lollard commentaries are not lollard, only that their tendencies to

instruct their readers and criticize contemporaries who profess holiness while departing from the words of the bible into "curiouse" language are not what distinguish them as lollard. What is more distinctive in the lollard expositions (though by no means heterodox) is their intensive focus on feeling and intention. Distinctive too, and potentially divisive by implication since it could be developed into a rejection of some ways of life valued in the institutional church, is their insistence that prayer without ceasing should be accomplished in and through daily actions accompanied by properly directed feelings and intentions, ones that serve as an instructive example for others, far more importantly than through words. In making these points they self-consciously return to, but also modify, what they derive from Augustine's Letter 130, to Proba, and Edmund's *Speculum ecclesie*.

Fifteenth-Century Reactions

Against the backdrop of the common ground between lollard and other commentaries on prayer, it is fifteenth-century respondents to this tradition—especially respondents to lollardy—who look startlingly unusual. What is more, it is hard to characterize their efforts as establishing a new "orthodox" tradition. Instead, their comments look more like self-conscious responses to a center ground where they are no longer comfortable. This discomfort does not characterize fifteenth-century religion outside lollardy as a whole. Most of the manuscripts I have been quoting were copied in the fifteenth century; the center ground shared by mainstream and lollard writers continued to be available to readers, to copyists, and to those writers who were not laboring to distance themselves from it. Indeed, the entirely superficial efforts at distance made in three fifteenth-century copies of the *Speculum vitae* help to demonstrate this point: they claim that no reader should condemn the work, for it was examined for heresy in Cambridge in 1384 and found to be without any defect, for if it had not been, it would doubtless have been burned.[72]

Lydgate's remarks about the comparatively narrowed scope of his Pater Noster commentary, mentioned earlier in this chapter, similarly introduce not an innovation in form, nor any real change in content, but a modification of framing. His refusal to dilate his commentary into a wide-ranging cosmology expatiated in foursomes is a gesture of comparative restraint. But it is no more than a gesture, and surely a playful one: even the most expansive of fourteenth-century commentaries in English does not cover what he

---

72. See Somerset, "Censorship," 249. See also Hope Emily Allen, "The *Speculum Vitae*: Addendum," *PMLA* 32 (1917): 133–62.

refrains from providing. In contrast, though, Reginald Pecock is yet more assertive than the *Speculum vitae*, and far more unorthodox than Lydgate. In his *Donet* he recommends that readers pray by thinking about the meaning of each petition of the Pater Noster in turn. He recommends the commentary in his own *Reule of Cristen Religion* as a guide to the meaning of each petition. Thus far he differs little from Edmund's remarks on the relationship between commentary and prayer in the *Speculum ecclesie*. However, Pecock goes on to transfer to his own commentary the sort of tripartite praise typically given to the Pater Noster itself:

> If þou wolte preie . . . þan I wole þat þou take þin vndirstonding of þe pater noster þoruȝ [through] eche of þe peticiouns, which vndirstonding is sette forþ in þe vij trety [seventh treatise] of þe first party [part] of "þe reule of cristen religioun." . . . And perauenture [perhaps] it schal be to þee so ryche, so swete and so preciose þat þou schalt desire aftir noon oþire [yearn for nothing else], for, certis [certainly], of alle þe exposiciouns and vndirstondingis which euer I siȝe [saw] vpon þe pater noster, þilk [that same] exposicioun and vndirstonding þere i-sett [put there] beriþ þe price [wins the prize].[73]

However typical of Pecock this strenuous promotion of the value of his own instruction may be, here it rather disturbingly makes his own commentary a kind of substitute for the Pater Noster itself.

Nicholas Love's commentary on the Pater Noster, interpolated into his *Mirror* in the commentary on the Sermon on the Mount in chapter 18, is perhaps the most thoroughgoing reconsideration of what a Pater Noster commentary might try to accomplish. His praise of the Pater Noster above all other prayers goes to extraordinary lengths to avoid saying anything negative about any kind of prayer whatsoever, reversing distinctions made conventional in a long tradition of commentary beginning with the gospels themselves.

> Bot miche folke [many people] as [behaving like] seruantes and hirede men haue more wile to [more want to] praye for speciale mede [a particular reward] þat þei coueyten [desire] here þan as [behaving like] trewe sones, [and praying] for þe loue and þe plesyng of oure fadere God of heuen. And so þei setten more hir likyng [direct their desire] and bisinesse [zeal] in [toward] a priuate praiere made of man

73. Reginald Pecock, *The Donet*, ed. Elsie V. Hitchcock, EETS, o.s. 156 (London: Oxford University Press, 1921), 204/10–14, 20–24.

to oure lady or to oþer seyntes of heuen þen [than] þei done in [direct it toward] þis generale praiere made of God himself, þe which without dout is most pleisyng to him and most spedeful [beneficial] to vs, and þerfore þei bene deceyued in many maneres. I speke not here of þe sawter [psalter] and þe seruice in holy chirch.

Neuerles also oþere deuout praieres made to God and to oure lady and oþere seyntes bene gude to be seide [good to say], after þat [as far as] þe deuocion of men is stired to sey hem in conable [fitting] tyme, so [provided] þat þei sette not hir affeccion þe lasse vpon þis most worþi praiere pater noster.[74]

In striking contrast with the lollard writers discussed here, and indeed with their mainstream contemporaries as well, Love cannot bring himself to criticize any religious practice, or any specific social group, without extensive qualification. Many people have more desire to pray for some special reward rather than for the love of God, as if they were God's servants and hired men rather than his true sons. Yet the "seruantes and hirede men" counterposed to the "trewe sones" are in their allusion to Galatians 4 evasively metaphorical. What is being described is a petitionary attitude, rather than a social status, and one that anyone engaged in prayer, not members of some specific group, might exhibit. Where a lollard writer might pursue the point to develop a contrast between the conduct of members of the true church and covetous members of a false church who insist on excessive compensation, Love's next sentence shifts ground rather than pursuing the issue. What is wrong with private prayers now is not so much their intention (reward) as their direction (Mary and other saints, rather than God himself) and their content: the prayer God made is surely best. Yet, Love hastens to add, he is not disparaging the psalter or the divine office. And, "neuerles also" (piling qualification upon qualification) prayers to Mary and the saints are fine as long as they are said with commensurate devotion, at the right time, and without neglecting the Pater Noster.

Love does not want to appear censorious of any accepted religious practice. But his cautious wording is also motivated by a concern, like that of several of the lollard writers we have examined, with his reader's intentions. Love agrees, for example, that the Pater Noster is often said without proper devotion. He has some choice words on those who "bene to [too] negligent

74. Love, *Mirror of the Blessed Life of Jesus Christ*, 84/32–85/2. Punctuation, word division, and capitalization have been modified, and further citations are parenthetical.

and rablene [babble] it forþ without deuocion," with "bedes . . . trillyng on þe fingeres, and waggyng þe lippes" (85/5–6, 84/10–11). His solution is unusual, as is his understanding of the role of commentary:

> whoso wole ȝiue his entent [attentively] fort [to] sey it with deuocion and haþ an inwarde desire to þe gostly [spiritual] vndurstondyng þerof, settyng his herte þerto [on it] als miche [as much] as he may when he seiþ it boþe in comune and in priuate, he shale . . . fynde in his soule, whan god wole ȝife [grant] his grace, with gret likyng [great pleasure] diuerse vndurstandyng þerof [a different kind of understanding of it] most pertynent [most fitting] to his desire. And þat oþere [that understanding will be different] þan is writen in þe comune exposicion þerof, or perantere [perhaps] þan he can telle. (84/21–24, 28–31)

Rather like the lollard commentators we have examined, Love foregrounds the devotion and desire for understanding of the person praying. These, properly disposed, will produce direct from God an individually tailored "diuerse vndurstandyng," "oþere þan is writen in þe comune exposicion þerof" and quite possibly beyond the recipient's ability to recount. In his assertions that correct understanding may come to the one praying by God's grace and that the Pater Noster contains many different understandings, more than can be told, Love steers close to the position of lollard commentators. But in his surprising suggestion that a reader may find interpretations of the Pater Noster "most pertynent to his desire," ones that diverge from the "comune exposicion," by directing his attention inward and away from the words of Love's own commentary, Love is on his own. Lollards embrace the "comune exposicion," even if they adapt it; Love's strikingly individualistic divergence from it here seems almost to efface the role of commentary altogether and places surprising trust in the anticipated results of his readers' inward reflections.[75]

Conclusion

This investigation points toward a new way of reading the group of texts that Matti Peikola has suggested form an "alternative Wycliffite catechetical programme."[76] Commentaries or expositions of the Pater Noster, as well as other canonical prayers on which lollard writers provide commentary,

---

75. On Love's emphasis on inwardness throughout his text, see further Jennifer Bryan, *Looking Inward: Devotional Reading and the Private Self in Late Medieval England* (Philadelphia: University of Pennsylvania Press, 2008), 50–51.

76. Peikola, "'And after all, myn Aue-Maria,'" 273 and n. 4.

aim to produce deeper devotion and understanding in the person praying, whether they pray aloud or "in þe herte." While the words of the Pater Noster themselves remain the most highly prized, and are the best form of prayer, other words can be valuable as well. Reflection on the words of prayer commentaries—except in Love's strikingly unusual formulation, in which those words encourage the reader to look within himself or herself instead— is the chief means by which a reader's prayer may be deepened and follow its own new course within that reader's heart. Thus far most mainstream and lollard writers, compilers, and book producers engaged in the production of miscellaneous religious manuals across the late fourteenth and fifteenth centuries would agree, if we may judge from the contents of a quite large number of extant manuscripts.

Where there might be room for more disagreement among these producers of religious writing, as well as lack of accord with those pursuing heresy, would be on the questions of who should have access to these forms of commentary and what sort of forming and augmenting of love, understanding, and desire their commentaries should be engaged in. I say "lack of accord" rather than "conflict" because there is no evidence that heresy prosecutions ever sought out the producers of suspect books seized in heresy proceedings.[77] Instead, they went after their owners, and—as has intermittently puzzled scholars of heresy—as far as we can tell from the brief titles or descriptions they give, they recorded their possession not of what we would consider obviously polemical lollard books but of any vernacular religious material whatsoever, even including pastoral material, commentaries on the ten commandments, biblical writings, and saints' lives.[78]

---

77. See Anne Hudson, "Lollard Book Production," in *Book Production and Publishing in Britain, 1375–1475*, ed. Jeremy Griffiths and Derek Pearsall (Cambridge: Cambridge University Press, 1989), 137. In the London trial of John Claydon in 1415, Chichele does make some attempt to discover the whereabouts of the scribe who copied the *Lanterne of Liȝt* Claydon had commissioned, yet apparently without success. E. F. Jacob, ed., *The Register of Henry Chichele, Archbishop of Canterbury, 1414–1443*, 4 vols. (Oxford: Oxford University Press, 1938–47), 4:132–38. For more on lollard book producers, see Maureen Jurkowski, "Lollard Book Producers in London in 1414," in *Text and Controversy: Essays in Honour of Anne Hudson*, ed. Helen Barr and Ann M. Hutchison (Turnhout: Brepols, 2005), 201–26.

78. McSheffrey, "Heresy, Orthodoxy, and English Vernacular Religion," 61–68. McSheffrey's view that the books named must be orthodox is based on the assumption that these books were printed books: see Shannon McSheffrey and Norman Tanner, eds. and trans., *Lollards of Coventry, 1486–1522*, Camden Fifth Series 23 (Cambridge: Cambridge University Press, 2003), esp. 323–24. However, books circulated among lollard communities in the late fifteenth and early sixteenth centuries might well have included earlier handwritten books, copies made by hand from those books, and printed books modified by marginalia. And while their content might not have been heterodox, nonetheless it might have foregrounded lollard emphases.

That these otherwise unobjectionable reading materials were in the wrong hands certainly seems to have been part of the problem: what a member of a religious order, or the nobility or gentry, might own and read more openly seems to have raised suspicion when it was shared among more ordinary readers. Yet that suspicion arises because it is expected that these readers will put their books to the wrong use. Even books with no polemical content—even books that select all of their quotations from the mainstream Christian tradition—might form and augment these readers' desires in the wrong direction when read in certain ways. Lollard Pater Noster commentaries give us evidence of some of the possible readings that could have worried bishops, as for example when in expounding "give us this day our daily bread," *PN Arnold II* forms and augments its readers' desire for the "lore of Godes word." If, through the negligence of bishops and others, that lore is not well taught, *PN Arnold II* encourages them to pray to Christ, "byschepe of oure soule [bishop of our soul], þat he ordeyne prechours in þe peple to warne hem of synne, and telle hem þe truþe of God."[79] These preachers among the people ordained by the bishop of our souls sound very much like the unlicensed preachers, not authorized by local bishops, whose suppression was one focus of heresy investigations from the 1380s onward.[80] Yet lollard commentaries also present more subtle examples of lollard emphasis that bishops and later commentators may not have noticed, as when *PN Arnold I* (in which Talbert and Kellogg could find "no evidence of Wyclifism") quietly develops its unusual opening formulation—that the Pater Noster surpasses all other prayers not just in "profit" but in "profit to Cristes cherche"—into a lightly drawn but no less firmly asserted lollard ecclesiology where Christ's church consists only of those who shall be saved.[81]

Yet even the mainstream Christian tradition as represented in the *Catena aurea* might, if lay villagers used it to discern the misdirected desires and actions in the world around them, give fuel to lollard uses of the Pater Noster. Consider, for example, the reported views of Thomas Hellis of Brenchley in the Weald of Kent, who was in 1431 recorded as believing "that men and wymmyn devout in devyn service, lifting her handis and here

---

79. 105/32–106/15, quotations from 105/33 and 106/8–10. There is a similar passage, adapted to address the broader issue of biblical translation (as many of the materials in this manuscript were), in CUL Ii.6.26: see *EA*, 118–20.

80. On the licensing of preachers, see Forrest, *Detection of Heresy*, 60–68.

81. See 94/9–10, "men *worþi to be herd* moten be knyt togidere [knit together] in charite and meeknesse of herte"; or 94/25–27, "Þe rewme [kingdom] of þis Fadir is clepid holi cherche þat at þe day of doom schal go hennys to hevene" (emphases mine). For more on Wyclif's and lollard views on membership in the church of those that shall be saved, see chap. 4.

yen [eyes] to goddis blessyd bodi and ymage, prayng and about the chyrch walkyng in here prayers, beth to be blamed and laughed to scorn and beth hypocryetes."[82] Historians have been bemused that this view is not one conventionally associated with lollard doctrinal positions, and indeed, none of the views Hellis is accused of holding matches up neatly with, for example, William Thorpe's confessional lollard assertions.[83] But nobody has remarked that Hellis's view on this point could have been derived from the *Glossa ordinaria* on Matthew 6:5–6, or Thomas Aquinas's recension of it into the *Catena aurea*, or the lollard *Glossed Gospel* on Matthew, each of which quotes pseudo-Chrysostom, *Opus imperfectum*, on excessively ostentatious prayer, in ways that lollard compilers, too, found appealing and included in their own reference works.

Here, for example, is the *Glossed Gospel* on Matthew's extended version of the same quotation, quoted here from Oxford, Bodleian Library, MS Laud Misc. 235:

> *In synagogis* God forbediþ not [does not forbid us] to preye in gaderynge [gathering] of men. But he forbediþ to preye in gadrynge of men for þat [fol. 36va] purpos, *to be seyn* [seen] *of men.* He þat preyeþ so, for to be seyn of men, his soule biholdiþ [beholds] not God, but men þat ben þere. But þe soule of[84] man preyinge biholdiþ God oonly if þe ilke our [at that same time] his mynde is as he [is disposed as if he] haue no man aboute hym. For his soule seeþ [sees] no man, for he preyeþ for no man, þat is, for preysynge `of´[85] no man [for no man's praise]. And þerfore þou3 [although] he preye in synagogis, neþeles [nonetheless] he semeþ to preye in pryueyte [in private] anentis hymsilf [as far as he himself is concerned]. A man preyinge do [should do] no new þinge whiche þing men biholde: neþer crie bi voys þat [so that] he be herd of oþer men, neiþer holde abrod [spread wide] his hondis as þe farise [pharisee] dide in þe temple, þat he be seyn of many men, neiþer smyte his breste openly—but priuely, as þe pupplycan [publican] dide in þe temple, neþer vnschamfastly [brazenly] reise his y3en [eyes] `in´to[86] heuene þat he be maad knowen [to make himself known]. And þus also

<hr/>

82. Quoted in Robert Lutton, "Lollardy, Orthodoxy, and Cognitive Psychology," in *WC*, 97. I thank Rob for our discussions of this case and its implications.
83. See Lutton, "Lollardy, Orthodoxy, and Cognitive Psychology," 97–98.
84. of] *prec. by canc.* þa
85. *suplin.*
86. in] *suplin.*

whom no man hereþ crynge, no man seeþ doynge, ony syche þing, ȝhe [indeed] he stondinge mong [among] many is in preuyte [private].[87]

Novel, ostentatious signs of devotion such as lifting the hands and eyes are, according to pseudo-Chrysostom, reliable signs of prayer wrongly directed toward impressing other men rather than addressing God. In compiling commentary on Matthew 6:5–6, this *Glossed Gospel* weaves an assertion of the greater benefit of silent prayer in the heart over loud and ostentatious prayer aloud out of a sequence of quotations drawn from Augustine and pseudo-Chrysostom by turns, many expanded to far greater length than what the compilers would have found in the section of the *Catena aurea* that was apparently the starting point of their composition.[88]

Similarly, the *Rosarium* in its entry on "oryson" distinguishes prayer of the heart, of mouth, and of work and begins its explanation of prayer of the heart by using quotations from Augustine's sermons to insist that proper prayer should be directed inward and should not involve raising the eyes or hands.[89] Shannon McSheffrey's suggestion that it was not the contents of books owned by suspected heretics that mattered so much as the use to which they were put has obvious bearing here.[90] The doctrinal positions we might extract from Hellis's testimony do not resemble those traditionally associated with lollardy. But it seems they may have been derived from reading, interpreting, and discussing Matthew 6, perhaps as part of the kind of reading community often sought out by bishops in pursuit of lollardy and in very much the ways that the vernacular reference books produced by the early lollard movement encouraged their readers to do so.

It is an irony that Hellis was forced to abjure positions that his examiners might have extracted from any of the widely available glosses on the New Testament. But perhaps they were not so far wide of the mark. As he reflected on how he himself aspired to pray, and what he found objectionable in the prayer of some members of his broader community, Hellis was reading like a lollard. He may have learned this way of reading and thinking about his neighbours from a Pater Noster commentary or from a gospel commentary, perhaps even a copy of the *Glossed Gospels* or *Rosarium*, perhaps as a product

---

87. Oxford, Bodleian Library, MS Laud Misc. 235, fol. 36rb–36va.

88. On the process of composition of the *Glossed Gospels*, the relationships between the texts, and their use of the *Catena aurea*, see *PR,* 249–59. For a convenient version of the pseudo-Chrysostom quotation in the *Catena aurea*, see Thomas Aquinas, *Catena aurea*, ed. and trans. J. H. Newman, 4 vols. (Southampton: St. Austin Press, 1997), 1:218/20–25.

89. Cambridge, Gonville and Caius College, MS 354/581, fol. 87v.

90. McSheffrey, "Heresy, Orthodoxy, and English Vernacular Religion," 64–68.

of group reading and discussion of one of these texts. Hellis reads like a lollard; he may have prayed like a lollard, and he may have regarded himself as a
lollard—even if the doctrinal assertions that were drawn from his testimony
by his prosecutors bear very little resemblance to what early lollard writers
aiming to present a confessional lollard creed, such as the writer of the *Testi-*
mony of William Thorpe, were most anxious to impart to their anticipated lay
readers. In part 2, we will move on to consider in closer detail how lollards
used parabiblical as well as biblical reading to develop a structure of feeling
and account of human willing and action that is in some ways distinctively
lollard in style and emphasis, in others more broadly characteristic of their
cultural moment.

❧ Part Two

CHAPTER 4

Lollard Tales

In this chapter I investigate a very common and widespread characteristic of lollard writings: their use of narrative forms, especially but not only drawn from the bible, to give their readers models for holy living. In these narratives they provide their readers with a training in feeling. Lollard writers use stories, that is, to show their readers how to feel like saints. Yet lollards are usually thought to disapprove of stories—and they do, at least some of the time, avoid narrative. The *English Wycliffite Sermons*, as Hudson has noted, contrast strongly with most other contemporary sermon collections in that they contain no exempla, no illustrative stories whatsoever.[1] Popular sermons containing entertaining stories were especially associated with the friars; lollards criticize this kind of preaching, and what is more, they do not practice it.

The following quotation from *Piers the Plowman's Crede* is one example of how lollards express disapproval of stories, among many others that might be given.[2] Here Piers is speaking, setting the narrator straight after he has

---

1. *PR*, 269–70.

2. Elizabeth Schirmer cites others in "William Thorpe's Narrative Theology," *Studies in the Age of Chaucer* 31 (2009): 267–99. I am grateful to Liz for allowing me to read her article in draft. Schirmer's account of the narrative aspects of the *Testimony of William Thorpe* is marvellous. I disagree, however, that lollard writings more broadly are sharply hostile to narrative forms. Within the wider context of how lollards use stories to talk about sainthood, the *Testimony* does not seem so anomalous.

listened to the conflicting blandishments and mutual condemnations of a representative from each of the four orders of friars:

> Swiche a gome godes wordes grysliche gloseth;
> Y trowe [believe], he toucheth nought the text but taketh it for a tale.[3]

This sort of man glosses God's words in a horrifying way. He does not touch the text—but why, and what does he do with it instead? There is a telling ambiguity here. In taking the text for a tale does he use the text as a pretext for his own, unrelated story, taking it and creating from it a tale? Or does he ignore the text's meaning because he disparages its literal sense, takes it as nothing but a tale? In the first case, the lollard Piers rejects a friar's "tale" because it is extraneous to the bible's meaning—a familiar complaint, here. But in the second case, it is a friar here (by Piers' report, at any rate) who is rejecting a "tale"—again, the complaint that friars disregard the bible's literal meaning is also familiar. It is not a lollard who rejects a tale here, not this time. The "tale" this friar might find in the "text" is one he considers not worth touching. If this second reading seems less convincing, we might remember that friars certainly do themselves disparage tales earlier in the poem, as where the Franciscan claims that Carmelites "lieth [lie/lay] on our Ladie many a longe tale" (49); here, the Franciscan dismisses Carmelite tales about Mary as specious inventions. As this poet portrays them, it seems that lollards and friars agree that tales, one subclass of stories, are not worthy of attention. What they disagree about is which stories can be classified as tales: which stories should not be touched, and which should. Some stories are not worth serious attention. But some require serious attention, of a kind that this poet thinks they do not get from friars.

Admittedly, Piers does not specify which part of "godes wordes" his friar is taking for a tale. Some parts of the bible are not stories, nor are they amenable to narrative exposition by anything but the most strenuous effort. It could be that what is in question is not a story at all, and indeed (though this does not seem to be the intended meaning within *Piers the Plowman's Crede*) the Middle English term "tale" can refer to discursive forms that are not in any way narrative: an argument, a conversation, a numerical accounting.[4] However, as we will see, lollards find narrative in the bible wherever they can.

---

3. *Pierce the Ploughman's Crede*, in Helen Barr, ed., *The Piers Plowman Tradition* (London: Dent, 1993), lines 585–86.

4. See *MED*, s.v. "tale," as, for example, in senses 3, 4, 5, 7, 8, 9, 10. The same may be said of the Latin verb "narrare," as used repeatedly by Richard Wyche in his *Letter*, for example: see D.R. Howlett et al., *Dictionary of Medieval Latin from British Sources*, 14 fascicles to date (London: Oxford University Press for the British Academy, 1975–), s.v. "narrare," 1, 2, 3.

They too, like the friar criticized in this quotation, are strongly motivated to take bible text as story, though apparently in what they think is a different, more deeply engaged way. What would it mean to touch a text as it should be touched? What counts as a good story, for lollard readers and writers, how should it be told, and how does that mode of storytelling differ from taking the text for a tale?

One kind of evidence for what lollards might consider a good story can be found in the records of heresy trials in Coventry in the early sixteenth century, where a volume of saints' lives was reportedly one of the books lollards read in group meetings.[5] This evidence seems at first confusing. Not only are lollards usually thought to reject hagiolatry, but volumes of saints' lives have been thought of as an unexceptional aspect of late medieval orthodoxy.[6] While some recent work has found in saints lives evidence of reforming or even radical ideas, nobody has ever suggested that they were typical lollard reading.[7] Would lollard writers in the early years of the movement have endorsed this sort of reading? Or is it anomalous, an element of mainstream practice inconsistently retained by some, perhaps especially in the later years of the movement, and remarked on in these trials only because, in seeking out potentially suspect reading practices, the inquisitional process had cast its nets as wide as possible?

While as far as I know there are no early lollard texts that explicitly exhort their readers to read saints' lives, I will show here that there is plenty of evidence in lollard use of narrative forms from the early years of the movement that helps to make sense of this late reading practice as a coherent development from core lollard ideas. Narrative is for lollards an important tool for evoking and sustaining appropriate emotion, as a means to train the will toward living in virtue. Telling and recalling stories are means of touching

5. See the deposition by John Spon on November 3, 1511, in Shannon McSheffrey and Norman Tanner, eds. and trans., *Lollards of Coventry, 1486–1522*, Camden Fifth Series 23 (Cambridge: Cambridge University Press, 2003), 133, where Spon reports hearing Roger Landesdale reading saints' lives and Paul's epistles on five or six occasions. As this chapter and the next will demonstrate, saints' lives and Paul's epistles might indeed have formed part of lollard group reading. Shannon McSheffrey also cites the example of Alice Cottismore, tried in 1521 in Lincoln, who had a copy of the *Legenda aurea* ("Heresy, Orthodoxy, and English Vernacular Religion, 1480–1525," *Past & Present* 186 [2005], 66).

6. On lollard disdain for the mainstream cult of saints, see *TWT*, lvi; and *PR*, 302–3; but see also Christina von Nolcken, "Another Kind of Saint: A Lollard Perception of John Wyclif," *Studies in Church History Subsidia* 5 (1987): 429–43; and Robyn Malo, "Behaving Paradoxically? Wycliffites, Shrines, and Relics," in *WC*, 193–210.

7. Karen Winstead, *John Capgrave's Fifteenth Century* (Philadelphia: University of Pennsylvania Press, 2006); Catherine Sanok, *Her Life Historical: Exemplarity and Female Saints' Lives in Late Medieval England* (Philadelphia: University of Pennsylvania Press, 2007).

the text, an essential element in one of the lollards' most dominant modes of engagement with the words of the bible, and through the bible their sense of self and of community. Stories of the saints are central to this touching of tales, both when lollards are reading about biblical or later saints and when they are composing life narratives that cast themselves as saints. Both these kinds of narratives, in lollard writings, involve a kind of training in feeling. Reading about saints is how lollards feel like saints and aspirationally position themselves among the little flock of those who shall be saved. Aspirationally rather than with smug certitude: as I will explain in closer detail toward the end of this chapter, lollards are not predestinarians in that they think their salvation is predetermined and necessary, as some critics have supposed. Instead, like Wyclif, they think that God's knowledge of the future, however certain, does not constrain human choice.[8] Sin is terribly destructive; it is also unavoidable. Only constant striving to repair our bonds with God and each other, love and trust as constant as we can muster, and reliance on God's mercy and grace can dispose us to be saved. Any choice could be our last and could save or damn us; these choices most especially include the choice of which stories to read, which to attempt to live out, which to avoid.

Bad Tales, Good Tales

The most extended discussion of what kind of stories should be avoided known to me among extant lollard writings appears in the *Dialogue between a Wise Man and a Fool,* extant in a unique copy in CUL Ii.6.26.[9] The dialogue's full title in the manuscript is "A dialoge as hit were of a wyse man and of a fole denyi[n]ge þe trweþe wiþ fablis": the Fool likes tales, fables, and other forms of idle speech, and the Wise Man attempts to persuade him toward better choices. Their dialogue is (though this bias is not unique among lollard dialogues) very one-sided: the Fool's objections are few but of special interest as a caricature of incorrect thinking about narrative and its uses.[10]

The first topic of debate raised by the Wise Man is which tales should be chosen and which avoided. Idle tales, merrily told, are a form of spiritual murder and violate the fifth commandment. They include "liynge, flatereynge, bacbitynge, slaundrynge, swerynge, cursynge, and wordis of rebawdie [ribaldry]" (130/17–18). In their place one should choose (citing Jerome

---

8. Wyclif's position is very fully explained in Ian C. Levy, "Grace and Freedom in the Soteriology of John Wyclif," *Traditio* 60 (2005): 279–337.

9. "Cambridge Tract XII," in *EA*, 130–42; henceforth cited by page and line numbers. Modernized with the title *Dialogue between a Wise Man and a Fool* in *WS*, 247–62. See also the Conclusion.

10. For a similarly one-sided dialogue, see the *Dialogue between Reson and Gabbyng,* in *FWD*, 43–53.

here) "wordis þat . . . turnen to þe goostli profiȝt [spiritual benefit] of þe speker or of þe herer," a topic on which the Wise Man expatiates at length (130/15–16, continuing to 134/161). Eventually the Fool begs him to leave off and tell a "mery tale . . . of summe welfarynge man [man who does well]," naming among his examples the stories of English heroes including Guy of Warwick, Bevis of Hampton, Libeaus Desconus (that is, the Fair Unknown), or Robin Hood (134/162–63).[11] The Wise Man counters, at length, that his opponent is showing himself to be among those who do not want to hear the law of God, but only pleasant things, for "þes geestis [deeds] and rymes of fiȝters, lechours and þeues [thieves] iben couitud of [are desired by] synneres bi þe idel [idle] ymaginacioun of þere [their] hertis" (135/168–69).[12] Idle imagination (though not all imagination is idle, as we will discover later) leads to a desire only for stories that are pleasing, not for what what would be most edifying.[13]

The Wise Man's criticism of the Fool's improperly directed desires produces a shift in the grounds of debate: away from the stories themselves and toward the feelings they produce and to what end. The Fool retorts that the Wise Man simply wants everyone to be miserable: "Be þi tale [by your account] we schulden neuere be merie, but euer [always] sory. For it semeþ þou woldist [you want to] haue alle men to speken of Goddis lawe, and to þenke on peynes þat ben ordeyned [ordained] for synners, and also of here eendynge [their last end]. And þis wolde make hem [them] die for sorowe" (136/230–33, punctuation modified). Reversing the usual condemnation of the merry or idle "tale" here, the Fool insists that by the Wise Man's "tale," everyone will become so sad that they will simply pine away. In reply the Wise Man strings together a great many quotations, mostly scriptural (Wisdom, Psalms several times over, Augustine twice, Job, Christ's words as reported by Matthew then John then Matthew again, three times, Paul, Proverbs, Ecclesiasticus, and Deuteronomy), in support of his claim that there is no greater delight, sweetness, and joy to be found than in knowing and keeping God's commandments, for they allow "louers and lyuers after [those who love and live

---

11. For more details about each of these heroes and the extant written versions of their tales, see Charles W. Dunn, "Romances Derived from English Legends," and Helaine Newstead, "Arthurian Legends," both in A *Manual of the Writings in Middle English, 1050–1500*, vol. 1, ed. J. Burke Severs (New Haven: Connecticut Academy of Arts and Sciences, 1967), 25–31 and 68–70 respectively; and David Fowler, "Ballads," in A *Manual of the Writings in Middle English, 1050–1500*, vol. 6, ed. Albert Hartung (New Haven: Connecticut Academy of Arts and Sciences, 1980), passim.

12. Reversing Dove's emendation of "couitid" to "contriuid"; at this point, in my view, the Wise Man is still focused on the idle desires of listeners.

13. For the "moral fantasy" or "moral imagination," see chap. 6.

according to] Goddis lawe" to dispose themselves toward the endless bliss of heaven, whereas the merry way of life the Fool incorrectly embraces will lead to endless sorrow and pain (137/234–138/283).

The Fool now attempts to refute the Wise Man's account of how tales should be relevant to their reader's way of life. The Fool's protest resembles that of characters in a number of well-known extant literary texts in that it deploys proverbs as a source of conventional wisdom—the Fool may in fact be quoting from works ranging from *Piers Plowman* to bird-debate poems, such as John Clanvowe's *The Boke of Cupide* or Jean de Condé's *Messe des oiseaux*, to Chaucer's *Pardoner's Tale*.[14] But equally, the writer of this dialogue may simply be employing a common literary strategy used to question conventional wisdom. In each proverb, what is at issue is the relationship between ethical behaviour and its consequences for salvation. The three proverbs do not all provide the same solution—the third indeed is fragmentary, providing no solution at all—but rather mounting skepticism:

> 3e, 3e, [Yes, yes] man, whanne þou haste al seid þer is namore [nothing more] but "do wel and haue wel," and as good a soule haþ an owle as a cockow, and I trowe [believe that] as longe as þou hast lyued þou sawist neuer [never saw] soule goo a-blacberied [blackberrying]; þerfore, be my rede [advice] lat us be merye and sele carre [ignore our cares], for amonge an hundrid men, be þei seculeris or prestis, þou schalt scarsly [you can hardly] fynde oon [one] þat wole telle suche talis as þou doist, and whoso doiþ after [whoever acts like] most men schal be blamed of leste [fewest] men. (138/284–89)

The Fool here urges contempt for one's possible future fate, enjoyment of the present, and conformity with popular opinion rather than with the "talis" the Wise Man is telling; again, he goes out of his way to refer ironically to the Wise Man's teaching as tale-telling, when this would scarcely be the most obvious description of the Wise Man's strings of quotations. In replying point

---

14. For "Do well and have well," see George Kane, ed., *Piers Plowman: The A Version*, rev. ed. (London: Athlone, 1988), 8.98–99; George Kane and E. Talbot Donaldson, eds., *Piers Plowman: The B Version*, rev. ed. (London: Athlone, 1988), 7.112–13; Derek Pearsall, ed. *Piers Plowman: A New Annotated Edition of the C-text* (Exeter: University of Exeter Press, 2008), 9.289–90. The owl and the cuckoo are both named as unclean birds in Deut. 14:15, but given the Fool's reading preferences, it seems more likely that he is referencing bird-debate poems where the natures and virtues of different bird species are debated, such as Jean de Condé, *La "Messe des oiseaux" et le "Dit des Jacobins et des Fremeneurs,"* ed. Jacques Ribard (Geneva: Droz, 1970); or John Clanvowe, *The Boke of Cupide,* in *The Works of John Clanvowe,* ed. V. J. Scattergood (Cambridge: Brewer, 1967), 35–53. For souls "goon a-blakeberied," see Geoffrey Chaucer, "Pardoner's Tale," in *The Canterbury Tales,* ed. Jill Mann (London: Penguin, 2005), VI.406.

by point the Wise Man again quotes copiously from the bible and urges the Fool yet more strongly to mindfulness of his end (138/291–141/377).

Following this second, more strongly urged "tale" from the Wise Man, though for reasons that are not made entirely clear, the Fool experiences a sudden conversion:

> O, now I se [see] yn my sowle þat Crist is kynge aboue alle kynges and lord aboue alle lordis. Also I se his lawe is sufficient to be saued wit [with], and þat alle oþere lawes contrarie to hit [that contradict it] of [by] trwe men schulden be dispised. But, good frende, howe schal I do [act] to geete [get] mercy of [from] þis kynge for my fol þouȝtis [foolish thoughts], myn ydele [idle] wordis and for my wyken werkes [wicked deeds]?[15] (141/378–82)

The Fool declares his faith, and his now properly ordered imagination ("I se yn my sowle"). He asks for advice on attaining God's mercy. In the remainder of their conversation, the Wise Man advises him to follow the example of the Three Kings, who "sowten [sought] oure Lord fro fer cuntre [from a far-off country], and whanne þei haden fonden [found] him þei ofreden him gold, encence [incense] and myrre [myrrh]. And whan þei haden slept þei wenten home by anoþer weye" (141/383–86). This example is also, for the first and last time in the Wise Man's "tale" telling, what we would recognize as a story. He goes on to explain its moral import. Like Peter, Paul, Mark, Matthew, and many others, the kings did not return to their sins again, when they had left them, but continued and ended their lives in virtue (142/424–26).

Literary scholars in particular may find themselves in sympathy with the Fool at some points here: it would be a hard thing to do without romances altogether, and the Wise Man's recommended reading may seem less obviously entertaining. But most of what the Fool says is supposed to be obviously wrong, however occasionally appealing, and was far more widely disapproved of than simply by lollards. Complaints about laypeople spending their time on the wrong sorts of reading are very common in a wide range of works presenting more improving reading as an alternative, as for example in Robert Mannyng's *Handlyng Synne*, where "many beyn of swyche manere [of the kind] / Þat talys and rymys wyle bleþly [happily] here [hear]" (4/45–46), or Robert of Gretham's *Miroir*, where "mult amez oir e lire / Chancon de geste e d'estoire" ("Many love to hear or read / Songs of brave deeds or about

---

15. Dove adds the pronoun "I" to the first and second sentences here, producing a first-person confession of faith. It is also possible that "se" may be an imperative addressed to the reader, implying the confession of faith but also making the Fool's experience overtly exemplary.

history") (2/4–5).[16] Similarly, when the Fool disdains any attentiveness to the future and is reluctant to abandon the customs of his ancestors, he is voicing kinds of intransigence elsewhere attributed to the sinful. His preference for popularity among his fellows in the present, instead of adherence to the truth, is rather more pointedly aligned with the typical lollard emphasis on adherence to truth regardless of what scorn or peril this might bring, but still not entirely unconventional.[17]

There are more unusual features of this exchange, though. The Fool persists in calling both his own preferred reading and the Wise Man's alternative teaching a "tale." What the Wise Man offers is not, precisely, a story—not until the brief narrative of the Three Kings at the very end. Rather, most of what he has to say consists of point-by-point argument, backed up by proof texts (most of them biblical, others patristic) for what is wrong with the Fool's claims. Yet nowhere does the Wise Man disparage storytelling as such. And while the semantic scope of "tale" might encompass utterances that lack narrative form, the Fool is by no means wrong that what the Wise Man is proposing to him is an alternative narrative (see above, n. 4). Whether stories should be told at all is not what they are arguing about.

Instead, as I have already sketched out, the disagreement progresses from what stories should be told to how the right sort of stories should make their readers feel and what these stories should then make them want to do. The Fool's merriment at idle tales is misplaced. His preferred stories lead him to value too highly the customs of the past, agree with the opinions of the majority in the present, and ignore his future. He ignores, that is, the narrative of his own life. The problem, up to the point in the dialogue where he suddenly experiences a change of heart, is not so much that the Fool takes stories too seriously, for he is plainly an avid reader, as that he does not take them seriously enough. He does not pay attention to the stories that matter most to his future, and his idle imagination ignores their applicability to himself; his

---

16. Robert Mannyng, *Handlyng Synne*, Medieval and Renaissance Texts and Studies 14 (Binghamton, NY: Center for Medieval and Early Renaissance Studies, 1983), abbreviations expanded; Thomas G. Duncan and Margaret Connolly, *The Middle English "Mirror": Sermons from Advent to Sexagesima* (Heidelberg: Universitätsverlag, 2003). Both cited by page and line number. There are many other examples of this common topos.

17. Consider, for example, the wayward behavior of the title character in *Mankind*, who eventually overcomes despair and attains God's mercy through a quasi-sacramental dialogue with the allegorical character Mercy. What is characteristically lollard about the *Dialogue between a Wise Man and a Fool* is less its mistrust of popular entertainment than the singlemindedness of its reliance on the commandments and on biblical examples in developing a positive example of virtue. *Mankind* is, undeniably, more entertaining.

failure of imagination here is also a failure of emotion, more specifically of empathy, and of will.

This dialogical narrative of a Fool who experiences conversion through biblical persuasion is, as far as I am aware, the only sympathetic presentation of a negative example of life narrative anywhere among extant lollard writings. It is only sympathetic, of course, because the Fool is exemplary in finally abandoning his error. However, the dialogue pays only scant attention to the positive model the Fool comes to exemplify, let alone the conversion of feeling and imagination by which he arrives there. For more fully fleshed-out positive models, we will need to look to other lollard writings.

Confessing Faith

Narrative confessions of faith, of the kind the *Dialogue between a Wise Man and a Fool* eventually arrives at, are central to lollard identity as presented in the lollard literary corpus. They present readers with a model of how to act, how to feel, and how to imagine and perform their own role, deftly fashioning their models from the implied narratives of the psalms, from more straightforwardly narrative biblical episodes into which readers are encouraged to insert themselves, and from the autohagiographical narratives of exemplary lollards themselves. We will examine each of these increasingly encompassing confessional modes in turn. I aim to show that lollard writers frequently (rather than only rarely, as some critics have claimed), and in a variety of modes, provide exemplary and even participatory models for sainthood.[18]

Consider, for example, this closing passage from the lollard *Five Questions on Love*:

> "O Lord, I confesse to þee þat I *am þi servaunt*, in bodie, soule,—*and I am son of þin hand-mayden*, for Y am trewe child of holy Chirch. *Þou hast brokun my bondis*, of synne, and bondis bi whiche my soule loveþ my flesche; *to þee I schal sacre an ost of heriyng*. And þus *Y schal clepe inne to me þe name of þe Lord*, to dwelle in me." And þes same wordis maie martris seie, þat loven so miche Goddis lawe, þat þei wole suffre peyne of deeþ, for love and mayntenyng of þis lawe. And bettere cause of martirdom schewid God never to plese him. And siþ a man mut nedis [must necessarily] die, and Goddis lawe haþe nowe manye enemyes, a

---

18. On the rarity of lollard exemplary models, see, for example, *TWT*, lvi.

man schulde wisely putt him forþ [himself forward] to suffre now þus
gloriously.[19]

I have already shown elsewhere how the vernacular *Five Questions* adapts and
develops a Latin letter, probably by Wyclif, that responds point for point to
Richard Rolle's *Form of Living* in order to provide an alternative account to
Rolle's of the best way of life in this world.[20] In closing, the *Five Questions* stops
defining and explaining properly ordered love and gives a demonstration. It
recommends the recitation of an interpolated version of Psalm 116:16–17.
Only the italicized words are direct biblical quotation; the *Five Questions*
writer's interpolations make of the psalm a confession of faith. Positioned
at the end of the *Five Questions*'s response to Rolle, this biblically mediated
confessional meditation is explicitly an alternative to mainstream devotion to
the Holy Name of Jesus of the kind that Rolle and others recommended, a
different way for lollard readers to call the Lord to dwell within them.

For the reader who recites or meditates on Psalm 116 mindful of what
the lollard writer has interpolated here, the words "O Lord, I am your servant
and the son of your handmaiden, you have broken my bonds, to you I will
sanctify a host of praise" carry with them their interpolated gloss: they are
in themselves a confession of faith and an affirmation of the reader's status,
body and soul, as a true child of holy church. These words may martyrs
say. In this lollard confession of faith, aspiring martyrdom becomes not just
a mode of death but, dispositionally and metaphorically, a practice of daily
life and orientation toward what is to come. Not only the mode of biblical
citation but the mode of this passage as a whole is interpolative: it inserts any
speaker who takes on its "I" voice, any community that joins together in
this posture, into a place in time and a structure of feeling.[21] The confession
implies a narrative, and by this means a disposition toward present, past, and
future: I am your servant (present), you have broken my bonds (past), I will
praise you (future). Here, as in so many other instances in lollard writings, the
practice of meditation on and recitation of the heavily interpolated biblical
text works to foster, to affirm, and to amplify a sense of fellow feeling and
of "feeling like saints."[22]

---

19. Arnold, 184/31–184/4.

20. Fiona Somerset, "Wycliffite Spirituality," in *Text and Controversy from Wyclif to Bale: Essays in Honour of Anne Hudson*, ed. Helen Barr and Ann M. Hutchison (Turnhout: Brepols, 2005), 375–86. For a translation of Wyclif's *De amore* and modernization of the *Five Questions*, and further discussion, see *WS*, 84–87, 162–64.

21. On structures of feeling, see further chap. 5.

22. For more discussion of interpolation, see chap. 6.

Confessional Impersonation

These words may martyrs say. This confessional poetics of self-interpolation becomes even more than that in a number of fuller treatments in other lollard texts: it becomes a poetics of impersonation. As it is narrated or recommended (or both at once) in a range of texts, lollard confession of faith commonly involves imitating the behaviour of a named character, placed in a narrative biblical episode, speaking in the first person. This poetics of impersonation draws, probably self-consciously, on contemporary trends in learned literary and biblical interpretation, in which "I" statements are often interpreted as "speaking in the person of" another in order to elaborate on their point of view, their spiritual significance, or the grounds that make them true.[23] As with self-interpolation, this mode of impersonation entails intensive emotional identification, conformity of words and actions, and a temporal displacement—usually a dual temporal displacement, as the reader speaking like the biblical character imaginatively inhabits the past, while the biblical character's suffering and vindication evokes both the figural fulfillment of that past moment in Christ's passion and the imitation of Christ by later martyrs continuing, in a future as yet unrealized, to the present speech of the lollard reader.

Let us consider a more fully developed example: David's "pleying" or "pleynyng" speech as he dances before the ark, as it is treated at the end of the *Tretise of Miraclis Pleying*.[24] The *Tretise* is rather unjustly famed as a paradigmatic lollard rejection of the practice of publicly reenacting biblical scenes—when, that is, its lollardy is not being doubted because publicly performed biblical drama is not discussed anywhere else in lollard writings.[25] In my view Lawrence Clopper is quite right to doubt that the *Tretise*'s primary target is

---

23. Ralph Hanna et al., "Latin Commentary Tradition and Vernacular Literature," in *The Cambridge History of Literary Criticism*, vol. 2, *The Middle Ages*, ed. Alastair Minnis and Ian Johnson (Cambridge: Cambridge University Press, 2005), 400–402. The authors trace this technique to a fourth-century commentary by Servius on Virgil's *Bucolics*, show its prevalence in commentaries on the *Consolation of Philosophy* of Boethius, and point out its importance to John Gower, to Dante, and in the *querelle de la Rose*. The technique is also prevalent in biblical exegesis, in lollard vernacular writings, and in a wider range of learned vernacular religious writers. For its frequent use in the Middle English summary of the bible in Oxford, Trinity College, MS 93, see chap. 5. See also *The Holi Prophete Dauid*, in *EA*, 150/1; and for more examples, *MED*, s.v. "persoune," n. (1) 5b and 5c.

24. Clifford Davidson, ed., A *Tretise of Miraclis Pleyinge*, rev. ed. (Kalamazoo, MI: Medieval Institute Publications, 1993). Cited by page and line numbers.

25. Jonas Barish excoriates the *Tretise* for rejecting dramatic representation in his *Antitheatrical Prejudice* (Berkeley: University of California Press, 1981), 67–79. Lawrence Clopper doubts the work is lollard and doubts that its focus is the public performance of biblical drama: "Is the *Tretise of Miraclis Pleyinge* a Lollard Tract against Devotional Drama?," *Viator* 34 (2003): 229–71.

the performance of biblical drama and saints' plays of the kind extant in (for example) the York Cycle or the religious plays of Oxford, Bodleian Library, MS Digby 133, though I do think the writer of the *Tretise* quite deliberately gives the terms "miraclis" and "pleying" a very wide range of meanings, one that includes items that sound like some kind of dramatic production. However, the account of "pleying" that the *Tretise* does give in its second half (as sensitively explored by Ruth Nisse) is not, by any means, evidence that the text cannot be lollard, as Clopper tries to suggest.[26] Rather, as we will see, this account of "pley" is precisely where the text's lollard affiliations are most evident.

In contrast with the incorrect forms of "pleying," exemplified in sinful ways of living, that it surveys over its second half, the text's peroration offers an alternative lollard form of "pleying." The proper way to play, the right kind of Christian performance of the bible, is to play as David did, dancing before the ark and responding to Michol's scorn with a confession of faith:

yif we [fol. 21r] wilen [if we want to] algate pleyen [play in another way], pleyne [lament] we as Davith pleyide [David played] bifore the harke [ark] of God, and as he spac [spoke] byfor Michol his wif, dispising [who was mocking] his pleyinge, wherfore [and for that reason] to hir he seide [spoke] in this wise [way]: "The Lord liveth, for I shal pleyn [play OR lament] bifore the Lord that hath chosen me rather than thy fadur, and al the hous of him [all his house], and he comaundide to me that I were duke upon [I should be leader of] the puple [people] of the Lord of Israel, and I schal pleyn [play OR lament], and I schal be maad fowlere more [made more foul] than I am maad, and I schal ben meke in min eyen [in my own sight], and with the handwymmen [servants] of the whiche thou speke I schal more glorious aperen [appear more glorious]."

So this pleyinge hath thre parcelis [three parts]. The firste is that we beholden in how many thingis God hath given us his grace passinge [more than] oure neghyeboris, and in so myche more thanke we him [let us thank him], fulfilling his wil and more tristing in him agen [regardless of] alle maner reproving of [every kind of reproach from] oure enmys [enemies]. The secound parcel stant in continuel [consists in continually] beinge devowt to God almighty and fowl [foul]

26. Ruth Nisse, "Reversing Discipline: The *Tretise of Miraclis Pleyinge*, Lollard Exegesis, and the Failure of Representation," *Yearbook of Langland Studies* 11 (1997): 163–94. On the work's discussion of the ethics of play, see Glending Olson, "Plays as Play: A Medieval Ethical Theory of Performance and the Intellectual Context of the *Tretise of Miraclis Pleyinge*," *Viator* 26 (1995): 195–222.

and reprovable [blameworthy] to the world, as Crist and his apostelis schewiden hemself [showed themselves to be] and as Davith seide. The thridde parcel stant in beinge as lowly in oure owne eyen [eyes] or more than we schewen us withouteforthe [what we outwardly reveal], settinge lest by in us silf [considering ourselves least] as we knowen mo sinnes of us silf [know more of our own sins] than of ony other, and thanne befom alle the seintis of hevene and biforn Crist at the day of dome and in the blisse of hevene we schul [shall] ben more glorious in as muche as we pleyn betere [play OR lament better] the thre forseid perselis heer [parts described here], the whiche thre perselis wel to pleyn heere and after [afterwards] to comyn to hevene, graunt the holy Trinite [may the holy Trinity allow us]. Amen. (114/724–115/749)

The second part of the *Tretise* has followed Nicholas of Lyra by exploring various instances of the wrong kind of "pleying" through the Hebrew Bible: Ishmael's playing with Isaac, the playing of the followers of Abner and Joab, the playing of the Israelites with the calf of gold, the playing of the children with Elisha's baldness. These are not mistranslations or misunderstandings of biblical usages of "ludere" as well as derivative verbs, as some have suggested; after all in linking and relating these examples they follow Lyra and through him rabbinic commentary.[27] Nor is the way they are deployed atypical of the kind of exegetical argumentation found elsewhere in lollard writings.[28] But what they do permit is a flexible, wide-ranging exposition of how the contemporary church and broader Christian community engage in preaching for profit, idolatry, mockery of Christ's passion or prophets, religious and priestly hypocrisy, lack of charity to the poor, disdain for the preaching of the word of God, and misplaced piety.[29] Now, finally, the author provides a positive account of play in a concluding exhortation to his readers.

In playing before the ark, and in defending his play against Michol's criticism, David figures Christ and his apostles; he also models, for readers, what

---

27. For disparagement, see Barish, *Antitheatrical Prejudice*, 71–74, esp. 72. See also Clopper, "Is the *Tretise of Miraclis Pleyinge* a Lollard Tract?," 258. For the use of Lyra, see Nissé, "Reversing Discipline," 177–78, giving more detail but also citing Lawrence Clopper, "Miracula and the *Tretise of Miraclis Pleyinge*," *Speculum* 65 (1990): 900.

28. Clopper claims "it would be untypical of [lollards] in polemic to read scripture as the texts are read in the *Tretise*"; he would expect instead "simple" literal biblical exegesis: "Is the *Tretise of Miraclis Pleyinge* a Lollard Tract?," 254 n. 95. For more on scholarship that expects "simple" literal exegesis from lollard writers, see chap. 6.

29. See 109/552–58, 112/647–54, and perhaps 108/521–23, 527–32, 113/681–85, 692–93, 109/539–41, 111/598–99, 112/631–33, 114/717–24. All of these, except the point about mockery of Christ's passion, are common lollard complaints.

they should say, how they should behave, what they should feel, how they should develop in themselves the virtues of faith, hope, and charity. David's actions and his words, his playing and his speaking, are consistent and mutually corroborative: "as [he] pleyide . . . and as he spac." David speaks to defend and explain the significance of his play, in a form of auto-exegesis, prophecy of his own future, even perhaps self-figuration: he will play before the Lord who has chosen him as leader, he will be brought lower than his true status, he will be meeker still than his apparent status, but eventually appear yet more glorious. He plays ("I shal pleyn"), but his playing also resonates, punningly, with mourning ("pleynen," rather than "pleyen"), as he is brought low and despised. Although it is not quoted, I think that "beati qui lugent" ("blessid ben they that mornen") lurks behind the lollard writer's final promise here of eternal bliss: "in the blisse of hevene we scul ben more glorious in as muche as we pleyn betere . . . heer," when to "pleyn betere" is to accept the world's reproofs and humble ourselves yet further in awareness of our own sin.[30]

The lollard writer's exposition of David's words exhorts readers to model themselves upon David, and like David on Christ and his apostles, in their response to persecution. They should reflect on their superior gifts of grace. (The tone here is rather unfortunate and illustrates the difficulty of making a spiritual leader into a model for the whole community.) In consequence they should thank God, fulfill his will, and believe in him the more for the reproofs they receive from his enemies. They should love God the more as the world despises them, just as David said and as Christ and his apostles showed. And they should humble themselves yet more in their own eyes, in their own knowledge of their own sin, in hope of future glory in heaven.

Confessional episodes presented as a model for imitation, like this one in the *Tretise*, show up across a wide range of lollard writings. They appear both in more polemical writings, like the *Tretise*; and in the more devotional and meditative kinds of lollard writing that have received far less scholarly attention. As an example from a more devotionally focused text, consider the longest and fullest of the three interpolated versions of Rolle's *English Psalter* (RV3), commenting on Psalm 86:4, "Myndful I shal be of Raab and Babylon þorouȝ knowyng me."[31] Here, the lollard writer tells us, the psalmist

---

30. The translation of the Vulgate's Matt. 5:5 is drawn from LV: see Forshall and Madden, *Holy Bible*, 4:10. Compare also with *Book to a Mother*'s explanation of David's dance before the ark "þat þe ten hestis [commandments] weren inne": *BM*, 28/14–29/9.

31. RV3 is extant in a single, incomplete copy divided between two manuscripts: London, Lambeth Palace, MS 34 contains a version of revised version 1 (RV1) to Ps. 84:5, then RV3 for Ps. 84:6 to Ps. 88, while London, British Library, MS Royal 18.C.xxvi contains Ps. 89 to Ps. 118:1. A thorough

speaks in the person of Christ, voicing Christ's promise to remember those who confess belief in him, with the aim of comforting sinners who might otherwise despair of God's mercy.

Raab, the commentary recounts, was a whore dwelling in Jericho. The writer retells her story at length, drawing attention to her feelings and actions and then presenting them as a model for sinners in the present.[32] She hears of the might of God. She marvels, she is astonished, she feels fear, and she performs an act of charity, hiding God's messengers. She converts to faith and confesses her faith aloud: "forsoþe [truly] þe Lord ȝoure God he is God in heuene aboue and in erþe byneþe [beneath]." The messengers acknowledge her "trewe shrifte [confession] to God" and pronounce that the red rope she gave them for their escape will be a token that not only she but all those she gathers into her house will be saved. Similarly, sinners should fear their offense to God, cease from their sin, and perform charity toward their neighbours, "knowelechynge [acknowledging] þe trewþe" in a way that almost seems to merge confession of faith with a kind of extrasacramental penance.[33] The red

---

explanation of the relationships between the three revised versions RV1, RV2, and RV3 appears in the first volume of Anne Hudson's edition of RV1 and RV2, Anne Hudson, ed., *Two Revisions of Rolle's English Psalter Commentary and the Related Canticles*, 2 vols. (of 3 projected, the last to be published as o.s. 343), EETS, o.s. 340–41 (Oxford: Oxford University Press, 2012–13), 1:xxiii–xxxiv. I am grateful to Anne Hudson for sharing with me her insights into the relationship between the versions before her edition went to press, and also for sending me her transcription of RV3 Psalm 86 before I obtained a microfilm of the manuscript.

32. For the whole of the commentator's exegesis on this verse, far too lengthy to quote in full here, see the modernized version (here given the modern numbering, Psalm 87) in *WS*, 229–41, on 231–36.

33. The commentary on this verse occupies Lambeth 34, fols. 184rb–185vb: the first two quotations in the text are from fol. 184vb, the third from fol. 185rb. Amid an extended exposition, the following quotation from fol. 185ra encapsulates most of the sequence of emotions and actions (underlined) that would-be repentant sinners should learn from Raab: "Þis is a <u>comfortable</u> [comforting] sentence to alle synneres, and specialy to hydouse stynckynge lechouris, avoutereris [lechers and adulterers], ȝif þei wolen <u>cese `of her yuel´</u> [leave their sin], hauynge in hemsilf <u>drede</u> of þe offense of God, cesyng fro her synne as dide Raab for <u>drede</u> of Goddis vengeaunce. And þanne þe <u>charyte</u> of siche <u>verrey repentaunt</u> shal strecche to her neiȝboris, <u>hauyng pyte</u> of hem whanne þei shulden be <u>wrongfully tretide</u> eiþer putte in <u>disese</u> [distress] as hadde Raab of Goddis messangeris. For <u>pite</u> is verreyly had [once someone truly has pity], al oþir ȝiftis of þe Holy Gost suynge þeraftir [will follow after] wiþ <u>werkis of mercy to mennes euencristen</u> [fellow Christians]. And þees blissid godly vertues drawen lederis of hem in <u>feiþfulnes</u> so nyȝ [near] to God, ioynyng [joining] hem so faste togedre þat <u>eiþer delitiþ so myche in oþer</u>, þat <u>eiþer is made cheer or dere</u> [cher, or dear] to oþer. And <u>siche cheerte or deerte</u> [dearness] of <u>God to man and man to God</u> is clepid [called] <u>charite of God and man</u>, for <u>eiþir wole</u> [wills, desires] <u>as oþir wole</u>. Þis charite of God was shewid in Raab [exemplified by Raab] whanne she, sett in [placed amid] <u>so grete dreede</u> on eche side, seyng [seeing] dyuers [various] regiouns distroyde for her synne, and hir cite for to be [about to be] distroyde, and hirsilf vnclene and synful, <u>feiþfully knowlechid</u> and seyde to þe messangeris 'forsoþe þe Lorde ȝoure God is God in heuene aboue and in erþe bineþe.' Þis forsoþe [truly] <u>knowleching of treuþe</u> made hir so <u>cheer</u> [dear] <u>to God, and God to hir</u>, þat fadir and modir, breþeren and sisteren, and to alle þingis

rope symbolizes what Christ's followers will willingly suffer for the truth; it also symbolizes Christ's passion and the Trinity:

> Þis reede [red] rope, verrey [true] signe of saluacioun, is þe þrefolde roope þat þe Wise Man spekiþ of, þe whiche byndiþ [binds] God to helpe man and man to serue God. Þis is þe trewe byleue of þe holy Trinitee, whiche most truly is contenyd [contained] in þe gospel of Crist. And whosoeuer trewly, þat is in werke and worde, knowelechiþ `þis gospel [to be] Goddis word, knowlechiþ´[34] Crist to be Goddis sone and to haue comen in fleishe. And *alle whoeuer shal confesse* [acknowl-edge] *me byfore men, þe sone of man shal confesse* [acknowledge] *him bifore þe aungelis of God.* (Lambeth 34, fol. 185va)

All who confess faith, all who believe in the Trinity and truly acknowledge Christ in their actions as well as their words, will be saved. What is outlined here amounts to an abbreviated, alternative creed, performed through works as well as words: true belief in the holy Trinity entails publicly acknowledg-ing that the gospel is God's word and acting accordingly. But it also involves inwardly (and perhaps in part visibly) mirroring an exemplary sequence of emotions. The sinful should, like Raab, be astonished by God, they should feel fear, they should feel pity and help others, they should confess their faith, and they should turn from sin.

Just like the writer of the *Tretise*, the writer of this psalm commentary fore-grounds a narrative sequence of emotions and explicitly urges their imitation by readers who aspire to similar virtue. David is exultant, defiant, humbled, triumphant. Raab is astonished, fearful, pitying, resolute, secure. Each suffers and is then saved. David's example focuses more heavily on resolve in face of the negative consequences of confessing faith, where Raab's focuses on the emotional difficulty of conversion from sin. But each, so each lollard writer affirms, gives fearful Christians seeking the resolve to act as they should a model not only of how to behave but of how to feel.

Autohagiography

The fullest development of this lollard poetic of impersonation occurs in writings that provide a first-person, exemplary account of how to respond

---

of hem [as pertained to all their possessions] al hir axing was to hir grauntid." The words between ` and ´ are inserted from the margin. For other examples where lollard writings formulate a kind of extrasacramental penance, see chap. 1 and chap. 7.

34. *insert from marg.*

to persecution and confess one's faith: what to believe, what to say, how to feel, how to model oneself on holy predecessors and join them in anticipating or imitating Christ. These models are rare among lollard writings: we have only the *Letter of Richard Wyche*, recounting events in 1402–3 and completed and sent by 1404, and the *Testimony of William Thorpe*, recounting an episode in 1407, and probably using the *Letter of Richard Wyche* as a model.[35] But while rare, these models are not isolated; they are simply the fullest development of a far more broadly diffused lollard posture. Each of these texts features a first-person narrator who describes his response to persecution in the course of proceedings associated with investigation for heresy; each has strong hagiographic overtones. Each narrator describes his changing emotions with considerable immediacy. Each recounts a moment of crisis in which he vividly recalls, and empathizes with, a holy predecessor's response to persecution, and each makes emotional demands of its readers as it tells them, in turn, how they should behave.

For William Thorpe, the story is Susanna's. Asked by the archbishop to swear that he will forsake all opinions associated with lollards, will in future not favour anyone holding these opinions, and will not preach until the archbishop is sure that he will contradict all that he has taught before, Thorpe at first does not reply:

> And I heerynge þese wordis þou3te in myn herte þat þis was an vnleeful askynge [unlawful request], and I demed [judged] mysilf cursid of [to be cursed by] God if I consentid herto; and I þou3te how Susanne seide "*Angwysschis* [anguishes] *ben to* [there are for] *me on euery side*," and forþi þat [for that reason] I stood stille musynge and spak not. (35/365–68)

Pressured to agree against his convictions, Thorpe at first reflects rather than speaking. His momentary silence is significant in other ways for readers

---

35. Hudson suggests in her edition of the *Testimony of William Thorpe* (cited by page and line number in what follows) that Thorpe modelled his *Testimony* on Wyche's *Letter*. see *TWT*, lviii–lix. For the *Letter of Richard Wyche*, see F. D. Matthew, ed., "The Trial of Richard Wyche," *English Historical Review* 5 (1890): 530–44 (cited by page and line number); Christopher G. Bradley, ed. and trans., "The Letter of Richard Wyche: An Interrogation Narrative," *PMLA* 127 (2012): 626–42. For other documentation about William Thorpe, see Maureen Jurkowski, "The Arrest of William Thorpe in Shrewsbury and the Anti-Lollard Statute of 1406," *Historical Research* 75 (2002): 273–95. For the trial and other life records of Richard Wyche, see M. G. Snape, "Some Evidence of Lollard Activity in the Diocese of Durham in the Early Fifteenth Century," *Archaeologia Aeliana*, 4th ser., 39 (1961): 355–61; Anne Hudson, "Which Wyche? The Framing of the Lollard Heretic and/or Saint," in *Texts and the Repression of Medieval Heresy*, ed. Caterina Bruschi and Peter Biller (Woodbridge: York Medieval Press, 2003), 221–37; Richard Rex, "Which Is Wyche? Lollardy and Sanctity in Lancastrian London," in *Martyrs and Martyrdom in England, c. 1400–1700*, ed. Thomas S. Freeman and Thomas F. Mayer (Woodbridge: Boydell, 2007): 88–106.

steeped in lollard thought. Although Thorpe does not comment overtly on the resemblance, his silence recalls and imitates Christ's silence before Pilate, as he will recall it again more overtly near the end of his narrative.[36] In his introspective moment here Thorpe also deploys Wyclif's theories that consenting to sin is a culpable form of participation in that sin and that sin excommunicates the sinner ("I demed myslif cursid of God if I consentid herto").[37] What no reader can fail to notice, though, is that at this conflicted and uncertain moment, Thorpe remembers the story of Susanna; more precisely, he recalls her description of her feelings when beset on every side. In describing his "musynge" Thorpe reports his own sensations, thoughts, and conclusions; but Susanna's feelings, or rather his memory of her description of them, stand in place of his own. Readers are invited, I think, to imagine, and participate in, this moment of narrative empathy, one that amplifies Thorpe's conviction and strengthens his resolve through his memory of Susanna's example. Pressed again by the archbishop to answer yes or no, Thorpe now explains his reasons for defiance at length.

There is much more to be said about narrative more broadly in the *Testimony of William Thorpe*, but many aspects have been sensitively explored in an article by Schirmer.[38] Instead we will pass on here to the *Letter of Richard Wyche*, Wyche's account of his detention and repeated examinations in a long letter apparently written to supporters outside prison. Wyche's *Letter* has received less scholarly attention than Thorpe's *Testimony*, in part because it is preserved in only a single poor copy in Latin in Prague; it seems likely that the original letter was in Middle English.[39]

In his *Letter* Wyche recounts imprisonment and repeated interrogation stretching over many weeks, culminating in a sentence of excommunication and continued suffering in prison at the moment of writing. He draws extensively on biblical models, both to help his readers understand his own suffering and to show them why they should want to emulate it in pursuit of truth. At the midway point, after he has sworn a version of the bishop's oath and his intentions in doing so have gone badly awry, he undergoes three days of especially intensive mental anguish in prison; during these days, his prayers and meditations focus on the example of Daniel, and on quotations

---

36. As Schirmer also notes, "William Thorpe's Narrative Theology," 297. See *The Testimony of William Thorpe*, in *TWT*, 92/2226, 93/2228.

37. On consent, see chap. 1. On how sin itself excommunicates the sinner, see below.

38. See n. 2. Schirmer mentions Thorpe's use of Susanna in passing but does not quote it ("William Thorpe's Narrative Theology," 283).

39. In this I agree with Christopher Bradley (email communication). See also chap. 2, n. 18. All translations used here are my own, though I have subsequently read Bradley's.

from Psalms, Ecclesiasticus, and Exodus that similarly recount or promise deliverance after suffering (536/24–537/12). But for the most part, across the whole of the narrative sequence, his aim is to show readers how his suffering is an imitation of Christ's.

Wyche repeatedly compares himself with Christ, both overtly and more covertly, by modelling his reported words and actions after those familiar from the narrative of Christ's passion. He repeatedly echoes Christ by affirming that he wills only what God wills should happen to him.[40] He is struck (metaphorically, by God, with the legal case).[41] High-ranking churchmen challenge him with claims about his earlier preaching, he remains silent when questioned, a seeming friend betrays him, and a high-ranking layman who had seemed to believe him stands by rather than intervening.[42] The people deny him, he is mocked and scorned by his various audiences, and he suffers intense physical pain.[43] In response to questioning on the eucharist, he repeatedly quotes parts of the biblical narrative of the Last Supper, especially Christ's words describing the eucharist, insisting that what the bible says should be the only answer required.[44]

Twice Wyche impersonates Christ, albeit hypothetically, in order to pursue his argument. Just before his excommunication, defending himself on the eucharist, he picks up a piece of straw and says "If it were possible that Christ himself were standing here and saying 'This is my body,' should I not believe that this is his body?"[45] Directly after his excommunication and hereticatation are read out, Wyche is asked once again to give his views on the eucharist and confronted with the oath he had earlier agreed to swear, but only (as earlier agreed in his conversation with a knight) according to his own

---

40. For Wyche's conformity of will, see 533/3–4, 533/14, 533/46, 534/37, 536/33–34.

41. "ut ostenderet michi Deus viam per quam ambularem, percussit me casu penali" (531/3–4). See also 531/28.

42. Challenges occur in every scene of interrogation, and Wyche specifies by name, or sometimes merely rank and affiliation, who each of his interrogators is. For Wyche's silence when questioned, see 531/26–27, 534/48, 540/14. The seeming friend is the high-ranking knight who at first seems trustworthy ("apparuit michi quod ille esset solidus homo," 534/4) but then denies (539/45) that he suggested Wyche swear the oath as limited in his own heart ("in corde tuo limitatum," 534/30).

43. The people deny that they agree with Wyche's eucharistic views at 532/19. Nevertheless, Wyche appeals to them twice more, at 539/1 and 541/17–19. For mockery, see 533/4 and 533/33. For physical suffering, see the quotation that follows in the text.

44. For Wyche's declarations or defenses on the eucharist (some summarized rather than rehearsed in full), see 532/3–7, 532/26, 532/29–32, 535/34, 537/41–45, 539/1–5, 540/10–11, and finally 541/17–19. On this final occasion he calls the people to witness that he has stated his belief six times in the same form: for quotation, see below at n. 45.

45. "Si possibile esset quod Christus personaliter hic staret et diceret 'Hoc est corpus meum' numquid non crederem hoc esse corpus suum?" (540/43–44).

interpretation of how it applies to himself. He impersonates Christ once again as he defends himself against the accusation of heresy, then continues to compare himself with Christ as he recounts his subsequent suffering:

> "What?" I said, "Why am I a heretic? I have said nothing that goes beyond the law of our God. Certainly, if it were possible for Christ to stand before you in person, you would judge him a heretic, as you have me." And I said to the people "I ask you to witness that this is my belief, as I have stated six times before these men: I believe that the worshipful sacrament is the true body of Christ, and true blood, in the form of bread."
>
> And so they put me in prison. There I remain, with adequate food and drink, thanks be to God. And our good God from his grace has visited me with great constriction in the belly, from which I have, and have had, great pain at times in emptying (*purgare*) my bowels, for sometimes I have gone for nine days without a single movement (*purgacio*). And hemorrhoids have twice afflicted me and have bled quite severely, in such a way that it is shameful to relate. Nonetheless I must do so, or I might not live, and my suffering (*purgacio*) is hard, like his suffering (*purgacio*).[46]

This final scene of interrogation is followed by brief directions about receipt of his letter and sending of news to others, then by more general teaching about how all those who follow Christ should behave if they wish to be saved:

> And so, if they will to be in God's household, they must expose themselves, for God their savior, to the humble suffering of scorn and detractions and scandals of this kind. And they should picture Christ, the father of their household, before their mind's eye, in his suffering of (as it were) infinite pain for our sins. And (then) these scorns will not harm them, but lead their souls to exult and bring God's blessing, as that

---

46. "'Et quid, dixi, pro quo essem hereticus? Nichil aliud dixi preter legem Dei nostri. Pro certo si possibile esset Christum personaliter coram vobis stare, iudicaretis ipsum hereticum, sicut et me.' Et dixi populo: 'Rogo testificetis quod hec est fides mea quam sexies coram eis dixi: Credo quod venerabile sacramentum est verum corpus Christi et verus sanguis in forma panis.'

"Et sic misit me in carcerem. In quo continuo etc. habens cibum et potum competenter, gracias agens Deo. Et bonus Deus noster ex sua gracia visitavit me per magnam strictitudinem in ventre, per quam habeo et habui magnam penam aliquando purgare ventrem meum, quia aliquando per novem dies non habui quantitatem unius purgacionis et emeraudes tenuerunt me bis et sanguinarunt quodammodo fortiter, et sic quod pudor est dicere. Tamen oportet me ita facere vel non vivere et purgacio mea est dura sicut purgacio eius" (541/14–27).

same teacher has attested: "*You are blessed when men hate you and scorn you and spurn your name as evil for the sake of the Son of Man.*"[47]

In this final defiance Wyche strongly asserts his conformity with the word and example of Christ, recalling Christ's own trial and passion as he does so. If Christ himself stood before them, they would label him a heretic as well—so Wyclif had similarly retorted, as Wyche probably knew.[48] In response the bishop's officials send him into prison, where he remains at the time of writing. There God, in his grace, has sent him great physical suffering from constipation and hemorrhoids, of a kind that it shames him to describe. Nonetheless he needs to do so, in order to live, and his (Wyche's) *purgacio* is hard, like his (Christ's) *purgacio*.[49] If they want to be in God's household, his readers must, like Wyche, expose themselves to suffering mockery and scorn, to an evil name rather than the holiest of names, and they must keep Christ's suffering of infinite pains for our sins before their mind's eye. If they do so then other men's hatred will not harm them, but instead lead their souls to exult in God's blessing.

Wyche's narrative empathy with Christ in this passage is more complex and polysemous than Thorpe's relatively straightforward emotional

---

47. "Ideo si voluerint esse de familia Dei, exponant se pro Deo Salvatore suo ad humiliter paciendum exprobria et detracciones et huiusmodi scandala, et respiciant Christum patrem familias ante oculos mentis penas quodammodo infinitas pro peccatis nostris pacientem. Et ista non nocebunt sed inducent animam exultantem et Dei benediccionem, ut ille magister testatur: Beati eritis cum vos oderint homines et exprobraverint et eiecerint nomen vestrum tanquam malum propter filium hominis" (541/41–47).

48. See, e.g., John Wyclif, *De blasphemia*, ed. Michael H. Dziewicki, Wyclif Society (London: Trübner, 1893), chap. 4, 62.

49. Rita Copeland, *Pedagogy, Intellectuals, and Dissent in the Later Middle Ages: Lollardy and Ideas of Learning* (Cambridge: Cambridge University Press, 2001), 162 n. 43, instead translates the line as "However, I must do so or not survive, and my purgation is as difficult as the 'purging' of it," with the note, "I take this to mean that, despite embarrassment, he must mention these afflictions to his custodians or friends outside (perhaps they would procure medical attention for him) or risk dying there in prison." She is quite right that there is no antecedent anywhere nearby for "eius," which she translates as "of it" rather than "his." And I agree with her that part of the difficulty Wyche refers to here is his emotional conflict about speaking out—she may also be right that he is hoping to get medical attention by this means. But that Christ must be the antecedent for "eius" is clear from the surrounding context of pervasive imitation of Christ's passion, reiterated and endorsed further before this quotation, and also in the advice to individuals that follows. The passage is yet more multivalent than she suggests: the difficulty of *purgacio* is that of imitating Christ's passion, as well as that of revealing the shame of Wyche's particular affliction, not less that of voiding his bowels. The analogy with Christ's suffering cannot be exact, of course, since Christ himself suffered without being sinful and had no need to purge himself of anything. Yet Christ's *purgacio* refers to Christ's purging of the sins of humanity, as it does in the lollard *Wordis of Poule on Tribulacioun*, quoted here from CUL Nn.4.12: "Seynt Poul clepeþ Crist heere . . . auctor of feiþ, for in cause of feiþ he purgeþ alle synnes" (fol. 44r). See also SS74, sermon 46 (described in Appendix B).

identification with Susanna and demands a more complex response from its readers as well. Much of this hinges on his sequential development, in what we might call not only an autohagiography but an auto-allegoresis, of the meanings of "purgare/purgacio." These range from a prosaic bodily voiding or purging, through more abstract spiritual forms of emptying or purification, to proving and vindication through suffering.[50] What does it mean for Wyche's purging, proving, or suffering to be hard like Christ's, especially given that Wyche fears for his life as well as his salvation and feels all the squeamish shame at relating these details, all the fear of scorn, that we might expect him to (as he is at pains to tell his readers)?

In assuming his role as man of sorrows here, Wyche compels his readers into intimacy, even risks their amusement at the notion that bleeding hemorrhoids are an imitation of Christ's passion. Yet the risk is theirs, if they scorn rather than empathize, that they will be cast as mockers and scorners rather than sufferers vindicated by mockery and pain. Wyche has run the risk of intimacy before, during his trial, in taking the advice of the knight who advised him to swear the oath and then betrayed him. His readers, like the knight, have the choice whether to scorn his shame, or on the other hand aid his hard purgation and join him in picturing Christ's suffering as they too invite mockery.

In inciting his readers to join him in empathetic meditation on Christ's passion and in inviting the scorn of their fellows as they follow Christ, Wyche gives us new insight into lollard interest in this genre of affective devotion—an interest that some have denied, or found incongruous, but that is strongly attested by frequent lollard references to Christ's passion as well as his active earthly ministry.[51] Indeed, as the example of David figuring Christ and his apostles as he plays before the ark has already suggested, lollards imagine Christ's active ministry, his passion, and his injunctions to the apostles and their subsequent fulfillment as a seamless whole. The lollard confessional poetic, involving self-interpolation or even full-on impersonation, is diffused across a wide range of lollard writings rather than confined to the only two extended first-person accounts that we have. It gives the readers of these writings a model for lollard speech (saying what martyrs may say), lollard action (charity as well as true speech), lollard feeling (sorrow and joy, pleyning and play, suffering and vindication, fear and love), lollard identity. Even if few readers of lollard writings eagerly embraced the opportunity for martyrdom,

---

50. See Howlett et al., *Dictionary of Medieval Latin from British Sources*, s.vv. "purgare" and "purgatio."

51. David Aers and Lynn Staley, *The Powers of the Holy: Religion, Politics, and Gender in Late Medieval English Culture* (University Park: Pennsylvania State University Press, 1996), 15–58.

we need not conclude that widely available and broadly disseminated models of this kind had no influence on readers' understanding of themselves as aspirational saints and members of the church of those that shall be saved.

Lollard Predestination

We might legitimately worry that exhorting church members to imitate the saints in martyrdom as the path to salvation—as several examples given in this chapter have done—is scarcely the way to build a durable community of faith. Michael Wilks has suggested that Wyclif's preoccupation with persecution is a means of casting himself as an apocalyptic prophet whose small band of followers prove the rightness of their faith through and by means of the fierce persecution they suffer: he concludes that "the notion of the suffering saints sustained the faith and enabled Lollardy to survive the long winter of the fifteenth century, but it had little more to offer."[52] This may be a fair criticism of the scope of Wyclif's vision of Christian community, but lollard narratives are both less and more successful than Wilks suggests. They are less successful in that even if they wanted this result, they did not produce martyrs in vast numbers. But they are more successful in that they did have more to offer by way of spiritual sustenance than bare survival in a chilly climate. They offered, as well, comfort and joy in the aspiration (if not the stable certainty) of dwelling with God in holy church.

Consider for example the commentary on the final verse of Psalm 86 in RV3, the interpolated version of Rolle's *English Psalter* we examined earlier in this chapter. This exposition shows its readers how to dwell in the "chirche of God" through "effectuel preyer":

> *Sicut letancium omnium habitacio est in te. As of alle ioying* [as it were, all rejoicing] *dwellyng is in þee* [is dwelling in you].
>
> In þees fewe wordis ben miche comfort. But hastily þei ben ouersliden and sone [soon] out of þe mynde [memories] of þe rederes, as her [their] werkis opynly (into greete confusyon of hem) wittnessen. For eche efectuel [effective] preyer haþ þis condicioun and strengþe [force] in it. First, it preieþ to be clansid [cleansed] of alle yuele [evil] bifore doon. And siþ to be defendid fro alle yuele to cumme. And þanne it desireþ and anxiþ [is anxious] after Goddis wille, to be an eyre of him

---

[his heir] in þe blysse of heuene. And so eche effectuel preyer to God
haþ in it sorowe and drede, desyre and hope, þe whiche alle togedre
[together] spryngen oute of byleue. For who þat byleuiþ not haþ noon
[none] of þees condiciouns. And so it semeþ þat feiþ of many men and
wymmen is dede [dead] and her [their] preyeris voyde. For þei ben but
nakid wordis, whiche whanne þei ben multiplyede stynken bifore God,
fro whom [against which] he closiþ his eeris. And no wondir, siþ [since]
þe most [greater] part of mankynde, as opyn werkis beren wittnesse,
ben sette in ypocrisye and coueitise [greed]. And siche [such people]
[fol. 187rb] resceyuen her mede [receive their reward] here no doute.
Effectuel preyer stabliþ [stabilizes] and makiþ sadde [constant] him þat
[the one that] preieþ in vertue, drawynge [withdrawing] hym fro al
vnspedy [unprofitable] occupacioun inward and outward. And siþ eche
man mot nedis haue summe occupacioun, he þat is wiþdrawen fro yuel
mot nedis be occupied wele, and aȝenward [the same for the contrary].
And siþ men and wymmen, whanne þei comen fro her preyeris, ȝhe
prestis fro her massis, ben seen occupyde in vanyte [vanity] worldly and
fleishly, who may gesse [suppose] þe preyeris of siche to be seide [said]
in sorowe and drede. And siþ siche ben not preysable to [praisewor-
thy for] God in his chirche, no wondre þouȝ þei ioyen not of [do not
rejoice at] þe vntellable comfort of seyntis dwellyng in þe chirche of
God, seyinge "dwellyng in holy chirche is as of alle ioyinge," as who
seye, no ioye is gretter. For siche duellyn in God, and God in hem. Be
þanne God [May God, then, be] in vs and dwelle we [let us dwell] in
him and ouer þat [beyond that] may noone be þouȝt and telde oute
[openly said]. We shuln ioye in the moste perfit ioye of alle men ioynge.
(Lambeth 34, fol.187r)

The words of the last verse of Psalm 86 slide quickly out of the mind of
readers who read them as "nakid wordis" while continuing to live sinfully.
"Effectuel preyer," in contrast, begins with meditating on the words of the
psalm as mediated by extensive commentary, issues forth in better forms
of occupation in the world, and produces the comfort of dwelling in holy
church. The content of the commentary that effects this change is a training
in feeling like a saint—in positioning oneself in the narrative of the psalm
and praying its words with correctly disposed emotions. The author lays out
for his readers how the affective and cognitive content of the feeling and
thinking that accompanies their prayer should be disposed with respect to
past, present, and future. Meditating on what is before and what is to come
brings "sorowe and drede, desyre and hope, þe whiche alle togedre spryngen

oute of byleue." He shows them how they ought to feel, if they want to feel like saints, rejoicing in the "vntellable comfort of seyntis dwellynge in þe chirche of God, seyinge 'dwellyng in holy chirche is as of alle ioyinge,' as who seie, no ioye is gretter." The comfort the author promised when he began, "In þees fewe wordis ben miche comfort," is delivered in repeating the psalm verse with an interpolated gloss: dwelling in holy church (his gloss on "in te") is "sicut omnium letancium," as of all joying. His readers pray the words of the psalm not as naked words but with this proper understanding, and as a result they withdraw from "al vnspedy occupacioun inward and outward." Saying the psalm in this interpolated form, with the proper affective and cognitive disposition, constitutes "effectual preyer." Religious practice and religious experience coalesce: praying effectually is dwelling in holy church and evokes in its practitioners the feelings of the saints.

It is well recognized, of course, and very clear in this quotation, that "holy chirche" is for lollards an equivocal term: it refers not to the ecclesiastical institution with which they find themselves at odds, but (in the words of the *Lanterne of Liȝt*) to the "congregacioun or gedering [gathering] togidir of feiþful soulis þat lastingli kepen feiþ and trouþe, in word and in dede, to God and to man, and reisen her lijf [life] in siker [certain] hope of mercy and grace and blisse at her [their] ende, and ouer-coueren or hillen [cover] þis bilding in perfite charite þat schal not faile in wele [well-being] ne in woo."[53] But the sedulous concern for the disposition toward the future of their readers that all of the writers we have discussed here display may seem incongruous to many readers in the light of lollards' reputation as stringent predestinarians. If lollards are convinced that they are the true church of those that shall be saved, while all others will be damned, then what is the point in attempting to instill the correct disposition in readers who are not lollards? And why does it matter so much what lollard readers feel, provided that they believe the right things and belong to the right church?

The solution to these apparent difficulties lies in recognizing that lollards, like Wyclif himself, are predestinarians in only the very softest sense (see n. 8). Yes, God knows the future, but God is atemporal in any case. God's knowledge in no way constrains or determines human choice. What is more, no human being can know the future: no person knows for certain whether he or she, or indeed any other person, will be saved. No person knows for certain who is in the true church and who is not. All of a person's choices, culminating in his or her last choice at the point of death, together with

---

53. Lilian M. Swinburn, ed., *Lanterne of Liȝt*, EETS, o.s. 151 (London: Kegan Paul, 1917), 25/2–7. Abbreviations expanded, punctuation modified.

God's unknowable mercy and grace, produce an outcome that cannot be foreseen by anyone and cannot be known for certain by those remaining here after the fact.

Faced with this uncertainty, how can lollards attempt to forge an alternative sense of community, a congregation of faithful souls? One important understanding lollards share, though it is disregarded by some critics who would take lollards to task for their rejection of institutional church authority, is that most of their consequent choices will have to be based in uncertainty.[54] Drawing directly on Wyclif's most widely circulated work, the *Dialogus*, they map out carefully what they can and cannot know.[55] The *Dialogue between Reson and Gabbyng*, a free translation of the first twelve chapters of Wyclif's *Dialogus*, explains it this way:

> Summe wordes men graunten [grant], for þei witen [know] þat it is soþe [true] before God, as ben poyntis of beleeue and oþur treuþis þat we seene [evident truths]. Summe wordis men denyen, for þei witen þat þei ben false, as ben wordis contrarie to truþe þat we han grauntid for þe first truþe. Þer ben on þe þrid maner [a third way] summe wordis þat we douten wheþer þei ben soþe or false for contrarie euydens þat we han [because we have some contrary evidence]. But þere ben on þe fourt maner summe wordis þat we supposen to be soþe or ellis false aftur þe euydens þat we han. As, I haue herd of a prelate moche truþe and Goddis werkis. I suppose þat he is a good preest and Goddis childe. But ȝitt [still] I beleeue not [do not believe] þis. For I beleeue not ȝitt of my silf þat I schal come to blisse. But I hope þis surely, and of oþur [about other] men I suppose. Summe I suppose schal be dampned, for her wickud lijf þat I knowe; and of oþur I suppose þat þei schulun be saued, for her good lijf. And ȝitt I beleeue neiþur of þise, for if God wole þei may falle or fayle [fail]. But beleeue is so certeyne þat it may not fayle on no maner. Bi þis may Cristen men see and answere to wordes feyned aȝeynes truþe. A man may wele and medefuly speke aȝeyns þe courte of Rome if he wit wele þat it synneþ aȝeyns Goddis lawe and harmeþ his churche. And þus he schuld do bi charite for loue of þe churche—in charite þat, as seynt Jame seiþ, heliþ [covers over] þe

---

54. See David Aers, who is critical of lollard "hermeneutic confidence," as for example in *Sanctifying Signs: Making Christian Tradition in Late Medieval England* (Notre Dame, IN: University of Notre Dame Press, 2004), 93.

55. Wyclif develops an account of the relationship between hopeful uncertainty for the self and careful scrutiny of others in *Dialogus, sive Speculum ecclesie militantis*, ed. Alfred W. Pollard (London: Trübner, 1886), 24/6–25/1.

multitude of synnes,[56] witouten wiche charite neyþer [neither] man ne [nor] womman may plese God.[57]

This vocabulary, of granting, denying, doubting, and supposing or guessing, is remarkably consistently applied across a wide range of lollard writings.[58] The points of belief and God's law are matters of certainty, grounds for granting or denying. Whoever insists that these grounds should be rejected must be resisted; this is why Thorpe is so sure his judgment is better than Archbishop Thomas Arundel's, and why Wyche, similarly, is so sure that his judgment is better than Bishop Skirlaw's. When it comes to assessing the spiritual condition of individual Christians, however, and whether they are members of holy church, the congregation of faithful souls who dwell in God and God in them, no certainty is possible in this life. This is why Wyclif, and his followers, strongly opposed ecclesiastical excommunication: sin itself excommunicates a sinner, but no ruling or ritual of the institutional church may do so, except to pronounce what it cannot know for certain.[59] About salvation we can only hope and suppose.

The congregation lollards attempt to build can only ever be an aspirational one. But this is its affective strength. Consider how RV3's commentary on Psalm 86 begins:

Þis salme is short in noumbre of wordis and long in sentence [wisdom], makynge mencioun of heuenly Ierusalem, þat is holy chirche þe whiche is a gostly cyte [city], of whiche oon [one] part fiȝtiþ in erþe [is fighting on earth] and oo [one] part regniþ in heuene. Here ben shewid [showed] verrey sparklis [true glimpses] of knowynge who in þis lijf is of þe chirche of God and who not. For alle þe tyme of þis liif, [fol. 184ra] oon or oþer [the other] eiþer al togedre [or all together], þat is, eiþer þe deuil or þe world eiþer [or] mannes owne fleishe, enforsen hem aȝenus [do battle against] man; and whoeuer in her asseylynge [at their assault] is founden fiȝtynge, shewiþ hem [shows themselves] not to be consentynge to her [their] aduersarie, and so to be membris of holi

---

56. This is actually 1 Pet. 4:8, but cf. James 5:20.

57. *Dialogue between Reson and Gabbyng*, in *FWD*, 54/358–78.

58. For other discussions of what can be known and what should be doubted, see Fiona Somerset, *Clerical Discourse and Lay Audience in Late Medieval England* (Cambridge: Cambridge University Press, 1998), 205–8. For a broader study of a range of late scholastic views on these issues, see Ilkka Kantola, *Probability and Moral Uncertainty in Late Medieval and Early Modern Times* (Helsinki: Luther-Agricola Society, 1994).

59. For analysis of Wyclif's and Wycliffite positions, see Ian Forrest, "William Swinderby and the Wycliffite Attitude to Excommunication," *Journal of Ecclesiastical History* 60 (2009): 246–69.

chirche. Ri3t [Just] so eche man, hauynge þes forseyde [these previously
mentioned] aduersaries, enforsyng him not a3enus [not doing battle
against] hem [them], shewiþ him [reveals himself] eiþer to be ouerco-
men of hem [overcome by them] eiþir consentynge to hem, and so to
be a membre of þe deuil. (Lambeth 34, fols. 183vb–184ra)

Membership in the church of God is an act of will. All who are struggling
against the world, the flesh, and the devil are not consenting to their adversary
and are members of holy church—while they persevere, that is. Whoever is
not struggling is not a member of holy church—at least not as long as he or
she continues consenting to the world, the flesh, and the devil. We cannot
know the membership of either church, but we are given "verrey sparklis of
knowynge" on the basis of observed behavior.

Still, holy church is not a congregation each of whose members struggles
alone. Instead, it is a community. In particular, those in heaven give active
help to those still struggling:

Þe foundementis [foundation] of holy chirche is Crist chefly [mainly],
and holy prophetis and apostlys duellynge [dwelling] in holy hilles,
stabely and perseuerauntly [stably and perseveringly] lastynge in hi3e
vertues wiþ bemys [beams] of pyte and charyte, 3yuynge ly3t [giv-
ing light] to lowe valeys, þat is to meke folke in whom pryde neiþir
veynglorye lordshipiþ not [does not dominate]. For to Crist propirly
perteyneþ [properly belongs] pytee and to his seyntis charytee. Þe Lord,
þat is þe fadir of heuene, louiþ 3atis [gates] of Syon. Þe forseyde foundementis [foundation previously mentioned] ben þe 3atis [gates] bi
whiche eche [every] man entriþ into blisse. Þees 3atis ben louid ouer
[more than] alle þe tabernaclis of Iacob, for of alle men obeyinge to þe
byleue [obeying faith] eiþir stryuynge þerfore [or striving toward it],
þees forseyde [these previously mentioned] blyssid seyntes enforseden
hem [did battle], puttynge hemsilf [putting themselves forth] wilfully
to bateyle in þe shiltrone [phalanx], shedyng her bloode to þe deeþ
[death] for þe treuþe, 3yuynge [giving] ensaumple and comfort to her
aftircomeris [those who come after], loueres of treuþe, to goo boldly þe
same wey most surely ledyng to endeles blysse. (Lambeth 34, fol. 184ra)

Lollard writers may express doubts about the value of intercessory prayer to
saints. But as this quotation makes clear, this does not mean that they think
the heavenly host is indifferent to the fates of those on earth. Rather, they
believe saints will help their fellow aspiring saints with their struggle unasked,
out of charity, just as aspiring saints on earth give help to one another and to

the poor. Those engaged in the struggle for salvation can of course rely on Christ's pity and his love. But they can also expect help from the saints. All who strive toward "obeyinge to þe byleue" can count on the active support and involvement of the holy prophets and apostles, eager to assist the "aft-ircomeris" who aspire to follow the same surest path in their love of truth.

❦ CHAPTER 5

Lollard Parabiblia

The governing intention of the Wycliffite bible translation project has often been asserted or assumed. Lollards translated the entire text of the bible, Hebrew Bible and New Testament, into English because they wanted laymen and laywomen to be able to read all of its very own words for themselves, rather than having to rely on adulterated versions, interlarded with glosses and exempla that distort its message, as for example in sermons and pastoralia. The problem with this conventional wisdom is not that it is entirely wrong. After all, one lollard translator makes something like this claim: the final chapter of what is known as the *General Prologue* to the Wycliffite Bible is concerned throughout to establish that the translators have created a "trewe and hool [complete] translacioun" that will allow for better lay understanding of the bible, and similar concerns with lay access to the biblical text may be found elsewhere in lollard writings, especially in the short works collected in CUL Ii.6.26.[1] Rather, the problem is that this conventional wisdom cannot on its own account for what the manuscript record shows us about how the bible was used, nor even for what the *General Prologue* itself explains, and demonstrates, about its purposes.

---

1. For new critical editions of all of these texts, see *EA*: on the "trewe and hool translacioun," see esp. 83/2891–94. Compare Dove's evaluation of this claim, "Wyclif and the English Bible," in A *Companion to John Wyclif, Late Medieval Theologian*, ed. Ian Christopher Levy (Leiden: Brill, 2006), 396–406.

To begin with the manuscript record, few of the 250-odd extant copies of the whole of the Wycliffite Bible contain the full text of Old and New Testaments.[2] Plainly, comprehensiveness was prized by the translators of the bible, for otherwise why would they have completed the whole. But not all book producers, not all readers, wanted the whole text. Probably there are a number of reasons why: expense is certainly one of them, and another may be that the bible was rapidly disseminated to book producers and readers who may have had very different agendas than the bible's translators. Yet we should be wary of explaining away every aspect of the bible's reception that does not meet our expectations as a corruption or dilution of the translators' original intent; it may be that our expectations are what need adjusting. For it seems clear enough that the audiences who used partial texts included lollards: many biblical texts mentioned in heresy trials were partial copies.[3] Nonetheless, manuscripts containing selections or excerpts from the Wycliffite Bible have received comparatively little attention in comparison with manuscripts of the whole bible, or at the very least the whole Old or New Testament, as if the evidence they provided about readership were less significant.

Scholars have also been reluctant to pay attention to some of the items that may accompany the text of the Wycliffite Bible in its manuscripts. The polemical prologues have had plenty of attention, and Mary Dove has done extensive work on explanatory glosses provided by the translators, while Matti Peikola has looked closely at the mise en page of a large sample of the manuscripts and at the developing forms of lectionary (that is, schedules of reading across the liturgical year) provided in these early, substantially complete copies of the Old or New Testament or both together.[4] Michael Kuczynski has examined compiled excerpts for liturgical or argumentative purposes, reproduced within bible manuscripts and elsewhere.[5] Fascinating, but largely neglected, is a concordance to the bible.[6] While the massive compilation of

---

2. I will refer to the Hebrew Bible as the Old Testament in this chapter on occasions where I am describing the understanding of my sources.

3. See, for example, the list of biblical books named in Coventry heresy trials in Shannon McSheffrey and Norman Tanner, eds. and trans., *Lollards of Coventry, 1486–1522*, Camden Fifth Series 23 (Cambridge: Cambridge University Press, 2003), Appendix 2, 343.

4. *FEB*, esp. 152–72, 210–21. Matti Peikola, "Aspects of *Mise-en-page* in Manuscripts of the *Wycliffite Bible*," in *Medieval Texts in Context*, ed. Graham D. Caie and Denis Renevey (Oxford: Routledge, 2008), 28–67; Peikola, "'First is writen a clause of the bigynnynge therof': The Table of Lections in Manuscripts of the Wycliffite Bible," *Boletin Millares Carlo* 24–25 (2005–6): 343–78.

5. Michael P. Kuczynski, "An Unpublished Lollard Psalms *Catena* in Huntington Library MS HM 501," *Journal of the Early Book Society* 13 (2010): 95–138.

6. Sherman M. Kuhn, "The Preface to a Fifteenth-Century Concordance," *Speculum* 43 (1968): 258–73.

traditional commentary known as the *Glossed Gospels* has discouraged attention through its sheer bulk, still it has not been ignored.[7]

Yet even these are still items of parabiblia designed to facilitate access to the bible's own words. They show that critical apparatus and purposive extracts of kinds already in use in the schools were being translated to new audiences, as part of the means by which the Wycliffite Bible made the authentic, unmediated words of the bible more accessible to more people. Potentially more troubling to the conventional emphasis on the bible's exact words are parabiblical materials that take the forms of summary, interpretation, paraphrase, or other renderings of biblical material other than in the bible's own words in a way that might more readily provide a substitute for reading those words. These may appear in marginal or interlinear glosses, prologues either original or adapted from previous sources, capitula summaries that briefly describe a book's content at its head or in a separate list, and freestanding biblical paraphrase: each of these kinds may draw on the others.[8]

These renderings of the bible in words other than its own words might seem deeply at odds with the intentions of the translators who produced, in the course of several years of hard work, a translation of all of the bible's own words were it not for the fact that fully two thirds of the *General Prologue* to the Wycliffite Bible, chapters 3 through 11, is itself a biblical summary that focuses especially on what the bible has to say to laypeople.[9] This fact has been rather unwelcome to most scholars: chapters 12 through 15 of the *General Prologue* are frequently cited, but the much longer biblical summary has generally been ignored or briefly disparaged.[10] Yet in providing a biblical summary as part of instructions about reading the bible itself, the *General Prologue*'s writer is following in a venerable tradition.[11] Jerome's Letter 53, to Paulinus, exhorting study of the bible, used as the first of two prefaces to

---

7. See, e.g., Henry Hargreaves, "Popularising Biblical Scholarship: The Role of the Wycliffite *Glossed Gospels*," in *The Bible and Medieval Culture*, ed. Willem Lourdaux and D. Verhelst (Louvain: Louvain University Press, 1979), 171–89; *PR*, 248–59; and for editions of the various prologues and epilogues, *EA*, 172–86.

8. On how copies of the Wycliffite Bible adapt prologues and glosses conventionally used, see Christopher De Hamel, "English Wycliffite Bibles," chap. 7 in *The Book: A History of the Bible* (London: Phaidon, 2001), 166–89; *FEB*, 83–102, and more diffusely 103–36, 152–72.

9. *FEB*, 120–88: for her new critical edition, see n. 1.

10. Dove suggests that the writer was merely marking time while waiting for the resources he most needed to appear. *FEB*, 121; further comments on how a full biblical paraphrase would have frustrated "the whole purpose of the translation project" on 122–23, continuing to 129.

11. For a wider view of this tradition, from its beginnings in the processes of canon formation in the Hebrew scriptures up to recent manifestations in the songs of Bob Dylan, see Lucie Doležalová and Tamás Visi, eds., *Retelling the Bible: Literary, Historical, and Social Contexts* (Frankfurt am Main: Peter Lang, 2011).

his translation of the bible and usually found at the beginning of Genesis in copies of all or part of the Vulgate from the earliest extant copies through to print, is also, over most of its length, a biblical summary.[12] Jerome's letter is translated into English and used as a biblical prologue in most of the manuscripts of the Wycliffite Bible containing all or most of the Earlier Version (EV) Old Testament, as well as four Later Version (LV) manuscripts.[13] The *General Prologue* writer plainly knows it well since he cites it in his own prologue. In adapting and developing Jerome's model for introducing the bible, the *General Prologue* writer bends biblical summary to his own ends. Rather than being an embarrassing oddity, then, the *General Prologue*'s biblical summary helps us understand how lollard writers thought summarizing the bible could contribute to better reading of the text.

The kind of biblical summary we find in the *General Prologue* is, of course, only one of the many forms of biblical redaction available to late medieval English audiences. These range from encyclopedic works presenting a kind of chronology of world history, to verse narrative renditions of specific episodes, to cycle drama; these forms of biblical retelling seem to have been extraordinarily popular.[14] Many of them draw, at some remove, on Peter Comestor's *Historia scholastica*, a summary of the bible used as part of the standard course of instruction in the schools; biblical summary was not only for the uneducated, though its uses among schoolmen have been very little studied.[15] We may speculate that scholars thought their students, at least as much as lay audiences, needed help in grasping the biblical whole that emerges from all its disparate component parts, in seeing where the bible's historical narratives fit within the larger narrative of the past, and in understanding how that larger narrative in turn, and the personal as well as communal or national episodes out of which it is made, fit within the yet wider arc of salvation history.[16]

---

12. De Hamel, *The Book*, 20–24, describes how Jerome's prologues were derived from his letters and lists the components of the later medieval Latin Vulgate.

13. For an edition, see Conrad Lindberg, ed., *Middle English Bible: Prefatory Epistles of St. Jerome* (Oslo: Universitetsforlaget, 1978). Updates in *FEB*, 199 and 281–306.

14. For a descriptive guide, see James H. Morey, *Book and Verse: A Guide to Middle English Biblical Literature* (Urbana: University of Illinois Press, 2000).

15. James H. Morey, "Peter Comestor, Biblical Paraphrase, and the Medieval Popular Bible," *Speculum* 68 (1993): 6–35. For a new edition of *Historia scholastica* on Genesis, supplementing the *Patrologia Latina* edition (*PL* 198, cols. 1053–1644), see Agneta Sylwan, ed., *Scolastica Historia: Liber Genesis*, Corpus Christianorum: Continuatio Mediaevalis 191 (Turnhout: Brepols, 2005). See the review by Daniel Hobbins, *The Medieval Review*, June 4, 2005, at http://quod.lib.umich.edu/t/tmr/. See also Mark Clark, "Peter Comestor and Peter Lombard: Brothers in Deed," *Traditio* 60 (2005): 85–142.

16. On how mnemonic verse summaries may have aided scholars in grasping the bible as a whole see Lucie Doležalová, "*Biblia quasi in saculo: Summarium Biblie* and Other Medieval Bible Mnemonics,"

It is unclear whether lollard writers disapproved (as is usually assumed) of most of the forms of biblical redaction that were already available to the laity: they do commonly list chronicles among kinds of idle storytelling that should be avoided, but without mentioning the possibility of biblical content, and while one work, the *Tretise of Miraclis Pleying*, is sharply critical of the staging of biblical stories, this may be a minority position.[17] What is clear is that lollards read and produced one kind of biblical redaction in a profusion that scholarly embarrassment with their use of it has obscured. Lollard writers strongly favored comprehensive prose summary and narrative harmonization of either the whole or extensive parts of one or both testaments, with the aim of providing an overall reading of biblical narrative that brings, in any given case, a small cluster of related themes to the surface throughout. Often the result is to read the whole of the bible, or a large portion of the bible, in relation to themes most prominent in some part or parts of it. In some cases the summary is part of a hybrid form, where parts of the bible—perhaps the ones that ground the reading of the rest—are translated closely, while other parts are summarized. In other cases the text is summarized throughout, but at greater length and with more intensive attention in the sections of greatest interest. Implicit in these efforts, it seems, are both an impulse toward comprehensiveness and a willingness to embrace partiality: unevenness of texture and attention seems to be the norm in these productions.

The form of engagement with the biblical text I am describing is by no means unique to lollardy—or to England. It should sound, among other examples, like Guiart des Moulin's *Bible Historiale* and the even more comprehensive *Bible Historiale Complétée* (BHC), French composite bibles made up of parts of the translated Latin bible, selections from a translation of the *Historia scholastica*, a gospel harmony (in the first case) or a version of the New Testament from *La Bible française du XIIIe siècle* and additional Old Testament books (in the second case). These biblical redactions, and especially the BHC, were available in widely varying forms, in England as well as France, in the early fifteenth century.[18] It should sound like the whole

---

Medium aevum quotidianum 56 (2007): 17–19. On the *Historia scholastica*, see also John Van Engen, "Studying Scripture in the Early University," in *Neue Richtungen in der hoch- und spätmittelalterlichen Bibelexegese*, ed. Robert E. Lerner and Elisabeth Müller-Luckner (Munich: Oldenbourg, 1996), 30.

17. Clifford Davidson, ed., A *Tretise of Miraclis Pleyinge*, rev. ed. (Kalamazoo, MI: Medieval Institute Publications, 1993). See Ruth Nissé, "Reversing Discipline: The *Tretise of Miraclis Pleyinge*, Lollard Exegesis, and the Failure of Representation," *Yearbook of Langland Studies* 11 (1997): 163–97. For doubts about the work's lollardy, see Lawrence Clopper, "Is the *Tretise of Miraclis Pleyinge* a Lollard Tract against Devotional Drama?," *Viator* 34 (2003): 229–71. See also chap. 4.

18. On French biblical versions, see Clive R. Sneddon, "The 'Bible du XIIIe siècle': Its Medieval Public in the Light of its Manuscript Tradition," in Lourdaux and Verhelst, *The Bible and Medieval*

pseudo-Bonaventuran tradition of meditation on the life of Christ, which produced a profusion of translations into English, not just Nicholas Love's *Mirror*.[19] It should sound like the treatment of the bible as a whole in the Middle English biblical version edited by Anna Paues (known as the "Paues version"); like the biblical rendering in *Book to a Mother*; like *Oon of Foure*, a Middle English gospel harmony with links to the Wycliffite Bible EV revisions, the *Glossed Gospels*, and the LV's *General Prologue*;[20] and like the rendering of each chapter of the whole of the bible in turn in a virtually ignored Middle English example of biblical summary that quotes extensively from the Wycliffite Bible, in Oxford, Trinity College, MS 93.[21] Examples could be multiplied further.

Ralph Hanna has influentially suggested that once it became available, the Wycliffite Bible first infiltrated, then supplanted, works such as these, first producing idiosyncratically assembled manuscript anthologies that display an impulse toward comprehensive engagement with the whole bible yet do not reproduce the whole text, then "destroying the circulation of competing biblical versions."[22] His analysis of these anthologies is important for its assertion that book producers and readers did indeed view what may look to us like cobbled-together substitutes for the bible itself as a means toward

---

Culture, 127–40; Éléonore Fournié, "Les manuscrits de la *Bible historiale*: Présentation et catalogue raisonné d'une oeuvre médiévale," *L'atelier du Centre de recherches historiques* 3.2 (2009), online at http://acrh.revues.org/index1408.html; and Margriet Hoogvliet, "The Medieval Vernacular Bible in French as a Flexible Text: Selective and Discontinuous Reading Practices," in *Form and Function in the Medieval Bible*, ed. Eyal Poleg and Laura Light (Leiden: Brill, 2013), 283–306. I thank Margriet for much discussion of French biblical versions.

19. On versions of the pseudo-Bonaventuran *Meditationes Vitae Christi* in England, see the online project, John Thompson, ed., *Geographies of Orthodoxy: Mapping English Pseudo-Bonaventuran Lives of Christ, 1350–1550*, 2007–10, at http://www.qub.ac.uk/geographies-of-orthodoxy/.

20. Anna C. Paues, ed., *A Fourteenth Century English Biblical Version* (Cambridge: Cambridge University Press, 1904; repr. New York: AMS Press, 1974); *BM*. No edition of *Oon of Foure* has yet been published, but see Paul Smith, "Could the Gospel Harmony *Oon of Foure* Represent an Intermediate Version of the Wycliffite Bible?," *Studia Neophilologica* 80 (2008): 160–76; and Elizabeth Schirmer, "Canon Wars and Outlier Manuscripts: Gospel Harmony in the Lollard Controversy," *Huntington Library Quarterly* 73 (2010): 1–36.

21. This manuscript remained unnoticed until Neil Ker published a short description with excerpts: N. R. Ker, "A Middle-English Summary of the Bible," *Medium Aevum* 29 (1960): 115–18 (see also Neil R. Ker, *Medieval Manuscripts in British Libraries*, 4 vols. [Oxford: Oxford University Press, 1969–92], 3:713). It has been edited in a PhD dissertation: Robert Reilly, "A Middle English Summary of the Bible: An Edition of Trinity College (Oxon) MS 93" (University of Washington, 1966). Brief notices appear in David Fowler, "A Middle English Bible Commentary (Oxford, Trinity College MS 93)," *Manuscripta* 12 (1968): 67–78; Morey, *Book and Verse*, 111; *FEB*, 52, 303. The most recent attempt to date the manuscript is that of Ralph Hanna (email July 2011) who thinks that the manuscript's neat anglicana hand with some secretary features may be dated s. xv[in].

22. Ralph Hanna, "The End of Early London Literature," in *London Literature, 1300–1380* (Cambridge: Cambridge University Press, 2005), 305–13. Quotation from 310, punctuation modified.

biblical study. However, my own view is that summaries and hybrid summaries such as these were not always merely a substitute for access to the bible's authentic text, necessitated by the constraints of a textual culture of scarcity and discarded once the text itself became more readily available. Biblical paraphrase was not superseded by the Wycliffite Bible but persisted alongside it, often within the same manuscripts. It was not always a substitute for unavailable parts of the bible; sometimes it was a supplement to them.[23] Instead, these summaries have much to teach us about the value writers and readers attached to summary as a hermeneutic tool. They show us how these book producers yoked summary with other parabiblical tools in order to provide new and more expert readers of the bible alike with a heavily mediated encounter with the bible's own words—one that enables them to perceive the bible as a unified whole of a certain kind and conveys to them an interpretation of its overall meaning and import.

Individual and group reading appear to have been important social practices among lollards, to judge from evidence preserved in heresy trials. Yet we know so frustratingly little about what was in the books these defendants admit to reading and how they went about reading them and discussing their content.[24] If we want to know more about how the "bible men" (as Pecock called lollards) read the bible, then we should look beyond the words of the translation itself, beyond even its scholarly apparatus and liturgical framings and explanatory glosses, to examine the forms of biblical summary they seem to have thought valuable. Rather than assuming that every form of biblical redaction linked with the Wycliffite Bible is distinct from and at odds with the long-term collaborative project that produced it—a position the manuscript evidence does not support—we would do better to examine how these works are consistent with what we know about lollard biblical reading from other lollard writings, and how indeed they might support and extend our understanding of what we learn from trial depositions. In what follows I will first examine how the summary material in the *General Prologue* both draws on and departs from Jerome's own biblical prologue in his Letter 53, to Paulinus. I will then discuss the much longer Trinity 93 bible summary.

---

23. Thus, I differ with Elizabeth Schirmer ("Canon Wars and Outlier Manuscripts") in her carefully attentive analysis of individual biblical manuscripts, in that she is, I think, too ready to regard her manuscript examples as idiosyncratic outliers and to follow other critics in seeing standardization and uniformity elsewhere.

24. We know that it involved memorization, reading aloud, and discussion of content and argument. For a survey of the evidence, see *PR*, 191–200; for further discussion, see Shannon McSheffrey, "Heresy, Orthodoxy, and English Vernacular Religion, 1480–1525," *Past & Present* 186 (2005): 47–80. We can speculate that it may have involved studying biblical commentary: see chap. 3.

Biblical Summary in the *General Prologue*

Before examining the *General Prologue* we should recall that it appears in full in only five copies of the Wycliffite Bible and is excerpted in ten more. Its use in full as a prologue to the Old Testament or both Old and New Testaments, as in Forshall and Madden's printed edition of the Wycliffite Bible, is the exception rather than the rule.[25] However, we would be hasty to conclude that the *General Prologue*'s relatively limited circulation is a reason to dismiss the evidence it provides. Few lollard writings are extant in as many as fifteen full or partial copies; the *General Prologue* remains an unusually broadly disseminated work, even if it was far from a standard item in every fifteenth-century reader's experience of the Wycliffite Bible. The questions of whether it was intended to appear in every copy of the bible and, if so, why it was dropped would bear further consideration; plainly the writer was closely involved in the bible translation project, even if his is the voice of only one collaborator, and one who at the time of writing (judging from his limited access to needed reference works) may have been reduced to a more peripheral role.[26] While I disagree with Dove that the extended

---

25. All of the following information derives from *FEB*, 120 nn. 80–83, but must be retrieved by compiling information from the opening list of sigla, Appendix 1, the Index of Manuscripts, and her main text. It is gathered here for the reader's convenience, but without independent checking. The complete copies are in Oxford, University College, MS 96, where they accompany gospel lections in the LV; Princeton, NJ, Scheide Library, MS M.12, LV MS of both OT and NT also including a lectionary; Edinburgh, National Library of Scotland, MS Advocates 18.6.7, with an EV NT including some revisions and a lectionary; Cambridge, Corpus Christi College, MS 147, LV MS of both testaments with lectionary; and Dublin, Trinity College, MS 75, MS of both testaments including two lectionaries, one with some LV content. A freestanding copy lacking most of chap. 15 is in London, British Library, MS Harley 1666. CUL Kk.1.8 lacks most of chap. 10; this manuscript has part of the OT, the NT, and a lectionary, with lections in LV. The same part of chap. 10 is missing in Oxford, Lincoln College, MS Latin 119, LV MS of both testaments in which the first three chapters of the Prologue are used as a preface to Genesis, while the biblical summary chapters are modified and distributed as prologues across the Old Testament books that they discuss; this copy also omits chaps. 12–15. Two manuscripts include only chap. 1: London, British Library, MS Royal 1.C.viii, LV copy of both testaments, and Oxford, Bodleian Library, MS Bodley 277, revised LV copy of both testaments. Portions of the biblical summary appear alone in San Marino, CA, Huntington Library, MS HM 501, a biblical miscellany (section on Psalms), as well as its separated opening; Keio, University Library, MS 170 X 9.6 ("part of" chap. 11, also of the polemical chaps. 12–15). The sections on Psalms only also appear in Dublin, Trinity College, MS 72, LV MS of Psalms and Canticles with lectionary, while the section covering Psalms to Ecclesiasticus appears in London, British Library, Additional MS 31044, LV MS covering Psalms to Ecclesiasticus, and Worcester, Cathedral Library, MS F.172, including Psalms 1–83 in Latin and English and Acts, both in LV, as well as works by Rolle and Hilton and the Gospel of Nicodemus. Finally, the opening of chap. 12 on the four senses of scripture appears in (again) San Marino, CA, Huntington Library, MS HM 501, and in London, British Library, Additional MS 10046, LV MS containing Psalms and Canticles.

26. Mary Dove has suggested that the heavily polemical portions, especially chap. 10 and part of 13, may have scared away compilers (*FEB*, 127). Henry Ansgar Kelly, "Literal versus Literal: The

biblical summary that occupies most of the Prologue's length was written to kill time while awaiting the arrival of books needed for the final chapters, I would agree with her that the work is scarcely a highly crafted and carefully organized persuasive whole ideally pitched to invite new readers.[27] Self-indulgent and somewhat rambling it certainly is, but in ways that give us greater, rather than lesser, insight into how its writer read and wanted others to read the bible.

Even before it embarks on biblical summary, the *General Prologue* is deeply concerned with the relationship between part and whole. It begins with a rather dry and pedantic survey, closely dependent on Jerome's biblical prologues, of which books of the bible, on the one hand, are canonical "books of faith" bearing the full weight of authority and which, on the other hand, are useful and worthy of inclusion as a means of edifying the people. The writer is concerned with establishing the exact constituents of the whole; yet he also allows the admission of other edifying matter clearly labelled as lesser in authority.[28] Adjoined following this display of learning is the reassurance that no simple man should be afraid to study the bible, just as no clerk should be proud of his knowledge of it, for (drawing on Augustine here) its most obscure parts contain the same wisdom as its most open teachings, and every part of the whole teaches the same meekness and charity.[29]

This assurance that any one "open" part of the bible contains the whole of the bible's truth does not prevent the writer from going on to present a comprehensive summary of the Old Testament, spanning the nine chapters from chapter 3 to the end of chapter 11, in which only the prophets, who had been given their own prologue written before this prologue, are quickly skipped over. This summary's central purpose is not altogether unlike Jerome's in his Letter 53, to Paulinus. In listing out the bible's books Jerome establishes the shape of the whole, as the *General Prologue* writer had in his first chapter. In summarizing the Old Testament Jerome insists, for each book covered, on the

---

Two Versions of the Middle English Bible (fka Wycliffite Bible)," and Andrew Brock Kraebel, "The Wycliffite Bible Prologues and the Translation of Academic Discourse," papers presented at the International Congress on Medieval Studies, Kalamazoo, MI, May 12–15, 2011, have each suggested that the prologue was composed by a satellite member of the translation project, working on his prologue at some distance from the main project.

27. *FEB*, 121.

28. Edited as "Prologue to the Wycliffite Bible," in *EA*, 3/1–5/75. Further citations to page and line numbers in parentheses in the text.

29. "Prologue to the Wycliffite Bible," 5/78–82: "þe same sentence is in þe derkest places of hooli writ which sentence is in þe open places; and ech place of hooli writt boþe open and derk techiþ mekenesse and charite, and þerfor he þat kepiþ mekenesse and charite haþ þe trewe vndurstonding and perfeccioun of al hooli writ, as Austin preueþ in his sermoun of þe preisyng of charite." See Augustine, Sermon 350, *PL* 39, col. 1534.

hidden figural mysteries rewarding close study that it contains. The *General Prologue* writer is similarly motivated to uncover the continuing relevance of the Old Testament, book by book, and similarly has recourse to figural interpretation in this effort. However, Jerome gestures toward hidden mystery whose content is for the most part left unexplained, as for example in his comment on Leviticus: "þe book of Leuytes is opun [clear], in þe which alle sacryfices, ȝhe [indeed] and almost alle silablis [syllables] and þe cloþis of Aaron and þe hool [whole] ordre of Leuy shewen [symbolize] heuenly sacramentis."[30] Jerome's prevailing mode throughout his whole biblical summary is irony: in urging the obviousness of meaning of each biblical book in turn, while pointing in his following description toward its hidden depths, his overall aim is to frustrate the facile engagement he seems to encourage and instead exhort close study.

In contrast with Jerome, when the *General Prologue* writer says something is "open," he means it.[31] After surveying all the canonical books in the first chapter, for example, he recommends that "cristen men and wymmen, elde and ȝonge [old and young], shulden studie faste [hard] in þe newe testament, for it is of ful [great] autorite and opene to vndurstonde [open to the understanding] of symple men as to [as concerns] þe poyntis þat ben moost nedeful to saluacioun" (5/75–78). In keeping with this conviction that the knowledge needed for salvation is openly accessible in the text of the New Testament, and in contrast with Jerome, whose description of the New Testament is progressively more laden with disclaimers about his inadequacy to describe its meaning fully, the *General Prologue* writer does not include the New Testament in the biblical summary that follows.[32] He precedes his biblical summary with a careful demarcation, in his second chapter, of what in the Old Testament has continuing relevance (the moral commandments) and what, on the other hand, must be interpreted with caution (the judicial content of Mosaic law, which has been superseded by the "lawe of merci and of charite;" and "cerymonyals," ritual practices such as sacrifices, that

---

30. Quoted from Lindberg's edition of the revised version of this prologue, abbreviations expanded and modern word division imposed. See Lindberg, *Middle English Bible: Prefatory Epistles of St. Jerome*, 105/8–12. Lindberg provides on the same page Jerome's Latin: "In promptu est Leviticus liber in quo singula sacrificia, immo singulae paene syllabae et vestes Aaron et totus ordo leviticus inspirant caelestia sacramenta." Jerome of course by "sacrament" meant something like "mystery," not "sacrament" in the sense that the eucharist is a sacrament, and the translators appear to have understood this, whether or not their readers did.

31. Usage of "open" to refer to what is obvious, apparent, or easily accessible is common in lollard writings. For a scattering of examples in a wide range of writings, see *MED*, s.v. "open," adj., 2.

32. For Jerome's account of the New Testament, see Lindberg, *Middle English Bible: Prefatory Epistles of St. Jerome*, 135/211–143/265.

are now only superseded figures for the "lawe of grace") (*General Prologue*, 6/103, 95–96, 115–16). It is clear, then, that despite the bible translators' decision to translate the biblical text as a whole, this participant, at least, shares the implicit or explicit conviction of many late medieval schoolmen that some parts of the bible are more easily accessible than others.[33] Yet his summary covers much more than these parts. In surveying each book in turn he spells out what he thinks it means, rather than following Jerome by gesturing toward its confounding profundity.

Beyond the historical events each book of the bible may recount, the *General Prologue* writer sums up its "moral comaundementis" (6/95) by describing their import for readers' emotions, will, and actions. He shows readers what each book "shulde stire cristen men" to feel and do, or (in a few cases) what it "shulde make cristen men" feel, and how they should then act in consequence: his motivations are, then, very similar to those of the writers we surveyed in chapter 4.[34] Some of these injunctions are general, address everyone, and convey basic, fundamental instruction that holds few surprises: for example, Genesis "shulde stire [stir] cristen men to be feiþful and for to drede and loue God, and in alle þingis do his wille" (7/149–50). Others sound as though they anticipate a lollard audience: for example, the hint at imitating Christ by withstanding persecution in Leviticus, whose sacrifices are said to figure the passion and death of Christ: "þis process [exposition] of Leuytici shulde make cristen men afeerd [afraid] to breke Goddis heestis and ioiful [joyful] to kepe þo [in keeping them] to liyf and deþ, for reward of God in euerlastinge blis" (8/186–88). Still other "moral commandments" are more status specific, more pointed, and in some cases addressed at far greater length.

Rather than giving each book of the bible equal attention, like Jerome, the writer of the *General Prologue* instead varies his level of engagement. What he dwells on seems to be what interests him most. One book of general relevance to all "cristen men" comes in for extraordinarily detailed summary: in concluding the summary of Deuteronomy, which occupies four printed

33. See esp. "Prologue to the Wycliffite Bible," 47/1577–82: "þou3 kingis and lordis knewen neuere more of hooli scripture þan þre stories of the ij. bookis of Paralipomenon and of Regum, þat is, þe stori of king Iosaphat, þe storie of king E3echie and þe storie of kyng Iosie, þei my3ten lerne sufficientli to lyue wel and gouerne wel her puple bi Goddis lawe, and eschewe al pride, and idolatrie, coueitise and oþere synnes." Job, the Psalter, Ecclesiastes, and the Song of Songs, on the other hand, are especially difficult to understand (57/1959–59/2023, 59/2040–60/2062). For a perceptive account of late scholastic biblical hermeneutics, see Christopher Ocker, *Biblical Poetics before Humanism and Reformation* (Cambridge: Cambridge University Press, 2002).
34. See, for example, "Prologue to the Wycliffite Bible," 7/149–50, 10/236–38, 15/441–42, etc., or on the other hand 8/170–72, 8/186–88, etc.

pages, the writer notes that "Cristen men shulden myche rede and here and kunne [know] þis book of Deutronomy, þat comprehendiþ [encompasses] al þe lawe of Moises and disposiþ men for to bileue in Crist and here and kepe his wordis" (13/383–14/385). Because it contains the "lawe of Moises" or ten commandments, because of their universal applicability, the writer slows down.[35] But the books that draw the writer's closest attention are those that he feels should have targeted impact on specific statuses within society, most especially the cluster of biblical books he stresses are especially useful to kings and lords: 1, 2, 3, and 4 Kings and 1 and 2 Paralipomenon. Summary of these six books occupies some thirty-one pages in Dove's edition, followed by a seven-page polemical coda before the summary of Esdras begins: this is more than half of the biblical summary's full length of fifty-six pages.

In this writer's rendering, the books of Kings become a miniature Fall of Princes catalogue. Except for good king Josiah, and with the occasional leavening of a thoroughly bad king who does no good throughout his reign, king after king starts out well, only to meet with one sin or another, or be undermined by his people's corruption, and end his life out of God's favor. And then, in Paralipomenon, they do it all again. Even though Paralipomenon repeats the same narrative sequence of episodes found in Kings, the *General Prologue* writer cites Jerome's Letter 53, to Paulinus, on Paralipomenon's crucial importance to an understanding of the bible, pointing out that these books both include stories left out of Kings and elucidate "questeouns vnnoumbrable [countless questions]" of the gospels (34/1122–27). The writer does not pursue this tantalizing claim about the gospels as he goes on to summarize Paralipomenon. But he does give the same sequence of kings different emphases the second time around, reporting in direct discourse the words of prophets to kings and describing various attempts at reform and their reasons for success or failure.[36]

While elsewhere in his bible summary the writer provides descriptions of how a given book should "stir" its readers, in Kings and Paralipomenon these directives mostly address "kyngis and lordis" and are presented as advice to rulers. In the second book of Kings, for example, the writer spins from this strain of advice a tiny Mirror for Princes encouraging kings and lords to learn from David's example:

> Þe processe [exposition] of þis secounde book ouȝte to stire [should move] kyngis and lordis to merci and riȝtfulnesse, and euere [always] to

---

35. On lollard emphasis on the commandments, see chap. 2, and *WS*, 8–12.

36. Jerome, Epistle 53, *PL* 22, col. 548; and see Lindberg, *Middle English Bible: Prefatory Epistles of St. Jerome*, 130/183–132/191.

be war of idilnesse, þat brou3te Dauiþ to auoutrie [adultery] and oþere
myschefs [mishaps], and euere to be meke to God and hise prestis, and
soore repente of [sorely repent] her mysdedis and make amendis to
God and men, and wilfuli [willingly] for3yue wrongis don to hem, and
euere be war [wary] of pride and extorciouns, lest God take veniaunce
[vengeance] on al þe puple as he dide on Dauiþ and his puple, and euere
[always] to be pacient and merciful, as Dauiþ was, to gete remyssioun
[obtain remission] of synnes bifor don, and to gete [gain] pees and
prosperite and heuenli blisse wiþouten ende. (19/578–86)

From David's adultery, kings and lords can learn to avoid idleness; from his
repentance, they learn making amends; from forgiveness of others, they learn
penitent mercy. Still, it emerges clearly across these books that if even David
or Solomon can fall, then nearly all rulers will sin. Repentance, rather than
perfection, is the goal.

Now, admittedly, works ostensibly advising rulers in the later Middle Ages
commonly had a far wider audience than kings and lords alone and typically acknowledge their own broader applicability. In this case, though, the
writer's switch in focus does signal, I think, a real narrowing of attention.
There is advice here specifically for kings and lords. But there is also some
rather different advice for other readers. Repentance is the product not only
of self-discipline but of willingness to accept and act upon the advice of
true prophets, as the third book of Kings advises lords and kings at its close:
"take councel at [advice from] hooli scripture and trewe profetis, and triste
not to [do not trust] false profetis, be þei neuere so many [no matter how
many they are] and crie faste a3enus [against] oon [one] or fewe trewe men"
(24/764–66). Even as it advises lords and kings, and increasingly in Paralipomenon where the focus shifts to prophets and what they advise, this section also exhorts lollard readers to believe the truth no matter how few its
speakers and join in speaking it regardless of the consequences.

The polemical coda to this section, which occupies most of chapter 10,
emphasizes that lollard behaviour should influence contemporary kings
and lords even as it also complains about those kings' and lords' behaviour.
Some lords are "cristen lordis in name, and heþene in condiciouns [disposi-
tion]," since they prevent God's law from being known, kept, and preached
(47/1596–97). Such unwise lords should recall the example of Elijah or of
Micaiah, who alone had the truth of God despite the opposition of many
false prophets. Similarly, "now a fewe pore men and idiotis in comparisoun
of [to] clerkis of scole moun [may] haue the treuþe of hooli scripture a3enus
[against] many þousynde prelatis and religious þat ben 3ouun to [devoted

to] worldli pride and coueitise, symonye, ipocrisie and oþere fleischli synnes; moost siþ [especially since] þese pore men desiren oneli þe treuþe and fredom of þe hooli gospel" (48/1616–21). The reasons why these "pore men" are persecuted are also the behaviors that readers should aspire to imitate: "to absteyne fro nedeles othis [oaths] and vnleueful [unlawful], and to eschewe [avoid] pride, and speke onour of God and of his lawe and repreue [reprove] synne bi weie of charite is matere and cause [the reason] now whi prelatis and summe lordis sclaundren men and clepen hem lollardis, eretikis and reisers of debate and of tresoun aȝenus þe kyng" (52/1793–97). The writer's sympathy, quite plainly, is with the "pore men," not the prelates and lords who collude in slandering them. He presents his "pore men" as an example of virtue for all readers and exhorts all readers to aspire to the truth of holy scripture. If the *General Prologue*'s biblical summary covers the familiar territory, in lollard polemic, of exhorting kings and lords to repent, to reform the churchmen who are leading them astray, and by that means to reform the realm, then it also offers other readers a way to contribute to that reform. What began as advice only for lords and kings becomes, in this sequence of biblical retelling, a process of participatory reform through the cultivation of virtue.[37]

Biblical Summary Writ Large

The very long Middle English biblical summary (*MEBS*) in Trinity 93—a small, closely written volume originally including around 220 folios, copied and corrected by a single scribe around the turn of the fifteenth century—is less overt about its intended import. Trinity 93 is the single extant copy of this summary, and the manuscript contains nothing else; there are no recognized overlaps with any others of the many prose and verse retellings of parts of the bible extant in Middle English, and this is the only known English work that summarizes every book of the Hebrew Bible and New Testament—if, that is, we assume that the Catholic epistles and Revelations are missing only because the end of the manuscript has been lost.[38] The summarizer plainly had access to the Wycliffite Bible: his biblical quotations commonly match up with the wording of the LV, less often the EV.[39] Any writer producing

---

37. For very similar advice to ordinary people about how to deal with heathen lords, see *A Schort Reule of Lif* in Mary Raschko, "Common Ground for Contrasting Ideologies: The Texts and Contexts of *A Schort Reule of Lif*," *Viator* 40 (2009): 410/75–77.

38. Morey, *Book and Verse*, 110–11, finds no overlaps with other Middle English biblical redactions.

39. In *MEBS*'s fairly frequent short quotations from the biblical text in English, Reilly finds that its wording corresponds frequently with the LV of the Wycliffite Bible, less often with the EV, and

biblical materials for a lay audience in the fifteenth century might draw on the Wycliffite translation, regardless of affiliation, but the *MEBS* writer does more. As we will see, he incorporates commentary that closely resembles the content of the Wycliffite Bible's extant glosses and prologues, to the point where the circumstantial evidence of common sources and interpretations suggests some collaborative relationship with the bible translators.[40] And as he amplifies the bible's significance, his summary frequently echoes or evokes lollard writers' readings of the bible elsewhere, and commonly extends them too. While this particular effort at biblical redaction was not, as far as we know, widely disseminated, it is a treasure-house of information about lollard biblical reading.

Features consistently present across the whole of *MEBS* strongly suggest that it is the product of one writer's sustained effort, even as marked differences in the writer's approach to different books demonstrate his varying level of interest, his sense of what the book in question demands (for there are some systematic variations that align with genre), and even perhaps what sources he draws on. Throughout, famous verses or episodes catch the writer's eye, though typically they are evoked through truncated quotation rather than rehearsed in full. The ten commandments, for example, are mentioned but not listed, and the same goes for the beatitudes and the Pater Noster: this is not a work with any interest in conveying the pastoral essentials. Nor is it any kind of index to the topoi of Wycliffite political polemic (indeed, Wycliffite polemicists rarely quote the lollard bible): unlike the *General Prologue*, this summary does not digress into extended complaint. Nor is the story what grips this writer's attention: while he brings narrative to the surface in books where there is a narrative, though sometimes with glaring omissions, the summary is only rarely interested in retelling parts of the biblical story in a gripping or novel way.

Yet this rendering of the bible compels our interest, as it seeks to compel that of its readers. Its swooping and opportunistic attention to true speech and its consequences, persecution and vindication, and the forging of an imagined

---

differs from both fairly often as well; he also finds that the content of its commentary often reproduces the *Wycliffite Bible* glosses ("Middle English Summary," xviii). However, his analysis is based on Forshall and Madden's edition, whose limitations as a record of the contents of the two versions and of the glosses are analysed in *FEB*, 154–55, 210–21; more comparison with other manuscripts might tell us still more and help to pinpoint the stages of the bible's production during which *MEBS* itself was composed and revised.

40. Reilly arrived at similar conclusions in preparing his dissertation edition, even with his more limited knowledge of other lollard writings, but did not pursue this research topic any further: "Middle English Summary," xviii.

community of true believers attests over and over to a lollard structure of feeling—one easily recognizeable from any number of other lollard works. While the *MEBS* may not be as interested in retelling stories as the *General Prologue* or the works surveyed in chapter 6, it shares their interest in feeling: in describing the feelings of biblical speakers, and in explaining how the bible seeks to "excite" or "stir" or "move" its readers. As we will see, these are the verbs it uses most often in commenting, as it frequently does, on the feelings the biblical authors intend to evoke.[41]

I choose the term "feeling," as opposed to "emotion" or "affect," to reflect the pervasive close interactions between emotion and cognition, from sensation of externals through to action in response, that the modern semantic range of "feeling" largely reflects. Like many of their contemporaries, lollard writers understood these processes as closely and pervasively interactive, even if they demarcated them into the operation of various separate powers or faculties for the purpose of analysis.[42] In lollard writings (and indeed far more broadly, though not always in the same ways) feeling is variably and provisionally structured by narrative (where sensations and emotions follow one upon another sequentially), by catechesis (where lists and hierarchies, visual or expository, aid the memory and give shape to experience), by metaphor (as for example the aspiration toward dwelling together in God and God in us), and by allegory (where personified feelings inhabit or are part of imagined landscapes, buildings, and cities).

My term "structure of feeling" draws on the work of Raymond Williams, although none of the examples he discusses are medieval, nor are they closely concerned with religion, and he does not elaborate upon its ramifications as I have just done. Williams's description of structures of feeling is deeply sensitive to the relationships between as well as within social groups and to the ongoing processes by which any human understanding of emotion develops in tension with lived experience, as well as with cultural norms articulated

---

41. The writer of this summary, like the *General Prologue* writer, may be aware of Richard Fitzralph's theory of "excitative speech," explained in his written defense at the papal curia and widely published across Europe together with his *Defensio curatorum*: see Fiona Somerset, "Excitative Speech: Theories of Emotive Response from Richard Fitzralph to Margery Kempe," in *The Vernacular Spirit: Essays on Medieval Religious Literature*, ed. Renate Blumenfeld Kosinski, Duncan Robertson, and Nancy Bradley Warren (New York: Palgrave, 2002), 59–79.

42. See Sarah McNamer, "Feeling," in *Oxford Twenty-First Century Approaches to Literature: Middle English*, ed. Paul Strohm (Oxford: Oxford University Press, 2007), 241–57; Fiona Somerset, "Emotion," in *The Cambridge Companion to Christian Mysticism*, ed. Amy Hollywood and Patricia Z. Beckman (Cambridge: Cambridge University Press, 2012), 294–304; on the inner and outer wits, see further chap. 6, and the references given there.

through both social practice and written texts.[43] In these ways it seems well suited to the study of lollard writings—more so, finally (although I have learned much from them), than the work of historians of emotion who seek to analyse "emotional communities," "emotional scripts," or "emotives" deployed within "emotional regimes" and "emotional refuges."[44]

The writers and readers of lollard writings are, after all, not so much an identifiable, cohesive local group as variously fixed persons, usually (as far as we can tell) cohering in smaller units, who strive toward communion with the saints amid especially fraught personal and social tensions, many of which may be the product of their own efforts. Not a community, then, emotional or otherwise; indeed, their feelings are not so very differently named or evoked than in mainstream writings, except in the extremity of their emphases.[45] That extremity complicates any effort to see a written text's description of feeling as a reflection of larger cultural norms—an "emotional script." And while analysing "emotives" deployed in "regimes" and "refuges" allows attention to the relationships between texts and the dynamic structures of lived and imagined experience in a larger culture whose norms are fragmented and conflicting rather than cohesive, the contrast between regimes of suffering and refuges of comfort finds little purchase on a persecuted medieval subculture that strives toward an intensification of suffering even as it offers comfort and seeks to instill in its readers an unusually rigorous set of emotional responses to that suffering.[46] There is no refuge from regime in lollard writings.

---

43. On "structures of feeling," see especially Raymond Williams, *Marxism and Literature* (Oxford: Oxford University Press, 1977), 128–35; and for its deployment in cultural criticism, Williams, *The Country and the City* (London: Chatto and Windus, 1973).

44. On the history of emotions, see the review essay by Barbara H. Rosenwein, "Worrying about Emotions in History," *American Historical Review* 107 (2002): 821–45. The term "emotional community" is Rosenwein's: *Emotional Communities in the Early Middle Ages* (Ithaca, NY: Cornell University Press, 2006). Talk of "scripts" for emotions has been in circulation for several years: while some scholars use it to finesse the difference between writing and lived experience, sophisticated analysis may be found, e.g., in Robert A. Kaster, *Emotion, Restraint, and Community in Ancient Rome* (Oxford: Oxford University Press, 2005). For "emotives" and "emotional regimes" and "emotional refuges," see William M. Reddy, *The Navigation of Feeling: A Framework for the History of Emotions* (Cambridge: Cambridge University Press, 2001). Another study that rethinks the relationships between self, group, and a larger regime of governance is Daniel Lord Smail, *The Consumption of Justice: Emotions, Publicity, and Legal Culture in Marseille, 1264–1423* (Ithaca, NY: Cornell University Press, 2003).

45. As Barbara Rosenwein agrees: I thank her for much sustaining conversation during the writing of this book, as well as for reading the whole of it in a near-final draft.

46. Reddy, *Navigation of Feeling*, esp. chap. 3, 63–111. I treat regimes and refuges as plural in response to Reddy's more recent reflections on the relationship between the two, in Jan Plamper, "The History of Emotions: An Interview with William Reddy, Barbara Rosenwein, and Peter Stearns," *History and Theory* 49 (2010): 242–43.

Thus, the interplay between suffering and comfort is prominent through-out the *MEBS*. Any summary of a large and disparate work must foreground the themes it wants to emphasize through a process of selection, choosing what parts best represent the whole its writer apprehends and wants to convey. It will succeed, if it succeeds, through demonstrating both how it perceives the shape of the whole and how that larger whole's less representative or more difficult parts are related to the more obvious or clearer parts the writer foregrounds. The *MEBS* writer, like Jerome and like the writer of the *General Prologue*, sketches in the shape of the whole bible by including all of its books, even if the attention he devotes to them is very uneven. He achieves his emphasis of the parts that matter most to him through any number of means, but there are two I want to focus on: his introduction of a common terminology across the whole of the bible (bolded in every quotation in this chapter, to aid readers of this book in recognizing it), and his repetition and resonance between different time scales—individual life narratives, stories of kings and their realms, the history of the Jewish people, the whole of salvation history—of the narrative arc he wants to convey, from suffering to salvation.

The *MEBS* writer's cluster of keywords repeats and varies his favored narrative themes: Good beginners, perfect men, true men, good men, saints, ill men, heretics. Patience, persecution, adversity, tribulation, suffering. Predestinate, ordained. Excitation or stirring, assent or consent, witnessing, speaking in the person of, true confession. Those that shall be saved. These words and phrases are repeated and varied across long stretches of the summary, as if we should already know what they mean. Many of them crystallize into full lucidity in the context of a key quotation and its exposition: several of these fuller explanations occur in the Pauline epistles, fewer in the prophets. They are reinforced, often, through cross-referencing, especially between the epistles, Psalms, Job, and major and minor prophets, but also elsewhere. Some of these terms are strongly prevalent in lollard writings elsewhere, while others are more idiosyncratic. But the significance of these words is not that they might form a "sect vocabulary" that allows us to identify the text as lollard, but that their sustained development and elaboration across the whole bible summary requires readers, over and over, to position themselves in salvation history, between stories of the past and prophecies of the future in an uncertainly positioned, aspirational here and now.[47] This self-positioning in

---

47. On the concept of a "sect vocabulary," see Anne Hudson "A Lollard Sect Vocabulary?," repr. in *Lollards and Their Books* (London: Hambledon, 1985), 165–80, a sensitively developed, exploratory study whose conclusions have sometimes been crudely applied in attempts to identify texts as lollard.

biblical history is repetitive and also recursive: the *MEBS* writer is fascinated, as we will see, with the bible's own repeated attempts to apprehend and comment upon its own story, in part or as a whole.[48]

Like the *General Prologue*, then, this biblical version strives to make it possible for readers to grasp the bible as a whole while closely understanding certain parts of it. The summary also shares in another common impulse among lollard writers: to convey to his readers not only the conclusions but also the methods of the academic study in which he was trained. There is much evidence in *MEBS*, everywhere, of the use of academic tools for biblical study, old and new, and of an effort to make them available to a wider range of readers. Thus, the writer incorporates the Latin tags that had long identified liturgical items, especially in Psalms, and draws on the capitula lists briefly summarizing the content of biblical books that had served as finding aids to locate specific items before a fuller chapter and verse citational system was developed around the turn of the thirteenth century.[49] He also provides chapter references in the left margin through most of the manuscript, or his copyist does; but there is evidence to suggest they were one and the same person or else working in collusion and sympathy. The manuscript is very carefully copied and corrected throughout in the hand of the single scribe; the way that text is crammed onto the page in some places is suggestive of augmentation during copying; and marginal *notae* in the scribal hand appear by a range of significant passages clustered in the major and minor prophets, Maccabees, and the Pauline epistles.[50] The *MEBS* writer or copyist incorporates, as well, very extensive cross-references in situ throughout. These cover overt references and quotations in the text of the bible itself, as in Paul's interpretation of Isaac and Ishmael in Galatians 4 or Stephen's quotations from Genesis, Exodus, Deuteronomy, Amos, and Isaiah. They also cover associations created more recently, of kinds that could easily be compiled into (or may have been compiled out of) an analytical concordance, a

---

48. For the *MEBS* writer's attentiveness to the bible's own recursive summaries of its earlier content, see the discussion of Heb. 12 below, at n. 82.

49. On the development from capitula lists to chapter and verse divisions, more traditionally thought to have been an innovation of the Paris Bible, see Laura Light, "French Bibles, c. 1200–30: A New Look at the Origin of the Paris Bible," in *The Early Medieval Bible: Its Production, Decoration, and Use*, ed. Richard Gameson (Cambridge: Cambridge University Press, 1994), 155–76.

50. For marginal *notae* indicating passages of interest, see fols. 88r–v, 89r, 102v, 103v, 104r, 105v, 106v, 113r–v, 116r, 121r–v, 123v, 128r, 147v, 150r. For examples of cramming, see fol. 5r four lines down, where "of þe gift of first frutes, and of þe maner of offering of þem" is shoehorned in. Modern punctuation, capitalization, and word division are silently imposed in all manuscript transcriptions, and abbreviations are silently expanded, but the text is otherwise reproduced without alteration. As elsewhere in this book, direct quotations of the biblical text are italicized.

compendium of historical events across the Hebrew Bible, and a harmony of the four gospels.

So extensive are *MEBS*'s glosses in some books that the work might be viewed as a bible commentary as much as a biblical summary.[51] Since these glosses are especially extensive in Job and the prophets, and since the commentary on Job partly corresponds with fragmentary marginal glosses in two Wycliffite Bible manuscripts, it is tempting to compare them with the *General Prologue* writer's justification for passing quickly over Job and the prophets—that he has already produced a "glos" on Job and the major prophets and has nearly finished a similar "glos" on the minor prophets.[52] Clearly both writers view summary and commentary as complementary or even equivalent activities. It seems possible that the *MEBS* summary may be the "glos" the *General Prologue*'s writer refers to, and quite likely that the *General Prologue* writer's "glos" may be one of the *MEBS* writer's sources.[53]

The glosses include not only explanatory notes that inform readers, for example, about Hebrew burial customs,[54] not only textual notes about different titles or textual divisions or readings in different Latin versions,[55] but also

---

51. Fowler has been the only critic to call the text a "commentary," but he too agrees that it is "in part mere summary, and in part exegesis" ("Middle English Bible Commentary," 78). Commentary and summary often blend into one another in the Middle Ages; see Cédric Giraud, "Introduction to Part III," in Doležalová and Visi, *Retelling the Bible*, 185–88; and also the contribution to this section by Sabrina Corbellini, "Retelling the Bible in Medieval Italy: The Case of the Italian Gospel Harmonies," 213–28.

52. The *General Prologue* writer moves briskly through Job for this reason: "for I haue declarid in parti in þe glos hou þe harde sentenses of Ioob shulden be vndurstonde þerfor I passe ouer liȝtli now" ("Prologue to the Wycliffite Bible," 57/1963–65). He surveys the prophets quickly not only because they already have their own prologue, but because he has been working to explain them elsewhere: "for I declaride sumdel þe Greet Profetis and in parti þe Litle Profetis, and þenke soone to make an ende, wiþ Goddis helpe, of þe glose of þe Smale Profetis" (60/2079–81).

53. Notice, too, that the *MEBS* writer's commentary on Ezekiel 34 includes a complaint about fantastical biblical exposition in the present day that closely resembles that in the *General Prologue* writer's prologue to the prophetic books. Here is *MEBS* on Ezekiel 34: "þe lord demes bituix beste and beste, bituix simple men and wilde men. And also bituix wheþers and buk geet, þat are princes of flockis, whome he blames for þey defiled and disturbliden þe remenaunt of her pastures and of her waters, þat were holy scriptures þat þey hade to be fed wiþ, <u>wiþ wrong exposicions after her fantasies</u>" (fol. 127r). Here is the "Prologue to Isaiah and the Prophets": "Þerfor men moten seke þe treuþe of þe text and be war of gostli vndurstonding eþer <u>moral fantasie</u>, and ȝyue not ful credence þerto, no but it be groundid openli in þe text of hooli writ in o place eþer oþer, eþer in open resoun . . . it haþ disseyued grete men in oure daies, bi <u>ouer-greet trist to her fantasies</u> (*EA*, 87/46–51). See also chap. 6.

54. *MEBS*, fol. 104r, gloss on Jer. 8.

55. Heb. 12: "Lira þof þe wordes be diuerse þe sentence is al one" (*MEBS*, fol. 194v). This quotation from Lyra is a favorite of the *MEBS* writer's. See also 1 Cor. 1, fol. 170r: "Lira þof oþer wordes be in þe chapitres of Ysai in oure translacion þen are here rehersed of Paul neþeles þe sentence is al one." In Rom. 9 the writer notes that Paul is quoting all his authorities using the translation of the seventy interpreters (Septuagint) (*MEBS*, fol. 167v).

interpretative notes. While the writer's glosses of all these kinds are replete with citations from Lyra, the *Glossa ordinaria*, Jerome, Gregory, and others, any reader should be wary of concluding on this basis that his commentary is ideologically neutral. (To suggest that it should be, of course, is also to impose a kind of privileging of unmediated or minimally mediated access to the bible's own words that the *MEBS* writer plainly has no use for.) Even in drawing on the mainstream tradition he selects passages of lollard interest, as for example on fol. 166r, in a gloss on Romans 5, where he adds at the bottom of the page a point he draws from Lyra that finds benefit in suffering: "Nota Lira. Tribulacion wirkes pacience, as oft herping makes þe craft of herping." And he augments or even alters what he quotes, both to explicate it more fully and to turn it toward his own concerns. On Jeremiah 7, for example, where God commands Jeremiah to tell the Jews not to trust lying words, the writer presents as Jerome's commentary on the passage an interpretation that lies much closer to his own concerns than Jerome's:

> Seynt Ierom vnderstandes þerby [by this] þat we shold not set oure trist in feyre chirches and clad walles, for þe verrey [true] temple of þe lord is where true beleue and oþer vertues duellen, and þerfore sues [this it follows, that], if 3e do blessed dedes and deme right betuix [judge rightly between] a man and his neghbor, etc., God shal duelle wiþ 3ou, etc.[56]

What the writer attributes to Jerome matches closely with what lollards usually say about the true church where God dwells, and there is a marginal *nota* at the beginning of this discussion of the temple to draw it to the reader's attention.

In addition, the writer invents his own commentary. He incorporates his preferred terminology in order to draw episodes into the orbit of his overall themes. He adds textual notes that go beyond Lyra's. And he comments often on the interpretation of narrative voice, pausing to explain, for example, that in a given psalm David speaks in the person of a meek man, or that Jeremiah expresses the horror the sensual part of his soul feels. In these ways he strives to teach his readers that the truth of statements depends on who or what their speakers represent and on what they mean by them.[57] Irony, too, is a special concern, prominently glossed and fully explained.[58] His concern

---

56. *MEBS*, fol. 104r. This interpretation does not appear in Jerome's commentary on Jer. 7, as the writer implies: cf. *PL* 24, col 753A. It does, however, strongly resemble the architectural allegories lollard writers develop elsewhere.

57. Ps. 74 on fol. 50v, Jer. 20 on fol. 108r of *MEBS*, and see below.

58. See marginal glosses in *MEBS* on fols. 97r and 171r. See also 103r, 107v, 140r, 174r, 177r, 181r.

with giving his readers tools of analysis goes further: he commonly identifies and explains tropes and forms of discourse including the literal, figurative, allegorical, prophetic, moral, and disputational.[59] This book is not merely a work intended for personal reference nor a coterie production designed for an educated group. It is designed to convey information to others, and the level at which the writer's glosses are pitched suggests that the anticipated audience included members with little formal schooling.

The *MEBS* writer's treatment of the books of the bible is, nonetheless, very uneven, in a way that might surprise scholars who would expect greater uniformity in what was obviously a sustained, concerted effort.[60] As in the *General Prologue*, what the author dwells on at length and how he tries to shape his readers' consequent feelings and actions are fairly reliable measures of his depth and intensity of engagement, though perhaps not the only possible ones. Some books are summarized very briefly, as a sequence of key summary phrases and truncated direct quotations, little more than a capitula list.[61] The Song of Songs, for example, is nothing but a list of phrases occupying less than a single folio, with no analysis whatever; and there is little expansion in any of the Wisdom books, though they are everywhere infused with the writer's characteristic idioms and vocabulary.[62] This style of summary might seem evidence of lack of interest, but we should bear in mind the benefits of such a list as a finding aid and how important key evocative phrases could be in remembering the bible.[63] Abbreviated direct quotations

---

59. On literal speech, see the comment at the end of Psalms (quoted above), Isa. 45 (*MEBS*, fol. 93r). On figures, figuring, or the figurative, see *MEBS*, fols. 60r, 84v, 137r, 147r, 173r–v; on allegory, see fols. 36r, 183v; on prophecy (seeing or saying before), see fols. 39v, 43r–v, 45v, 189r. Most psalms end with a "moral" exposition. For comments on or rehearsal of disputation or debate, see fols. 35r–v, 99v, 105v.

60. Dove, for example, assumes that the same depth would have been intended throughout (*FEB*, 161–62).

61. On capitula lists, see part 1 of Donatien de Bruyne, *Sommaires, divisions et rubriques de la Bible latine* (Namur: Auguste Godenne, 1914), 1–423.

62. For the Song of Songs, see *MEBS*, fol. 74r–v. For some examples of the writer's idioms and vocabulary in the wisdom books, see Prov. 1, where those who perfectly serve God need not be afraid and will attain bliss (fol. 68v); Prov. 24 on the perdition of those who assent to backbiters, as well as backbiters themselves (fol. 71v); Wisd. 6, where the writer reportedly speaks in the person of Solomon (fol. 75v); Wisd. 10, which becomes a miniature biblical summary where the names of those alluded to are added in (fol. 75v); Ecclus. 11:9, where "consent not to wrong dome [judgment]" adapts the biblical text, exactly as the LV gloss on the same verse does (fol. 77v and cf. J. Forshall and F. Madden, eds., *The Holy Bible, Containing the Old and New Testaments, with the Apocryphal Books, in the Earliest English Versions, made from the Latin Vulgate by John Wycliffe and his Followers*, 4 vols. [Oxford, 1850; repr. New York: AMS Press, 1982], 3:143); Ecclus. 27, where the temptation of tribulation proves the just (fol. 79v), and chap. 42, where "he made seyntes to tel oute his merueyles" (fol. 82).

63. On the use of mnemonic triggers, see Doležalová, "*Biblia quasi in saculo*"; Daniel Hobbins, *Authorship and Publicity before Print: Jean Gerson and the Transformation of Late Medieval Learning*

appear in books treated at more length, as well, and there they often appear at sites of especially intensive interest. (The highest-interest quotations, perhaps, are those included at length, rather than truncated, as at John 14:15, the lollard favorite "If any man luf [loves] me he shal kepe my worde and my fadre shal luf hym" [fol. 164r].)

For the most part, and in stark contrast to the *General Prologue*, the narrative books of the bible are summarized briefly and with little reference to the moral import that might be drawn from their stories. Acts gets the longest and most discursive treatment of any narrative book, seemingly because of the importance of its events to the founding and constitution of the Christian church. The books from Genesis through to Esther are surveyed briefly except where narrative event allows the writer to develop his favorite themes. There are flashes of topicality, as when the account of God's resolution of potential schism in Numbers 16 explains that after the earth engulfs Dathan and Abiron and all their kin, "Eleaʒarus þe son of Aaron made plates of þe censours and festend [fastened] þem to þe awter [altar] in mynde [remembrance] and token [as a symbol] þat in tyme comyng oþer [others] shold not take vpon hem wrongfully þe office of prestehod"—a symbolic action whose implications are here implied to extend up to the present.[64] The treatment of the gospels is if anything even more cursory than that of the historical books of the Hebrew Bible: a brief narration of main events, evocative partial quotations, cross-references to the prophecies its events fulfil, and heavily cumulative cross-referencing of the contents of previous gospels. On the other hand, the persecution and resistance of the Jews in 1 Maccabees, though now incomplete owing to missing leaves, provides the writer with a telling analogue for his own present and prompts elaboration as well as detailed retelling. The writer expatiates on the scene in chapter 3 where the Jews fast and "spred bokis o brode [opened up books] to shewe þat þey were redy to put hemself to perrel [in danger] of deþe for þe lawe," in preparation to dispute the interpretation of the bible with "heþen men þat were letterd" who argue that it authorizes the worship of "simulacres [images]" (fol. 150r). This moment is almost too rich with present resonances and is one of those accompanied by an approving marginal *nota*.

(Philadelphia: University of Pennsylvania Press, 2009), 171–72. More generally, see the essays in part 1 of Lucie Doležalová, ed., *The Making of Memory in the Middle Ages* (Leiden: Brill, 2010), 31–213; and for a useful introduction and a range of translated texts, Mary Carruthers and Jan M. Ziolkowski, eds. and trans., *The Medieval Craft of Memory: An Anthology of Texts and Pictures* (Philadelphia: University of Pennsylvania Press, 2002).

64. *MEBS*, fol. 7r. For lollard interest in this episode elsewhere, see the *Dialogue between a Wise Man and a Fool*, edited as "Cambridge Tract XII" in *EA*, 139/339–140/355.

Treated at far greater length and through the insertion of extensive commentary are Job, the major and minor prophets, the Psalms, and the Pauline epistles. The writer develops his commentary on each of these in distinctive ways that require separate discussion. Job is the difficult book whose varied content spurs him to develop analytical techniques he will use again more fully in commenting on the prophets and on the Psalms. Psalms is treated in extraordinary detail, at great length, using the analytical technique of division into parts developed in Job. The prophets are the occasion for some of the text's most argumentative and presentist moments. The Pauline epistles are different again: full of evocative part-quotations on the one hand, and more concerned than any other book to explain the concepts that undergird the writer's whole commentary on the other. Here more than anywhere else in this range of books that present lyrical first-person speaking of the truth, commentary focuses on how the speaker—here Paul—means what he says, and thus how it is that his words contain truth: in what person, in what voice, in what mode. One of the writer's favorite annotations is "yronice, as who sey, 'nay,'" and another is that X is speaking "in the person of" Christ, or the church, or a part of himself, or someone different from himself.

The book of Job is not easy to summarize: at full length it is an uneasy amalgam of ponderous narrative, lengthy speeches that form a protracted dialogue, and lyrical, evocative expressions of complaint and faith. For the book's narrative portions, the *MEBS* writer falls back on his usual strategy of briefly listing events. The book's famous sayings he presents as truncated quotations: "I cam naked into þis world etc."[65] Its dialogue prompts him to develop an analytical approach that divides argument into parts, one that he will use much more extensively in Psalms. In chapter 3, for example, he makes the following observation, citing Lyra:

> þis chapitre is parted into ij: First Iob curses to þe begynning of his life and to þe tyme of his begynning. In þe second parte þere *Why is light gyuen to þe wrech* etc. he weyles [bewails] þe continuacion of þe life of wreched men in general and telles of his owne sorw [sorrow] in special [particular]. (fol. 32r)

While the writer may indeed have learned these analytic habits of thought from reading Lyra, Lyra himself does not divide the chapter in this way at the outset in his commentary on Job: his characterization of the overall argument of the chapter is dispersed across his analysis and takes considerable acumen to extract.[66]

---

65. Job 1:21; see *MEBS*, fol. 31v.

66. There is no modern edition of Lyra's *Postilla on Job*, but scanned pdfs of the unfoliated Venice 1488 edition are readily available: see http://www.umilta.net/nicholalyra.html.

Still, what prompts extended analysis of Job 3, from both Lyra and the
MEBS writer and from the authors they cite among others, is not its overall
form but its troublesome content. Job's cursing and complaining requires
some explanation, given how much the Christian tradition more generally,
and the *MEBS* writer in particular, values patience in response to tribulation.
So it is that an excursus between the summaries of chapters 2 and 3 develops
one of this writer's longest explanatory glosses:

> Here is to vnderstand [we should understand] þat þe wordes of Iob in
> þe thrid chapitre and after, þat semen to a fleschly man þat hace not þe
> gostly [spiritual] vnderstanding of scripture as [as if] þey sowned [tended
> toward] inpacience or blasfemy. Þem most outher [they should either]
> be vnderstanden gostly, as Seynt Gregori in his Morals and oþer doctours
> expoune hem; or elles þey are spoken after þe disposicion of þe sensual
> parte þat often suffers peynes wiþ heuynes [heavily] þat reson þorw þe
> vertu of pacience re[fol. 32r]ceyues wiþ greet gladnes. Or elles, as Lira
> seys, þem most be taken noght þat Iob spekes þem of his owne sentence
> [wisdom], bot as wordes dryuen owte by disputacion of [in disputing
> with] þe errand [erring] wordes of þem þat disputed wiþ hym. For þof
> [although] his frenedes seyd many tru þinges, ʒit þey erred in summe
> þinges. And so Iob concluded of her erring sentence many wordes þat
> shold sue of [follow from] her errours. Þus to vnderstond Iob, shal `he´[67]
> neþer be noted of inpacience nor of blasfemy. (fols. 31v–32r)

The *MEBS* writer cites the explanations by Gregory and Aquinas that Lyra
discusses (though without naming Aquinas as the source of the second) before
arriving at his own. He may also know the closely similar glosses on Job 3 found
in two LV manuscripts, for his explanation differs from Lyra's, and resembles
that of the LV glosses, in that he does not choose between the alternatives he
proposes.[68] Instead, he stresses what his readers should conclude, whichever
explanation they may favor: despite appearances, Job is not impatient.

Later on, however, in commenting on Jeremiah 20's similarly troubling
complaint, the writer favors, several times over, Aquinas's explanation that
these complaints express the horror at persecution felt by the sensory part of
the soul. Here, this horror is the beginning of a narrative episode in which
Jeremiah repudiates these impulses:

---

67. *insert from marg.*

68. For the glosses, see Forshall and Madden, *Holy Bible*, 2:676. The two manuscripts are London,
British Library, Cotton Claudius E.2 and Royal 1.C.ix. Both were originally complete copies of the
bible produced in the first decade of the fifteenth century: see *FEB*, 163.

Lord þou hace deceyued me etc. þat is, for þou send me to **prophecie**
I suffre mycle [much] yuel [evil]. Þise are þe wordes of Ieremy expres-
sand þe horrour of his sensualite [expressing how his senses recoil] in
regarde of [when contemplating] **persecucion** þat he sufferd, al þof
[even though] he sufferd paciently such **persecucion** after þe dome
[judgment] of his reson. As it seyde like [similarly] before of Iob, in his
boke sone after þe begynnyng. *Þou was strengher þen I*, bowand [bow-
ing] my wille to þi wille, and made me to **prophecie**, which office
I dred after my sensualite [feared with my senses], for disese þat ap-
pered [the discomfort it caused], for þe peple scornes me, for I cry at þi
bidding [order] þat þey shal be wasted [destroyed] for her wickednes.
And I seyd in my þoght after þe **stiryng** of sensualite, "I *shal no more
speke in þe lordes name.*" Bot þe worde of God was in *my hert as fire* [like
a fire] þat wold brest [burst] oute, *and I myght not suffre*. Bot me most
execute [I had to take up] Goddes **stirryng** wiþinforthe [within] and
prophecie, not wiþstanding þat I here [hear] and knowe þat I shal be
despised of many men, and þat men lig [lie] in weyte [wait] to pursue
me, etc. Bot ȝit he was **conforted** in þat, þat he felid þat þe lord as
a strong werrioure was wiþ hym, and þerfore his pursuers shold falle,
which vnderstode not euurlasting shenship [cursedness] of helle. And
þirstand þe rightwisnes of [fol. 108v] God [thirsting for God's righ-
teousness], he askes vengaunce on þem and **excites** oþer men to hery
[praise] God wiþ hym. *Cursed be þe dey wherein I was borne* etc. In þise
wordes Ieremy declares [explains] þe hydousnes [hideousness] of his
sensualite in comparison of [with] sorwe and **traueile** þat he se [sees]
to cum [coming], as is bifore seyd. (fol. 108r–v)

This is a compellingly detailed and empathetic description of emotional conflict over speaking the truth under persecution: a briefer gloss on the passage
containing some close verbal echoes appears in full in nine LV manuscripts,
truncated in two more.[69] As will also be the case in the summary of Paul's
epistles, the commentary shifts between first-person voicing of Jeremiah's
inner struggle and third-person commentary upon it, in a way that both
invites and bespeaks empathy with its difficulty. As was the case with Judas's
followers in Maccabees spreading their books abroad on the eve of battle, the

---

69. Quoted with full details about the manuscripts in *FEB*, 163: "þese ben not wordis of Jer-
emie vnpacient and dispeiringe [impatient and despairing], but in þis he declareþ þe hidousnesse of
sensualite in comparisoun of euil neiȝinge [coming near], which euil, þat is peyne [suffering], þe
resoun suffrede pacientli, as seint Joob, ensaumpler [exemplar] of pacience, seide *þe dai pershe* [may the
day perish] *in which I was born*, and þis is þe sentence [meaning], *cursid be þe dai*, etc., þat is, if I suede

resonances with the writer's present-day situation (and perhaps that of his anticipated readers) are hard to miss. It is easy to understand why the commentary introduces a comfort ("Bot ȝit he was conforted") that the biblical chapter itself, in contrast, never expresses.

From the beginning of his summary of Jeremiah, the *MEBS* writer is fascinated with the model for true speech Jeremiah might provide. In commenting on Jeremiah 1, he provides us some insight into why lollard writers are strangely preoccupied in other writings, for reasons they do not explain, with Jeremiah's hallowing in his mother's womb:

> He was **predestinate** or he were fourmed. He was halwed in his modre wombe, purged of original synne. . . . Þe lord . . . wold be wiþ hym hymself to delyuer hym, gifing hym **pacience** wherby he ouercam alle his **tribulacions**. (fol. 101v)

There is, of course, no mention of patience during tribulations in Jeremiah 1: here Jeremiah becomes a sort of proto-martyr as well as a proto-Christ, modelling predestinate patience for the summary's readers.[70]

Another telling linkage between Christ's passion and Jeremiah's mission that echoes lollard discourse elsewhere emerges in Jeremiah 25 and in the *MEBS* writer's unprompted reference to that interpretation in commenting on Isaiah 27. In Jeremiah 25, Jeremiah takes the cup of God's anger—accepting his prophetic authority—and offers the tribulation it promises to the recipients of his prophecy, promising vengeance upon Jerusalem, the cities of Juda, Pharaoh and his servants, and many other kings and their lands. If they refuse the cup, disbelieving his prophecy, they will drink it whether they will or no.[71] Earlier, in Isaiah 27, the *MEBS* writer introduces the same motif,

---

[followed] þe hidousnesse of sensualite I shulde curse þe time of my birþe, Lire here." I omit Dove's interpolated explanatory notes.

70. Other writings that discuss Jeremiah being hallowed in his mother's womb include "On Feigned Contemplative Life," in Matthew, 188/22–26; and Rolf H. Bremmer, Jr., ed., *The Fyve Wyttes* (Amsterdam: Rodopi, 1987), 2/12–14. A more oblique reference that does not name Jeremiah appears in the *Dialogue between a Friar and a Secular*, in *FWD*, 35/111–13.

71. *MEBS*, fol. 110r: "þen Ieremy is biden to take þe cup of wyne of Goddes wodenes [anger] and birl [offer] etc., þat is to sey þat he prophecie to heþen men how God shal ponysch hem, and þey shal be disturbeld and as wode [like madmen] for drede of suerd [sword] and sorwe þat shal cum to hem. He toke þe cup and birled, þat is, he toke auctorite of God and prophecied first ageyne Ierusalem and to alle þe citese of Iuda, etc. what tribulacion shold cum to hem. Þen he prophecies ageyne Pharao þe king of Egipt and his seruantes etc., and ageyne many oþer kinges of oþer landes whose names he expresses. And he seys to þem, '*Drink ȝe and be ȝe dronken* etc.,' þat is to sey, as a dronken man hace no wit nor myght of withstanding [power to withstand], so ȝe shal not mo wiþstand þe vengaunce of God. And when þey nil [do not want to] take þe cup etc., þat is, þat þey refuse his prophecie as fals, he is biden [ordered] to sey þat wille þey, nil þey, þey shal drink of þe cup of peyne,

despite lack of any warrant in the biblical text. When it is his saints who are in question, God takes pains to explain that he offers tribulation to them not out of indignation but to ensure their salvation: "þe lord seys þat it is not of indignacion þat he birles [offers] or gifes [gives] drink of tribulacion in þis world to his seyntes. Bot he kepes hem night and dey vndur his ʒerd [rod], lest it be visited ageyn þem [brandished against them] in þe dey of dome"; there is a marginal "Nota" by this passage (fol. 88r). In Isaiah 51, in contrast, God offers a cup of indignation to the Jews who denied Christ and were then later destroyed at the siege of Jerusalem by the Romans but also promises to take the cup away if they will do penance (fol. 95r). In contrast with this rich layering of comparison and historical resonance in prophetic discourse on the drinking of a cup, the cup of his passion that Christ offers to share with his apostles in Matthew 20:22 and Mark 10:38 is scarcely mentioned.[72]

The resonances developed here help to explain the rich concatenation of associations with drinking the cup of Christ's passion deployed in the *Dialogue between a Wise Man and a Fool*:

> Bere we gladly [let us gladly bear] þis cros of tribulacioun, be ensanple [at the example] of Crist and his holy apostlis, þat ʒeden [went] ioyynge [rejoicing] fro þe biholdynge [sight] of wicked princes (Acts 5:41–42), and þe cause whi was þis, þat þe kynge of mercy made hem able and worþi to suffre peyne and dispite for shewynge of his name to þe peple. Þerfore, drynke we gladly of þe cuppe of Cristis passioun, trustynge stidfastly in Poulis wordis, seiynge on þis [fol. 64r] wise "ʒif *ʒe ben parteners* [partners] wiþ Crist *in tribulaciouns* and peynes, þan dar ʒee not doute *ʒe schal be parteners of* his eendeles *blessis*" (2 Cor. 1:7; cf. Rom. 8:17).

And a few lines later,

> For þese counfortable wordis of oure Aʒenbiere and of hise holy folowers, eche trewe soule [should] take þe vois of [take on the voice of, that is, speak in the person of] holy Dauiþ seiynge þus: "I *schal take* gladly þe holsum *cupe* of tribulacioun, *and* in drynkeynge of Cristis cuppe

---

for siþen God began at Ierusalem to tourment it, where his name was clepid [called] to help, heþen folk þat wirchipped ydols shold not be as innocentis wiþoute peyne, for *þe lord shal rore fro an hy* [roar from on high], *ponisching his feyrenes* [beauty], þat is, Ierusalem and þe temple."

72. Admittedly, Matt. 20 was on a missing leaf after fol. 153, and it is possible that it has been removed because of its content—though to have expatiated on drinking of a cup here would be inconsistent with the writer's practice elsewhere in his exposition of the gospels. There is the barest mention in Mark 10: see *MEBS*, fol. 156v.

I *schal* ynwardly *clepe* his *name* to helpe" (Ps. 116:13). (*EA*, 133/107–13, 121–24)

The Wise Man exhorts the Fool toward an apostolic joy in drinking the cup of Christ's passion and suffering pain and contempt when he shows forth Christ's name. But only the rich associations of the prophetic books explain why taking on the voice of David means taking a cup of tribulation, why taking the cup of tribulation means accepting prophetic authority and speaking the truth, why drinking Christ's cup entails suffering followed by vindication and is different from merely suffering God's indignation, why the psalm quotation at the end of this passage is so heavily interpolated (only the italicized words are biblical) in order to bring all these associations together. This concatenation of significance may also give us insight into why the Coventry lollard group in the early sixteenth century chose "May we all drink of a cup" as a password by which they identified themselves to one another.[73]

With the precise historical anchoring in an individual life narrative that the *MEBS* writer provides in his summaries of the prophets, and reinforces in these books through frequent cross-references to the larger historical events recounted in Kings and Paralipomenon, and with the anticipation of what is to come that fuels prophetic discourse and its later accretions of typological import, comes the freedom to range across salvation history, from Christ's passion to the siege of Jerusalem to the Day of Judgment. But if the prophetic books are where history really comes into the picture for the *MEBS* writer, then that history comes in principally to give evidence about sin, suffering, and vindication either occasioned by or occasioning the true speech of true believers who complain at and celebrate it. This writer does not have the kind of interest in the rise and fall of kings, and their import for kings and lords in the present, that we saw in the *General Prologue*. Instead, the prophets provide a series of divinely inspired or authenticated statements about past, present, and future that allow the *MEBS* writer to position the reforming aspirations of true believers in a dynamic economy of suffering and vindication, both for the individual Christian and across the narrative of salvation history. After giving this sense of history a very full airing here, he evokes the sense of history he instills here more briefly and allusively throughout Psalms, and he revisits it in developing the relationship between Acts and the Pauline epistles.

The careful attention the *MEBS* writer gives to the book of Psalms should come as no surprise. Lollards devote extensive attention to the Psalms

---

73. McSheffrey and Tanner, *Lollards of Coventry*, 182–83, 117.

elsewhere: they interpolate Rolle's *English Psalter*, and copies of their translation of Psalms that are heavily glossed, redacted into catenae of quotations
with or without interspersed commentary, and supplied with multiple prologues show their intensive interest in this book. Two of the four prologues
supplied for Psalms in manuscripts of the Wycliffite Bible are adapted from
Rolle's prologue to his *English Psalter*, and some of this material finds its way
into the *General Prologue* as well, both in the brief summary of Psalms common to most copies of the *General Prologue* and in the extended treatment of
Psalms adjoined to the *General Prologue* in Dublin, Trinity College, MS 72.[74]
Even in the brief summary common to most copies, the writer explains that
Psalms condenses within itself all the narrative and mystery of the bible as
a whole:

> Þe Sauter comprehendiþ [encompasses] al þe elde [old] and new tes-
> tament and techiþ pleynli þe mysteries of þe Trinite and of Cristis
> incarnacioun, passioun, risyng aʒen and stiyng [ascending] into heuene
> and sendyng doun of þe Hooli Goost and prechyng of þe gospel, and
> þe comyng of antecrist, and þe general doom [judgment] of Crist, and
> þe glorie of chosun men to blisse and þe peynes of hem þat shulen be
> dampned [fol. 12ra] in helle; and ofte rehersiþ þe stories of þe elde
> testament, and bryngeþ in þe kepyng of Goddis heestis and loue of
> enemyes. (58/2007–14)

The notion that the Psalter epitomizes in some sense the truth contained in
the bible was widespread in the Middle Ages.[75] What is telling about this
quotation is just what it includes in its brief account of the whole of biblical
truth. In contrast with the prologue by Rolle that the *General Prologue* writer
is adapting, this account gives us a compressed account of salvation history,
the "stories of þe elde testament," and the commandments: just the priorities
we would expect from a lollard writer or indeed on the basis of the *General*

---

74. For details on this material I am indebted to Michael Kuczynski for his careful work on
lollard commentary on the psalms, and especially several conversations about his edition of Oxford,
Bodleian Library, MS Bodley 554. I also thank him for allowing me to read his article on HM 501
in advance of publication (see n. 5). I am grateful to Liz Schirmer as well, for stimulating conversations about individual lollard manuscripts and for allowing me to read her "Canon Wars and Outlier
Manuscripts" in draft (see nn. 20, 23).

75. Compare with the prologue to Rolle's *English Psalter*, in Jocelyn Wogan-Browne et al., eds.,
The Idea of the Vernacular: An Anthology of Middle English Literary Theory, 1280–1520 (University Park:
Pennsylvania State University Press, 1999), 246/37–46. For a very full survey of the patristic sources
for understanding the Psalms as an epitome, see Anne Lake Prescott, "King David as a 'Right Poet':
Sidney and the Psalmist," *English Literary Renaissance* 19 (1989): 131–51. Thanks to Clare Costley
King'oo for this reference.

Prologue as a whole. Rolle instead summarizes "the lare of the Ald Testament and of the New" as a catalogue of life stories that morphs into indirect advice about the best way of life in the world:

> Tharein is discryved [described] the medes [rewards] of goed men, the pynes [punishment] of ill men, the disciplyne of penaunce, the waxynge [growing] in rightwise lif, the perfeccioun of haly men the whilk passis til [goes up to] heven, the lyf of actyf men, the meditacioun of contemplatifs and the joy of contemplacioun, the heghest that may be in man lifand [living] in body and feland [feeling]; alswa what synne reves fra [takes away from] mannys saule and what penaunce restores.[76]

That the life stories in the bible might spur readers toward contemplation and penance is understood, rather than explained. The *MEBS* writer, in contrast, surveys the implications throughout salvation history up to the present day, the historical occasion as he understands it, and the moral import of each psalm in turn in a way that suggests that he agrees quite closely with the *General Prologue* writer about what it is that comprises the Psalter's comprehensive content.

In concluding his summary of the book of Psalms, the *MEBS* writer comments overtly on how he incorporates and cites the commentators he consults:

> It is to wit [we should understand] þat in þis declaracion [explanation] of þe psauter, Lira shewes þe litteral sense and þe glose, þat is þe comyn glose [*Glossa ordinaria*], oþer senses. Wherfore where þe declaracion of Lira diuerses [differs] noght or litel fro þe comyn glose, þere is not rehersed distinctly what Lira seys and what þe glose seys. Forþermore, where þou findes þis worde "Morali" wiþ a shorte shewing of moral vnderstanding in þe endes of declaracion of psalmes, þat is comynly taken of Lira. (fol. 68r)

He admits here to a certain economy of reference: where Lyra and the *Glossa ordinaria* give the same interpretation he will not distinguish between them, and where he gives a moral interpretation in closing he may be citing Lyra even where he does not say so. But even in describing his own imprecisions of citation, he implies a heavy dependence on previous commentary, most especially where he presents moral teachings. The writer may in fact believe

---

76. Wogan-Browne et al., *Idea of the Vernacular*, 246/39–44. Punctuation modified.

his own claims here about how derivative his commentary is. But that does not prevent him from selecting emphases and terminology that further his overall themes, and in the pursuit of tendentious implications that these commentaries did not originally have, as when in commenting on Psalm 14 he tells us that "after þe glose, þe intencion of þe Prophete here is to confounde þem þat seyne þey are of Goddes chirch and are not" (fol. 38r). His aim is not so much to disguise as to authorize departures from the norm, as he harps on persecution, tribulation, vindication, men of true belief, a community of saints including past martyrs and present sufferers, definitions of the church that include only those who shall be saved, good beginners, the perfect, speaking in the person or voice of another, and the confession of faith and praise as well as, or rather than, that of sin.[77]

In commenting on Psalms the *MEBS* writer uses an unusual scheme of analytical division into parts. His method is not entirely new: similar techniques appear in commentaries on the Pater Noster, Ave Maria, and creed, for example, and he had developed it in commenting on Job, in imitation of Lyra's commentary. But his method contrasts with the usual conventions of commentary on the Psalter and with what Lyra and the *Glossa ordinaria* provide: a detailed, lemmatized exposition in which the kind of compressed synthesis the *MEBS* writer seems to favor does not appear. His analytical compression facilitates linking the present with the past, as a sample from Psalm 43 will show:

> It is diuided into iij. First þe prophete telles what benefices [benefits] God hace shewed to **gode begynners** in þe world, and what shal be gifen to **parfite men** in heuen. Þe second þer *Bot now þou hace put abak* he noumbers illes þat **gode men** suffer here and ȝit þey forgeet not God. Þe thrid þer *Rise vp, why slepes þou lord* he preyes for Goddes help, telling how **seyntes** meken [humble] þer saules, sending pouder on þeire heedes, prostrate þeire belies to þe grounde. (fol. 43v)

The analytical division into three parts makes of David's words an ethical commentary upon the present day as well as his own. God confers favor on good beginners, still more on the perfect who persevere long enough

---

77. This is an impressionistic rather than an exhaustive list of where topics favored by lollards are treated in the Psalms: on persecution, see Pss. 3, 9, 27, 30, 63, 82, 92; on tribulation 16, 27, 106, 122; on vindication 63, 91, 92, 106; on men of true belief 5, 9, 15, 16, 27, 28, 51, 96; on the community of saints 4, 9, 12, 28, 29, 43, 44, 49, 67, 76, 82, 97, 120, 121, 136, 143, 149, 150; on the church of those that shall be saved 3, 14, 15, 45, 50, 76, 78, 85, 122, 124, 128, 131, 146, 147; on good beginners 43, 99, 133; on the perfect 1, 11, 43, 99, 132, 133, 149; on speaking in the person of another 11, 12, 34, 36, 39, 48, 76, 79, 87, 89, 93, 122, 129, 131, 144; on confession of faith 9, 29, 59, 105, 106.

to attain heaven. Good men suffer ill fortune here but do not forget God. Saints humble themselves in prayer. Each of the writer's key terms, bolded here, is treated in far more detail elsewhere.[78] The role of the psalm commentary is not to define terms but to create memorable, emotionally charged associations with the present-day situation of readers, ones that might then be reinforced by reading the psalms and witnessing or participating in their liturgical performance.

In contrast, the Pauline epistles, more even than Job and the prophets, are where the *MEBS* writer explains in more detail what he has used the Psalms to evoke. Here he justifies lollard sharp speech, authorship, and the publishing (his term) of scripture. He explains what the true Christian church consists in, and he establishes how contemporary Christians should view biblical history.[79] Like the Psalms, and for that matter the prophets, it is not surprising that a lollard writer should have chosen the Pauline epistles as a key point of reference. Even more so than for the mainstream Christian tradition, Paul's constitution of the primitive church and exemplary consolation of its tribulations was of special interest to lollards, as for example the treatment of Paul's epistles in the *English Wycliffite Sermons* on the Sunday Epistles, the separate series of Sunday Epistles sermons in *SS74*, and the *Letter of Richard Wyche* help to demonstrate. This is not to suggest, however, that the *MEBS* writer's treatment of the Pauline epistles is uniformly expository.

While in commenting on Psalms he was far more consistent, the *MEBS* writer's work with Paul's epistles resembles his approach to the book of Job: his treatment varies in response to local texture and indeed in keeping with his level of interest. Some chapter summaries are little more than catenae

---

78. For topics explained more fully in the Pauline epistles, see n. 79. The relationship between membership among the "seyntes" and true speech is most fully explained in the books of the prophets, where figural interpretation allows those who speak the truth to replace the Jews as God's people. This phenomenon in Christian commentary more broadly is addressed well in Deeana Copeland Klepper, *The Insight of Unbelievers: Nicholas of Lyra and Christian Reading of Jewish Text in the Later Middle Ages* (Philadelphia: University of Pennsylvania Press, 2007). Thus, in Jer. 23, "Iuda, þat is ich man truly knowleching Criste, shal be saued" (*MEBS*, fol. 109r). Picking up on the same interpretation of "Iuda," Isa. 26 sheds light on several psalms in making the same promise: "Here is how **seyntes** in heuen, þat is þe land of Iuda of **true confession** or knowleching, [fol. 88r] preysing God, shal syng þis song. . . . And here is of þe openyng of þe ʒates of heuen to **seyntes**, and of þe closing of þem fro vniust men" (fols. 87v–88r).

79. On sharp speech, see 2 Cor. 7, 10, and 12. On how "we" should preach even on pain of death, see 2 Cor. 4. On publishing Christ's word, see Rom. 10, 14, 16, and 1 Thess. 1. On the importance of reading together where not everyone knows Latin, see 1 Cor. 14. On the church as all saints in heaven, earth, and purgatory, see Eph. 1; on the church as the congregation of the faithful, see Heb. 3. On "seyntes," see Rom. 15, 1 Cor. 6 and 15, Eph. 6, 1 Thess. 4, 2 Thess. 1, Heb. 9 and 10. On good beginners versus "parfit," see Col. 1 and Heb. 5. On "parfit" or "parfitly," see Rom. 14, 1 Cor. 2, 1 Cor. 3, 1 Cor. 7, 1 Cor. 14, 2 Cor. 5, 2 Cor. 13, Eph. 4, Heb. 4, Heb. 5.

of evocative, abbreviated quotations, some incorporate the writer's favoured themes and terms, some are commentary that expatiates on the writer's understanding of Paul's key point, and some seize the occasion to explain a key term at length. Most incorporate very full cross-references elucidating Paul's frequent references to the Hebrew Bible and New Testament. Resonances with the Psalms are especially common, reinforced not only by marginal cross-references but by reduplicated keywords. The effect can perhaps best be demonstrated by examining the writer's treatment of Romans 8:26–39, a kind of evocative catena. As elsewhere in this book, biblical phrases, or near echoes of them, are italicized in this quotation, while interpretative glosses and modifications of the biblical text are left in roman type.

> *We wot not what is bihouely* [fitting] *for vs to prey, Bote þe spirit axes for vs*, etc., þat is, þe Holy Gost makes vs to prey etc. Þe Holy Gost, from whome no hert is hid, makes **seyntes** to prey after þe wille of God. *Alle þinges wirken togidre into gode of hem* þat are ordeyned to be saued etc. *Þilk þat God bifore ordeynd to blis, hem he called* etc. *If God for vs, who is ageyn vs, þat spared not his owne son* etc.? *Who shal accuse ageyn þe chosen of God* etc.? *Iesus preyes for vs. Who shal departe vs fro þe charite of Crist, tribulacion or anguysch* etc.? Þat **seyntes** shold suffre such **tribulacions** he allegges (Ps. 43). I *am certen þat neþer deþe nor life etc. mey departe vs fro the charite of God.* (fol. 167r)

As will readily be apparent, this rendition is little more than a string of key phrases. These seem to be aides-memoire or perhaps study aids. As in the writer's quotation of key phrases to develop his analytical divisions in Psalms, it seems likely that he either expects his readers to remember the whole of the epistle based on his quotations or expects readers to use them as reference points in referring to a copy of the whole text. The only nonbibical interjections are respectively an interpretative expansion, a paraphrase, and a cross-reference, all seemingly with the aim of ensuring correct understanding.

In his first two sentences the writer incorporates Lyra's glosses (given separately, for example, in manuscripts of the Wycliffite Bible) to reassure his readers that the Holy Spirit ensures that "seyntes" pray as God wills.[80] With "þat are ordeyned to be saued" he elegantly incorporates the combined

---

80. The LV of the Wycliffite Bible, complete with glosses taken from London, British Library, MS Harley 5017, provided in the margin in Forshall and Madden, *Holy Bible*, 4:320, col. 2, and here in square brackets with underlining: "And also the spirit helpith oure infirmyte; for what we schulen preie, as it bihoueth, we witen not, but the ilke spirit axith [that is, makith us to axe. Lyre and Austyn and the Glos here] for vs with sorewyngis, that moun not be told out. For he that sekith the hertis, woot what the spirit desirith, for bi God [that is, at Goddis wille. Lire here] he axith for hooli men."

wisdom of Augustine, the *Glossa ordinaria*, and Lyra on how to translate
"secundum propositum" in the Vulgate's "iis qui secundum propositum vo-
cati sunt sancti," or as the Wycliffite Bible LV renders it "hem that aftir
purpos ben clepid seyntis."[81] He also in the process omits a biblical reference
to the saved as "sancti"—even if he himself uses the term in his first and
third added passages—in favor of explaining what it means: those who are
ordained to be saved. Toward the end of the passage quoted here, notice that
rather than elaborating on the "tribulacion or anguysch etc." that cannot
separate "seyntes" from God's charity, he instead provides us a cross-reference
to Psalm 43. But rather than suppressing the theme of suffering, this cross-
reference amplifies it. Recall that the *MEBS* writer's analytical division of
Psalm 43, quoted above, emphasizes how tribulation plays a role in a narrative
of spiritual growth. "Gode begynners" see evidence of God's goodness but
then undergo suffering on their way to become "parfite men" in heaven.
Rather than rejecting God as they suffer adversity, they humble themselves
and pray. Combined, as the cross-reference encourages readers to combine
them, the two expositions offer redoubled reassurance: tribulation cannot
separate "seyntes" from God, and what is more, it brings them closer to him.

In a biblical summary fascinated with the bible's own recursive summarizing of its own content, the interpretative biblical summary of Hebrews
11–12 becomes perhaps this writer's most telling precedent for his own endeavor. In addition to frequent orientations of specific events in relation to
a larger historical narrative, the *MEBS* writer dwells in turn on no less than
five summaries of history provided in the bible itself: those in Wisdom 10,
Daniel 2 and 7, Acts 7, and Hebrews 11–12. The last of these becomes in
his hands perhaps the most elliptical and allusive biblical summary anywhere:

> *Feyth*[82] *is substaunce of þinges to be hoped* etc. Fadres of þe old lawe hade
> witnes of godenes of God for merit of her feyth. *By feyth we vnder-
> standen þat worldes were made* etc. Ensaumples of old fadres, what þey
> wroȝten of her feyth [did out of faith]. Of þe feyth of Abel, of Enoch.
> *It is impossible to plese God wiþout feyth. It bihoues a man comyng to God to
> bileue þat he is* etc. Of þe feyth of Noe. Of þe feyth of Abraham etc. And
> how Abraham bileued þat God wold haue reysed Ysaac fro deþe to fulfil

81. LV with Harley 5017 glosses in square brackets with underlining: "And we witen, that to men that louen God, alle thingis worchen togidere in to good, to hem that aftir purpos [that is, pre-destynacioun ether bifore ordeynyng by grace. Lyre, Austyn and the Glos here] ben clepid seyntis" (Forshall and Madden, *Holy Bible*, 4:320, col. 2).

82. The two-line capital that should be an F at the opening here has been incorrectly executed as an H.

his biheste [promise] þof [even if] he had sleyne hym in to sacrifice, and
he vnderstode þe offering of Ysaac was a parable or figure of Cristes
passion. Of þe feyth of Ysaac. Of Iacob and how he, lenyng on þe ouur
[top] ende of Iosephs ӡerd or staf, wirchipt [worshipped] þe lord, or
elles by þe hyӡnes [height] of þe ӡerd is vnderstanden Crist, by whome
Ioseph had þe septre [sceptre] of lordchip in Egipt. Of Ioseph. Of þe
feyth of þe fadre and modre of Moyses. Of þe feyth of Moyses. *By feyth
þe walles of Iericho fel doun* (Josh. 6). Of Raab. Of þe feyth of Gedeon,
Barach, Sampson, Iepte, Dauid, Samuel and oþer prophetes which by
feyth ouurcamen rewmes [overcame kingdoms]. And many oþer grete
dedes he reherses [repeats] þat þey did by feyth. And what **tribulacions**
þey **suffred** for feyth. Fadres of þe old lawe receyued not ful ioy [the
full joy] of body and saul, bot after þe general resurrection boþe þey and
seyntes of þe new lawe shal receyue ful ioy of body and saul. (fol. 194v)

The figural significances seeded into the summary of chapter 11 here are traditional rather than unprecedented, even if the author of Hebrews only explicitly
mentions the first, that Abraham understands that Isaac is a parable or, as medieval readers understood this, a figure of Christ.[83] The summarizer here inserts the second traditional interpretation, that the height of Joseph's staff may
symbolize Christ, and infuses some of his favorite keywords here at the end.

The beginning of chapter 12 is more startling: here the writer steps back
from allusive evocation of the text interspersed with interpretative expansion
in order to consider, in a more expansive expository mode, what effect he
thinks its author intends upon readers in the present:

He **stires** vs to **pacience** by ensaumple of so many **seyntes** þat are
witnesses of feyth, which by her ensaumple refreschen vs in þe hete
[heat] of **tribulacion** and reynen [rain] on vs her holy doctrine, wherfore [for which] þey are lickend [likened] to cloudes. And specialy
by þe ensaumple of Iesus Crist etc. Also by auctorite of scripture
(Prov. 3), *My son nil þou despise* [do not despise] etc., *for þe lord chastises
hym þat he loues* etc. Lira: þof [although] þe wordes be diuerse [differ-
ent], þe sentence is al one. If ӡe [you] be wiþout chastesing wherof al
þe sones of God are partineris [partners], þen are ӡe sones of þe world
or of þe `flesch´,[84] auoutrere [adulterers] and not of God. (fol. 194v)

---

83. For an example of the use of this interpretation by Nicholas Gorran, and the complications
in the late medieval understanding of the relationship between allegory and history that it suggests,
see Ocker, *Biblical Poetics*, 47.

84. The inner margin has eroded here, leaving a hole in the page.

The examples of the "seyntes" who have suffered tribulation in witnessing faith, and most especially the example of Christ, refresh "vs," the *MEBS* writer and his audience, in the heat of tribulation and stir "vs" to patience. All the sons of God are partners in tribulation, and all of them, if they witness faith, can expect the same reward. Here, in a very few words, is a compelling attestation of the importance of interpretative biblical summary, no less than the bible's own words, to the lollard movement.

The central importance of interpretative biblical summary for lollard writers has been largely overlooked in scholarship, perhaps mainly because of the emphasis, in English religious history, on lollard translation and provision to the laity of the bible's own unmediated words. Yet in retelling the bible lollards respond to its own recursive tendencies. These are especially marked in the medieval Christian tradition as it cumulatively recasts the Hebrew Bible as an anticipation of a New Testament everywhere marked by figural anticipation and fulfillment. But they are also present across the course of the Hebrew Bible, and within the New Testament itself, in a long sequence of recursive summary retellings and evocations that were seemingly part of the Jewish tradition of collecting sacred writings from its earliest stages.[85] In participating in this recursive pattern lollards are also, of course, responding to a broader recursive impulse in Christian history itself.[86]

---

85. On the scope of this tradition, with attention to these early stages, see Tamás Visi, "Introduction," in Doležalová and Visi, *Retelling the Bible*, 13–43.

86. Here I differ with Lee Patterson, who claims that for medieval writers, Christian history is linear and dominated by a sense of decline from perfection, but that Chaucer uses the repeated recursions of Theban history to consider "questions about historical origin and the legitimacy of the historical life itself." See *Chaucer and the Subject of History* (Madison: University of Wisconsin Press, 1991), 23; see also 18 (on Augustine's sense of history) and 19–26 (on Chaucer). The cyclical patterns of "Thebanness" do not provide Chaucer with an alternative to a single, dominant Christian view of history, but rather allow Chaucer to engage (albeit with his customary indirection) with a range of recursive Christian historical models. On the dissemination of alternative Christian historiographies in England, see Kathryn Kerby-Fulton, *Books under Suspicion: Censorship and Tolerance of Revelatory Writing in Late Medieval England* (Notre Dame, IN: University of Notre Dame Press, 2006).

🍂 Part Three

❧ Chapter 6

Moral Fantasie

Normative Allegory in Lollard Writings

I begin with two lengthy quotations from late medieval English writers concerned to educate their vernacular readers in biblical exegesis. Both develop a metaphor of reading the bible with proper understanding as eating a sweet food, hidden at first, that pleases and nourishes the soul. Both of these writers insist, drawing implicitly or explicitly on 2 Corinthians 3:6, that the proper understanding of the scriptures must be spiritual, "gostly," rather than according to the letter, or "fleschly." Both stress that "gostly" understanding depends not only and not even primarily upon study but upon one's whole way of life. Anyone who wants to understand scripture must walk with the Holy Ghost: they must be properly disposed to virtue, they must live a good life, they must receive God's grace. On the other hand, "fleshly livers" and heretics will be denied understanding. The understanding both texts praise is "gostly" in that it is conferred by the "Holi Goost," a gift of grace; it is also "gostly" in that it deploys the contrast between modes of biblical reading for which 2 Corinthians 3:6 was customarily invoked: it involves moving beyond "the letter," the sometimes obscure words of the biblical text, to "the spirit," the bible's figural or allegorical interpretation.[1] Part of the point I want to underscore is that

---

1. As will already be clear, there is no way to modernize "gostly" while maintaining this fluidity and breadth of meaning, from metaphorical to allegorical to typological to nonbodily to spiritual.

few, if any, readers will find it easy to identify which of these passages has been called "lollard" (let alone "heresy") and which is by a well-known writer who is considered "orthodox":

> Holy writ haþ þe lyknesse of a tree þat beriþ fruyt—note [nut], peer or appel. Whanne it is þikke leued [thick with leaves], litil or nouȝt is seen of his [its] fruȝt, but whanne men schaken [shake] þe tree þe fruyt falliþ doun faste and þike [thick], and þan swetenesse is knowe þat was hidde aforn [before], and whanne men eten it, it plesiþ hem wel. So it fareþ bi holy writ. Þe letter semeþ derk and harde [obscure and difficult]. But ȝif a man sette his herte to see þe gostly witt [spiritual meaning] þat is þereynne [within], and ȝif he schake it wel, þat is to seie, þorouȝ studyynge þerof [study of it] and by good lyuynge, by þe grasce [grace] þat God wole [fol. 52r] þanne do to hym, myche good fruyt he schal fynde þerynne, þat ben sentenssis [wise sayings] of manye good maneris [kinds], and þe swetnesse þerof schal turne him to gret goodnesse, whiche þat a man vnderstondeþ not tyl [until] it be drawen and schaken into his owne langage. . . . Poul seiþ *"þe letter sleiþ,"* þat is, fleischly lyuers [those who live by the flesh] brekynge þe comaunde-mentis [fol. 52v] of God. *But þe spirit quikeneþ* [gives life to] alle þoo þat lyuen feiþfully after þe gostly vnderstondynge of holy writte. Wherfor Poule seiþ, *"be ȝee ledde oþer walke ȝee wiþ þe Holy Goost and ȝe schullen not fulfile þe synful desires of ȝoure fleische."*

> To a clene [pure] soule that hath the palet [palate] purified from filthe of fleschli love, Hooli Writ is liyfli [life-giving] foode and sustenaunce delitable. It savoreth wondir sweteli [tastes marvellously sweet] whanne it is weel chewid bi goostli undirstondynge. For whi [The reason why is that], the spirit of liyf is hid thereinne, that quykeneth alle the myghtes [powers] of the soule and filleth hem ful of swettenesse of hevenli savour and goosteli delite. But sotheli him nedeth [he needs] for to han white teeth and scharpe and wel piked [clean] that schulde biten on this goostli breed, for fleschli loveres [lovers of the flesh] and heretikes mowe not touche the inli flour of it [flour within]. Here

---

I will use the term "gostly" throughout this chapter, but I will also paraphrase using modern ter-minology to foreground whichever of its senses is most prominent in a given situation. Some key resources for understanding medieval uses of figural language and placing them in a broader perspec-tive are Eric Auerbach, "Figura," in Auerbach, *Scenes from the Drama of European Literature: Six Essays* (New York: Meridian, 1959), 11–76; Giles Constable, "Medieval Latin Metaphors," *Viator* 38 (2007): 1–20; Rita Copeland and Stephen Melville, "Allegory and Allegoresis, Rhetoric and Hermeneutics," *Exemplaria* 3 (1991): 159–87; Jon Whitman, ed., *Interpretation and Allegory, Antiquity to the Modern Period* (Leiden: Brill, 2000).

[Their] teeth aren blodi and ful of filthe, and therfore aren thei fastynge from feelynge [they fast from the feeling] of this breed. Bi teeth aren undirstonden inli [inward] vertues of the soule, the whiche in fleschli loveres and in heretikes aren blodi, ful of synne and of wordli vanyté; thei wolden, and thei kunnen not, come bi the curiousté [vain curiosity] of her kyndeli [natural] wit to the sothfast [true] knowynge of holi writ. For here witte is corrupt bi the original synne and actuel also, and is not yit heelid [healed] thorugh grace, and therfore thei don but gnawen upon the bark withoute. Carpe [Speak] thei nevere so moche thereof, the inli savoure withinne thei feelen not of. Thei aren not meke, thei aren not clene for to seen it; thei aren not frendis to Jhesu, and therfore he scheweth [shows] hem not his conceil. The priveté [secret knowledge] of holi writ is closid undir keie [key] seelid [sealed] with a signet of Jhesuis fyngir, that is the Holi Goost; and forthi, withouten his love and his leve [permission] mai no man come in.

The first of my two excerpts comes from one of twelve short treatises in favour of biblical translation in the lollard manuscript CUL Ii.6.26.[2] While the comparison between holy writ and a tree developed here is derived from the prologue to Robert of Gretham's *Miroir*, this version extensively interpolates then diverges from that prologue in order to develop a lollard account of "gostly" understanding, explained in more detail below. My second excerpt, in contrast, is from Walter Hilton's *Scale of Perfection*, book II, chapter 43.[3] Both the lollard writer and Hilton persuasively argue that only the virtuous can interpret scripture correctly: in any reader who hopes to discern what God has hidden in scripture, both affect and intellect must be correctly disposed. While the tone in each case is admonitory rather than permissive, each writer nonetheless makes a promise. Readers who do have the "love" and "leve" of the Holy Spirit, who set their hearts on it and work hard, will

2. "Cambridge Tract XI," in *EA*, 126–29, 126/1–10, punctuation modified. See also Nicholas Watson, "Lollardy: The Anglo-Norman Heresy?," in *Language and Culture in Medieval Britain: The French of England, c. 1100–c. 1500*, ed. Jocelyn Wogan-Browne et al. (Woodbridge: York Medieval Press, 2009), 334–46. Thanks to Nicholas for identifying the relationship with Gretham when I was first working on it, long before Dove's edition was published, and for productive discussions of its interest. See also Simon Hunt, ed., "An Edition of Tracts in Favour of Scriptural Translation and of Some Texts Connected with Lollard Vernacular Biblical Scholarship," 2 vols. (D. Phil. thesis, University of Oxford, 1994). I thank Simon for allowing me to borrow and read his thesis, and first drawing my attention to this manuscript, in 1995.

3. Walter Hilton, *The Scale of Perfection, Book II*, ed. Thomas H. Bestul, *TEAMS Middle English Text Series* online, at http://www.lib.rochester.edu/camelot/teams/hilfr2.htm, lines 3322–39 (paragraphing modified). Michael G. Sargent is preparing a critical edition; I thank him for much discussion of this text.

enjoy scripture's sweetness. Claims of this sort, when presented to new readers of the bible in the vernacular, have sometimes been viewed as populist,
contradictory, or even "disappointingly anti-intellectual."[4] Even when passages like these ones exhort their readers to study the bible carefully as well
as to set their hearts on understanding it, their descriptions of that study are
resolutely metaphorical; as "gostly," that is, as their exhortation to love. They
fail to demonstrate what techniques might be deployed in order to produce
correct interpretations, perhaps leaving the impression that once the heart is
set, all else will fall into place.

A suspicion that the very real difficulties in understanding and obstacles
to study that new readers might face are being glossed over, or even deliberately ignored, might seem all the more pressing where other writers more
fully substitute virtuous living for conventional scholarship. When Piers
Plowman tells a priest that "Abstynence þe Abbesse myn a b c me tauȝte, /
And Conscience cam after and kenned me muche more," for example, the
contrast is even more striking: this is a curriculum vitae that refuses to explain
the fluent biblical exegesis that Piers has just deployed in terms of intellectual formation through a recognized course of study.[5] The same point
might be made about Walter Brut's claim, in his written testimony sent to
Bishop John Trefnant in the early 1390s, to be "peccator, laycus, agricola,
cristianus" ("a sinner, layman, farmer, and Christian") even as he composes
a lengthy defense in Latin.[6] But as Piers's and Brut's evident learning may
also suggest, the assertion that virtue and grace and right living are just as
necessary as study for any correct interpretation of the bible has a long history in the learned Christian tradition, stretching from Augustine's *De doctrina Christiana* through the writings of thirteenth-century scholastics such
as Bonaventure and Aquinas, as well as fifteenth-century conciliar reformists
such as Richard Ullerston and Jean Gerson.[7] Affective piety and intellectual

---

4. Mary Dove, "The Lollards' Threefold Biblical Agenda," in *WC*, 219. See also Kantik Ghosh,
The Wycliffite Heresy: Authority and the Interpretation of Texts (Cambridge: Cambridge University Press,
2002), chap. 4, 112–46.

5. George Kane and E. Talbot Donaldson, eds., *Piers Plowman: The B Version*, rev. ed. (London:
Athlone, 1988), B.7.138–39. I restore "much more" in place of Kane and Donaldson's emendation
to "bettre" (for metrical reasons?) drawn from CUL Gg.4.31: "more" does not imply, as "better"
would, that Conscience's teaching is superior.

6. William W. Capes, ed., *Registrum Johannis Trefnant* (London: Canterbury and York Society,
1916), 285/25. On Brut's claims about his social status, see Anne Hudson, "*Laicus Litteratus*: The
Paradox of Lollardy," in *Heresy and Literacy, 1000–1530*, ed. Peter Biller and Anne Hudson (Cambridge: Cambridge University Press, 1994), 222–36.

7. Ian Christopher Levy, *Holy Scripture and the Quest for Authority at the End of the Middle Ages*
(Notre Dame, IN: University of Notre Dame Press, 2012), 10–11, 12; Christopher Ocker, *Biblical
Poetics before Humanism and Reformation* (Cambridge: Cambridge University Press, 2002), 149–61.

engagement are routinely thought of as inseparable in this tradition, even where claims to simplicity may be deployed and learning disclaimed.[8] And even where learning is disclaimed, there may also be teaching: demonstration of exactly how to go about biblical exegesis is not always absent in the writings of lollards and their contemporaries, as we will see.

I juxtapose these quotations not in order to insist that their claims are identical. We will have ample opportunity to explore what is distinctive in lollard scriptural hermeneutics in what follows. Instead, what I want to emphasize is how extensive was the common ground, of both theory and practice, between lollards and their contemporaries both academic and extramural, as well as between lollards and mainstream tradition. This common ground has sometimes been denied, even now, by those who want to insist instead that lollards are fleshly adherents to the letter of the biblical sense, who "inspiciunt sacram scripturam et solum capiunt litteram et non sensum" ("search through holy scripture and take only the letter, and not the sense").[9] The roots of this rhetoric lie, of course, in just the passage that Hilton and the lollard adaptor of Gretham are referring to. In any conflict over biblical meaning, especially one that involves accusing the other side of heresy, 2 Corinthians 3:6 offers a way to label one's opponents as fleshly literalists. This accusation will not stick to lollard writers, any more than it will to Wyclif, for their biblical interpretations are just as devoted to uncovering the spiritual sense of scripture by means of the full range of interpretative methods available to them in the Christian tradition as those of any of their contemporaries. So it is that a rather more sophisticated version of the same smear suggests that Wyclif's and lollard interpretative practice is in tension with their theoretical claims (claims we will examine in more detail in a moment), while lollard assertions that only those who live rightly can interpret rightly are somehow especially vulnerable to the accusation of circular reasoning.[10] Instead, we need to appreciate that lollards and their contemporaries are often contending over the same ground.[11] Both make the circular yet

---

8. Ocker, *Biblical Poetics*, 112–23. On claims to simplicity, see also Gregory Heyworth, "Ineloquent Ends: Simplicitas, Proctolalia, and the Profane Vernacular in the *Miller's Tale*," *Speculum* 84 (2009): 962. See also Robert E. Lerner, "Ecstatic Dissent," *Speculum* 67 (1992): 33–57.

9. Patrick Horner, ed., A *Macaronic Sermon Collection from Late Medieval England, MS Bodley 649*, Studies and Texts 153 (Toronto: Pontifical Institute of Mediaeval Studies, 2006), 437/27; my translation. For claims that lollards are literalists, see, e.g., James Simpson, *The Oxford English Literary History*, vol. 2, *Reform and Cultural Revolution, 1350–1547* (Oxford: Oxford University Press, 2002), 471–75, and chap. 4, n. 29.

10. This is where I differ with Kantik Ghosh's otherwise excellent introductory discussion of Wyclif's and Wycliffite hermeneutics in *Wycliffite Heresy*, 39–42, 61–66, 143–46.

11. As Levy demonstrates in *Holy Scripture and the Quest for Authority*.

enabling claim, one that is by no means new, that only the virtuous are able to understand the bible. And both, at their more polemical moments, may claim the high ground of properly spiritual interpretation and label their opponents as fleshly adherents to the killing letter. Lollards are usually concerned to define themselves against the religious culture that surrounds them, but they do so not by making a sharp break, not through crude opposition, but through a series of coherent and carefully worked-out self-differentiations, developed in theory and carried through in practice.

"Gostly Vnderstondynge" in Lollard Writings

Comparing the lollard adaptation of the prologue to Robert of Gretham's *Miroir* with its thirteenth-century Anglo-Norman source, and with roughly contemporary versions of the Middle English *Mirror* translation, will allow us to trace these careful lollard differentiations more closely. In Gretham's *Miroir* and the Middle English *Mirror*, the comparison between holy writ and a fruit-bearing tree begins the second half of the prologue, right after the statement that the prologue—what seems at an earlier stage to have been conceived of as a shorter prologue—has come to an end. The first section of the *Miroir/Mirror* prologue contains much that would seem congenial to a lollard writer: it urges that writing about God is better for you than follies and trifles, lies and vanity. However, the lollard writer makes use only of the second half of the prologue, on holy writ and its interpretation. He extensively interpolates and adapts Gretham's discussion, far more so than any of the translations. His first paragraph follows Gretham closely through his first eighteen lines of verse, though diverging on key points, in his analogy between scripture and a thickly leaved, fruit-bearing tree. Gretham's next forty lines of verse elaborate a more extended agricultural metaphor, comparing obstructions to the understanding of scripture with a dark cloud and its exposition with life-restoring rain. The lollard writer retains the cloud analogy but elaborates it in a different direction, substituting quotations from Paul for most of its elaboration and deferring any further development of the agricultural metaphor until a passage near the end of his text, not shared with Gretham, on the "glorious gardyn of Cristis gracious gospel" (128/106–129/107). After his extended agricultural metaphor, Gretham develops in eight lines a model of the three estates. The lollard writer draws upon the brief description of each estate and expands this section considerably. From this point the two works diverge, though the lollard writer does at two later points make use of quotations from Lamentations 4:4 and Luke 6:38 also used by Gretham.

Returning to the much more closely similar first paragraph, we see that the lollard writer gives greater emphasis than had Gretham to the operations of both affect and intellect, as well as the kinds of work that further them. Differences from Duncan and Connolly's edition of the translated Gretham prologue are underlined in the quotation of the interpolated Gretham prologue that follows and the variant content included in footnotes, while the Anglo-Norman version provided for facing-page comparison in the same edition is included below the quotation.[12] A man must "sette his herte" (not merely his intent, or "purpens") on "gostli" understanding. After the tree is shaken, the sweetness of its hidden fruit is known (rather than only pleasing). One shakes the tree not merely through "vndoinge" (as other translations would render "espundre"—a key term for scriptural exposition, though at this point it is not clear who is providing it, or to whom), but "þorouȝ studyynge þerof and by good lyuynge." And understanding cannot happen except by God's grace, and "tyl [scripture] be drawen and schaken into his owne langage":

Holy writ haþ þe[13] lyknesse of[14] a tree þat beriþ <u>fruyt</u>—note,[15] <u>peer</u> or[16] appel. Whanne it is þikke leued, litil or nouȝt <u>is seen</u> of his fruȝt,[17] <u>but whanne</u>[18] men schaken þe tree þe fruyt falliþ doun <u>faste</u> and þike,[19] and þan swetenesse <u>is knowe</u>[20] þat was hidde aforn, <u>and</u>[21] whanne men eten it, it plesiþ hem wel. So it fareþ bi holy writ. Þe letter semeþ derk and harde. <u>But ȝif</u>[22] a man sette his <u>herte</u>[23] to see þe gostly <u>witt þat is þereynne,</u>[24] and ȝif he schake it <u>wel, þat is to seie, þorouȝ studyynge þerof and by good lyuynge,</u> by[25] þe <u>grasce</u>[26] þat God wole <u>þanne</u>[27] do to

---

12. Thomas G. Duncan and Margaret Connolly, eds., *The Middle English "Mirror": Sermons from Advent to Sexagesima* (Heidelberg: Universitätsverlag, 2003), 7/19–27, and for the Anglo-Norman, 6/197–214. While the version of the Anglo-Norman provided here may differ from that used by the lollard writer, his divergences from the text are strikingly original enough that small differences in wording are unlikely to matter.

13. þe] a
14. of] vnto
15. fruyt—note] note
16. peer or] oþer
17. litil or nouȝt is seen of his fruȝt] of þe frout it lest litel oþer nouȝt
18. but whanne] ac ȝif
19. faste and þike] þicke and fair
20. is knowe] *om.*
21. and] *om.*
22. But ȝif] ac
23. herte] entente
24. witt þat is þereynne] writ
25. wel, þat is to seie, þorouȝ studyynge þerof and by good lyuynge, by] as þurȝth vndoinge
26. grasce] gode
27. þanne] *om.*

<u>hym</u>,[28] myche good fruyt he schal fynde þerynne,[29] þat ben sentenssis of manye <u>good</u>[30] maneris, and þe swetnesse þerof schal turne him to <u>gret goodnesse</u>,[31] whiche þat <u>a man vnderstondeþ not tyl it be drawen and schaken into his owne langage</u>.[32] (*EA*, 126/1–10, punctutation modified)

> Saint escripture ad la custume
> Del arbre qui port noyz u pume;
> Quant est fuillie esspessement
> Del fruit i pert petit u nient;
> Mais si l'em encust l'arbrecel
> Li fruit enchet espes e bel,
> E la ducur ke fu celee,
> Quant l'em en guste, mult li agree.
> Also est de saint escripture:
> La lettre pert obscure e dure,
> Mais qui i mettrat sun purpens
> Pur ueer l'espirital sense,
> E si l'escut cum par espundre
> Le bien ke Deus i uolt respundre
> Mult i uerrat pumettes cheres,
> Co sun sentences de maneres;
> E mult li sauura bien
> La dulcur dunt ainz ne solt rien.

Shaking the tree requires not only study accompanied by good living but a translated text. The stress here on translation pursues the interest in this topic found throughout CUL Ii.6.26 and is reiterated at the opening of the next paragraph, where it is not "þe letter of holi writ" (startlingly) but the fact that holy scripture is in Latin, Greek, or French that makes it a dark cloud to an Englishman before he has learned those languages. But the passage's underlying insistence that every person should have access to the truth, and that once they have that access, even laypersons are capable of discerning true teaching and its teachers and distinguishing them from the false, is far more broadly typical.

---

28. to hym] vs
29. þerynne] þerinne, and derworþ
30. good] *om.*
31. gret goodnesse] gode
32. a man vnderstondeþ not tyl it be drawen and schaken into his owne langage] aforn he ne vnderstode nouȝt

The writer's emphasis on the need for grace, and for right living as well as study, continues in his first lengthy interpolation, where he grounds his interpretation closely in biblical quotation. As before, divergences from the *Miroir/Mirror* are underlined, but since the texts diverge more widely here, only the lollard version is quoted.

> For <u>holy scripture in Latyn, Grew or Frensche to an Englische man</u> is as a derk cloude <u>til he haue lerned and vnderstondun þese spechis,</u> <u>but whanne by þe voys of his owne langage hit entreþ into his soule,</u> <u>it moyste[þ] alle hise wittis, boþe bodily and gostly, and makeþ hem to</u> <u>bere fruyt be þe goodnesse of Goddis spirit. Also, be þis derk cloude</u> <u>is vnderstonden wicked lyuynge, þe whiche blyndeþ so his louers þat</u> <u>þei wanten þe liȝt of gras truly to vnderstonde holy scripture.</u> For Poul seiþ *"þe letter sleiþ,"* þat is, fleischly lyuers brekynge þe comaundementis [fol. 52v] of God. *But þe spirit quikeneþ alle þoo þat lyuen feiþfully after* *þe gostly vnderstondynge of holy writte.* Wherfor Poul seiþ *"be ȝee* *ledde oþer walke ȝee wiþ þe Holy Goost and ȝe schullen not fulfile þe synful* *desires of ȝoure fleische."* Þei ben alle as[33] a <u>dreye</u> cloude þat vnderstonden not what þei don ne what <u>þei ben comaunded to do</u> ne what is forboden hem <u>to do,</u> neiþer be holy writyngis ne in her owne wittis. Þanne þei haue no reyn <u>ne dewe of grace</u> whanne no man techeþ hem <u>ne writeþ to hem holy scripture.</u>[34]

While for Gretham the "dark cloud" was the letter of scripture ("lettre de saint escripture"), here the "dark cloud" is first the untranslated text and second—eliding any difficulties that comprehending the literal meaning might otherwise be thought to present—the wicked living that would blind God's lovers and cause them to lack the grace they need to understand scripture. The dry cloud (where Gretham had "cum en nues") is those who lack understanding by means of either holy scripture or their own wits, because nobody has moistened either their bodily or spiritual wits (see line 3 of the passage quoted) with holy scripture.

For the lollard writer the cloud becomes a threefold metaphor, repeating and elaborating three reasons why the sinful lack necessities for eternal life: untranslated scripture, wicked living, and lack of understanding caused by

---

33. as] as in; Dove emends the text in line with *Miroir/Mirror*'s "cum en nues" ("as in a cloude"). I think the modification to "as a dreye cloude" is deliberate and develops the cloud metaphor.

34. "Cambridge Tract XI," 126/11–24. For the corresponding passages in the *Miroir/Mirror*, see Duncan and Connolly, *Middle English "Mirror,"* 7/28–9/10, and for the Anglo-Norman, 6/215–8/254. The prologue to the Middle English *Mirror* is itself highly critical of abuses in the contemporary church and of those who permit them: see 9/19–25, and see *PR*, 414–15.

lack of oral and written teaching. But this is not primarily a condemnation, except perhaps of the people who obstruct translation and oppose or neglect proper teaching. Rather, it is an implicit program for reform, and one that places considerable trust in the "wittis" of the lay readers, as well as in whatever internal or external force (this is left crucially unclear) it is that will dispel the cloud—dark or dry—that prevents understanding. This writer's version of life-giving rain is an utterance in one's own language, and for all those who receive it in grace and with proper understanding, it moistens all the bodily and spiritual wits so that they bear fruit. What is more, bearing fruit now has a much more specific import, repeated twice: knowing and keeping the commandments.

Previous scholarship might have labelled this passage's interest in the "gostli witt" and its imaginative development of extended metaphor atypical, or inconsistent with lollards' supposed literalism. Rather, what appears here is typically and even distinctively lollard. The lack of specificity in its metaphorically described process of lay instruction is common in lollard writings, but also in a wide range of mainstream writings. What is more distinctive is the passage's detailed elaboration of the means that might bring about broader "gostli" understanding among lay readers: learning, knowing, and living the truth of holy scripture, and especially the insistence that this process should be grounded in proper instruction in the commandments.[35]

"Gostly" understanding is, then, central to lollard religion and to the articulation of lollard reform. Expressing that "gostly" understanding in the vernacular for a mixed audience of laypeople as well as clerics is a means of rendering it more broadly accessible. Rather than being self-contradictory or vacillating in their approach to allegory, lollard writings display a sophisticated engagement with the terms and possibilities of what they most often call "gostli speche" or "gostli vndurstonding," one that gives credit to the capacities of human wit as well as the contents of holy writings.

As we have already begun to see in our first pair of examples, "gostli" is something of a cultural keyword in a fairly wide range of late medieval English vernacular theological writing.[36] The adjective refers to the Holy Spirit. The adjective and adverb are applied to items and actions that are "spiritual" and in some way the obverse of "bodily" or "material." But they also (and sometimes in closely related or deliberately ambiguous senses) refer to figural or allegorical language in the broadest possible sense: any speaking or understanding that might be thought of as other than literal, and sometimes, speech

---

35. For further explanation, see chap. 2.
36. See *MED* s.v. "gostli," adj. and "gostli," adv.

that is regarded as reliably true. Yet crucially, 2 Corinthians 3:6's opposition of "letter" and "spirit" notwithstanding, the "gostli" need not exclude the literal. Rather, it might expand its potential range, as lollards and their contemporaries deploy a polysemous range of potential oppositions variously capable of being reconciled as one and the same: body against soul; letter against spirit; word against thing; words against deeds; literal against allegorical, anagogical, or moral; historical against typological; literal meaning in the strictest sense of the grammatical meaning of the words against metaphor, figures of speech, or authorial intention.

"Gostly Vnderstondynge" and the Lollard Imaginary

To develop a more broadly based understanding of how lollard writers deploy and then reconcile these oppositions, let us consider an excerpt from the fullest explanation of scriptural interpretation that lollards give anywhere, in what is known as the *General Prologue* to the Wycliffite Bible. This passage has been cited to demonstrate the lollards' overwhelming bias toward the literal sense over the three most commonly distinguished spiritual senses of the bible, as well as to suggest that they did not understand the full complexities of Wyclif's thought on the subject.[37] But as we will see, there is far more to it than that:

> [H]ooli scripture haþ foure vndurstondyngis: literal, allegorik, moral and anagogik. Þe literal vndurstonding techiþ þe þing doon in deede [historical event],[38] and literal vndurstonding is ground and foundement of þre gostli vndurstondingis, in so myche as Austin in his pistle [epistle] to Vyncent, and oþere doctours, seyn oneli bi [say that only by] þe literal vndurstonding a man mai argue aȝenus [may a man argue against] an aduersarie. Allegorik is a gostli vndurstonding þat techiþ what þing men owen for to bileue [should believe] of Crist or of hooli chirche. Moral is a gostli vndurstonding þat techiþ men what vertues þei owen to sue and what vices þei owen to fle. Anagogik is a gostli vndurstonding þat techiþ men what blisse þei shulen haue in heuene. And þese foure vndurstondingis moun be takun in [may be taken from] þis

---

37. See, e.g., Ralph Hanna et al., "Latin Commentary Tradition and Vernacular Literature," in *The Cambridge History of Literary Criticism*, vol. 2, *The Middle Ages*, ed. Alastair Minnis and Ian Johnson (Cambridge: Cambridge University Press, 2005), 399; Alastair Minnis, "'Authorial Intention' and 'Literal Sense' in the Exegetical Theories of Richard Fitzralph and John Wyclif: An Essay in the Medieval Theories of Biblical Hermeneutics," *Proceedings of the Royal Irish Academy* 75, Section C, no. 1 (1975): 29–30.

38. "þe þing doon in deede" is a translation of *res gestae*.

word "Ierusalem," for whi [for] to þe literal vndurstonding it signefieþ an erþeli citee, as Londoun or sich anoþere; to allegorie, it signefieþ hooli chirche in erþe þat fiȝtiþ aȝenus synnes and fendis; to moral vndurstonding, it signefieþ a cristen soule; to anagogik, it signefieþ hooli chirche regnynge in blisse or heuene, and þo þat ben þerinne [those who are within it]. And þese þre gostli vndurstondingis ben not autentik or of bileue [are not authentic or a matter of faith] no but if þei ben groundid [unless they are based] openli in the text of hooli scripture, in oo place or oþer, or in open resoun þat mai not be distried [self-evident argument that cannot be invalidated], or whanne þe gospelers or oþere apostlis taken allegorie of þe elde testament, and confermen [confirm] it, as Poul, in þe pistil to Galatas, in þe iiij cᵒ, preueþ [proves] þat Sara, þe fre wiyf and principal of Abraham, wiþ Isaac hir sone, <u>signefieþ bi allegorie þe newe testament and þe sones of biheest</u> [sons of the covenant], and Agar þe handmaide, wiþ hir sone Ismael, <u>signefieþ bi allegorie þe elde testament and fleischli men that shulen not be resseyued</u> [received] <u>into þe eritage</u> [inheritance] <u>of God wiþ þe sones of biheest þat holden þe treuþe and fredom of Cristis gospel wiþ endeles charite.</u>[39]

Granted, the literal sense sounds limited, and limiting, at the beginning of this passage, where it is distinguished from other possible senses and made their ground. Yet the claim that "literal vndurstonding is ground and foundement of þre gostli vndurstondingis" is commonplace.[40] The writer seems to attach considerable importance to the restriction that only the literal sense may be used as the basis of an argument: he repeats it twice more in the later sections of this prologue.[41] Yet it was commonplace, too, to assert on Augustine's authority that "oneli bi þe literal vndurstonding [may] a man . . . argue aȝenus an aduersarie."[42] It makes little sense to label lollards as literalist extremists on the basis of statements that most of their contemporaries would agree with.[43]

---

39. "Prologue to the Wycliffite Bible," in *EA*, 63/2166–90.

40. See Beryl Smalley, "Use of the 'Spiritual' Senses of Scripture in Persuasion and Argument by Scholars in the Middle Ages," *Recherches de théologie ancienne et médiévale* 52 (1985): 44–63, and *The Study of the Bible in the Middle Ages*, 3rd ed. (Oxford: Blackwell, 1983). For reconsideration of Smalley's approach to the literal sense, see Lesley Smith, "What Was the Bible in the Twelfth and Thirteenth Centuries?," 1–15, John Van Engen, "Studying Scripture in the Early University," 17–38, and Robert Lerner, "Afterword," 181–88, esp. 183, all in *Neue Richtungen in der hoch- und spätmittelalterlichen Bibelexegese*, ed. Robert E. Lerner and Elisabeth Müller-Luckner (Munich: Oldenbourg, 1996); and see below, n. 43.

41. See "Prologue to the Wycliffite Bible," 74/2597–99, 76/2654–55.

42. Smalley, "Use of the 'Spiritual' Senses of Scripture."

43. See Levy's exposition of Gerson in *Holy Scripture and the Quest for Authority*, 209–21.

In implementation, even across the span of this quoted passage, the literal sense admits considerably more slippage than these initial claims would seem to permit. Again, this slippage is not unique to lollards but broadly typical of their cultural moment. Beryl Smalley has suggested that argumentation was not limited to the literal sense as stringently as the frequent citation of Augustine's restriction would seem to suggest. While the limitation seems to have had some impact on disputed questions and other similar scholastic genres across the late thirteenth to fifteenth centuries, it had absolutely no influence on genres involving persuasion, such as sermons and polemical writings.[44] Yet at the same time, it is unclear whether the authors Smalley surveys would always have agreed that they were transgressing the boundaries of the literal. For as Christopher Ocker has noted, biblical interpreters across these centuries seem to have experienced increasing difficulty in keeping literal and spiritual senses distinct: even as scholars became more interested in philology and history, definitions of the "literal" underwent a dizzying expansion, while self-styled literal exposition ranged far and wide, often without acknowledgement, over this new territory.[45] Rather than the grammatical meaning of the words and their immediate reference to historical event—a narrow sense of the "literal" retained throughout this period for its analytic usefulness—the literal sense might also include metaphors or other figures that are clearly intended by the author (as in Aquinas), or even the whole of the author's intended meaning regardless of how it is conveyed (as in Lyra), or the meaning God intended (as in Wyclif). There might even be more than one literal sense at once (as in Fitzralph's and many of his contemporaries' *duplex*, or Wyclif's *multiplex, sensus litteralis*).[46] The explanation at the end of this passage of how "gostli" meanings may be grounded demonstrates just this sort of expansion. The combination of any meaning expressed openly elsewhere in scripture, any meaning compatible with reason, and any allegorical significance of the Hebrew Bible assigned in the gospels or epistles points toward an extraordinarily broad range of possibilities for the literal sense. Not only strict grammatical meaning and historical events but any interpretation that can be confirmed elsewhere in the bible or even by "open resoun þat mai not be distried" might count as the "gostli" sense.

---

44. Smalley, "Use of the 'Spiritual' Senses of Scripture"; also Ocker, *Biblical Poetics*, 40.

45. Ocker, *Biblical Poetics*.

46. Minnis, "'Authorial Intention' and 'Literal Sense'"; Levy, *Holy Scripture and the Quest for Authority*, 11–23, 68–72, 211–12; Ocker, *Biblical Poetics*, 142–49. See also the translated excerpts in section 6, "Scriptural Science and Signification," in Alastair J. Minnis, A. B. Scott, and David Wallace, eds. and trans., *Medieval Literary Theory and Criticism, c. 1100–c. 1375: The Commentary Tradition* (Oxford: Clarendon Press, 1991), 197–276.

Only much later in the prologue, in his second, expanded version of the
Tyconian rules for biblical interpretation as explained by Lyra, does the writer
spell out that the "gostli" senses authenticated by the means he outlines may
be considered a part of an expanded literal sense and that all interpretations
associated with this expanded literal sense, rather than only the most narrowly
defined literal interpretation, may be used in argument.[47] But his final gesture
even here, in the earlier passage I have just quoted at length, demonstrates
the practice he will later justify. In the underlined phrases at the end of my
quotation the writer does indeed use allegory—Paul's allegory, stitched to his
own application of it—to authorize his own implicit argument and his own
aspirational position (one he hopes to share with his readers) as the "sones of
biheest," the true heirs of the true meaning of the Christian message. Paul's
allegory in Galatians 4 authenticates as quasi-literal the interpretation of Sara
as the gospel and Isaac as the gospel's authentic Christian interpreters, the
"sones of biheest." For Henri de Lubac, Galatians 4 is a sort of founding
moment for Christian allegory and a model authorizing its practice for a
long lineage of Christian allegorists.[48] Certainly it seems to be a founding
moment for lollards. Paul renders allegory quasi-literal here. But in drawing
attention to Paul's use of allegory in a passage that draws a contrast, as it is
interpreted here, between fleshly and "gostli," the old law and its fulfillment,
the damned and those who hold the truth and freedom of the gospel, the
writer also offers here a broader endorsement of allegory in general, as well
as of its practitioners. He grounds himself in Paul's insistence that the highest
truths in God's mind lie beyond history and select as their most suitable recipients those who are willing to affirm them. The imagined community this
lollard paraphrase asserts, the "sones of biheest þat holden þe treuþe and fredom of Cristis gospel wiþ endeles charite," is a community uniquely recep-
tive to its own inclusion in the biblical text as enabled by allegory. We have
already seen, in chapter 5, how this plays out (and see also below). Nothing
could make clearer the central role played by allegory in the lollard imaginary.

The Lollard Imaginary: Holy Church as Aspirational Edifice

The lollard community identifies its members, in lollard exegesis, with what
seems a blithely confident effort of interpolative imagination. Past and present

47. "Prologue to the Wycliffite Bible," 76/2640–60. This exposition also addresses Augustine's
claim that the "goostli" sense may not be used in argument. On the *General Prologue*, see further
FEB, 120–36, 145–48, 152, 160–62, 172–76, and 135 on the relationship between Lyra's version of
the rules of Tyconius and Augustine's.
48. Henri de Lubac, *Exégèse médiévale: Les quatres sens de l'ecriture*, 2 vols. (Paris: Aubier, 1959), 23.

come together, in the imagination, where interpolation brings the biblical words
and their asserted "gostli" understanding into direct conjunction, without any
apparent concern that they require proof.[49] Consider again, for example, how
the lollard adaptation of Gretham's prologue presents 2 Corinthians 3:6: "Poul
seiþ '*þe letter sleiþ*,' þat is, fleischly lyuers brekynge þe comaundementis of God.
But þe spirit quikeneþ alle þoo þat lyuen feiþfully after þe gostly vnderstondynge
of holy writte." Paul says the letter slays—that is, slays those living after the
flesh and breaking God's commandments. If we lay aside quotation marks that
might be added by a modern editor, there is no visible seam between the (italicized) biblical phrase and its supplemental predicate, any more than there is in
the next sentence, when the spirit gives life—that is, gives life to all those who
live faithfully after the "gostly" understanding of holy writ. This common lollard habit of abrupt, supplemental glossing that stitches word-for-word quotation from the bible to its asserted "gostly" sense aptly epitomizes how lollard
writers are at the same time literalists and allegorists. Allegory joins seamlessly
here with allegoresis, in a process of invention as discovery of the hoped-for
truth. All the bible's true senses, whether expressed, derived, or supplied, collapse into one: the imputed intention of the divine author.

Similarly, consider the careful ratification of Paul's allegory in the *English
Wycliffite Sermon* on Galatians 4, where the "foure wittis [senses]" of scripture
are carefully defined on the way to explaining that Paul is deploying the
second of them:

> [Þ]es tuo children of Abraham bytoknen [symbolize] two lawis of God,
> and two children þat God haþ: þe furste child schal be dampned, and
> þe secounde schal be sauyd. And so men seyn comunly [generally say]
> þat hooly writ haþ foure wittis: þe furste wit is of story [historical], or
> euene as þe wordis schulden toknen [what the words mean]; þe sec-
> ounde wit is allegoric, þat figureþ þing þat men schulden trowe [what
> people should believe], as þes two sonys of Abraham figuren [are figures
> for] þes two þingis; þe þridde wit is tropologic, þat bytokneþ wit of
> vertuwis [the moral sense]; þe fourþe wit is anagogic, þat bytokneþ þing
> to hope [what is to be hoped for] in blis. Poul swiþ here [is following
> here] þe secounde wit, and he hadde auctorite þerto [was justified in
> doing so]. (*EWS*, 1:556/13–557/23)

Yet contrast this careful anatomy and subdivision of scriptural senses with
the leap of faith some forty lines later that would assimilate Paul's discussion

---

49. On this mode of exposition, see also *WS*, 23–24; Fiona Somerset, "Wycliffite Spirituality,"
in *Text and Controversy from Wyclif to Bale: Essays in Honour of Anne Hudson*, ed. Helen Barr and Ann
M. Hutchison (Turnhout: Brepols, 2005), 384–85.

of the children of Abraham to the sense compatible (so the sermon writers think, at any rate) with "open reason":

> Poul descenduþ to þis figure [pursues his figural interpretation], and seiþ [says] in þis tyme of grace *we ben children of byheste* [the covenant] *as Ysaac* was Abrahammys sone. And so we ben children of þe free modyr, and schulden be tretude [treated] now as fre. But riȝt as [just as] þe sone of Abraham þat was first born, *fleschly pursuwede* [pursued] *hys goostly sone*, þat was born *spiritually, so it fallup now* on dayus [happens nowadays] of [concerning] men þat God haþ ordeyned to peyne, and men þat he haþ ordeyned to blis, and men of þe oolde lawe and of þe newe. (*EWS*, 1:558/61–68)

We (the lollard writers tell their readers) are the "goostly" sons, while our opponents are Ishmael. Having been born spiritually, we should be treated as free, but instead we are "fleschly" pursued. Yet no justification, other than the asserted common experiences of entitlement and persecution, backs up this claim to group identity.

Despite the confidence visible in such moments, lollards are certainly well aware that attempts to explicate the "goostly sense" of scripture may go awry. The prologue to the prophetic books of the Hebrew Bible, produced at an earlier stage of the work on the lollard bible translation, emphasizes instead the perils inherent in the work of imagination required to ground "goostly" understanding—though it offers, as well, a means of navigating them.[50] This earlier prologue's ratification of "gostli vndurstondyng" is far more cautiously specific in its terms and careful to corroborate its claims by reference to exegetical tradition:[51]

> Þe literal vndurstonding of hooli scripture is þe ground of al goostli vndurstonding þerof [of it], þat is, of allegorik, of moral and of anagogik. No gostli vndurstonding is autentik [authentic] no but [unless] it be groundid in þe text openli eþer [or] in open resoun suying of principlis [following the principles] eþer reulis [rules] of feiþ, as seynt Austin witnessiþ openli in his pistle to Vyncent Donatist, and in his book of *Soliloquies*, and Jerom on Ionas, and Lire on þe bigynnyng of Genesis and in many places of hooli scripture, and Ardmakan in his book of *Questiouns of Armenyes*. Þerfor men moten seke [should seek]

---

50. On the composition of this prologue and the extant copies, see *FEB*, 106–7. For the *MEBS* writer's very similar worries about imagination, cf. chap. 5, n. 53.

51. For a different interpretation of the relationship between the two prologues, see *FEB*, 113–19.

þe treuþe of the text and be war of [be cautious about] gostli vndurstondyng eþer moral fantasie, and ȝyue not ful credence þerto, no but
[do not fully believe it, unless] it be groundid openli in þe text of hooli
writ, in o [one] place eþer oþer, eþer in open resoun þat mai not be
avoidid [dismissed], for ellis it wole as likyngli [as easily] be applied to
falsnesse as to treuþe. And it haþ disseyued [deceived] grete men in
oure daies, bi ouer-greet trist to her fantasies [too much trust in their
imaginations].[52]

To explain "goostli vndurstonding" by glossing it as "moral fantasie" is not
to dismiss the "goostli" senses out of hand, however.[53] That would be to
enforce strict oppositions where the writer is instead making careful distinctions. Rather, the category of "moral fantasie" acknowledges and gives
credit to the activity of the imagination, the compounding and dividing
in the human mind, required in any such hermeneutic effort.[54] Still, the
writer is also concerned to remind us that any human effort can go wrong.
If the work of the imagination is to be moral, just as much as if the work
of the understanding is to be "gostli," then it must be "openli" grounded,
in either holy writ or reason. This pairing of holy writ with reason as equal
counterparts is very common in lollard writings, however much it may leave
unexplained as the writer warns us, in closing, about great men (which ones?)
who have trusted their imaginations too far (but how?) and been deceived
(about what?).[55]

The Lollard Imagination—Moral and Immoral

What, then, other than the bare assertion of open grounding in holy writ
or reason, can help us to be sure that the work of the imagination is moral,
rather than the deceptive product of "ouer-greet trist"? In the interpolated
Gretham prologue, the perils of deception are externalized: the dark cloud

52. "Prologue to Isaiah and the Prophets," in *EA*, 87/40-51.
53. For a different view, see Hanna et al., "Latin Commentary Tradition and Vernacular Literature," 399.
54. Recent studies of late medieval views on the role of imagination include Michelle Karnes,
Imagination, Meditation, and Cognition in the Middle Ages (Chicago: University of Chicago Press, 2011);
Alastair Minnis, "Medieval Imagination and Memory," in Minnis and Johnson, *Cambridge History of
Literary Criticism*, 2:239–74.
55. On the pairing of holy writ and reason in lollard writings, see Fiona Somerset, *Clerical Discourse and Lay Audience in Late Medieval England* (Cambridge: Cambridge University Press, 1998),
180–83. See also Kantik Ghosh, "Wycliffite 'Affiliations': Some Intellectual-Historical Perspectives,"
in *WC*, esp. 27–28.

of untranslated scripture deceives would-be readers only because it has not yet been translated and explained to them (yet by whom?). Perhaps this is a confidence no longer available to a writer who has already been engaged in the translation and explication of scripture over a period of years. In the prologue to the prophetic books, by contrast, the peril into which great men have fallen is that of self-deception, rather than deception by others. While there is no explanation here, beyond the directive to ground it openly in holy writ or reason, of how the imagination may be guarded from deception, commentary on the work done by the imagination and the ways in which its activity can be either moral or deceptive is common elsewhere in medieval writings. This topic emerges not only in learned treatises on human cognition and the physiology of perception or in encyclopedic compendia on human self-knowledge—the sources that have commonly been consulted in explaining the prominent role given to the personification Ymaginatif in *Piers Plowman* B.12, the wariness about the work of the imagination in the richly imaginative *Cloud of Unknowyng*, or Chaucer's sources in depicting Troilus's disordered imagination in *Troilus and Criseyde*.[56] Scarcely examined in this research, but probably far more accessible to readers of vernacular religious writings, are the vernacular commentaries on the internal senses, or inward wits, that appear frequently in pastoral and devotional manuscripts, sometimes as freestanding works, sometimes within either loosely or tightly organized collections providing basic instruction for lay readers.[57] In some cases, the inward wits are merely listed, with little to no comment, but in other cases, the writer of such a list will expatiate at length on how the senses might be used for good or bad. A survey (though scarcely an exhaustive one) of more or less distinctive treatments of the inward wits within lollard manuscripts will allow us to develop a better sense of how lollard writers expected their readers to distinguish moral from immoral imagination, amid the interactive workings of common sense, imagination, cogitation, and memory.

What the very brief discussion in the prologue to the prophetic books, learned discourses, and pastoral and devotional writings share in common is

56. Karnes, *Imagination, Meditation, and Cognition*, chap. 6, 207–36; Minnis, "Medieval Imagination and Memory"; see also Alastair Minnis, "Affection and Imagination in *The Cloud of Unknowing* and Hilton's *Scale of Perfection*," *Traditio* 39 (1983): 323–66; Mary F. Wack, *Lovesickness in the Middle Ages: The Viaticum and Its Commentaries* (Philadelphia: University of Pennsylvania Press, 1990).

57. P. S. Jolliffe lists works treating the internal senses under heading D, "Self Knowledge," in *A Check-list of Middle English Prose Writings of Spiritual Guidance* (Toronto: Pontifical Institute of Mediaeval Studies, 1974), 74–76. See also Robert Raymo, "Works of Religious and Philosophical Instruction," in *A Manual of the Writings in Middle English, 1050–1500*, vol. 7, ed. J. Burke Severs and Albert E. Hartung (New Haven: Connecticut Academy of Arts and Sciences, 1967), 2320, 2323, 2325–31, 2335.

a tension, or even discomfort, with the mediating role between bodily and "gostli" understanding played by the external and internal senses, one that may manifest itself in various ways and result in the assertions of greater or lesser reliability and importance for the imagination. Imagination was never regarded as a human capacity that could simply be dispensed with. Nobody thought that human reasoning and willing could do their work on the data provided by the external senses without any mediation whatsoever. Yet theorists differed in their accounts of how the functions of mediation were subdivided between internal faculties, of how embodied or how spiritual the work of the imaginative and fantastic powers (sometimes distinguished, sometimes not) might be, of whether these faculties accomplished their tasks in strict sequence, of the form in which their material or spiritual input arrived and from what sources, of how reliably they mediated sensory input to the reason or intellect (which were sometimes distinguished, sometimes further subdivided), and of whether in its highest functioning the mind might dispense with the aid of imagination entirely—after death, if not in life.[58] Not all of these differentiations and distinctions find their way into vernacular religious writings. But tensions over the imagination's reliability, materiality, and capacity for serving "gostli" understanding most certainly do, with widely varying results. These tensions ensure that questions about the role of the imagination in religious instruction are always, explicitly, moral questions. Like their written culture more broadly, lollard writers did not take up a single position on the troubled question of the imagination's role. But in rehearsing its difficulties they do tweak the moralizing discourses that surround them in distinctive ways—ones that help to amplify our understanding of the prologue to the prophetic books' brief and cryptic comments.

The Lollard Inward Wits

The two treatments of the inward wits, side by side, near the end of the third and final booklet in Bodley 938 are a nice illustration of the tensions over the role of imagination. Indeed, it seems likely that the second, shorter text may have been included to compensate for the rather extreme position on

---

58. On medieval theories of internal and external sensation and cognition, see Michael Camille, "Before the Gaze: The Internal Senses and Late Medieval Practices of Seeing," in *Visuality before and beyond the Renaissance: Seeing as Others Saw*, ed. Robert S. Nelson (Cambridge: Cambridge University Press, 2000), 197–223; Minnis, "Medieval Imagination and Memory"; Robert Pasnau, *Theories of Cognition in the Later Middle Ages* (Cambridge: Cambridge University Press, 1997); Dallas G. Denery II, *Seeing and Being Seen in the Late Medieval World* (Cambridge: Cambridge University Press, 2005); and Karnes, *Imagination, Meditation, and Cognition*.

imagination's unreliability taken in the first text—a position that must have appealed on some level to the manuscript's compiler, but that is also somewhat mitigated through interpolation. The second, unique text draws on encyclopedic works that anatomize the functions and location of the inward wits, in an Aristotelian tradition also influenced by the theories of cognition of Aristotle's Arabic mediators.[59] Here, it seems the inward wits are a corrective to the possible moral corruption of the outer senses: "Þe fiue wittis of þe fleisch [external senses] ben þees. Seyng veynly [frivolously], hering folily [foolishly], smellyng delicatly [daintily], taasting gloterously [gluttonously], touchyng to lustly [with too much pleasure]. But þere ben oþere fiue `inward´[60] wittis [five other inward senses] by whiche þees firste fiue ben ledde to inward knowing, as witt comoun [common], ymaginatif, estymatif, fantastyk, and memoratif" (Bodley 938, fol. 246v). Susceptible to sin as the external senses may be, their internal counterparts are nonetheless capable of arriving at "inward knowing." In the brief exposition that follows, the bodily rather than spiritual nature of each inward wit—its location in the head, the ways in which its functioning is also evident in other animals, its position in a linked chain of functions that draws upon the external senses—is stressed. Rather than leading to greater unreliability, it seems that the way these functions participate in a sort of shared animal nature validates their work. Indeed, this short text's only reference to deceptive cognition involves physiologically based dysfunction and externalized spiritual interference, rather than sin: "bi þis witt [by this sense (the fantastic sense)], seeke [sick] men and malencolious [melancholy] and siche [similar sorts of] men haue many fantastik siȝtis [sights] and horrible conceitis [imagine horrible things] `bi suffrance of kynde [in a way that nature allows] and troubling of spiritis in þer brayn´[61] [brain]" (fol. 247r).

The first treatment of the inward wits in Bodley 938 might at first seem an odd choice for a lollard manuscript: it consists of chapters 63 through 66 of the *Cloud of Unknowyng*, excerpted in this form in only one other copy, in CUL Kk.6.26, an anthology of writings attributed to the *Cloud* author, where it is not interpolated as it is here.[62] The title promises a "schort declaracion

---

59. See, for example, the detailed discussion of the inward wits as explained by Avicenna, Algazel, and Aristotle compiled by Vincent of Beauvais, *Speculum naturale*, chaps. 85–100. See also Aquinas's commentary on Aristotle's *De anima*, esp. book 2, lectiones 6 and 13.

60. *insert from marg.*

61. *insert from bottom of page*

62. For a critical edition of the version in the *Cloud* itself, see Phyllis Hodgson, ed., *The Cloud of Unknowing and Related Treatises*, Analecta Cartusiana 3 (Salzburg: Institut für Anglistik und Amerikanistik, 1982), 64/15–66/28. In addition to a short prologue and epilogue (shared, though with

of worching of þe fiue inward wittis of a mannis soule" (fol. 243v). But what these four chapters of the *Cloud* have to offer, rather unusually, is a sophisticated interactive synthesis (for Mynde both comprehends and does nothing else but "gostly" contain the other four powers *and* all the things in which they work) that is highly unusual in its stringent subordination of Ymaginacioun to Resoun and Sensualite to Wille. Resoun and Wille are principal powers, the only human powers capable of knowing the virtues, conditions, and causes of things, and the only ones capable of working spiritually "wiþouten any maner of bodilynesse" (fol. 244r) as they achieve their highest potential. Before man sinned, Resoun and Wille might not be deceived. Now, they are constantly deceived except when illuminated by grace. Their subordinates, the secondary powers Ymaginacioun and Sensualite, are their unruly servants, constantly prone to deception. Ymaginacioun, in particular, is especially inclined to confuse bodily with "gostly" concepts, in ways that may mislead Resoun.

Yet tellingly, in the interpolated version in Bodley 938, the example given of the imagination's disobedience fixes not, collectively, on "newlynges", novices in contemplation, but on any individual who (more topically) "now late [recently]" attempts "lasting" (in place of "contynowel [continual]") attention to "gostly þinges."[63] "Lasting" picks out a broader audience, and sets the bar for participation lower, than "contynowel," which suggests a vowed religious engaged in contemplative life rather than any reader who aspires to greater devotion. Any such aspirant to devotional prayer is likely to be plagued by "wondurful and . . . diuerse þoȝtis, fantasies, and ymagis þe whiche ben mynistrid and printid in his Mynde by þe liȝt and curiouste of Ymaginacion" (fol. 245v). Lasting meditation on "gostly þingis" (fol. 245r) such as human wretchedness, Christ's passion, and God's "kyndenes" (fol. 245v) is an activity that a properly ordered Ymaginacioun can serve, but only through the vigilant effort, enabled by grace, of Resoun:

but [unless] it be refreyned [restrained] or wiþdrawe [curbed] bi þe liȝt of grace in þe Resoun, ellys it wol neuere ceesse [stop], sleping or waking, for to portreie [portraying] sum diuerse vnordeyned [various

---

several minor variations, with the copy in CUL Kk.6.26), the Bodley 938 version interpolates throughout. It introduces explanatory doubling and (far more occasionally) substitution of terms, and it adjusts the text to address a more inclusive audience. The content of the copy in CUL Kk.6.26 is much closer to the content of the *Cloud*. I am grateful to Jack Harding Bell for his insightful course paper on these texts, which I hope to see become a published article. I have limited the discussion here to my own observations.

63. Bodley 938, fol. 245r, compared with Hodgson, *Cloud of Unknowing*, 65/33, 65/36.

disordered] ymagis of bodily creaturis or ellys sum fantasie þe whiche is not ellys but a bodily conseyt [conception] of a gostly þing or a goostly conseit [conception] of a bodily þing. And þis is euermore [always] feyned [feigned] and fals and yknyt [wedded] to errour. (fol. 245r)

This fastidious concern for a watertight separation between bodily and "gostly" understanding is unusual in descriptions of the imagination. Yet its revulsion against wrong ways of living and the falseness they give rise to, adapted here to address any person who might recently have erred in attending to prayer, would certainly have appealed to lollard readers.

Straightforwardly prescriptive descriptions of what good things imagination might accomplish can give us more insight into the work of the "moral fantasie." Lollard versions of pastoral teaching on the inward wits seem inclined toward providing these. The highly variable *Pride, Wrath, and Envy,* for example, a short pastoral text extant in a wide range of full and partial versions, many with lollard content, usually includes some version of a list of first the outward and then the inward wits.[64] In some of its lollard copies the list of inward wits takes the form of a brief description of how the work of each inward wit can be moral rather than immoral—inflected, especially when it comes to its description of Resoun, with typical lollard vocabulary. Consider this version from Rylands 85:

Here suen [follow] þe fyue wittis of þe soule. Wille, Mynde, Vndirstonding, Ymaginacioun, and Resoun. First, wille þou [you must will] þat þe will of God be fulfild bifore þin owne will. Þe secunde, haue mynde on [be mindful of] þe blis of heuene and eke [also] on þe peynes of helle. Þe þridde, vndirstonde what benefetis [benefits] God haþ don for þee and hou vnkynde [ungrateful] þou art aȝen [in return]. Þe ferþe, ymagyne good of [about] oþir men more þan of þisilf [yourself]. Þe fifþe, resonably ruli þisilf vndir þe foorme of Goddis lawe and [similarly rule] alle þo [those] þat ben vndir þee [your subordinates]. And wiþ þese fyue goostli wittis rule and gouerne þi fyue bodili wittis biforseid, or ellis alle goiþ to wrake [ruin] and meschif [wrongdoing].[65]

---

64. On *Pride, Wrath, and Envy,* see chap. 2, n. 7.

65. Rylands 85, fol. 13v. The relationships between the copies of this highly fluid text are still not well understood. For the most recent attempts, see Oxford, Bodleian Library, MS Laud Misc. 524, item 3, described in S. J. Ogilvie-Thomson, *The Index of Middle English Prose, Handlist XVI: Manuscripts in the Laudian Collection, Bodleian Library, Oxford* (Cambridge: Brewer, 2000), 53; and Cambridge, Corpus Christi College, MS 385, item 4, described in Kari Anne Rand, *The Index of Middle English Prose, Handlist XX: Manuscripts in the Library of Corpus Christi College, Cambridge* (Woodbridge: Boydell and Brewer, 2009), 94. See also Margaret Connolly, "Preaching by Numbers: The 'Seven

As in the second text on the inward wits in Bodley 938, but without any of its appeal to the technical vocabulary of contemporary faculty psychologies, the inward wits work together (rather than at odds, as in the *Cloud*) to direct the external senses toward good. Their operations in this brief account add up to a compressed account of virtuous lollard living "vndir þe foorme of Goddis lawe" and thus according to God's will, rather than one's own.

While in the Rylands 85 version of *Pride, Wrath, and Envy* the work of moral imagination is nothing more or less than to dispose its proponent toward charity ("ymagyne good of oþir men more þan of þisilf"), the more expansive account of the inward wits in the *Pride, Wrath, and Envy* version in Edinburgh, University Library, MS 93 explains several ways in which Ymaginacion might be a means toward attentive conformity with God's will:

> Of þis good wil cometh forth þe fourth gostely wit, þat is Ymaginacion, or bisie thynkynge, for a gode wil hath a bisie thynkynge how, whan and where it may moste plese God. Now with sorouful [sorrowful] hert mowrnynge [mourning] for synne by whiche God is offendid, now with deuout orysoun [prayer] preysynge his holy name, now in deuoute contemplacion, now in herynge [praising], now in stodyynge [studying], now in techynge, now to know his own vnwordynes [unworthiness], and to meke hym [fol. 17v] þerfore [humble himself for that reason]. Now hauyng compassion of þe nedy [needy], now bisi-lye thenkyng þerayene remedie [considering a remedy for them], and so about [engaged in] godly werkes, wherby endles peyne is eshewed [avoided], and about medefull [worthy] dedis wherby endles blisse is goten. A vertues lyuer [virtuous liver] is occupyed bisilie in his thought, and of suche a bisye thought commeth [comes] þe fifte gostely wit þat is Resoune.[66]

Imagination, on this account, consists in assiduous thought about how to apply the will toward actions that will be pleasing to God, and it issues forth into reason. Someone who lives virtuously is occupied busily in his thought: that is, he has just the kind of hardworking imagination that is described here, across the course of this exposition of the inward dispositions involved in virtuous living. Rather than merely a tautology, this is an attentive and

Gifts of the Holy Ghost' in Late Middle English Sermons and Works of Religious Instruction" in *Preaching the Word in Manuscript and Print in Late Medieval England: Essays in Honour of Susan Powell*, ed. Martha W. Driver and Veronica O'Mara (Turnhout: Brepols, 2013), 83–100.

66. C. A. Martin, ed., "Edinburgh University Library Manuscript 93: An Annotated Edition of Selected Devotional Treatises with a Survey of Parallel Versions," 2 vols. (PhD diss., University of Edinburgh, 1978), 2:368–69, citing fol. 17r–v. Punctuation and capitalization modified.

detailed description of what makes the imagination moral: just the range of activities, and inward dispositions toward them ingrained in the properly disposed will, imagination, and reason, that are here described. Anybody who lives virtuously will engage in the kind of "bisye thought" that issues forth in correct judgment by reason. That person's reason will be disposed toward not merely a kind of self-willed ratiocination but the ability to believe God's word and do as it requires:

> For Resoun kyndely dampneth [naturally condemns] all euel thynge and vicious, and it consentith with [consents to] trewth and apreueth [approves] it. For Resoun moueth [impels] a man kyndely [naturally] to rewle hym after [rule himself according to] God, þat is aboue mannes resoun, and to hate synne and to loue vertue, and to bileue Goddis worde withouten errour, and to doo þerafter [act accordingly]. Resoun also moueth a man to meknesse, and it loueth mercy; it sorowith of [is sorrowful about] euel; it ioeth of [rejoices at] godenes; it is a mirrour and a meen [means] to come to heuen blisse. Whoso sueth [whoever follows] Reson he goeth not amys [does not go wrong].[67]

The person who lives virtuously engaged in busy thought has a "kyndely" or natural capacity reliably to ground him- or herself in holy writ (here, "Goddis worde") and reason, ruling the self "after God, þat is aboue mannes resoun" and consenting only to truth, not to what is evil.

Thus, the imagination is moral, rather than deceptive, when it is "openli" grounded in reason or holy writ rather than at odds with them, and it is "openli" grounded in reason or holy writ when the person to whom it belongs constantly exerts him- or herself in living virtuously. Emphasized wherever holy writ and reason are adduced as means of validation (and they are adduced very frequently in lollard writings; see n. 55) is the claim that the truth can be demonstrated and the false shown to be erroneous. But like the "gostli" understanding, the "moral fantasie" is accessible not only to those who have been trained in the interpretation of holy writ or the validation of argumentation but to anyone who is virtuous and lives rightly. The very frequent references to "open" text and "open" interpretation or argument in lollard writings carry within them an assertion of the self-evident rightness of the writer's position, so obvious that any reader (or at least any virtuous reader) can see it. The corollary of this assertion is that what makes a "fantasie" moral, just as much as what makes an understanding "gostli," is

---

67. Martin, "Edinburgh University Library Manuscript 93," 2:369, citing fol. 17v. Punctutation, capitalization, and word division modified.

the rectitude of its reading community—a presumption, if this is presumed, with all too obvious pitfalls. But this rectitude is one that needs continual exhortation and aspiration; it is not something achieved, but rather a state of being dependent on continually renewed right action.

Virtuous disposition and right action provide the grounds for correct interpretation. To claim that correct interpretation can proceed only from a virtuous reader is conventional enough, as our paired opening quotations showed us and as recent work by Ocker and Levy has emphasized (see below). But placing greater emphasis on right action, and less (though without dismissing its importance) on the operations of grace, is more typical of (though not unique to) lollards. These differing emphases are highlighted in the quotations with which we began. Hilton describes those who are friends to Christ and those who are not as two stable groups, distinguishable by their inward dispositions. The teeth (that is, the "inli vertues of the soule") of lovers of the flesh "aren blodi, ful of synne and of wordli vanyté." Their understanding "is corrupt bi the original synne and actuel also" and "is not yit heelid thorugh grace": they can only "gnawen upon the bark withoute." In contrast, those who are meek and pure and healed through grace have the love and leave of the Holy Ghost to enter in. Of course Hilton does not place these lovers of the flesh irremediably beyond the scope of God's mercy and healing grace. But he does not offer much prospect, or any suggestions, on how they might arrive at God's mercy and grace. Their role in their metaphorical agricultural economy is that of consumers of its humanly produced end products, rather than workers who gather and share its naturally occurring fruits, as in the lollard writer's metaphor of the shaken tree. By contrast, the lollard writer uses far fewer descriptive "is" phrases and issues more positive injunctions. Acquire translated scripture and arrange for instruction, set your heart on understanding, keep the commandments, and you will then through grace find much sweetness. Even if the lollard writer does similarly contrast those who live according to the "gostli" understanding of holy writ with "fleischly lyuers," the lollard writer puts greater stress on holy living as a process, rather than a state of being, and describes a means of transition between these ways of life.

Similarly, the *Cloud of Unknowyng*'s account of the inward wits in chapters 63 through 66 everywhere emphasizes that they may not operate virtuously without the help of grace. By contrast, the versions of *Pride, Wrath, and Envy* we have examined focus on how the inward wits may be disposed toward virtue through the efforts of the person and community where they do their work. It would be simplistic to attempt to annex some of these descriptions of the moral operation of the inward wits to a works-based theory of salvation and others to a faith-based one, just as much as it would be to suggest that nobody else except lollards talks about practical charity and moral instruction. Yet it cannot be emphasized enough how often and how assiduously lollard writers seek to instill a disposition toward personal and communal amelioration in their readers, in a way that is hard to square with the reputation Wyclif and his followers have acquired, in post-Reformation historiography, as strictly determinist predestinarians who rigidly divide the saved from those foreknown as damned (see also chapter 4).

Lollard Imagination, Lollard Literature

Eamon Duffy, building on Kantik Ghosh's early work on Wyclif's and Wycliffite hermeneutics, has proposed that in contrast to later protestantism with its "powerful and positive message," lollardy could only deliver "disparagement of the sins of others." Lollards refused the "polysemic resourcefulness" of the late medieval church, and their writings were "religiously and imaginatively sterile," displaying a "literalistic hostility to symbol and metaphor."[68] Lollards and many of their contemporaries certainly did disparage others' sins as well as encouraging their readers to examine their own sins. But I would contend, against Duffy's assessment of the "sour diet" he finds in the *English Wycliffite Sermons*, that many lollard writings engage imaginatively with the resources they find in mainstream contemporary religion. Even if they do reject some aspects of contemporary religious practice, they develop their positive alternatives precisely by means of symbol and metaphor and by offering covert or even overt instruction in alternative means of reading scripture that are anything but "literalistic" in the narrow sense. Indeed, they are often playful about words, as well as attentive to their imagery: filled with punning, alliterative or metrical passages, and rhetorical figures, and concerned to assert or covertly demonstrate that their expository style is different from, and better than, the kind of scholastic discourse that was usually considered to be the most robust means of arguing against an adversary and arriving at the truth.[69]

---

68. Eamon Duffy, *The Stripping of the Altars: Traditional Religion in England, c. 1400–1580,* 2nd ed. (New Haven, CT: Yale University Press, 2005), xxvii–xxviii, citing Ghosh, *Wycliffite Heresy,* 32, 34.

69. On the literary qualities of lollard writings and their critical reception, see Shannon Gayk, "Lollard Writings, Literary Criticism, and the Meaningfulness of Form," in *WC,* 135–52. For a description of how Gerson, too, experimented with literary style and genre as a means of providing moral instruction to newly broadened audiences, see Daniel Hobbins, *Authorship and Publicity before Print: Jean Gerson and the Transformation of Late Medieval Learning* (Philadelphia: University of Pennsylvania Press, 2009), chap. 4, 102–27.

Lollard writers use the "gostli" sense to imagine what should be, or what could be, rather than describe the world as it is.[70] In doing so they frequently make use of structural metaphors in order to think about the self and the community and their parts and disposition; often, too, self and community may serve as metaphors for each another, in a way that the metaphor of a city, castle, church, or barn can allow to bend both ways, or collapse into one another. The structures in question are usually built, rather than simply naturally occurring, because typically these writers want to focus on the process and the effort involved in a lived structure and its effortful disposition. Architectural allegory is of course far from unique to lollardy: lollard writers are participating in, and in some respects adapting in distinctive ways, a wide-ranging and highly various literary tradition popular over several centuries and common in later medieval English writings more broadly.[71] We will look at some of these structuring metaphors in more detail in the final chapter, where we will examine how lollard writers use them to develop modes of religious life within, say, a "gostli" abbey (spiritual as well as metaphorical) that sidestep or even compete with the religious institutions that inhabit brick-and-mortar structures. In concluding this chapter, we will examine a little-known work in which the metaphorical building and inhabiting of both self and community is especially effortful, especially fraught, and perhaps for these reasons unusually various in its metaphors and the narratives in which they participate. Here, perhaps more than almost anywhere, the "moral fantasie" is hard at work.

The text we will examine is a unique item in Laud Misc. 23 that I will call the *City of Saints*.[72] The whole of *City of Saints* is an extended meditation on the ecclesiological and individual moral implications of Ephesians 2:19, "Vos estis cives sanctorum," "*you are citizens of saints*" or "*fellow-citizens with*

70. In addition to the works discussed in the remainder of chap. 6, in chap. 7, and in the Conclusion, readers interested in investigating how lollard writers imagine the world otherwise through "moral fantasie" might begin with SS74's architectural allegory (discussed in chap. 1), the revised versions of Rolle's *English Psalter*, and *Piers the Plowman's Crede*. See also Bruce Holsinger, "Lollard Ekphrasis: Situated Aesthetics and Literary History," *Journal of Medieval and Early Modern Studies* 35 (2005): 68–89.

71. See Christiania Whitehead, *Castles of the Mind: A Study of Medieval Architectural Allegory* (Cardiff: University of Wales Press, 2003), for an introduction.

72. Laud Misc. 23, fols. 61r–70r. For a modernized version of the full text, see WS, 276–90. For more on this text and its manuscript, see Stephen Kelly and Ryan Perry, "Devotional Cosmopolitanism in Fifteenth-Century England," in *After Arundel: Religious Writing in Fifteenth-Century England*, ed. Vincent Gillespie and Kantik Ghosh (Turnhout: Brepols, 2012), 363–80, where they "reject the assertion that it is a Lollard text" (376 and n. 40, citing WS). On this manuscript and other London books, see Margaret Connolly, "Books for the 'helpe of euery persoone þat þenkiþ to be saued': Six Devotional Anthologies from Fifteenth-Century London," *Yearbook of English Studies* 33 (2003): 170–81.

the saints" as most modern translations have it. *City of Saints* introduces its understanding of this city and its inhabitants by means of a story:

> The wyse man [Solomon] tellus in his bok, Ecclesiastes 9, þat þer was sum tyme [once] a lytil cyte [city] and fewe dwellers þerinne [within]. A gret kyng come [fol. 61v] aȝen [against] þis cite and besegid þis cite, and sette engynys þeraȝen [put siege engines around it]. But þer was a pore wise man wiþinne þis cyte, and he delyuerede [saved] þis cite þoruȝ [through] his wysdam. Gostly [Spiritually/metaphorically] þis cite is Cristendam [Christianity], or Cristen mennys religioun, as þe prophet Dauid seiþ, "*Ierusalem que edificatur ut ciuitas. Cristendam is ibildid* [built] *as a cite of pes.*" Þe fewe dwellers in þis cite aren þe lityl ch[o]syn noumbre [small number of the chosen] þat schal come to þe blisse. And so seiþ Crist, Luce 13, "*Nolite timere, pusillus grex, quia complacuit Patri vestro dare uobis,*" etc., þat is, "*Nil ȝe drede* [Do not be afraid], *my litil flok, for it plesiþ my fader to ȝeue ȝow a rewme* [give you a kingdom]." Austyn seiþ Crist clepiþ [calls] his schosun [chosen] a lytil flock in comparisoun of [with] þe grete noumbre [number] þat is to be dampned. And if we biholde inwardly þe multitude of þe hethyn, of Iewis, of Saracenys, and of fals Cristen men, þanne we schulde vnderstonde Cristis wordis, how he clepiþ his schosun noumbre a litil flock. (fol. 61r–v)

The figural story related here is anything but a sustained exercise in the exposition of the historical literal sense: instead, it provides readers with a means of imagining themselves, by means of the "gostly" sense, within the community of those that shall come to bliss.[73] What is provided is scarcely an argument for which a scriptural basis is provided. Clearly there is a sustained effort here to juxtapose texts in a way that confirms and allows the elaboration of their joint significance, yet one text does not "prove" another. Instead, what we have is a process of corroboration—of a kind of mutual strengthening of support beams in a structure—as the writer explains, on the basis of biblical quotations, how the inhabitants of his city should feel and how they should imagine their community in order to understand themselves.

The *City of Saints* grounds its architectural allegory of the city of Christendom in an apparently deliberate mistranslation and pun, one that may also lurk behind *Piers Plowman* B's designation of love as "ledere of þe lordes folk

---

73. The texts examined in chap. 4 and chap. 5 provide further evidence of how lollard writers use biblical stories to develop their readers' sense of aspirational group membership among the community of those that shall be saved.

of heuene / And a meene, as þe Mair is, bitwene þe commune and þe kyng."[74]
Love is also a mayor in the *City of Saints*:

> Þe meir [mayor] þat gouerniþ þese citesynys [citizens] dwellyng in þis
> cite of Cristendam is clepid charite, for þe apostel seiþ, Cor. 13, "*Maior
> horum est caritas*," þat is "charite is meir ouer þese cytycynes [citizens]
> of seyntis." And Iohun Euangelist seiþ, Io. 4, "*Deus caritas est*," þat is, þat
> *God* hymself *is charite*. Þanne it is knowen of þe beleue þat God himself
> is meir ouer þese citesynes. (fol. 62v)

The passage has the form of a syllogism providing a demonstration, on the
basis of biblical proof, of what can be "knowen of þe beleue": the mayor
is charity, God is charity, therefore God is mayor. Not a watertight major
premise, certainly. But of course, it scarcely needs proving that God governs
Christendom; the ease with which this might be demonstrated from "open"
scripture, or tested against reason, may help to license the mnemonic literary
wordplay that begins the treatise's extended personification allegory.

The personified mayor of this city has a great deal to tell his people: for
the bulk of this short treatise, his will be the voice imparting basic instruction
about the ten commandments, followed by briefer instructions for the three
estates: priests, knights, and commons. Occasional first-person interjections
remind us who is speaking, while his concluding remark—"þe meyr of þis
cite techiþ þis lore to 3ow þat ben cetecynis [citizens] of holy seyntis"—
restates the expository theme and reminds the audience of their status as
God's citizens (fol. 66v). Now, near the end, the allegory of the treatise becomes more explicitly architectural. Christ, as cornerstone, is the foundation
of the city. A brief account of the four evangelists and four senses of scripture
follows; it appears to be textually corrupt, since Luke and the allegorical sense
are missing. The three estates become the walls, towers, and dwellers within
the city, and the exposition morphs into a survey of biblical history, linked
through apocalyptic-sounding prophecy to the present, as readers learn how
the city is destroyed and how it may be rebuilt and unified. Finally, the scope
of the architectural allegory shifts from community to individual person.
After a brief recap of the entire treatise, the city's individual inhabitants are
anatomized in not one but two architectural allegories. The first focuses on
the body's outward appearance, itemizing first architectural structure, then
bodily correspondence; it is followed by lists of the conditions of charity and

74. *Piers Plowman* B.1.159–60. I am grateful to Jim Knowles for bringing this text to my
attention—his interest was the resemblance to *Piers Plowman*—and for excellent suggestions about
this chapter as a whole.

of the conditions of love, both called the "conditions of our Mayor." The second allegory focuses on the person's inward disposition:

> For mannis herte is clepid Goddis chambre; mannis soule, Goddis halle; mannis mynde, Goddis chapel; mannis strengþis [faculties][75] ben Goddis houses of offis. Þanne muste Feiþ be stiward in þe chambre, Hope, keper in þin halle; Charite wardeneþ [acts as warden] in þe chapel; Drede, porter of houses of office. For if Drede be porter at þe vtter ȝate [outer gate], no dowte þan ne shal [then, no doubt, shall] no enemy cum in to inquiete [disturb] þe lord God in his dwellyng place. But alle þyngis shal be rewlid [ruled] in þe trewe ordre of pees [peace]; þus shal ȝe cetesynis wiþ mercy and grace be browȝt [brought] to blisse wiþouten end. Amen. (fol. 70r)

This second allegory itemizes first the parts of the person, then architectural structure; it peoples its structure with personified virtues, then concludes with a final address to the citizens.

Now, *City of Saints* is not an allegorical work whose complexity of layered vision and indirection of voicing can rival the *Romance of the Rose* or *Piers Plowman*. But it does deploy sustained narrative as well as episodic reconfigurations that build upon one another's themes. It uses personification, voicing, wordplay, estates satire, and invitations to introspection. It moves fluidly between individual and community-based ways of building, or peopling, a conventional allegorical conceit, and it thoughtfully works out the possibilities opened by their juxtaposition and interplay. The final architectural allegory that concludes the text makes a characteristically lollard appeal to secular power, as a curb on the power and possessions of the church, calling for better control of society by knights: "alle þyngis shal be rewlid in þe trewe ordre of pees; þus shal ȝe cetesynis wiþ mercy and grace be browȝt to blisse wiþouten end." Jerusalem is the city of peace, as we saw in the text's opening. Knights, as the towers of the city, bring peace by means of the virtue they share with and derive from Christ, as is explained in the passage where Christ and the three estates are made part of the city's architecture and assigned their roles. Now, finally, rule in this true order of peace will bring the citizens to bliss.[76]

Yet alongside a covert polemical point, in this final peroration we see lollard writing in its most mystical mode, with an emphasis on mutual indwelling that is also prominent in RV3, the longest version of the interpolated

---

75. By "strengþis" the writer intends, I think, a compressed reference to the various faculties of the soul: the external senses, the will, the reason, the imagination, the common sense, and so on.

76. For more on lollard characteristics of this text, see *WS*, 277.

Rolle psalm commentary.[77] Man's heart, soul, mind, and strength are God's house; man's faith, hope, charity, and dread inhabit his house: God dwells within. The city of the soul jumps scales, in the final sentence, to become the city of the saved, as the citizens we met earlier in the text all participate in its final promise. This last allegorical description bears a close resemblance to the *Abbey of the Holy Ghost*, a contemporary Middle English work adapted from the French, that similarly peoples its internal cloister with personified virtues and human capacities that perform the various duties of the abbey.[78] It also resembles *Book to a Mother*, a Middle English advice manual addressed by the writer to his mother and all Christians and repeatedly preoccupied with forms of allegorical enclosure (see chapter 7). The lollard tract's punning personification of the "Mayor" of Charity may draw on *Piers Plowman*, and of course the tract's repeated shifts between allegories of self and of community, also found in the *Dialogue between Jon and Richard*, are a pervasive feature of the allegory of *Piers Plowman*.

The close affiliations between this example and other Middle English religious writings suggest that in their explorations of "gostli vndurstondyng" we find lollards engaged in some of their closest dialogues with the religious culture around them and some of their most considered and self-aware differentiations of their own beliefs and practices from those of their contemporaries. The moments when lollard writers are most invested in allegory are also, often, their most ambitious literary efforts. This conjunction prompts us to reconsider the category "imaginative theology," proposed by Barbara Newman.[79] For Newman, "imaginative theology" describes self-consciously literary writings, writings that make use of allegory, personification, and sometimes dialogue, among other devices, in order to think about the divine in ways that scholastic discourse cannot. Writing in these literary forms, she suggests, might allow authors greater conceptual freedom than making the same claims in an academic exposition, where they might be more closely scrutinized. For the most part, the writings she discusses were never viewed as heretical, and in the rare cases where they were, it was not

---

77. On RV3, see chap. 4.

78. The *Abbey of the Holy Ghost* does not have a published critical edition, but for versions based on individual manuscript copies, see George G. Perry, *Religious Pieces in Prose and Verse*, EETS, o.s. 26, 3rd ed. (London: K. Paul, Trench, Trübner, 1914), 51–62; and C. Horstmann, ed., *Yorkshire Writers: Richard Rolle of Hampole, an English Father of the Church and His Followers*, 2 vols. (London, 1895–96), 1:321–37. See also D. Peter Consacro, ed., "A Critical Edition of the *Abbey of the Holy Ghost*" (PhD diss., Fordham University, 1971).

79. Barbara Newman, *God and the Goddesses: Vision, Poetry, and Belief in the Middle Ages* (Philadelphia: University of Pennsylvania Press, 2003). On "imaginative theology," see esp. 291–304.

their use of allegory and personification to present aspects of the divine as female that caused the trouble.

It is hard not to agree with Newman that the kinds of imaginative thinking about the divine that interest her most, as well as a good few others, could evidently be expressed in literary writing without provoking censure. Yet it is obvious, too, that medieval authors used allegory, personification, and dialogue to cause trouble as well as to avoid it. Indeed, some of the works Newman examines, certainly *The Sacred Alliance of St Francis with Lady Poverty*, Mechtild of Magdeburg's *Flowing Light of the Godhead*, *Piers Plowman*, and Dante's *Divina Commedia*, may be as motivated by controversy over the proper conduct of the clergy as they are by imagining aspects of the divine as female. Newman interprets female goddesses as a corrective to an impoverished official religion, a very human desire to see God or at the very least his incarnate form as the image of both sexes rather than only of the male, but one that was not yet a direct challenge to the status quo. Divinity is imagined in a form that more closely reflects lived experience. In contrast, what lollards strive to imagine through allegory is that life in this world could be otherwise than their experience suggests. Life could be otherwise, that is, not in the relatively abstract ways imagined by scholastic debates over contingency—however absorbingly to their participants and cosmic in their scope—but rather in urgent, vital ways that have a direct impact on the bodily and "gostli" sustenance of their imagined and real communities.[80]

Lollard writings are imaginative in more the way that Raymond Williams insists that writing in its full multiplicity (beyond the narrower category of high-culture "Literature") is imaginative—and importantly more than *only* imaginative. They refuse the separation of the fictional from the possible and pursue what should be, even beyond what a writer and his readers have the power to effect and against the desires and interests of those who are most invested in the way things are.[81] These are certainly moments in which they do so in ways more conventional in their culture, and that most modern sensibilities (certainly mine) find repugnant, as when the Trinity 93 biblical

---

80. On debates over contingency, see Hester Gelber's marvellous study of the "conversational community" among the Dominicans at Oxford, *It Could Have Been Otherwise: Contingency and Necessity in Dominican Theology at Oxford, 1300–1350* (Leiden: Brill, 2004). For more lollard writings invested in imagining the world otherwise, see n. 70.

81. See Raymond Williams, *Marxism and Literature* (Oxford: Oxford University Press, 1977), especially the sections on "Literature" (45–54) and "The Multiplicity of Writing" (145–50). See also "Literature," in Raymond Williams, *Keywords: A Vocabulary of Culture and Society*, rev. ed. (London: Fontana, 1983), 183–88.

summary repeatedly asserts that the siege of Jerusalem was God's punishment of the Jews and figurally interprets "Iuda" as every man truly acknowledging Christ, in service of its systematic substitution of Christians for Jews as God's chosen people;[82] or when the *SS74* sermons, in their exposition of the eleven kinds of lechery, assert that women are the cause of men's lechery if their appearance leads men's sight astray.[83] But at times the lollard imaginary produces acutely felt demarcations between what is and what should be, of startling relevance.

Consider, for example, this description of the fishes in the sea of this life—the same sea, although the writer has strayed from this exposition for the moment, in which Christ tells the apostles in Matthew 13:47 that the net of the kingdom of heaven draws up all manner of fish, so that the fishermen may choose the good and throw out the bad:

> Þe fisches þat swymmen in þis see ben [are] alle þe peple þat lyuen in þis world, boþe good and yuel [evil] of euery degree [rank], of iche staate [status] temperel [secular] or spirituel [ecclesiastical]. But as þe greet [great] fisches eeten þe smale, so miȝti riche men of þis world deuouren þe pore [poor] to her bare boon [bones], eeting þe moselles [morsels] þat hem beest likeþ [please them best], as þe wise man seiþ, "*Venancio leonis onager in heremo, sic pascua diuitum sunt pauperes.*" "Þe hounting or þe pray [prey] of þe lioun is þe feelde-asse in wildirnes [wilderness]; so [similarly] *feding* [the food] *of þe riche men ben pore nedi men*" (Ecclus. 13:23). And whanne þe sunne schynneþ [shines] warme and in a mylde wedir [weather], þe grete fisches drawen nyȝ [approach] þe eire [air] and driuen doune þe smale. And if þer come an aile [hail] storm or a coolde cesoun [season], þise greet fisches falle to þe grounde and putt abouen þe smale [put the smaller ones above them]. So whanne riche men sen avauntage [see a position of advantage] or ony worldis wynnyng [worldy profit], þei risen abouen þe cloudis in vaunting of her richessis, and al tolaken [put all the blame on] þe symple comunes, and seyn [say] þei mai not paie, wherof [and for that reason] don þei entirmetenen hem [interfere with them (saying)] þei ben but verry [are truly nothing but] beggers. But whanne þer comeþ a charge [burden] to þe countre, as taxis, loones [loans], or ony oþir payment, þanne þe riche men fallen doun and feynen hemsilf nedi [pretend to be needy]

82. See chap. 5, n. 78, and at n. 70.
83. Sermon 19, *SS74*, fol. 50r.

and magnifien [exaggerate the wealth of] þe pore man þat wonneþ bisiȝde him [dwells beside them] and seiþ he is a pryue [secretive] man and hidiþ [is hiding] miche richesse [great riches].[84]

It seems obvious that the rich fish in this rather trenchant comparison will be the bad fish who the fishermen throw out at the Day of Judgment, recounted two paragraphs later. And indeed one solution to injustice—a familiar one, often unpopular with those who want social change in the present—is to wait for the end of time. But the dizzying disposition of space in the analogy between big fish and rich men disorients the reader: are we on land or in water, near the ground, at the surface, or in the clouds? In contrast to a stably imagined hierarchy, where all know their place and obey their superiors, here the small fish are jostled up or down or preyed upon at the whims and dissemblings and predatory impulses of their larger counterparts, with no reliable sense of whether their current position will work to their advantage—probably not. Tellingly, too, this is not a built structure, a home the fish have fashioned through their own efforts, but the water we all swim in.

More dizzying yet, this instability morphs in the following paragraph into a property of the sea itself, now "hidous wawis [waves]" that rise and fall. And by virtue of their natural capacity to withstand the motion of the waves, "quiuer [alert] and quik [alive] in plente [the fullness] of þe watir," the fish who had been the poor become the true faith that permits followers of Christ to withstand even the peril of death in the "watir of tribulacioun," "lyueli ioieyng [vividly rejoicing]" with a fearless conscience. In turning the sea from a metaphor for an unjust social structure to an anatomized psychology of defiant steadfastness, the text shifts its mood from complaint to exhortation. It also shifts the focus of its imaginary, from a hope for future stability to a resolve to withstand any vicissitude, stable in true faith amid whatever changes in circumstance, in order to "do and suffre as plesiþ God."[85] Whether lollard writings appeal to our own moral sensibilities or not, however, and in either case—whether imagination might use literary form to bring writing closer to lived experience, or on the other hand whether it might both insist upon and aspire to bridge the distance between that lived experience and what should be—it is perhaps less important that the imagined changes should form a coherent political program that might be achieved than that they awaken in turn the imaginations of their readers.

84. Lilian M. Swinburn, *Lanterne of Liȝt*, EETS, o.s. 151 (London: Kegan Paul, 1917), 45/34–46/19. Punctuation, word division, and abbreviation expansions modified.
85. Swinburn, *Lanterne of Liȝt*, 47/1–15, quotations from lines 1–2 and 12–13, modified as in n. 84.

❧ CHAPTER 7

Lollard Forms of Living

This final chapter turns to examine in depth a set of lollardy's most self-consciously literary writings: writings that are attentive to literary style and rhetoric and that develop with unusual thoroughness the possibilities of speaking "gostili." What they mean by "gostili" speech is nothing new for the readers of this book: it is the lollard habit of redefining in spiritual or metaphorical terms a concept usually presented as material, bodily, or closely defined by institutional convention.[1] As we learned in the previous chapter, lollard writers often deploy these spiritualizing redefinitions in the service of "moral fantasie," a mode of normative allegory that imagines what should be rather than describing what is, even as it refers to real-world conditions by way of contrast. In their efforts to reimagine the self and the Christian community through spiritualizing metaphors that leave room for uncertainty and aspiration, lollard writers draw deep on the tradition of architectural allegory whose resources Christian writers had been developing for hundreds of years. They also draw upon each other, in a mutually referential ferment where a topic or a turn of phrase or an extended metaphor can be developed to a variety of ends, within very different genres and rhetorical conventions, ranging from polemic to literary dialogue

---

1. See esp. chap. 6, and particularly nn. 1, 36, on the prevalence of the keyword "gostli," in lollard writings as well as more broadly in religious discourse in medieval England.

to confessional formula to instructional treatise to deinstitutionalized form of living.

The full range of lollard experimentation with these possibilities has not been easily accessible to scholars, largely because of a kind of definitional resistance that was unreceptive to the idea that there might be lollard writings that did not include the doctrinal propositions sought in heresy trials and were not primarily polemical. This resistance has also had difficulty with the proposition that lollard writings might have been engaged in conversation, with mainstream writings as well as with each other. So part of this chapter will need to make the argument that the *Book to a Mother* is not a reforming work from the 1370s that predates any written formulation of lollard ideas that might otherwise be thought to have influenced it, as its editor claimed, but a lollard form of living closely engaged with Wyclif's ideas and probably written in the late fourteenth or early fifteenth century, in close conversation with other lollard writings we will examine.[2] We have had cause intermittently in the course of this book to consider why the form of living was a genre that appealed to lollards; this chapter will be our most extended investigation of the "form of living" as both metaphor and genre.

We might define a form of living as any text that lays out a structure or daily routine or set of guidelines for living a life of exceptional virtue in this world in preparation for attaining salvation. The fortunes of Richard Rolle's *Form of Living* well illustrate the spreading popularity of this kind of writing: Rolle wrote the *Form* for an individual anchoress, Margaret Kirkeby, but it subsequently reached a far broader audience, and its preface was adapted in subsequent copying explicitly to address lay readers as well as religious.[3] Texts advising their readers on how to live as perfectly as possible in this world had long been written to address members of religious orders, or else extraregular religious living an ascetic life separated from the world; they might take the form of religious rules giving guidelines for daily conduct, manuals laying out a daily or weekly routine of meditation and prayer, architectural allegories elaborating the proper disposition of the well-ordered individual and community by comparison with a building and perhaps also the community it houses, or all of these combined.

---

2. See *BM*, hereafter cited by page and line number. On McCarthy's arguments for the *Book's* ideological stance and date, see below.

3. The *Form of Living* is edited, and there is some discussion of its textual tradition, in *Richard Rolle: Prose and Verse Edited from MS Longleat 29 and Related Manuscripts*, ed. S. J. Ogilvie-Thomson, EETS, o.s. 293 (London: Oxford University Press, 1988).

Lollard writers were by no means the only ones who took an interest in adapting these forms for lay audiences, nor the only ones to render them in the vernacular or translate them from one language to another in order to make them more accessible.[4] But lollard adapations of the genre do most certainly have a range of distinctive features that make them fairly easy to identify. In this chapter I will show how lollard writers deployed spiritualizing metaphors for religious structures in order to adapt what had been presented as a second-best means to holiness for those unable to join a religious order into an alternative presented as better than religious life, the only true form of religion, and one that all who want to be saved should embrace.

The Soul as Cloister

Let us begin with an easy case: a lollard engagement with mainstream forms of living in a strongly polemical lollard text, found in an early fifteenth-century manuscript everywhere linked with lollardy. The *Dialogue between Jon and Richard* is extant in a unique copy, the final item in the second part of Cambridge, Trinity College, MS B.14.50.[5] This polemical dialogue is extensively inflected by architectural allegory, specifically an allegory of the soul as cloister used to delineate the structure of a truly religious life. Jon invokes this allegorical trope at the dialogue's outset, when he begins by announcing the topic of the coming debate:

> Siþen þe most perel of [greatest danger to] hooly chirche standeþ in false freres, it were to [we should] bigynne atte hem and make hem more knowen. And for þe discriuynge [describing] of þings declareþ [explains] hem more, þerfore schulden we wete [know] wat is suche a frere. Þe grette clerke Grostehed discriueþ hym þus: "A fals frere þat wendeþ [goes] ouȝt [out] of þe cloyster of his soule is a dede caren cropon [crept] ouȝt of his sepulcur [grave], wappid [wrapped] in cloþes of deel [mourning] and oþer fals signes, and dryuen ouȝt of þe deuel for to drecche [destroy] men." Þe cloister of soule schulde be þus schapen, as is þe bodili cloister: gostili to speike, so þat foure cardinal vertues

4. For a recent study of attempts to make some version of religious discipline accessible to new audiences in England, see Nicole R. Rice, *Lay Piety and Religious Discipline in Middle English Literature* (Cambridge: Cambridge University Press, 2008).

5. For a full description, see *FWD*, xvii–xxiii. Quotations from the *Dialogue between Jon and Richard*, and later from the *Dialogue between Reson and Gabbyng*, will be cited from this edition by page and line numbers.

schulde be þe foure wallis keping þe soule fro þe worlde and worldely
þingis, and so iche vice brekeþ þis cloister. (3/6–16)

The underlined portions of the description of friars ascribed to Grosseteste
are a loose translation of a quotation from Grosseteste's Dictum 135, a sermon originally directed at monks:

> Qui vero ambicione dignitatis, aut libidine curiositatis, aut delectacione
> voluptatis, sub pretextu necessitate administracionis egreditur, nichil
> aliud est quam cadaver mortuum, pannis funebribus involutum, de sep-
> ulcro egressum, a diabolo inter homines motum et exagitatum.[6]
>
> [Whoever out of an ambition toward rank, or lustful curiosity, or
> delight in physical pleasure, goes out of the cloister on the pretext of
> needful administrative work, is nothing other than a corpse come out
> of the grave wrapped in a shroud, put in motion by the devil and sent
> out among men.]

Grosseteste's arresting image of a kind of zombie-monk driven from the
grave where he belongs by his improperly focused intentions is similarly re-
directed at friars in other lollard writings, for example the short tract entitled
"Lincolniensis," an interpolated commentary on the "Benedictus" found
with copies of Rolle's *English Psalter* as well as separately, and the *Apology for
Lollard Doctrines*.[7]

The *Dialogue between Jon and Richard*'s use of the quotation is unusual
in comparison with these examples, however, in that it displays awareness
of the quotation's context in Grosseteste's sermon, beyond what might be
gained from gleaning the quotation from a list of famous sayings useful for
preaching, like the one that appears earlier in *Jon and Richard*'s single extant
manuscript.[8] Specifically, the introductory phrase "a fals frere þat wendeþ
ouȝt of þe cloyster of his soule" reveals that the writer is aware of Grosseteste's distinction between the cloister of the soul and the cloister of the body,
developed earlier in Dictum 135. Monks should avoid leaving the cloister of

---

6. Robert Grosseteste, Dictum 135, quoted from the edition of the *Dicta* in Oxford, Bodleian
Library, MS Bodley 798, fol. 110ra, by Edwin J. Westermann, published online at *The Electronic
Grosseteste*, http://www.grosseteste.com/cgi-bin/dicta-display.cgi?dictum=135.

7. The texts using the image from Grosseteste against friars are "Lincolniensis" (Arnold, 230),
"Benedictus" (Arnold, 60/20–23), and *Apology for Lollard Doctrines* (Arnold, 105/2–5). It is applied
more generally to "possessioners," that is, members of religious orders that own property, in "Of
Clerks Possessioners" (Matthew, 123/31).

8. Cambridge, Trinity College, MS B.14.50, fol. 20r. For more details, see *FWD*, xx.

their abbey, Grosseteste begins by explaining. When they must do so in order to provide the community with necessities, then they should leave in body only; the soul should remain cloistered in meditation and contemplation even as they engage in worldly business.[9]

Even in this brief reference to the "cloister of the soul," we can see Grosseteste playing on an already well-established tradition of architectural devotional allegory in order to articulate norms for monastic conduct that require internal as well as external self-regulation; his concerns over internal self-regulation are indeed similar to those of his contemporary Edmund of Abingdon in his much-cited discussion of prayer in the *Speculum ecclesie* (see chap. 3). Grosseteste makes a distinction between the body, materially cloistered in the abbey, and the soul, able to wander at will in the world even while the body is cloistered, but on the other hand capable of dwelling in the cloister "meditans cum Maria" even while the monk is out in the world engaged in business. In making this distinction Grosseteste is alluding to a tradition of claustral allegory of the soul that goes back at least as far as the Augustinian canon Hugh of Folieto's mid-twelfth-century *De claustro animae*.[10] Hugh's work is hortatory in intent: it aims to consolidate its intended audience of monks and canons in properly virtuous religious life in the cloister. Book I gives a defense of the religious life; book II describes the regime of the material cloister of the abbey in detail; book III develops an extended allegory of the "cloister of the soul" in order to describe how the monks should regulate themselves internally; and book IV discusses the heavenly Jerusalem.

Hugh's cloister of the soul, in Book III, is a figurative space for contemplation:

Animae claustrum contemplatio dicitur, in cujus sinum dum se recipit animus, sola coelestia meditatur, separatur a terrenis, a turba cogitationum

---

9. Dictum 135, in Grosseteste, *Dicta*, fol. 109vb: "Pro indempnitate et necessitate fratrum bene licet corpore de claustro egredi, dummodo mente simplici cum Iacob habitet domi. Qui enim pociori sui parte, hoc est animo, in claustro habitat, licet corpore sit extra, nonne propter partem sui pociorem pocius dicetur in claustro esse quam extra? Et econtrario, qui animo est in mundo, licet corpore sit in claustro, nonne pocius est extra claustrum quam intra? Claustralis igitur qui pro necessitate fratrum corpore claustrum egreditur, animo et voluntate in claustro degens, eterna meditans cum Maria et transitoria exterius ministrans cum Martha, talis est in ierarchia humana qualis sunt angeli per contemplacionem assistentes, et similis per officia sibi deputata nobis ministrantes in ierarchia angelica."

10. On this tradition, see Christiania Whitehead, *Castles of the Mind: A Study of Medieval Architectural Allegory* (Cardiff: University of Wales Press, 2003). See also Roberta D. Cornelius, "The Figurative Castle: A Study of the Mediaeval Allegory of the Edifice with Special Reference to Religious Writings" (PhD diss., Bryn Mawr College, 1930); Gerhard Bauer, *Claustrum animae: Untersuchungen zur Geschichte der Metapher vom Herzen als Kloster*, 2 vols. (Munich: Wilhelm Fink, 1973).

carnalium longe ponitur, dulces carnis refugit affectus, vagos sensuum motus restringit, in Domino delectatur, angelica fruitur dulcedine, legit in libro vitae, pro silentio pacem tenet, in choro virtutum, servat concordiam morum, summi Patris bonitatem, angelicae creaturae, beatitudinem contemplatur, attendit bonitatem, cui nihil deest, beatitudinem, quae nullo indiget.[11]

[The cloister of the soul is called contemplation, and while the mind holds itself within it, it thinks only of heavenly things, it is divided from earthly concerns, and it is placed far from the jostling of carnal thoughts. Its feeling flees from bodily sweetness, its movement restrains the wandering of the senses, it delights in the Lord, enjoys angelic sweetness, reads in the book of life, is at peace in silence in the choir of the virtues, maintains a harmony of habits. It contemplates the goodness of the high Father, the blessedness of the angelic creatures, as it attends to that goodness, that blessedness, that is in no way lacking.]

Like *Jon and Richard*'s cloister of the soul, Hugh's has four walls, each equated with an aspect of virtuous behaviour. In Hugh's case these are contempt of the self, contempt of the world, love of God, and love of one's neighbour. "Sicut ex quatuor lateribus claustri materialis structura fieri solet, sic in quatuor virtutibus animi quadratura claustri spiritualis per similitudinem assignari potest, quae sunt contemptus sui, contemptus mundi, amor Dei et amor proximi" ("Just as the material cloister is built from four walls, so the four virtues of the soul can be assigned to the building of the spiritual cloister, virtues which are contempt of the self, contempt of the world, love of God, and love of neighbour").[12] Through the rest of book III Hugh elaborates his architectural allegory in great detail, linking each of the many enumerated features of his figurative monastery's buildings with a desirable behaviour or attitude.

The *De claustro animae* was widely read in subsequent centuries, and for a long time ascribed to Hugh of St Victor. The work was known to lollards, as we know from the citation of its distinction between material and spiritual cloister in the *Rosarium*'s entry on "monke": "*Item Hugo, De Claustro Anime,* 'Monkez makeþ þam cloysteris be wich [by which] þe vtter [outer] man may be holden, bot wolde God þat þei made cloisterez be wich þe inner man schulde ordinately be halden.'"[13] The *De claustro animae*'s later adaptations

---

11. Hugh of Folieto, *De claustro animae, PL* 176, cols. 1017–1182, bk. III, chap. 1, at col. 1087b–c.

12. Hugh of Folieto, *De claustro animae*, bk. III, chap. 2, col. 1088d.

13. Christina von Nolcken, ed., *Middle English Translation of the "Rosarium theologie": A Selection* (Heidenberg: Carol Winter Universitätsverlag, 1979), s.v. "monke." Punctuation modified.

include the much shorter, derivative Latin works "Introduxit me rex in cellam vinariam," which draws on the Song of Songs and switches the setting
to a wine-cellar—"quia corda letificat et debriat et confortat" ("because it
makes hearts joyful and drunk and brings them comfort")—but maintains
the focus on allegorization of architectural structures, and "In claustro animae Deus debet esse abbas," which may be the first work to shift the terms
of the allegorization of the cloister from a focus on architectural structure
to a personification allegory that closely aligns claustral allegory with psychomachia: "Deus debet esse abbas. Discrecio prior. Paupertas procurator.
Timor portarius. Vestiarius humilitas. Regula caritas. Lector veritas" ("God
should be the abbot. Discretion the prior. Poverty the steward. Fear the por-
ter. Humility the keeper of the wardrobe. Charity the rule. Truth the reader
at meals"), and so on.[14] There are also contemporary allegories of the soul as
cloister in German and French. But the mainstream religious writings on the
cloister of the soul from which the writer of *Jon and Richard* is developing a
lollard expression of spirituality include more proximate vernacular choices,
more likely to be familiar to the lollard writer's anticipated audience, such as
the late fourteenth-century *Abbey of the Holy Ghost*, itself a translation and
adaptation of the French *L'Abbaye du Saint Esprit*; the *Charter of the Abbey
of the Holy Ghost*, a Middle English sequel to the *Abbey of the Holy Ghost*
frequently associated with it in manuscripts; and the very brief *Eight Ghostly
Dwelling Places*, which appears along with the *Abbey of the Holy Ghost* in San
Marino, CA, Huntington Library, MS HM 744. An especially close relative, as we will see, is the *Book to a Mother*, composed probably in the west
Midlands, by a self-styled priest, and directed in the first instance to his own
mother but by extension to "euerych man and womman and child" (1/2).[15]

These Middle English works develop an implication of Grosseteste's model
that he himself left unexplored. These are works in which the potential of a

14. See Bauer, *Claustrum animae*, 1:282–309 (discussion and comparison of the three works) and
377–87 (edition of "Introduxit me rex in cellam vinariam"). For the first quotation, see 377; for the
second, the transcription of Melk, Bibliothek des Benediktinerstifts, MS 1605, on 311.

15. For introductory discussion of each of these works, see Robert Raymo, "Works of Religious
and Philosophical Instruction," in A *Manual of the Writings in Middle English, 1050–1500*, vol. 7, edited
by Albert E. Hartung (New Haven: Connecticut Academy of Arts and Sciences, 1986), 2267–68
(*Book to a Mother*), 2340–41 (*Abbey of the Holy Ghost*), 2341 (*Eight Ghostly Dwelling Places*), 2341–43
(*Charter of the Abbey of the Holy Ghost*); and Vincent Gillespie, "Anonymous Devotional Writings," in
A *Companion to Middle English Prose*, ed. A. S. G. Edwards (Woodbridge: Boydell and Brewer, 2004),
127–49. See also Rice, *Lay Piety and Religious Discipline*, chap. 1, 17–46, and chap. 4, 105–32. On
French and Latin works and images that "translate[] enclosure as a state of constant interior reform"
in preparation for divine indwelling, see Aden Kumler, *Translating Truth: Ambitious Images and Religious Knowledge in Late Medieval France and England* (New Haven, CT: Yale University Press, 2011),
161–237, quotation on 236–37.

"cloister of the soul" that allows an individual to live the perfection of religious life while engaging in the business of the world, meditating with Mary while laboring with Martha, is extended in order to develop a model of cloistered existence and even religious perfection accessible to lay readers who are not members of religious orders and who live very much in the world rather than in any form of material enclosure. Thus the *Abbey of the Holy Ghost* explains, "I seo wel þat monie wolde ben in religion but þei mowe not [may not] for pouert or for age or for drede of heore kin or for bond of mariage. And, þerfore, I make her a book of relygion of herte þat is of þe abbeye of þe Holy Gost, þat alle þo þat mouwe not ben in bodi relygion, þei mowe ben in gostly."[16] The *Charter of the Abbey of the Holy Ghost* develops a narrative of salvation history in which the abbey's proper disposition was destroyed by Adam and Eve's sin, sought throughout biblical history up until Christ, then restored by Christ's sacrifice to all those who keep the abbess "Charite" in their hearts, are counselled by Reason, Discretion, Patience, and Peace, and call on the Holy Ghost for help.[17] The *Eight Ghostly Dwelling Places* asserts that "Blessid is þat religioun of whiche þe temple is holynes, þe scole sooþnes [truth], and þe cloister stilnes, þe chapilte of equite, þe dortoir [dormitory] of chastite, and þe fermary [infirmary] pitee, þe fraitir [refectory] sobirnes and þe hostrie [guest house] largenes and charite. Þerfor who þat haþ þese viii placis goostly in his soule and outward in hise werkis, his religioun is perfiȝt."[18] The reference to perfect religion here is tantalizingly tendentious, by the way: this very brief piece of writing seems to claim, as lollard writers do, that religious perfection is available to anyone with a virtuously disposed soul that manifests itself in a virtuous life, regardless of their position in the world—hard though such a soul, and such a life, might be to maintain.

The *Book to a Mother* is far more tendentious in its contrast between the "noiouse [loathesome]" customs, signs, and ceremonies established by men and Christ's true religion, which is perfect all on its own and has no need for these trappings. This text exhorts its readers to maintain themselves "faste

16. D. Peter Consacro, ed., "A Critical Edition of the *Abbey of the Holy Ghost*" (PhD diss., Fordham University, 1971), 1/4–10. Also in C. Horstmann, ed., *Yorkshire Writers: Richard Rolle of Hampole, an English Father of the Church and His Followers*, 2 vols. (London, 1895–96), 1:321–27; and George G. Perry, *Religious Pieces in Prose and Verse*, EETS, o.s. 26, 3rd ed. (London: K. Paul, Trench, Trübner, 1914), 48–58; as well as Norman Blake, ed., *Middle English Religious Prose* (London: Arnold, 1972), 88–102.

17. Clara E. Fanning, ed., "The Charter of the Abbey of the Holy Ghost: A Critical Edition" (PhD diss., Fordham University, 1974). Also in Horstmann, *Yorkshire Writers*, 1:337–62.

18. The *Eight Ghostly Dwelling Places* is edited from its single manuscript, HM 744, in J. W. Conlee, ed., "The *Abbey of the Holy Ghost* and the *Eight Ghostly Dwelling Places* of Huntington Library HM 744," *Medium Aevum* 44 (1975): 137–44, here 142.

iclosed in a cloister of foure stronge wallis, þat ben riȝtfulnes, strengþe, sleiþe [prudence] and temperaunce" (120/26–121/2)—that is, with walls that are the four cardinal virtues—or later, with walls of "bileue, hope, charite and dede" (121/22): that is, the three theological virtues coupled with virtuous action. The writer promises

> ȝif þou kepe wel þis cloister and holde þe þerinne to þi liues ende, Crist, þat is Abbot and Priour of þis cloister, wol euer be þerinne wiþ þe whereeuere þou be, and teche þe his religioun, þat is mekenes and hu-milite. . . . [H]is religioun is most parfit bi hereself, and euere schal laste in heuene, and non oþer mai be good wiþoute þis. For what abite þer ben of ony religioun; customes, signes, or ony oþer serimonies; but [un-less] þei acorde wiþ Cristes religioun and helpe þerto, þei ben noiouse, and better hit were to leue such ordynaunces of men. (122/1–12, punctuation modified)

The precise terms of this claustral allegory are remarkably similar to those of *Jon and Richard*, as well as to those of the only other work in this particular tra-dition of architectural allegory that I have found that equates the four cardinal virtues with the four walls of a dwelling, that is, Wyclif's *Opus evangelicum*:

> [F]ides ista est fundamentum domus spiritualis anime cuius funda-mentum humilitas est sementum. Quatuor autem parietes sunt virtutes quatuor cardinales, scilicet iusticia, prudencia, fortitudo et temperancia. Tectum autem huius domus quoad meremium est spes beatitudinis et caritas. Tegumentum constat autem ex dictis et practica.[19]

> [Faith is the floor of that spiritual home in the soul, and its mortar is humility. The four walls are the four cardinal virtues, that is, justice, prudence, fortitude, and temperance. The timber roof of this home is the hope of salvation and charity. It is shingled with words and deeds.]

Granted, there are other works in the tradition of architectural allegory more broadly, ones possibly known to all of these writers, that label four walls as the four cardinal virtues, or as faith, hope, charity, and works.[20] Yet these examples do not focus their attention on moral exhortation that builds from

---

19. John Wyclif, *Opus evangelicum*, ed. J. Loserth, 2 vols., Wyclif Society (London: Trübner, 1895–96), 3:221/17–24.

20. See, for example, Ralph Hanna, "Verses in Sermons Again: The Case of Cambridge, Jesus College, MS Q.A.13," *Studies in Bibliography* 57 (2005–6): 80–83, for a macaronic sermon interspersed with verse couplets that develops an allegory of the temple of the soul in which the four cardinal virtues are the four walls. Many thanks to Ralph for sharing his transcription of this sermon with me long in advance of publication of his article.

yet also sidesteps traditional ecclesiastical structures in quite the same way as the cluster of writings under discussion here.

Of course the interest these works share, in developing models of virtuous living and even of devotional contemplation accessible to laypeople living in the world, is visible more broadly in Middle English works intended at least partly for lay audiences including translations of Edmund of Abingdon's *Speculum ecclesie*, Richard Rolle's *Form of Living* as well as other writings, the works of the writer of the *Cloud of Unknowyng*, the writings of Walter Hilton, perhaps especially his *On Mixed Life* and *Scale of Perfection*, the *Lyfe of Soule*, the *Pore Caitif*, the *Contemplations of the Dread and Love of God*, and some adaptations of *Ancrene Wisse* that broaden its terms of address to include laymen and laywomen.[21] Among these is a fourteenth-century adaptation of *Ancrene Wisse* that some scholars have associated with lollardy but that Ralph Hanna has argued must be too early to be associated with lollardy—though in conjunction with a sensitive reading of the text that demonstrates the bases of its appeal to Langlandian and lollard sympathies.[22] As *Jon and Richard*—and, as I will argue, *Book to a Mother*—help to show, the interest in making religious

---

21. For brief introductions to these works, see Valerie M. Lagorio and Michael G. Sargent, "English Mystical Writings," in A *Manual of the Writings in Middle English, 1050–1500*, vol. 9, ed. Albert E. Hartung (New Haven: Connecticut Academy of Arts and Sciences, 1993), 3116–17 (*Speculum ecclesie*), 3060–61 (*Form of Living*, and see 3051–68 for a broader survey of Rolle's writings), 3068–73 (works associated with the *Cloud* author) 3075–77 (*Scale of Perfection* and *On Mixed Life*), 3086–87 (*Contemplations of the Dread and Love of God*), and 3135–36 (*Pore Caitif*). Some of these works have a published critical edition that gives further information on their textual tradition: the *Form of Living* in Rolle, *Prose and Verse Edited from MS Longleat 29 and Related Manuscripts*; Phyllis Hodgson, ed., *Cloud of Unknowing and Related Treatises*, Analecta Cartusiana 3 (Salzburg: Institut für Anglistik und Amerikanistik, 1982); *Walter Hilton's "Mixed Life" Edited from Lambeth Palace MS 472*, ed. S. J. Ogilvie-Thomson (Salzburg: Institut für Anglistik und Amerikanistik, 1986); Helen M. Moon, ed., *The Lyfe of Soule: An Edition with Commentary* (Salzburg: Institut für Englische Sprache und Literatur, 1978); Margaret Connolly, ed., *Contemplations of the Dread and Love of God*, EETS o.s. 303 (Oxford: Oxford University Press, 1993); and Bella Millett, ed., *Ancrene Wisse*, 2 vols., EETS, o.s. 325–26 (Oxford: Oxford University Press, 2005–6).

22. Hanna dates the manuscript between 1365 and 1375 on the basis of its hand; Ralph Hanna, "English Biblical Texts before Lollardy and Their Fate," in *Lollards and Their Influence in Late Medieval England*, ed. Fiona Somerset, Jill C. Havens, and Derrick G. Pitard (Woodbridge: Boydell, 2003), 142–44. But he later describes its "rewriting of inclaustration into a purely metaphorical concept," detailing the incongruities of reference that the work's uneven revision in this direction produces (*London Literature, 1300–1380* [Cambridge: Cambridge University Press, 2005], 202–12, quotation on 204). Previously, Colledge had claimed the work was lollard, but Anne Hudson had explained inconsistencies amid what she identified as two layers of revision. See E. Colledge, "*The Recluse*: A Lollard Interpolated Version of the *Ancren Riwle*," *Review of English Studies* 15 (1939): 1–15, 129–45; *PR*, 27–28. As it remains to us now, this version has features untypical of lollard writings that make it unsuitable for detailed study in this book; equally, however, its use of metaphor reveals lollard or perhaps proto-lollard leanings. See also Christina von Nolcken, "*The Recluse* and Its Readers: Some Observations on a Lollard Interpolated Version of *Ancrene Wisse*," in A *Companion to "Ancrene Wisse,"* ed. Yoko Wada (Cambridge: Brewer, 2003), 175–96.

perfection more accessible to lay readers that all these works exhibit is one that lollards share but also develop in new ways.

Lollardy and Literature: "Gostili to Speike"

Jon and Richard self-consciously positions itself amid this burgeoning vernacular tradition and against the conventions of scholastic argumentation. Jon's insistence on speaking "gostili" rather than scholastically both urges the merit of literary discourse, and of allegory in particular, and widens its scope to include instruction and persuasion as well as diversion, thinking as well as feeling, lay as well as clerical audiences. Richard's challenge to Jon's initial claim calls attention to the mode of Jon's exposition, challenging its appropriateness:

> RICHARD: Þeise wordes may plese vertues men, but a sophester wolde schame for to speike hem, and þerfore, I preie þe, declare [explain] hem more. (3/17–19)

Although perhaps pleasing to the virtuous (this is, it appears, a small concession from Richard's point of view, though not from Jon's), Jon's words will not be effective. They are poorly expressed: a "sophester" would be ashamed of them, suggesting that they are neither logically well formed nor stylistically elegant. The intended referent of "sophester" may be those who have had some university training: in late medieval Oxford a student who had finished the first stage of his study in arts became a "sophista generalis,"[23] while in late medieval vernacular contexts, "sophester" is a pejorative term for someone who has great technical skill in argumentation but deploys it fallaciously or with the intent to deceive.[24] In repeating Jon's "declare hem more" but asking for more clarification, Richard is explicitly rejecting Jon's previous claim that "þe discriuynge of þings declareþ hem more." Richard is denying, that is, that speaking "gostili" as Jon has called it, drawing on its broader vernacular tradition and its associations with virtuous spirituality—that is, descriptive analogy and allegorical exposition through extended metaphor of the kind that Jon has provided—will provide the most effective explanation of the peril of false friars.[25] He insists that more explanation of these words is required, and of a kind that will please a "sophester."

---

23. See J. M. Fletcher, "Developments in the Faculty of Arts, 1370–1520," in *The History of the University of Oxford*, vol. 2, *Late Medieval Oxford*, ed. J. I. Catto and R. Evans (Oxford: Clarendon Press, 1992), 325.

24. See *MED*, s.v. "sophistre."

25. For more on "gostili" and its usages, see chap. 6, esp. at n. 1.

In reply Jon insists that his mode of address is carefully chosen to suit his primary audience. Further, Jon asserts that the "sentence and forme" appropriate for his audience will also stand up to criticism from the "sophistris of freres."

> JON: Aftur þe elde [age] of men and hereres of wordis [audience] schulde a man ordeyne his speche in sentence and forme, and I am certeyn þat alle þe sophistris of freres cannot pinche at [find fault with] þese wordis, ne dispreue her sentence [refute what they convey]. (3/20–23)

Even "sophistris" will be unable to disprove Jon's words. What this amounts to is something of an apology for allegory as an expository tool employed in the course of argumentation: even an answer to Augustine on this topic, or at least to those who quote him.[26] It is followed by a demonstration. Jon does go on to "declare . . . more," or explain further, his initial assertion. Yet in doing so he does not depart from his previous mode but rather extends and elaborates his allegorical description:

> Suche a frere is a dede careyne [corpse], as þeise clarkes seyn; for al if he be grett and fatte in his body, naþeles [nonetheless] siþen hym wantiþ [since he lacks] spirit of lijf, he is a deed body, stynkyng wiþ synne. He comeþ ouȝt of his cloister þat he clepiþ his sepulcrer [grave], for he is biried from þe worlde wiþinne fowre wallis and only heuene and heuenly þings ben opyn to his wittis, and grene gresse of vertues and fowles of heuene teche hym to clymbe euene to heuenewarde. . . . [in concluding his long second reply Jon returns to the theme:] . . . it dispergeþ [damages] not Cristis religioun siþen þei ben founded in liȝes [lies] contrary to trewþe, as [just as] ordour of worschipe [the honor of rank] is noþing fowled [not made foul] ȝif þer ben kynges and bischopis of harlatis [among rogues]. But siþen þe charite of Crist caccheþ men to councel, and freres ben fisches wiþouten water þat dwellen ouȝt of cloister, I wolde counsele hem come cleue to Cristis religion. Þane myȝte þei frely wander in cloyster of soule, and flodes of wateris of wisdam schulden renne of [run off] þer bodies, and þane nedid hem not [they need not] þus be ded as to Crist, ne galpe aftur gulles [gullets full] of grace as ffisses [like fish] wiþouȝten [out of] watur. (3/23–29, 4/57–65)

---

26. For how writers quoted and responded to Augustine's stipulation that only the literal sense may be used in argument, see chap. 6, at nn. 40–46.

We are given two explanations here for why a friar is equivalent to a dead body, in a form of double play on body as against soul and bodily as material that will continue throughout the dialogue as Jon extends his criticism to fraternal habits and churches as well as their dwelling places. First, since the soul has gone out of its cloister by transgressing against properly ordered behaviour, the body "wantiþ spirit of lijf," in that it is "ded as to Crist": in this sense the soul's cloister is read as metaphorically equivalent to the body. Second, the body was previously metaphorically entombed in the sepulcher of the material cloister, "biried from þe worlde wiþinne fowre wallis," and dead to the world in that only heavenly thoughts and actions were (or should have been) available to it. Now that the body has departed from the material cloister, it is like a dead body come out of the grave.

Given Jon's strong disapproval of the dwellings that friars do inhabit, and not only when they haunt "howses of lordes" and "chamboris of ladies" but also when they live in ornate buildings within cities (4/48, 49, 51), it may seem odd that the images of the cloister at the beginning and end of this passage are so strongly affirmative, in a style of rhapsodic elaboration that resembles Hugh of Folieto's or the *Abbey of the Holy Ghost* writer's descriptions of contemplation, even if the terms of comparison are different in each case. The friar is "biried from þe worlde wiþinne fowre wallis," with "only heuene and heuenly þings . . . opyn to his wittis" and "grene gresse of vertues and fowles of heuene" teaching him "to clymbe euene to heuenewarde." The friars may "frely wander in cloyster of soule," and "flodes of wateris of wisdam schulden renne of þer bodies." The space within the cloister seems an expansive landscape with a plenitude of natural goods, inflected even perhaps with a dream-visionary mode in which the green grass and birds and waters and fish are "opyn to [a dreamer's] wittis" and encourage "heuenewarde" wandering.[27] Yet this cloister's description is developed as a corrective to incorrectly disposed life in the material cloister: while at the outset the four walls encouraging a focus on heaven and heavenly things sound as though they might be those of the material cloister, the grass of virtues and fowls of heaven teaching the heavenly climb and waters of wisdom that Jon goes on to invoke clearly refer back to the allegorical cloister of the soul within the four walls of virtue from which the dialogue began.

Jon's self-conscious development of vernacular stylistics, too, becomes more and more pronounced, even exaggerated, in his reply to Richard's

---

27. On the importance of comparing literary dream visions with visionary literature rather than seeing them as distinct, see Barbara Newman, "What Did It Mean to Say 'I Saw'? The Clash between Theory and Practice in Medieval Visionary Culture," *Speculum* 80 (2005): 1–43.

challenge. Notice that by the end of his lyrical description of the cloister of the soul, his prose is heavily alliterative: "charite of Crist caccheþ men to councel, and freres ben fisches wiþouten water þat dwellen ouȝt of cloister, I wolde counsele hem come cleue to Cristis religion. Þane myȝte þei frely wander in cloyster of soule, and flodes of wateris of wisdam schulden renne of þer bodies, and þane nedid hem not þus be ded as to Crist, ne galpe aftur gulles of grace as ffisses wiþouȝten watur." The phrase "galpe aftur gulles of grace" in particular evokes *Piers Plowman*, especially Glutton's gulardous "glubbing" of a gallon and a gill in B.5, the "maister"'s anticipated "galping" after his guts rumble in B.13/C.15, and Conscience's "gradd"ing after "grace" at the close of B and C. Jon's is a self-consciously vernacularized "gostili" description, presenting an attractively idealized image of the cloister of the soul as a retreat where the soul, once it cleaves to Christ, may wander freely and disport itself in wisdom. Adherents of "Cristis religion" are already able to enjoy this retreat. Friars, on the other hand, are urged to leave antichrist's religion and return to their proper home.

It seems likely, then, that the writer of *Jon and Richard* knew *Piers Plowman*, and dream vision poetry more generally probably informs his description of this cloister of the soul's rather unusual internal landscape. And it seems obvious that the work draws deep on the tradition of claustral allegory and is well aware of the contemporary Middle English allegories that we have already noted, ones that like *Jon and Richard* use an allegory of the cloister of the soul to develop a model of religious perfection accessible to lay aspirations. What sorts of choices can we see him making among the possibilities these works present?

One choice present in the tradition from early on was that between a heavily populated cloister that develops its exhortations to virtue through a psychomachia staged between allegorical personifications, and an allegory based in the symbolism attached to the architectural features of the cloister. A range of possibilities are represented in Middle English. The *Abbey of the Holy Ghost* proceeds mainly through personification of the abbey's construction crew and inhabitants, all of them maidens or "levedys [ladies]," though there is also some minimal allegorization of the abbey's architectural structures. This work combines, as well, narrative description of the abbey's construction and defense with headily emotional description of the activity of contemplation possible therein. The combination of allegorical techniques and expository modes is, again, very much reminiscent of *Piers Plowman*. The *Charter of the Abbey of the Holy Ghost* is both longer and simpler: in this work the focus is largely on narrative biblical paraphrase, but the frequent brief references to the abbey are in terms of personification allegory, and again the inhabitants are women. The *City of Saints* tries out each alternative, briefly, in turn (see chap. 6). The *Eight Ghostly Dwelling Places* is exclusively architectural, though also very short: I have already quoted the whole. But *Jon and Richard*'s closest cousin by far is the *Book to a Mother*, which like *Jon and Richard* uses claustral allegory not as its overall organizing principle but instead as an intermittent generic inflection across the course of its similarly self-consciously literary exposition, in this case of how the woman being addressed (and, by extension, others) can avoid the temptations of the world and achieve salvation in Christ's religion, far better than they could by joining a religious order.

Christ's Religion over Antichrist's Irreligion: *Book to a Mother*

For *Book to a Mother*, the key to salvation is the avoidance of external signs of religiosity, in all their falseness, and choice instead to focus on the internal disposition of the self. The behaviour of women religious epitomizes for the writer what his mother should avoid, as we see in this loathing description:

> [Þ]ei haue a white, mysproude [improperly proud] and gai, smal, ridlid [pleated], lecherous wimpel; a þicke, ryuen [ornamentally slashed], lesinge [lying] abite [habit]; a ring, and a mantel treilinge aftur hem, wiþ a ueil þrefold ileid [veil triple folded laid] on here hed—for ellis þei helden not þer rule!—and þus be semeliche [are seemly] to turmentours þat comen to hem, not to lerne Godis hestis, wiþ daggede cloþis [clothes with slashed edges], longe cracowes [points] on here schon [shoes], wiþ a stirop [stirrup] aboute þer necke, þat þe deuel lepiþ wiþ upon his hors. And so þei treten [discuss] and conseilen [advise themselves on] hou þei mowen maintene anticristis irreligioun, and seien wiþ here dedis [actions] to antichrist, here [their] Abbot: "Sire, com whanne þou wolt; we haue araid [are dressed] for þe." (123/16–26)

Instead, the writer's mother should choose Christ as her abbot and remain within the cloister of the soul—though interestingly, there is very little, anywhere in the *Book*, by way of positive description of this cloister's or any of its other enclosures' "gostili" furnishings; in general the text is nervous about bodies and skittish about things that might be interpreted in terms of physical pleasure. As this quotation helps to illustrate, *Book to a Mother* shares *Jon and Richard*'s strong bias against organized religious orders, although *Book to a Mother* participates in some traditional topoi of antifeminism whereas in *Jon and Richard* women are never mentioned. Both works share a slippage between literal or figurative habitation and religious habit as a sign of lack of virtue, and both works achieve this slippage by allowing the bodily cloister to stand for both material building and material body. Both works label Christ as the proper abbot of the cloister of the soul, and adherents to religious rules as followers of antichrist. Christ the abbot is the only inhabitant described for each work's cloister; perhaps as a product of each writer's bias against the religious orders, there is no personification of virtues as the various officers of the abbey but rather a strict adherence to architectural allegory. Both works label the four walls of the abbey as the four cardinal virtues, and both give an extended account of what the four walls stand for. In fact, to my knowledge these are the only two extant works in the broad tradition of claustral allegory that name the walls as the virtues, although as we have seen this move has some precedent in the even broader tradition of architectural allegory (see above at n. 12).

Book to a Mother and *Jon and Richard* also have in common that both use the very unusual word "serimonies" to describe ecclesiastical ritual: this word is rare outside of lollard writings and lollard-affiliated works.[28] Both are heavily alliterative in places, fond of rhetorical figures, and in general have a self-consciously literary style. Both draw on a theory of dominion according to which sinful people cannot possess anything. Adrian McCarthy, the editor of *Book to a Mother*, is right that this theory is not unique to Wyclif and lollards but rather drawn by them from Richard Fitzralph. He is also right that its appearance in vernacular writings in or after the 1380s, when Richard Maidstone preached publicly in Oxford against John Ashwardby for propounding just this idea, strongly suggests that those writings are influenced by Wyclif's use of Fitzralph (*BM*, xxxiv, liii–lv). Both resemble a wide range of other lollard writings in that they emphasize the need for correct judgment and insist that, if well instructed, the laity are capable of such judgment by means of their wits.

The most detailed exposition of how laypeople should judge the evidence before their eyes by means of their wits (on which see chapter 4) appears at the end of a third lollard work, closely associated with the *Dialogue between Jon and Richard*: the *Dialogue between Reson and Gabbyng*.[29] For the most part, *Reson and Gabbyng* is a translation and adaptation of the first twelve chapters

---

28. In the *MED*, the only instances outside this circle are from Lydgate, John Capgrave, and Chaucer—all writers well acquainted with lollardy, of course.

29. The *Dialogue between Reson and Gabbyng*'s sources and resemblances with *Jon and Richard* are treated in the introduction to *FWD*, xlix–lii, and detailed more fully in the notes on *Reson and Gabbyng*, 97–107.

of Wyclif's *Dialogus*; providing the exposition of lay judgment with which it concludes was in my view one of its writer's main reasons for undertaking the translation. But *Reson and Gabbyng* closely resembles *Jon and Richard* as well, most of all in the lengthy excursus from translating Wyclif's *Dialogus* that occurs early in the dialogue, in Reson's second long monologue, and that contrasts Christ's religion with the false obedience of the "irreligiouse of antecrist" at length.[30] In this discussion *Reson and Gabbyng* refers to a more elaborate treatment in another work of how the institutional practice of auricular confession harms the virtue of both parties: just this topic is treated with great thoroughness, and similar wording, in *Jon and Richard*.[31] As we will soon see, *Book to a Mother* too is unusually skeptical, compared with some other lollard writings, that any good confessor might be found. In the same excursus, *Reson and Gabbyng* also develops the idea that Christ, rather than any human leader of a religious order, is our abbot, just as *Jon and Richard* and *Book to a Mother* do. It is unusual for lollard writings to describe Christ as an abbot in just this way, developing the comparison more fully than Wyclif does.[32] Providing Christ with a "gostli" version of high-ranking ecclesiastical status in order to assert his superiority as a spiritual leader to the real-world holders of these ranks is a fairly common lollard strategy, as when a lollard treatise on the sacraments refers to him as the bishop or priest of our souls, or when two of the *English Wycliffite Sermons* refer to Christ as abbot of the apostles, but making Christ the abbot of the whole church that shall be saved is more unusual.[33]

On the basis of these similarities it is irresistible to speculate about some direct line of influence between the writers of these three works. Perhaps they knew each other, were part of the same reading circle, or responded to one another's writings; these possibilities are strengthened, if not confirmed,

---

30. See *Dialogue between Reson and Gabbyng*, in *FWD*, 46/108–48/199: the quotation appears at 46/123.

31. For this example, and several other similarities, see the discussion cited in n. 29.

32. One of the *English Wycliffite Sermons* cites the example of how Paul and the apostles held to Christ's order "siþ þe abbot is betture," in a way that is obviously meant to be exemplary for the "men" who are being exhorted toward resistive obedience (*EWS*, 1:354/92–96). For Wyclif's presentation of Christ as the abbot of present Christians, see *De civili dominio*, ed. Reginald L. Poole and Johannes Loserth, 4 vols., Wyclif Society (London: Trübner, 1885–1904), 2:166/2, 3:5/5. For more commentary and more examples, see *FWD*, note to line 336 of the *Dialogue between Jon and Richard*, 76; Appendix B, sermon 33.

33. For the treatise on the sacraments and a quotation including this term, see below at n. 50. Nicole R. Rice, "A Defensive Devotion: A Lollard *Pore Caitiff* in British Library MS Harley 2322," paper presented at the International Congress on Medieval Studies, Kalamazoo, MI, May 13–16, 2010, has also noted that lollard writings refer to Christ as a bishop: I look forward to this work's further development.

by the dialectal similarities of the extant copies.[34] Perhaps the same person
wrote all three works: imagine a West Midlands lollard writer with an ear
for literary rhythm, a broad knowledge of rhetoric, a close understanding
of Wyclif's writings, plenty of time, and an inexhaustible fund of conviction. While these speculations may or may not finally be provable, McCarthy's proposition that *Book to a Mother* is not associated with lollard writings
seems weaker in the light of this evidence. We might wonder, instead, what
we might learn about the range of possibilities for lollard "moral fantasie"
if we consider these closely associated works together, rather than allowing
only the polemical dialogues to be classified as lollard, while the work of
religious instruction is instead dated earlier and labelled as "orthodox" or at
best "reformist."

Book to a Mother is a volume of religious instruction addressed by the
writer in the first instance to his mother, though the writer makes clear that
he also wants a wider audience, for in Christ, "I desire euerych [want every]
man and womman and child to be my moder"—all of them united to him
and to one another in his spiritual mother the church, with loving bonds that
transcend kinship (1/2–3). The *Book* begins, as so many devotional compilations do, with an exposition of basic pastoral instruction: the Pater Noster,
Ave Maria, creed, commandments, the counsels of perfection (interpreted as
accessible to all), the works of mercy (combined with commentary on the
Last Judgment), the seven gifts of the Holy Spirit, the beatitudes, and, after
treating parts of the first three chapters of the Song of Songs, a brief list of
the seven sacraments. An exposition of biblical references to the Book as the
source of salvation follows, then development of the theme that this Book is
Christ. This development takes the form of a meditation on episodes in the
life and teachings of Christ, interspersed with social complaint about abuses
in the present: it is in this section that the writer's mother is exhorted to ask
Christ for new wine like Mary at the wedding at Cana (see below) and to
follow her abbot Christ rather than join a nunnery. Then there follows a
long section of translated selections from the gospel of John, the first and
second epistles of John, Jude, James, the first and second epistles of Peter,
and Paul's First and Second Thessalonians, First Timothy, First and Second

---

34. All copies of the works in question have Southwest Midlands or South Midlands characteristics; an admixture of forms assigned by *LALME* to Huntingdonshire or nearby regions is typical of
lollard writings with generally West Midlands characteristics. On the dialects identified for the *Book
to a Mother* copies, see *BM*, xi–xvii; and see *LALME*, LP 4682 (London, British Library, MS Egerton
826: not analysed by McCarthy). For Cambridge, Trinity College, MS B.14.50 and the *Dialogue between Jon and Richard* in particular, see *FWD*, xxxviii–xxxix; and *LALME*, LP 6680. For the *Dialogue
between Reson and Gabbyng* and TCD 245 more generally, see *FWD*, xli–xlii; and *LALME*, LP 7990.

Corinthians, and Hebrews. This translation is interspersed with glosses, but only sparsely. A final interpretative summary follows, in which the mother is invited to learn to judge rightly based on the advice of the six judges Christ, John, Jude, James, Peter, and Paul, and to ignore the advice of Herod (that is, of members of religious orders and other clergy who would lead her astray).

The *Book* spans 204 pages in its published edition edited by McCarthy and is extant in one complete copy and three partial copies. The extant manuscripts are in fifteenth-century hands, the earliest dated to roughly 1400, and cannot provide direct help with the vexed question of the work's date of composition.[35] In every published discussion of the work's contents since it was edited and published, McCarthy's assessment that the work dates to the 1370s and is not directly associated with lollardy remains unchallenged. It is clear that McCarthy's assessment is under strain in the work of scholars well acquainted with a wide range of late medieval religious writings.[36] But rather than questioning his claims overtly, critics have instead used *Book to a Mother* to attempt to understand the relationships between "reformist" stances within the bounds of what they want to call "orthodoxy," as well as outside of them. The text becomes a kind of benchmark for how far "reformist" writing can go without being "lollard" (and by "lollard," "Lollard," or "Wycliffite" critics generally mean "heretical," or sometimes "what bishops would have seen as heretical"), and when and how this reformist stance was possible.[37] While questioning of the categories within which we understand late medieval religion is very much needed, there is a simpler solution to the difficulties of analyzing *Book to a Mother* as an "orthodox" religious treatise of the 1370s: to realize that it is not. The evidence for the work's "orthodoxy" and early date does not hold up under close scrutiny. Indeed, if it were not the case that this vernacular text has been so central to our understanding of how reformist writing parted company with lollard polemic, it would be discourteous to disagree at length with what was, after all, dissertation research of necessarily limited scope.

35. For further details, see *BM*, iii–viii.
36. See especially Nicholas Watson, "Fashioning the Puritan Gentry-Woman: Devotion and Dissent in *Book to a Mother*," in *Medieval Women: Texts and Contexts in Late Medieval Britain; Essays for Felicity Riddy*, ed. Jocelyn Wogan-Browne et al. (Turnhout: Brepols, 2000), 169–84; Elizabeth Schirmer, "Reading Lessons at Syon Abbey: The *Myroure of Oure Ladye* and the Mandates of Vernacular Theology," in *Voices in Dialogue: Reading Women in the Middle Ages*, ed. Linda Olson and Kathryn Kerby-Fulton (Notre Dame, IN: University of Notre Dame Press, 2005), 345–76; and Rice, *Lay Piety and Religious Discipline*, 105–32, 148–51.
37. Rice, *Lay Piety and Religious Discipline*, esp. 106–11. For similar benchmarking by means of *The Fyve Wyttes* (treated in the Conclusion), see Andrew Cole, *Literature and Heresy in the Age of Chaucer* (Cambridge: Cambridge University Press, 2008), 51–54.

McCarthy's chief impressionistic grounds for a date before 1380—and he makes this argument last, but it seems to me to be the basis for all his earlier claims—are that in 1380 Oxford parted company with Wyclif, heresy became sharply defined, and "the lollards bec[a]me a force to be reckoned with," so that after 1380 it became impossible for any "orthodox" author to write on the sorts of topics found here without issuing polemics against the lollards.[38] McCarthy introduces Nicholas Love's *Mirror* (ca. 1405–10) by way of comparison: if Love condemns lollards, then so would *Book to a Mother* if produced after 1380. The *Book*'s orthodoxy is something that McCarthy assumes rather than proves, though he does attempt to provide some corroboration by contrasting the *Book*'s claims with the errors of John Wyclif condemned at the Council of Constance in 1414–18. On that basis he also claims that the *Book*'s writer could not and would not have made a number of the sensitive statements he makes after they became firmly associated with Wyclif, and thus with heresy, in 1380. The one definitively lollard view McCarthy identifies, and he is quite right here—the comment in exposition of the creed that holy church consists of all those who shall be saved—he suggests may be evidence that some lollard views had more widespread acceptance before they became more firmly associated with Wyclif or may be an example of how lollard views are commonly interpolated into "orthodox" writings; both possibilities leave *Book to a Mother*'s own "orthodoxy" unchallenged.

These claims raise a number of objections. While there were some at Oxford who changed their minds sharply about Wyclif in the early 1380s— Adam Stocton is usually cited for having scratched his positive description of Wyclif in 1379 out of his manuscript and substituted a negative one—there were plenty who did not, nor need it have been possible to label all of them as "lollards"; Oxford resisted outside control, and continued to do so after Arundel's *Constitutions* of 1407–9 attempted to tighten that control as Jeremy Catto and others have shown.[39] Many vernacular devotional and pastoral writers working after 1380 and on well into the fifteenth century did not condemn lollardy: some covertly and some overtly support some of its tenets.

---

38. For McCarthy's dating arguments, see *BM*, xxx–xxxiv; for his arguments for the work's orthodoxy, see xlvi–lvii.

39. On Stocton and the manuscript he annotated, Dublin, Trinity College, MS 115, see Aubrey Gwynn, *English Austin Friars in the Time of Wyclif* (London: Oxford University Press, 1940), 238–39; he is mentioned, e.g., in *PR*, 86 n. 161; and indeed *BM*, xlvii. On the gaps between Arundel's attempts at reform and their implementation, and for a reassessment of his reputation, see Jeremy Catto, "Shaping the Mixed Life: Thomas Arundel's Reformation," in *Image, Text, and Church, 1380–1600: Essays for Margaret Aston*, ed. Linda Clark, Maureen Jurkowski, and Colin Richmond (Toronto: Pontifical Institute of Mediaeval Studies, 2009), 94–108. See also *PR*, 82–110.

Love's *Mirror* is far from representative, in that it aligns itself with Archbishop Arundel's hostile response to lollardy, and in any case it was written well after the 1380s, in 1405–10.[40] All of the evidence for what Wycliffites thought and how "orthodox" writers responded to them that McCarthy presents dates from the first two decades of the fifteenth century. While there are overt condemnations of lollardy in vernacular writings of this period, there are other writings that seem sympathetic, and mainstream and lollard writings were still being copied alongside one another; it is impossible to draw a timeline from which the expression of lollard views in wider contexts simply disappeared.[41] Further, the errors and heresies attributed to Wyclif at his posthumous condemnation for heresy at the Council of Constance are far from a reliable guide to his actual views—let alone the views found in lollard writings, which draw extensively upon but do not merely echo Wyclif's.[42] In order to find out how like or unlike other late fourteenth- or early fifteenth-century writings *Book to a Mother* is, and in what ways its idioms and concerns overlap with those of known lollard writings, McCarthy would have needed to read widely in this corpus.

The *Book*'s satirical idiom also points to a later date. McCarthy notes that the fashions criticized in the *Book*, for "crakowed" or pointed shoes, "dagged" edges on clothing, and the "paltok [short coat]" and "jakke [stuffed jacket]," came to England in the reign of Edward III (*BM*, xxx). It is true, as Richard Green has explained, that "crakowes" are first disparagingly mentioned in Latin chronicles of the 1360s. However, as Green also points out, many of these fashions were popular until nearly the end of the fifteenth century.[43] And while at some point familiarity may have made them immune to mockery, most Middle English (as opposed to Latin) satire referring to these fashions—and in particular, referring to "crakowes" by that name— dates from the fifteenth century. The early fifteenth-century lollard *Lanterne*

---

40. On Love's alignment, and the textual tradition of the *Mirror*, see "Introduction" in *The Mirror of the Blessed Life of Jesus Christ: Full Critical Edition*, ed. Michael G. Sargent (Exeter: University of Exeter Press, 2005), 54–96.

41. See Anne Hudson, "Who Is My Neighbour?," in *WC*, 79–96; and Fiona Somerset, "Censorship," in *The Production of Books in England, 1350–1500*, ed. Alexandra Gillespie and Daniel Wakelin (Cambridge: Cambridge University Press, 2011), 239–58.

42. On the condemned articles, see Margaret Harvey, "Adam Easton and the Condemnation of John Wyclif," *English Historical Review* 113 (1998): 321–35; Anne Hudson, "Notes of an Early Fifteenth-Century Research Assistant, and the Emergence of the 267 Articles against Wyclif," *English Historical Review* 118 (2003): 685–97.

43. Richard Firth Green, "Jack Philpot, John of Gaunt, and a Poem of 1380," *Speculum* 66 (1991): 331. See also Michael Van Dussen, *From England to Bohemia: Heresy and Communication in the later Middle Ages* (Cambridge: Cambridge University Press, 2012), 19 and n. 28.

of Liȝt complains about "crakowed" shoes; an early fifteenth-century poem on "the tixt of holy writ" in Oxford, Bodleian Library, MS Digby 102, a collection of satirical and polemical poetry clearly closely linked with lollardy and with *Piers Plowman*, refers to "crakowed" shoes and "dagged" clothes; an undated lollard polemical text on antichrist preserved in the fifteenth-century manuscript TCD 245 likewise complains about "crakowe pykis" and "tagged" clothes; the mid-fifteenth-century *Castle of Perseverance* associates "crakowes" with boasting; the *Book of Margery Kempe* refers to "dagged" clothes; and both Lydgate and Malory refer to the "paltoke."[44] The earliest Middle English reference I have found for any of these fashions is the reference to dagged clothes in Chaucer's *Parson's Tale*, that is, likely in the late 1390s. Again, this is a work linked, though not through direct condemnation, with lollardy, through the *Man of Law's Epilogue*, probably composed in the late 1380s or early 1390s and perhaps subsequently discarded, in which the Host calls the Parson a "Loller."[45]

The *Book's* closing reference to Herod similarly benefits from more context. McCarthy claims that the allusion to Herod, Herodias, and womanly rule refers to Edward III, John of Gaunt, and Alice Perrers and firms up a date in the period 1370–77 (*BM*, xxxi–xxxiii). Even though McCarthy is right that an opponent of Wyclif writing in Latin at Oxford in the 1370s makes a passing reference to Edward as Herod in criticizing Wyclif's bid for royal patronage, the *Book's* extended polemical exegesis on Herod and family, the most detailed one I have seen in Middle English, has rather different aims. The writer exhorts his mother to judge who the true Christians are by noticing whether they follow Christ's commandments. Mother, look to John, James, Paul, Peter, and Jude, he exhorts. Do not be like the three kings who asked Herod where to find Christ. Do not rely on man's help, but God's: God's help can be found in the bible with the help of the "liȝtinge of feiþ [illumination of faith] þat þe Holi Gost putteþ in a mannes soule" (193/25–194/1). In contrast Herod provides false pastoral teaching, that of fleshly men or worldly folk without faith such as "false feynynge nonnes, flateringe freres, oþer ony oþere þat wiþ false confessiouns and glosynge wordis disseyuen [deceive] mennes soules," or even "alle maner men, lered and lewede, þat ioyen hem [enjoy themselves] and desiren more to be glorious in þinges

---

44. See *MED* svv. "cracou" (n.), "daggen" (v.(1)), "paltok(e)" (n.). Note the new edition of the Digby 102 poem, as poem 20 (untitled), in Helen Barr, ed., *The Digby Poems: A New Edition of the Lyrics* (Exeter: University of Exeter Press, 2009), 270–81.

45. "The Epilogue to the *Man of Law's Tale*," in Geoffrey Chaucer, *The Canterbury Tales*, ed. Jill Mann (London: Penguin, 2005), 209–10, here 210/1173, 1177.

wiþoute-forþ . . . þan þei don in uertues wiþynne" (194/15–17, 20–22).
These members of religious orders, and the other men who resemble them,
delight in outward things and rich apparel rather than in virtue and have by
this means lost their true religion. Although these irreligious may tell you
to ask about Christ, their actions reveal their true nature as they, like Herod,
slay Christ and all the innocents of Bethlehem. Indeed they are worse than
Herod and have wedded Herodias out of lust for her daughter and promised
her half or all of the kingdom. All three have slain John the Baptist through
lechery, vainglory, and pride, and the "false reynynge of wommenliche men
[womanly men] þat ben ouercome wiþ Heredias and hire douȝter, as Heroud
was" is to blame for how difficult it is to attain the grace to continue in good
life in these times (195/17–18).

It is hard to agree with McCarthy that "Edward III in his dotage, and
John of Gaunt in his most influential period were in the mind of our author" in this passage (BM, xxxiii), or to draw a reference to Edward III, John
of Gaunt, and Alice Perrers from the final phrase here. Plainly the Book's
"wommenliche men" are in the first instance members of religious orders
and other clergy, not persons at court, and the passage strongly recalls not
Alice Perrers's influence on Edward III in his final years, but late medieval
English satire on corrupt clergy and members of religious orders that focuses
on their sexual depravity as an index to or even a substitute for any description of their perversions of faith. These men are "womanly" in that they
are sodomites, or hypermasculine woman-chasers, or even both. Chaucer's
Pardoner is perhaps the most famous example, but we might also recall the
rather hysterical "proof" of the sexual proclivities of men and women in
religious orders in the 1395 lollard Twelve Conclusions, or the description of
Oxford as a nest of sodomites in chapter 13 of the General Prologue to the
Wycliffite Bible, arguably referring to the parliament in which the warden of
Merton College, John Bloxham, was accused of sodomy, which was perhaps
the Wonderful Parliament of 1386.[46]

There are, then, no grounds for dating Book to a Mother before 1380. There
are, on the other hand, plentiful grounds for dating the Book to the 1380s or
later and for associating it with contemporary lollard writings. The Book's
affiliations are very clear: except in the manuscript where a partial copy appears alone, every extant copy of the Book appears in a manuscript containing

46. See the third and eleventh of the "Twelve Conclusions," in SEWW, 25/25–35, 28/154–62;
and in the General Prologue: "The Prologue to the Wycliffite Bible," in EA, 72/2515–20; for the
speculative dating, see EA, xxiv; and FEB, 110–13.

lollard writings.[47] What is more, the *Book* incorporates in its chapter 2 (or is perhaps the source for) a discussion of the seven works of mercy also extant in several short freestanding versions, all of them with lollard characteristics and most extant in manuscripts containing other lollard writings as well.[48]

The *Book's* associations with lollard writings are also revealed in many features of its content, most pervasively perhaps in the tendency toward "gostli" understanding and exposition of the kind that we have been examining in this and the previous chapter: that is, its tendency to describe material aspects of religious life in metaphorical terms that allow them to be imagined in new ways. The *Book's* rather covertly divergent presentation of some sacraments is, for example, achieved through "gostli" description. McCarthy had pointed to the list of sacraments at the end of chapter 2 with approval and cited the *Book's* repeated deployment of the phrase "sorew of herte and schrift of mouþe [oral confession] and satisfaccioun" as evidence for orthodoxy (*BM*, xlviii–xlix). Limited and qualified endorsement of the value of confession to the right sort of priest is fairly common in lollard writings, as we have seen (see chapter 1). Yet while this writer recommends "schrift of mouþe," he is in fact more hesitant than some lollard writers to endorse its value. Even though he repeatedly exhorts his reader to repent and reject her sins, there is no reference to confession to a priest: the writer's one reference to the confessing of sins specifies that his mother should "schrif þe [confess] to God" (50/17), while a later account of confession as direct appeal to Christ looks very like a metaphorical description of confession directly to Christ without human intermediaries. Notice how the underlined description is incorporated into the writer's exposition:

---

47. The manuscript containing only a copy of the first third of the *Book* is London, British Library, MS Egerton 826, described in Elisabeth Dutton, "Christ the Codex: Compilation as Literary Device in *Book to a Mother*," *Leeds Studies in English*, n.s., 35 (2004): 81–100. The only complete copy appears in Laud Misc. 210, described in Ralph Hanna, *The English Manuscripts of Richard Rolle: A Descriptive Catalogue* (Exeter; University of Exeter Press, 2010), 160–62; discussed in chap. 2. A copy missing the first third of the text is Bodley 416, discussed in chap. 3; the "short moral pieces" near the end of the manuscript are laden with lollard diction. London, British Library, Additional MS 30897 contains most of the text, as well as one of the interpolated copies of the *Pore Caitif* discussed in Sr. M. Teresa Brady, "Lollard Interpolations and Omissions in Manuscripts of *The Pore Caitif*," in *De Cella in Seculum: Religious and Secular Life and Devotion in Late Medieval England*, ed. Michael G. Sargent (Woodbridge: Brewer, 1989), 183–203. This manuscript also contains a short text on the beatitudes and a long commentary on the Ave Maria, both similarly containing lollard diction; it has been most fully described in M. T. Brady, ed., "The Pore Caitif" (PhD diss., Fordham University, 1954), xvi–xvii.

48. For the versions and their manuscripts, see Fiona Somerset, "Textual Transmission, Variance, and Religious Identity among Lollard Pastoralia," in *Religious Controversy in Europe, 1378–1536: Textual Transmission and Networks of Readership*, ed. Michael Van Dussen and Pavel Soukup (Turnhout: Brepols, 2013), 71–104.

Þenk also, bi þat he tok his modur a maide to kepe [that by preserving his mother's virginity], he schewede þat penaunce and goode werkes plesinge to him moste be kept wiþ clene þouȝtes and chast loue. And þerfore tast and asai ofte [often taste and test] þi wyn, þat þou turne it not into water; and ȝif þou do, cri wiþ Marie and sei: "Sone, þei haue no win," shewinge þi bodi and þi soule, and oþer men biside þe, as Marie dide. And be sori, doinge penaunce fort Crist haue turned hit [until Christ turns it] into wyn aȝeyn; and so þou shalt make glad and murie wiþ þi win þe grete Architriclin—þat is, þe Fadur of heuene— þat is þe grettest of þis wedlac [marriage], and alle seintes and alle angelis of heuene. (88/6–16)

This passage comes from the discussion of the wedding at Cana, in the *Book*'s extended meditation on Christ's life. The son exhorts his mother to taste her wine often—that is, engage in frequent self-examination to ensure continued chastity. If her wine should turn to water, the mother should cry out with Mary to Christ, be sorry, do penance, and by this means return to the communion of saints. The mother seems in some respect to be responsible for revealing to Christ the sins of "oþer men biside þe" as well as her own: she should cry out that *they* have no wine. But any audience this crying out may have other than Christ himself is not mentioned. She is in no way encouraged to reveal her sin to any other man, priest or otherwise.

The text's reference to a kind of metaphorical eucharist, too, is unusual in its emphasis on "gostli" rather than bodily, material reception of Christ. The following passage builds on an earlier comment that Christ wants us to eat him by learning the ten commandments and his counsels (27/1–3). This "gostli" eating of a book that teaches about Christ's life (that is, the *Book* itself) substitutes properly disposed bible reading and meditation for any institutionally mediated account of the reception of Christ's body and blood through the sacrament of the eucharist:

Þerfore, modur, lerne þis bok, as I seide raþer [earlier]; þat is, know þou þe liuinge of Crist and ofte chew hit and defie [digest] hit wiþ hot brennynge [burning] loue, so þat alle þe uertues of þi soule and of þi bodi be turned fro fleshliche liuinge into Cristes liuinge, as bodiliche mete þat is chewed and defied norschiþ [nourishes] alle þe parties of a mannes bodi. And þanne þou etist [eat] gostliche Cristes flesh and his blod whereuere þou be, as Crist seiþ, and ellis [otherwise] not, þouȝ þou seme to folis oþirweies [fools may think otherwise about you]; and in þis ben mony bigiled [tricked]. (32/12–20, punctuation modified)

The mother may spiritually eat Christ's flesh and blood wherever she may be if through meditation on Christ's life she turns her soul and body to Christ's way of life: the emphasis is upon her transformation from fleshly to Christian living, not on anything that might happen to bread in the eucharist. There is no other way than this to eat Christ's flesh and blood "gostliche," and this eating may take place anywhere, regardless of what fools may think, and even if many are deceived on this point. It seems very hard to find a way to read this passage other than as the development of an extrainstitutional, if not explicitly anti-institutional, understanding of communion with Christ.[49]

The *Book* does not reject the sacraments outright, as McCarthy might have expected a heretical work to do. But what it shares with other lollard writings is an impulse to treat them metaphorically, in a way that either sidesteps their institutionalized performance in favor of a more internalized religious experience or attempts to reinvest the conventional performance of the sacrament with spiritual meaning. In either case, the emphasis is on the recipient's virtuous disposition. An unpublished lollard treatment of the sacraments in Bodley 938 makes very similar moves, as we see in the following sequence of excerpts, developing a contrast between material "token" and spiritual truth:[50]

> [A] sacrament is as myche to sey as a token þat may be seen of a þing þat may not be seen wiþ any bodili iȝe [eye]. Þerfor prestis moun [must] mynistre to þe peple þe tokens of siche sacramentis, but þe spiritual grace wiþinne, þat we se not, is mynistrid to vs of [by] God, þat is prest and bischop of oure soules. (fol. 268r)

> [I]n schrifte, þouȝ [although] þou telle þi synnes to a prest and he putte on þee penaunce, þou art assoilid neuer þe raþer but if God [not absolved unless God], þat is þe prest of þi soule, se [sees] `þat´[51] þou sorwist [are sorrowful] wiþ al þin herte for þi synne and þat þou be in ful purpos and will [fully intend] to leue hem euermore after [to leave them forever]. . . . And so schrifte of mouþe [oral confession] maad to a prest is but a token of þe schrifte þat þou makist to God in þin herte. (fol. 268v)

> Þe resseyuing [receiving] of Cristis fleisch and his blod in liknes of breed and wyn: þou schalt vndurstond þat þat þing þat þou resceiuest of

---

49. For more on lollard descriptions of the eucharist, see the Conclusion.

50. Bodley 938, fols. 267v–270v. Each passage in the sequence of excerpts that follows is cited parenthetically.

51. *suplin.*

þe prestis hond `is noþing ellys but a tokyn´⁵² of þe bileue þat þou hast
in Crist þat is veri God and veri man. . . . And al þe tyme þat a man is
in þis bileue, and is bisy wiþ alle þe wittis of his soule and þe wille of his
herte to kepe Goddis heestis [commandments], he etiþ Cristis fleisch
and drynkiþ his blod. . . . [Þ]is gostli etyng of Cristis body is nedeful
to alle [fol. 269v] men þat schulen be sauid. (fol. 269r–v)

Only "gostli" eating of Christ's flesh and blood through belief and keeping
the commandments is needful for those that shall be saved, just as only shrift
to God in one's heart leads to forgiveness of sins by the priest and bishop of
our souls. Like the *Book*, this short treatise does not reject sacraments administered by ordained priests outright, but it does provide its readers with a way
to reimagine their meaning and to perform or participate in them in covertly
or overtly alternative ways.

The *Book*'s metaphors have other close resemblances with lollard writings. The way this writer elaborates on the common metaphor of Christ as
Book has a close analogue in the lollard *Testimony of William Thorpe*.⁵³ In their
treatment of Christ as Book both works follow Wyclif, and resemble a wide
range of lollard writings, in that they value the written page of the book less
than its "sentence," equate that "sentence" with the kingdom of heaven, and
insist that living in imitation of Christ is an essential part of "effectual vn-
dirstondyng" of his word.⁵⁴ Thorpe deploys this analogy to explain why he
will not swear on a copy of the gospels: *Book to a Mother* too eschews swearing, and while concerns about swearing are not unique to lollards—witness
Margery Kempe—they are characteristic of lollardy.⁵⁵

---

52. *erased, visible under ultraviolet light.*

53. *Testimony of William Thorpe*, in *TWT*, 78/1753–80/1826; and see Fiona Somerset, *Clerical Discourse and Lay Audience in Late Medieval England* (Cambridge: Cambridge University Press, 1998), 195–97.

54. On Wyclif, see Ian Christopher Levy, *Holy Scripture and the Quest for Authority at the End of the Middle Ages* (Notre Dame, IN: University of Notre Dame Press, 2012), 62–66. For lollard writ-ings that make similar claims, see chaps. 2 and 3 above. Crucially, Levy insists that Wyclif's claims should be situated in a broader tradition of interpretation stretching from Henry of Ghent to Jean Gerson and beyond, rather than seen as a radical departure from that tradition: see 1–53, esp. 2–11.

55. For Margery Kempe's reproofs of swearing, see Lynn Staley, ed., *The Book of Margery Kempe*, TEAMS Middle English Texts Series (Kalamazoo, MI: Medieval Institute Publications, 1996), 48/821–23, 844 (chap. 16), 121/2833–36 (chap. 50), 124/2914–18 (chap. 52), 135/3207–9 (chap. 55). Unlike William Thorpe in his *Testimony*, Margery never disapproves of swearing in the sense of taking an oath in court, and even takes such oaths when she can do so truthfully. She rejects only swearing in the sense of profanity. On Kempe's and Chaucer's deployment of complaints about swearing in association with lollardy, see Cole, *Literature and Heresy*, 166, 76.

Perhaps the most pervasive metaphor in the *Book* is that of enclosure. The *Book*'s depiction of the soul as cloister is certainly one of the text's more striking images, and its closest points of similarity with *Jon and Richard*, but the *Book*'s writer is preoccupied with a wider range of metaphorical enclosures throughout the advisorial sections of his text: the prison of this world (23/16), Mary's conclave where she was visited by Gabriel (33/5–15, 45/20), Mary's womb where Christ's Book was enclosed (33/6, 44/21–22), the stable of Christ's birth (34/2, 48/15–16), Christ's cradle (50/18), Anne's temple (52/12), the soul as a place where Mary may dwell (98/16–17), the house, gate, and grave from which Christ called the dead (128–30), the womb that gives birth to the child of sin (132–33), and three tabernacles built in the wounds in Christ's feet, hands, and heart (149/3–5), where his mother should "holde . . . euere wiþ Crist an heiʒ" by keeping his commandments (150/4–5). He exhorts his mother to avoid penetration of and excursions beyond these enclosures, literal as well as metaphorical: whatever else might be said of this son's attitude toward women, he is certainly uncomfortable with his mother's sexuality and in particular with her bearing of children.

As we have seen, the *Abbey*, the *Eight Ghostly Dwelling Places*, and *Jon and Richard* all describe their method of "gostli" exposition, and do so more or less as soon as they embark upon it. While the *Book* considers it equally important to make its "gostli" method clear, its emphasis emerges more gradually throughout its opening catechetical section and as a means of establishing its imagined reading community of those interested in spiritual development. A "gostli" enclosure first appears in the exposition of the works of mercy (this section appears in varying forms widely distributed among lollard manuscripts, remember) where the writer's concerns about Christian community are for the first time explicitly raised. The works of mercy are here interpreted throughout in "gostli" senses, as deprivation of knowledge of God's commandments and consequent entanglement in sin rather than literal hunger, thirst, sickness, imprisonment, and so on. The alternative that the reader is encouraged to urge by her own example is to enter the house of Holy Church. The seven gifts are portrayed as those by which God makes man's soul his house. The ultimate reward linked with the seven gifts and beatitudes is provided in a lyrical (though physically nervous) description of the pleasures of contemplation with God, found in the flower-strewn bed, in the cedar house, under the apple tree, and in the wine cellar, all as described in the Song of Songs—and as similarly subjected to architectural allegory elsewhere, as the writer of the *Book* surely knew (11–13). Readers should join those in the wine cellar:

In þis wyn seler oure Lady was loken [locked] with seuen ʒiftes of þe
Holy Gost whan Gabriel here grette [greeted] in þe conclaue [meeting].
Forto holde him in þis wyn seler Ion þe Baptist wente into deserte and
cloþed him with a skyn of a chamule [camel]. Of þis wyn Poule hadde
dronke whan he seyde: "I am crucified to þe world and þe world to me," and
alle þe seyntes þat Poule spekeþ of, þat were in wildernesse, in spelunkes
[caves] and in cauernes of erþe. Þis wyn made þe Aposteles and martirs
glad and ioyful to suffre schame and parsecucioun; þis wyn made Seynt
Cecile bere euer [carry always] þe gospel of Crist in her herte and secede
not [never cease] nyʒt ne day [night or day] fro holy speche. (13/7–17)

Other writers might celebrate the pleasures of wine and liken them to communion with Christ. This one fixes his attention on the resolve of constancy
and even joy in the face of martyrdom that enclosure in the wine cellar and
drinking of the wine symbolize for him. The martyrdom that faces those enclosed in the wine cellar is not necessarily literal, physical martyrdom (though
it is not always clear that it is not) as much as it is spiritual or metaphorical
martyrdom—"goostli" martyrdom—as a way of life in Christ. The Book's
writer wants his mother drunk on "goostli" martyrdom, and his description
of living metaphorically enclosed and mindful of death is a systematic recon-
figuration of what should count as religious life.

Paul's remark when he has drunk the wine, that he is "crucified to þe
world," is a lollard favourite. William Thorpe similarly uses it to describe
his opposition to Arundel and his clerks near the end of his Testimony, written around 1407, and the Lanterne of Liʒt, from around the same date, tells
its readers that all those who live virtuously, as well as (if not as severely as)
those who are martyred for truth, are crucified to the world, exhorting all
Christians to join the cross to their bare flesh.[56] Lollards dwell in Christ in
that they are at odds, "crosse wyse" as Thorpe puts it, with the world around
them.[57] In rather the same way that members of religious orders are taught
to consider themselves dead to the world, lollards dispose themselves toward
possible martyrdom as a way of cleaving to Christ.[58] What is more, as the
writer goes on to elaborate here, drinking the wine of the wine cellar by
being crucified to the world purifies and strengthens the "gostly wittes"

56. Testimony of William Thorpe, 93/2245–47; Lilian M. Swinburn, Lanterne of Liʒt, EETS, o.s. 151
(London: Kegan Paul, 1917), 79/23–80/19.

57. Testimony of William Thorpe, 93/2246.

58. See also Fiona Somerset, "Wycliffite Spirituality," in Text and Controversy from Wyclif to Bale:
Essays in Honour of Anne Hudson, ed. Helen Barr and Ann M. Hutchison (Turnhout: Brepols, 2005),
383–86.

(13/18–15/8). Adam lost his "gostly" wits in Paradise through sin, but "þe more a man loueþ God [that is, the more he drinks the wine of the wine cellar], þe more clere ben his gostly wittes" (13/21–22)—and thus, the more likely he is to agree with the *Book* writer's "gostly" exposition, here and throughout. Just as in Richard's concession that Jon's "gostili" argumentation will please the virtuous but not sophesters, the *Book*'s writer here suggests that any virtuous reader will share his "gostli" understanding.

But perhaps the *Book*'s most revealing illustration of a metaphorical ascesis of enclosure is its description of the womb of sin and its child who should never have been born. This passage is only tangentially based on Gregory's *Moralia in Job*, the source McCarthy identifies:

> Þe furste wombe of synne is þe furste þou3t [thought] of synne, or mynde [recollection]; and 3if a man slow [should slay] þe furste þou3t, he schulde bringe forþ none wickede werkes. Aftur þat, þou3t is brou3t forþ bi likinge [pleasure] of alle his wittis, þat ben soget to do synne in dede wiþouten-forþ [outwardly], as þe child is leid [laid] on his modir [mother's] knees; and so þe synneful man 3eueþ [gives] his cursede child souke [nurses his cursed child] wiþ two tetis [teats] of his fyue wittis, and norischeþ [nourishes] hit wiþ fals bileue and hope of Godis merci, wiþ fals excusaciouns and wickede defendinges þoru3 [through] yuele ensample of oþere synful men. And þus þe modur baþeþ hure [bathes her] child and swaþeþ [swaddles] hit wiþ a cursede swaþe [cloth] bond of alle maner synnes—for as mony uices, so mony bondis—forte [until] hit be an olde scherewe [wicked thing], þat his fadur fecche [fetch] him wiþ his cursede modur to dwelle with him eueremore in þe peine of helle . . . and so dede men birien dede men wiþ fals fauour, wickede preisinges and defendinges in þer sinnes. (132/14–133/12)

A virtuous man will slay his "furste þou3t" of sin in its "furste wombe," in his mind, while a less virtuous man will mother it and nurse it with his five wits and bring forth wicked deeds, nourished by false faith and hope, bound together with a band of other sins of all kinds, with the help of false excuses and wicked defendings and evil examples from other sinful men. The writer focuses, at least at the outset here, on the individual's consent to his or her own sin, rather than the social consent to the sins of others that more typically preoccupied Wyclif and his followers and that he does himself treat in more detail elsewhere.[59] But in providing a "gostli" description of even one

---

59. As explained in chap. 1, Wyclif's theory of consent translates the private, personal sin of acting upon or even just fantasizing about one's own individual urges—this is the sin of consent that

person's consent to his or her own sin he also reconfigures that very personal, internal process as a family romance of improper nurturing. The father and mother who nurture their sin into an "olde scherewe" closely echo other lollard descriptions of the importance of providing children with proper training; they may indeed deliver an all too personal reproach to his mother, and all the more so, perhaps, the writer's dead father—especially when we remember his earlier description of "cursede hosbondis þat wollen not lerne Godis hestis ne holde hem ne teche here children to holde hem" and who scorn their children who are not like them.[60] Recall Christ's advice to the man who wanted to bury his father before following him (Luke 9:60). Let the dead bury the dead, Christ says—as the *Book*'s writer tells his mother that they do when they consent to one another's sins. Instead, you should preach the kingdom of God.

Even if *Jon and Richard* and *Book to a Mother* resemble one another closely in several ways, the differences in how they depict the soul's susceptibility to sin are clearly visible in the contrast between this description of the womb of sin and *Jon and Richard*'s later elaboration on the cloister of the soul. These differences are richly suggestive and support my larger point that a narrow focus on the assertions made in lollard polemical writings gives us only a very partial account of how lollards felt about their beliefs. For as Jon describes it, the soul's activity within its cloister sounds unusually effortless. Even in its most celebratory moments *Piers Plowman* does not find the "craft of loue," as Jon too calls it, so easy to maintain (*Jon and Richard*, lines 859–60; cf. *Piers Plowman* B.20/C.22.207–8). Similarly, the *Abbey of the Holy Ghost* is imperiled by assaults from the "foure douȝtren" of a "tiraunt"/"fende," "Envye," "Pruide," "Grucchinge," and "Fals-Demynge-of-Othere," and can only be preserved by earnest prayers to the Holy Ghost from the ladies of the abbey (*Abbey of the Holy Ghost*, 38/9–39/3). While the peril of these assaults is delayed until near the end of the *Abbey of the Holy Ghost*, the narrative of salvation history that takes up the bulk of the *Charter of the Abbey of the Holy Ghost*

---

concerns Augustine, and many penitential writings—to the realm of social responsibility, with the result that we become directly responsible for the sins of others. His conclusion is that not only anyone who commits a sin but anyone who fails to help to prevent or at the very least openly censure a sin has consented to that sin and is also guilty of it. Wyclif's deployment of this theory has its basis in legal theory from the twelfth century onward, but in developing it into a justification for dissent he articulates it in an extreme form. His followers go even further, in that they lay the imperative to act against the sins of the clergy at the feet of laypeople, in a wide range of vernacular writings. In the *Book*, the writer grounds his claims about consent in Rom. 1:32 but attributes the imperative to withstand and even destroy sinners to "seintes": see 119/23–120/14.

60. See 78–79, and esp. 78/3–5, 79/1–6. See chap. 2 for lollard writings that urge parents to instruct their children in the faith, above all by teaching them the commandments.

is deployed in response to an initial assault on the abbey by the "tiraunt . . .
Sathanas" that is finally repulsed only with Christ's sacrifice, yet requires
continuing vigilance and prayer to the Holy Spirit to maintain (*Charter of
the Abbey of the Holy Ghost*, 11/8–9). Even though the *Book to a Mother*, like
Jon and Richard, is focused during its claustral allegory on blaming the faults
of religious orders in contrast with the virtue of "Cristes religioun," the
reader's success in maintaining that "religioun" remains very much an open
question and in fact the *Book to a Mother's* major concern throughout its
length, rather than a foregone conclusion. No "gostili" mother can succeed
in killing all her "gostili" sin-children before they bring forth any wicked
works whatsoever. For Jon, in contrast, the rejection of religious rules seems
to make religious perfection easy: "our abbot is þe best, siþen he is God and
man" (12/336–37), and "God haþ ȝeuen a sufficient reule, as oure feiþ techiþ,
þat is more liȝt and more fre to iche Cristen man to holde" (27/879–81).

This apparent certitude about salvation might seem to be the product of
a rather odious smug dogmatism stemming from Wycliffite predestinarian-
ism. However, as discussed in more detail in chapter 4, predestination does
not always entail determinism nor always produce certitude; there is ample
evidence elsewhere that it did not do so for lollards, any more than it had
for Wyclif. In my view the difference in attitude here is largely situational.
Rather than having pious exhortation as its chief focus, like the *Abbey of the
Holy Ghost* and *Charter of the Abbey of the Holy Ghost* and to a lesser extent
the *Book to a Mother*, *Jon and Richard's* primary focus is polemic. Rather than
encouraging his lay readers to fortify the cloisters of their souls despite their
inability to remove themselves from the vicissitudes of life in the world, it is
most helpful for Jon's argument for him to claim that his vernacular readers
are already doing a far better job of maintaining their virtue and aspiring to
Christian perfection than are the friars. There is an exhortation to proper
conduct embedded in Jon's first use of the trope: "Þe cloister of soule *schulde
be* þus schapen, as is þe bodili cloister: gostili to speike, so þat foure cardinal
vertues *schulde be* þe foure wallis keping þe soule fro þe worlde and worldely
þingis, and so iche vice brekeþ þis cloister." But the overwhelming emphasis,
both here and in what follows, is on fraternal vices rather than the possibility
of lay vices.

Thus Jon's fullest deployment of claustral allegory comes in reply to Richard's claim that friars live a more perfect life than lay people. Jon cannot agree:

As freres in many þings contrarien [act contrary to] Crist, so þei han
brouȝt in customes to manye þat ben contrarie to Godes maneres. . . .
Se how oponly þei lie in suying [about following] of Crist. And þerfore

no drede [no doubt] þei parten hem [separate themselves] fro Cristis children and schewen hem brolles [show that they are children] of antecristis couent. . . . siþen foure cardenal vertues schulden be foure wallis to holde þese freres in cloyster of þer soule, and þei breke alle þese and turnen to vices, it is opon [obvious] þat þei ben false in bodily cloysteris. Iusticie is þe first wal þat Cristes religion axiþ [requires], þat techiþ Cristen men to obesche to mesure [observe the moderation] of Goddis lawe. But þis wal han þei broken and clumben þerouer. Þe secunde vertu is strengþe to stonde in þe limites [stand within the limits] þat Goddes lawe haþ sette wiþou3t sclidyng [sliding] awaye. But þis wal is broken, and new wal maked for to stonde stifely [stand stubbornly] in þer owne ritis [rites]. Þe þred vertu is prudence, þat þei han forsaken, siþen it is no prudence to drynke trubily and venemous watur [stirred-up, venomous water] and forsake water of wisdom of God. Þe fourte vertu of þis cloyster is clepid [called] temperance, þat þese freres han broken in maner of þer lyuyng. For take heede to þer numbre, and efte [again] to þer houses, and eke [also] to þer reules, and al þat þei vsen, and we may opinly see þat temperance faileþ. And þis erroure haþ brou3t þe pope and þe pepul in more depe erroures be freres ypocricie [hypocrisy]. . . . In þis mesure God 3af his lawe and his ordur so þat eche mi3t frely and li3tly holde it. But in þis mesure failen þe freres more þan pharises in þe newe lawe þat wolde kepe þe rites of þe olde lawe, and þerwiþ þe fredom of þe lawe of Crist. (13/388–89, 14/406–8, 14/419–34, 15/438–42)

Rather than taking on a special religious vow that gives them access to a kind of perfection that laypeople cannot attain, friars are transgressing against a kind of virtuous soul-cloistering in virtue that is easily accessible to all laymen and laywomen who seek it out. Laypeople who "frely and li3tly holde" Christ's law are the "mesure" for friars; this presentation of the laity as reliable judges of the clergy is of course very common in lollard polemic.[61] Rather than acting as a cynosure, the friars fail to measure up to a common standard accessible to all—and they fail in ways that all can easily measure. The friars are false in their bodily cloisters because they break all four of the walls of the cloister of their souls by transgressing against the four cardinal

---

61. For examples, and for discussion of the wider conversation in which this lollard confidence participates, see Fiona Somerset, "'As just as is a squyre': The Politics of 'Lewed Translacion' in Chaucer's *Summoner's Tale*," *Studies in the Age of Chaucer* 21 (1999): 187–207; and Somerset, "'Mark him wel for he is on of þo': Training the 'Lewed' Gaze to Discern Hypocrisy," *English Literary History* 68 (2001): 315–34.

virtues. It is telling, I think, that the claustral allegory begins to break down here even as do the walls of virtue: this writer finds no pleasure in negative imagination. There is no wall in the description of prudence, though there is a reference to the waters of wisdom that we encountered within the allegorical landscape of the cloister of the soul. And the description of temperance and "mesure" departs from allegory entirely, as the writer's concern to give specifics of just how the friars fail in obeying the "mesure of Goddis lawe" through their failures of temperance takes over from allegorical exposition.

The *Book to a Mother*, on the other hand, helps us to understand that lollards are not so certain of their salvation as the lay-authorizing argumentative moves staged in *Jon and Richard* might make them look. If they were, then the striving toward difficult perfection characteristic of claustral allegories would not have been so appealing to them in the first place: they have many other resources for creating arguments that authorize the laity without having to draw upon the discursive resources of forms of the religious life. *Book to a Mother* certainly helps us to see that lollard writers are far from certain of their own or their readers' salvation. The self-doubt and fear for his mother's as well as his father's salvation most acutely visible in the *Book* writer's allegory of the sin-child might give us new insight into how it felt to be a lollard. It certainly demonstrates the importance of reading lollard writings across their full range of genres and rhetorical modes, and with attention to what they share with mainstream religion as well as how they differ, if we want to comprehend this religious movement's widespread diffusion in English religious culture and fathom the appeal of a spirituality so severe upon, yet invitingly inclusive of, its participants.

Conclusion

In summary of this book's findings, this Conclusion examines a largely neglected short text that eschews polemical declaration but that nonetheless within its short length touches on all the characteristic emphases in lollard writings that we have discovered across the course of this book, compactly providing us with an occasion to draw them together and to demonstrate how they allow us to identify and describe lollard writings more effectively. Like the *Book to a Mother*, the *Fyve Wyttes* was classified as "orthodox" by its student editor—in this case Rolf Bremmer, now a well-known scholar of Old Frisian and Middle Dutch as well as Old and Middle English, but at the point of writing at work on an MA thesis.[1] When the *Fyve Wyttes* has been mentioned in the years since, discussion has focused more or less exclusively on the text's use of the word "lollarde," and it has been presented as an example of "orthodox" tolerance for lollardy.[2] Far from it: the text is instead a good example of how lollard writings encourage their readers' active engagement in the discovery of truth by teaching them

---

1. Rolf H. Bremmer, Jr., ed., *The Fyve Wyttes* (Amsterdam: Rodopi, 1987). Subsequent quotations will be cited by page and line numbers.

2. *PR*, 435 n. 194; Andrew Cole, *Literature and Heresy in the Age of Chaucer* (Cambridge: Cambridge University Press, 2008), 51–53, 162; Ian Forrest, *The Detection of Heresy in Late Medieval England* (Oxford: Clarendon Press, 2005), 168.

to doubt and question. What is more, it provides a final example of how late medieval usage of "lollard" was often more flexible than that in some recent scholarship: the *Fyve Wyttes* deploys "lollarde" as a verbal noun, one that describes persons only when they are behaving in certain ways, rather than treating "lollarde" as a static category of personhood (see Introduction).

The single extant copy of the *Fyve Wyttes* appears in Harley 2398: the same manuscript in a Gloucestershire dialect that also contains the single copy of the longest and most heavily influenced by Wyclif of many related commentaries on the commandments (discussed at length in chapter 2).[3] The *Fyve Wyttes* follows directly after this lengthy commandments commentary, within the same booklet. Nobody has yet noted that the *Fyve Wyttes* appears to have been excerpted from a longer treatise, no longer extant or as yet unrecognized as its source: the text begins in medias res, yet with a five-line, elaborately decorated initial capital that suggests its copyist was presenting this excerpt as a freestanding item. Like *Book to a Mother* this text has a penchant for architectural allegory and for ornate prose (see chapter 7). To excite man to love, the *Fyve Wyttes* begins, God builds him the royal palace of the world. Its description is lyrically alliterative: "dyuers," "delyte," "dalyaunce," "desporte" (1/5). Within that world is man's private dwelling, the hall of the body, and within that body, the little private closet of the heart. We discover, later, in the author's creative translation of Matthew 5:28's "in corde suo" ("in his heart") as "in his conscience byfore God" that the closet of the heart, for this author, is also the house of conscience (3/35). Yet man's true home is not this house, not the closet, not the hall, not the palace, but dwelling in love with God in heaven, and the world should excite every man in that direction, "hom [home] to his loue" (1/3), by means of the five senses.[4]

The rest of the treatise addresses each of the hall's five windows in turn: just over twelve pages of the published edition are on sight, nine and a half on hearing, one on smell, four on taste, and five on feeling. Lists of the five senses in the course of religious instruction are common in Middle English writings and often focus on the ways in which the senses might lead one toward sin (see also chapter 6). Extended treatments of the kind found in the *Fyve Wyttes* are rarer: the only other one known to me is books 2 and 3 of the *Ancrene Wisse*, themselves redacted in the fifteenth century into a freestanding treatise addressed to laypeople.[5] But neither *Ancrene Wisse* nor

---

3. For a description of Harley 2398, see Appendix A.

4. Mutual indwelling is a pervasive metaphor in lollard writings and a means of imagining an alternative church: it appears in every chapter in this volume, but see especially chap. 7.

5. On this treatise, see Robert Raymo, "Works of Religious and Philosophical Instruction," in *A Manual of the Writings in Middle English, 1050–1500*, vol. 7, ed. Albert E. Hartung (New Haven: Connecticut Academy of Arts and Sciences, 1986), 2323.

the fifteenth-century redaction of its second and third books is similar to the *Fyve Wyttes*. Our author has independently developed a treatise on the five senses into a guide to lay religious conduct, a form of living for the everyday world, one that focuses on how the senses can become windows toward properly trained discernment in the "myrour of ymaginacioun" (14/28).

Even if it is modeled on the kind of advice about daily conduct found in a religious rule or in an adaptation of that genre intended for extraregular religious persons and lay readers, the text as a whole emphasizes not introspection, self-knowledge, and care of the self, as would be more typical in this genre, but social responsibility, care of others, and right action in the world.[6] It assigns the moral guidance of others not only to priests but to everyone. In advice on the window of sight, for example, all are required not only to turn their eyes from vain sights to the "verray ly3t of trouþe" (3/10) but to watch out for the good of others. To behold Christ's sinful limbs and help and comfort them. To read the law of God and live by it, rather than false new rules. To see and follow the example of good men. To watch that their subordinates follow God's law, or else forfeit their own souls. This emphasis on communal responsibility and this insistence that God's law is better than new rules are distinctive and characteristic of the lollard writings we have encountered (see especially the commandments commentaries in chapter 2).

The same interest in how the senses mediate human relationships found in the *Fyve Wyttes*'s discussion of sight also pervades the discussion of the window of hearing, where it is not hearing but speech—backbiting, foul speaking, flattering, and blasphemy—that takes center stage. All are required not only to avoid hearing or commiting these sins of speech but to do all they can to keep others from them too. When your subordinate engages in backbiting, for example, you should reprove him. When your equal does so, you should smite him with the sword of scripture, explaining to him why his behaviour is wrong. When your master backbites, you should not answer, but "schewe þyself as þyn herte ys . . . loþ of his wordes"—subject him to an eloquently disapproving silence (16/28–17/1, here 16/30–31). Just this concern with the obligation to speak the truth not only to inferiors but to equals and superiors as well, and just this kind of advice on how a speaker should modulate his rendition of the truth to suit his audience, is also prominent in the lollard *Schort Reule of Lif* and in the long lollard *SS74* (see chapter 3, chapter 1).[7]

---

6. On Middle English adaptations of guides to religious life for lay readers, see Nicole R. Rice, *Lay Piety and Religious Discipline in Middle English Literature* (Cambridge: Cambridge University Press, 2008).

7. On lollard formulations of the obligation to speak truth, see chap. 1. For description of how the Christian obligation to correct others is described differently by lollard than by mainstream writers, see Edwin D. Craun, "Discarding Traditional Pastoral Ethics: Wycliffism and Slander," in *WC*,

Against the backdrop of his pervasive theme of social responsibility, the *Fyve Wyttes* writer brings up the term "lollarde" in his discussion of blasphemy, the last kind of speech treated in the discussion of hearing. It will be crucial to attend to the writer's artful involution in this passage, his play with voicing and the social meanings of speech, rather than to treat the passage reductively and assert what it really means to say. This close attention will require a lengthy quotation:

Þe fourþe wynde is blasfemye whiche I calle errour and heresye contrarie aȝenst Cristes lore. Aȝenst þis most þou principaly [most especially] stoppe þy wyndow, for what þat euere he be, on or ouþer, þat wolde induce or teche þe eny nywe adinuenciouns [new fabrications] in nywe and sotel conceytes [conceits] oþer þan haue ben vsed by holy seintȝ and doctours of Holy Churche, contrarie or impertinent [irrelevant] to Iesu Cristes gospel—to whiche in soþe [truth] þer nys no lore impertinent, bot oþer he is þerwiþ [with that] oþer euene contrarye [contrary to it], as himself seyþ: "*Qui non est mecum, contra me est.*" "*Who that is nouȝt wiþ me, he is aȝenst me.*" And among alle oþer þynges he nedeþ to be war now in tyme of opynyouns whiche þat faste encreceþ [increase], oþer, soþ for to say [to tell the truth], longe tyme haue ben hyd and now begynneþ openly to be schewed, blasfemynge God and his seintȝ, vsynge, meyntenynge and defendynge liberte of synne, so þat no man dar cheyrly [charitably] do, as he scholde, repreue synne [reprove sin as he should] þat þey ne wole falsely desclaundre [slander] hem and, in al þat þey may, trauayle [work] to destrue hem, so þat þey myȝte frely fulfille þe lustes and lykynges [pleasures] of þe wordle [world] to pleysynge of here flesch. Consente þou nouȝt [Do not consent] to þis errour ne þis blasfemye. *Videte ne scandalizetis vnum ex pusillis istis,* þough þey be called heretykes or lollardes. Bot be war, [fol. 118r] consente þou nouȝt to calle hem so, ne leue nouȝt lyȝtly to [do not easily give credence to] þe commune sclaundre or clamour of fooles, yf þey preche trewely Crist and his gospel. And þerto [in doing so], ȝe knoweþ non oþer bot [know nothing else except] þat þey leneþ[8] [give] þer all ȝe nedeþ.

_____

227–42. On the *Schort Reule*—itself an adaptation of the religious rule for lay readers—see chap. 3, and Mary Raschko, "Common Ground for Contrasting Ideologies: The Texts and Contexts of *A Schort Reule of Lif,*" *Viator* 40 (2009): 387–410. For a description of Cambridge, Sidney Sussex College, MS 74, see Appendix A.

8. I emend Bremmer's reading, "leueþ": he has mistaken an "n" for a "u." "Lenen" is used very commonly in West Midlands dialects of this period to mean "give" or "bestow," especially when the giving involves practical charity or spiritual benefit. See *MED*, s.v. "lenen," v. (3), 1.

Nou3t ly3tly do oppon [Do not lightly open] 3oure herte to þulke [those] þat dampnede hem, for vtterly men lyeþ muche oppon hem [men tell many lies about them], and it is betere to be in doute of hem [remain undecided about them], whaþer þey be goede men or badde, þan presumptuously to deme hem or ly3tly consente to hem þat demeþ hem. If þey preche pouert, so dyde Crist and was pore himself. Yf þey repreue pride and precheþ mekenesse, so dyde Crist and was meke himself. Yf þey repreue swerynge, Crist forbedeþ it ne swor he nou3t himself. Yf þey repreue gret aray, Crist repreuede it and seyde þat þe ryche man, ycloþed in purpur and bysse [linen], was beryed in helle. Lete God alone wiþ hem: yf it be of God, it schal stande, who þat euere wiþstande, yf it be nou3t goed, it wol be destroyed, þough 3e do nou3t þerto; ne deme hem nou3t [do not judge them] at al. (18/29–19/26, punctuation modified)

The Latin quotation in the underlined section of the first quoted paragraph, just before the text's reference to "heretykes or lollardes," should catch our attention. "Videte ne scandalizetis vnum ex pusillis istis" is the only Latin quotation in the whole of the *Fyve Wyttes* that is not translated into Middle English and then interpreted, but rather absorbed macaronically into the writer's argument. What is more, the Latin matters: the untranslated quotation makes clear that the writer is not merely quoting Matthew 18:10 (the reference Bremmer supplies) but conflating it with Matthew 18:6, where the verb "scandalizetis" appears in place of Matthew 18:10's "contemnatis," and with Luke 17:1–3, where those who scandalize the little ones are linked to the negative connotations of lolling through the Latin verb "suspendere"; recall Wyclif's punning on "suspendere," discussed in the Introduction. "Qui autem scandalizaverit unum de pusillis istis qui in me credunt expedit ei ut suspendatur mola asinaria in collo eius et demergatur in profundum maris" ("Whoever brings scandal upon any one of these little ones who believe in me, it would be better if a millstone were hanged around his neck and he were drowned in the depths of the sea").

Once its range of multilingual reference is unpacked, then, this conflated quotation responds to the verbal aspect of "loll," indicating that those who slander persons they call lollards should themselves be hung about with millstones. It vindicates the persons it labels as "pusillis," since they, as the rest of Matthew 18:10 asserts, will see the face of God in heaven. In Luke 17, on the other hand, it is followed by positive suggestions for reproof and forgiveness that reinforce the ones that the *Fyve Wyttes* has already articulated in its discussion of backbiting, providing materials for the reproof of equals by means of the sword of scripture and an example of how to go about this criticism. This range of reference would certainly not be immediately apparent to all readers of a vernacular treatise on the five wits, although it is possible that the intention behind leaving the quotation untranslated was to allow an expositor to expatiate on its implications in reading aloud. Certainly these implications defy any word-for-word translation, even if they could, like "in corde suo" and in a manner that we have seen is common elsewhere in lollard writings, have been rendered briskly in an interpretative paraphrase.[9] Still, what the *Fyve Wyttes* packs into this untranslated Latin phrase, it also develops more fully across the whole of the discussion of blasphemy just quoted.

The *Fyve Wyttes* introduces blasphemy here by making it equivalent to both error and heresy. Canon law would disagree.[10] But for this writer, anything contrary to the gospel is against Christ, for whoever is not with Christ is against him (a favorite quotation in lollard polemic).[11] Blasphemy has grown so widespread, the writer complains, that none dare to reprove blasphemers for their sin, for fear that they will be slandered as heretics or lollards. Notice the shifts in perspective here. All of us, readers and writer, had temporarily inhabited the identity of the reprover a moment earlier, as we opposed new fabrications that reject the right path held by holy saints and doctors. Now, at "no man dar cheyrly do," readers become onlookers, or rather hearers (recall that the larger discussion is about sins of hearing), as "þey"—the slanderers—call the man who might reprove the blasphemers a heretic or lollard. Do not consent to this sin, the writer cautions his readers. One sin of hearing, then, is the sin of agreeing too readily with what one hears. Do not consent to slander against those who would reprove sin. Instead, take a stand: for whoever is not with me is against me. As we have learned, lollard writers commonly exhort their readers to social responsibility by alluding to a theory of consent to sin that Wyclif, too, frequently cited

---

9. For similar examples of interpretative paraphrase, see chap. 5, chap. 6, *WS*, 23–24.

10. As R. H. Helmholz explains in *The Spirit of Classical Canon Law* (Athens: University of Georgia Press, 1996), 263–83, blasphemy only acquired precise legal definitions in both canon and common law in the sixteenth and seventeenth centuries; before this point, the concept was more nebulously defined as any kind of insult to God. Heresy, on the other hand, acquired a quite precise legal definition in the twelfth century: a person was a heretic if they refused to submit to correction after being instructed about the errors in their beliefs. Thus, an error might be heresy if the person who held this incorrect belief refused to renounce it, and an error or heresy might be blasphemous, especially if it were forcefully asserted in strong terms, but not every error or blasphemy was a heresy. See Forrest, *Detection of Heresy*, 14–19.

11. For a sampling of quotations or paraphrases of Matt. 12:30 and Luke 11:23, see *EWS*, 1:280/1–2, 549/18–550/19, 570/57, 2:55/16–20.

and developed in the same characteristic way.[12] We are guilty not only of consenting to our own sins, when we give in to our baser impulses, but also of consent to any sin by another person that we do not attempt to prevent. In a startling shift, what constitutes blasphemy in this passage is not merely the teaching of newfangled ideas but any slander against the true preacher of Christ's gospel who criticizes those ideas or even any failure to speak out against this slander.

Rather than presumptuously judging or being too ready to believe others' judgments, readers of the *Fyve Wyttes* should maintain a state of uncertainty: "it is betere to be in doute of hem." Especially if the reproofs of sin issued by these so-called lollards imitate Christ's, we should not blame them: it is not good for the bad to reprove the good lest we blaspheme against the Holy Ghost. It is the name-callers, finally, and those who too easily follow their example, who are the blasphemers. The importance of remaining uncertain in order to arrive at a properly measured discernment on topics where there is room for doubt was a widespread topic of late scholastic discussion.[13] But, as we saw in chapter 4, it is Wyclif who develops this topic into a means for asserting the validity of his own judgments, and those of the readers he urges to agree with him, over and above those of the institutional church. He insists that only God can know whether a person is a true Christian or not and whether that person will be saved. This conviction leads him to protest that ecclesiastical excommunication is invalid; it also leads him to urge his readers to maintain a hopeful uncertainty about their own future fate, as a spur toward continued effort, and to form their own judgments about whether their priests are virtuous and provide adequate spiritual instruction and are thus worthy of monetary support. Wyclif's development of these ideas is deployed far and wide in lollard writings, from the *Dialogue between Reson and Gabbyng* that translates Wyclif's *Dialogus* to the third version of the interpolated *English Psalter* of Richard Rolle to the *Testimony of William Thorpe* to *Of Dominion*.[14]

This lollard insistence on uncertainty also provides a better framework within which to understand how the *Fyve Wyttes* treats the eucharist. The text's discussion of the eucharist was the basis of Bremmer's conclusion that the text cannot be lollard, even if it shows sympathy for "lollardes." His attempt to describe the text's ideological affiliations is well reasoned and

12. See esp. chap. 1, chap. 7 at n. 59.
13. See Rudolf Schüssler, *Moral im Zweifel*, 2 vols. (Paderborn: Mentis-Verlag, 2002–6); Ilkka Kantola, *Probability and Moral Uncertainty in Late Medieval and Early Modern Times* (Helsinki: Luther-Agricola Society, 1994).
14. See chap. 4 at nn. 35 and 55–58 for most of these citations. See also chap. 1 at n. 15. For the chapters on lay judgment of the clergy in *Of Dominion*, see Matthew, 289–93.

coherent, even if mistaken.[15] Bremmer notices the close resemblance between the *Fyve Wyttes* and a brief list of authoritative statements on the eucharist from TCD 245 (printed in *SEWW*, 110–12): each of them provides an account of Christ's life in place of a technical description of what happens in the act of consecration. (So, for that matter, do the *Letter of Richard Wyche* and the *Testimony of William Thorpe*, and in closely similar terms: see chapter 4.) However, Bremmer thinks that the inclusion of the word "substancialy" in the *Fyve Wyttes* indicates that the writer of the *Fyve Wyttes*, unlike the author of the Dublin text, must accept transubstantiation. Here is the passage:

> þou schalt byhalde þy saueour in sacrament wiþ sadde deuocioun and stablenesse of mynde, fully bylyuynge and þenkynge in þyn herte þat vnder þe forme of bred and wyn þer is verrayly, holly and substancialy þe same persone in flesch and blood, boþe God and man þat was bore of Blessed Virgine, suffrede deþ vpon þe cros for redempcioun of mannes soule, was beryed, aros fro deþ þe þrydde day, styed into heune, is to come for to deme euery man as he haþ deserued. (5/22–29)

Bremmer is unaware, however, that what the author says is entirely compatible with a theory of consubstantiation, one Wyclif himself found appealing, although his thinking on the eucharist developed over time, and his positive statements on the topic are rarer and less straightforward than his negative ones.[16] Moreover, in suggesting that a Wycliffite author would certainly have taken the opportunity to elaborate on his heretical position, Bremmer is incorrect. Instead, it is a pervasive and widespread characteristic of lollard writing about the eucharist to refuse to explain what happens to the bread and wine at consecration. Even the *Tractatus de oblacione iugis sacrificii*, the single lengthiest lollard treatment of the eucharist, rehearses a long string of possible interpretations of "Hoc est corpus meum" only to conclude that what all of them miss is the true foundation of belief in Christ's words.[17]

---

15. Bremmer, *Fyve Wyttes*, xxix–xxxiii.

16. See Stephen E. Lahey, *John Wyclif* (Oxford: Oxford University Press, 2009), 102–34, for an introductory discussion of Wyclif's writings on the eucharist and their philosophical underpinnings.

17. See Anne Hudson, ed., *Works of a Lollard Preacher*, EETS, o.s. 317 (Oxford: Oxford University Press, 2001), 207/1978–209/2068. On positions taken in lollard writings, see further Fiona Somerset, "Here, There, and Everywhere? Wycliffite Conceptions of the Eucharist and Chaucer's 'Other' Lollard Joke," in *Lollards and Their Influence in Late Medieval England*, ed. Fiona Somerset, Jill C. Havens, and Derrick G. Pitard (Woodbridge: Boydell, 2003), 127–38. See also chap. 7. For a survey of lollard writings and trial evidence about the eucharist, see Patrick Hornbeck, *What Is a Lollard? Dissent and Belief in Late Medieval England* (Oxford: Oxford University Press, 2010), 68–103. Hornbeck perceptively charts doctrinal variations but misses a broader consistency in reluctance to explain the eucharist's mystery.

When they provide positive accounts of how their readers should understand the eucharist and participate in the sacrament, as we saw in chapter 7, lollard writings emphasize "gostili" or spiritual reception through knowing about Christ's life, believing he is God and man, and keeping the commandments. This tendency to treat the sacraments metaphorically or insist on their spiritual significance, but not flatly to refuse participation in them or deny their efficacy, is typical of lollard treatments of the sacraments more broadly (see chapter 1). The *Fyve Wyttes*'s concern for the correct disposition of readers' emotions when regarding the eucharist, as well as this passage's emphasis on believing that Christ is God and man and knowing about Christ's life, seem entirely typical of lollard treatments of the eucharist.

For the *Fyve Wyttes* writer, then, "lollard" is not a fixed identity stably attached to a fixed group—even if the slanderers who reportedly label followers of Christ as heretics or lollards in this passage may indeed think of it that way. Instead, as it is lived by the true preachers whom slanderers *call* lollards, it is an allegiance to truth, a structure of feeling (see chapter 5). The discerning readers that the *Fyve Wyttes* as a whole is laboring to create are encouraged here to try this allegiance on, like the "lollare" clothing Will wears in *Piers Plowman* C.5.2.[18] In so doing, they might speak in the person of those who speak the truth in the gospel, feel like saints, and imagine their participation in the church of those that shall be saved (see chapter 4, chapter 6).

Those who reserve judgment on so-called "lollardes" and hold the window of their hearing open to the law of Christ that those so-called "lollardes" preach (21/1–2) could scarcely be more lollard, as we have developed the meaning of this term across the course of this book. For they, and the writer of this text, are implementing some of Wyclif's more dearly held and often repeated convictions in a way that is recommended over and over in lollard writings. The *Fyve Wyttes* acknowledges that slanderers deploy "lollard" as an insult, even an accusation. It does not attempt to reclaim the word by assimilating the defiance it recommends to the positive senses of lolling, as the *Dialogue between a Wise Man and a Fool* does, for example, by asserting that the most blessed loller that ever was or shall be was Christ and all who wish to loll toward God should imitate his followers by lolling on his right hand and speaking out against the sins of the people.[19] But it does invite its readers to imagine that refusing to consent to the condemnation of so-called

---

18. Cf. Cole, *Literature and Heresy*, 69. I agree that *Piers Plowman* is engaged in discussion of the same term, within the same discourse, rather than advancing a separate meaning of the term "loller" that would be superseded by its use to describe lollards, as Scase and others have suggested.

19. "Cambridge Tract XII," in *EA*, 131/36–46. For more on this text, see chap. 4.

"lollardes," when those "lollardes" are in fact true preachers of Christ and his gospel, could be a moral obligation.

When the *Fyve Wyttes* asserts, without any qualification and on Christ's authority, that any teaching not confirmed by the gospel is against Christ, it does not explicitly urge its readers to disregard the instructions of their priests and bishops where they do not confirm the gospel, as more polemical lollard writings do. But it clearly does so implicitly and in a way that invites them to form their own judgments about who among them are the truest followers of Christ. As the text goes on to encourage readers to exercise their discernment when they witness true preachers being condemned as "lollardes," the writer similarly places no limits on whose condemnations its readers should exercise their discernment upon. There is no difficulty in disregarding "þe commune sclaundre or clamour of fooles" when the slanderers and fools are mere rumormongers: canon law stipulated that only well-founded suspicions, not malicious rumors, were legitimate grounds for the investigation of heresy, and the author of the *Fyve Wyttes* surely knows this.[20] But what if these slanderers and fools are themselves members of the clergy? In both repressive and reforming discources, as they remain to us in written sources, "lollard" is an insult deployed by clerics, often for audiences that include laypeople, in order either to provoke or to suspend wider agreement that the recipient is a heretic. Far more so than his position on the eucharist, the *Fyve Wyttes* writer's insistence that his readers should make up their own minds about the legitimacy of the preachers they hear, and on the basis of those preachers' conformity with the gospel rather than what others who use the word "lollarde" may say about them, is a persuasive indication of his own lollard views.

We have learned that lollard pastoral and devotional writings are in many ways similar to, and often derived from, more mainstream religious writings in the same vein. Nonetheless, lollard writings have characteristic emphases, many of them derived from Wyclif's own concerns. These key topics to do with lollard belief are not points of doctrinal difference, like the lists of propositions found in a condemnation for heresy or sought in a heresy trial. Rather, they address the practice of everyday life, urging their readers to imagine the world otherwise and to conduct themselves as if it were. A rigorist impulse in everyday religion is by no means distinctive to lollardy, among late medieval vernacular religious writings intended for and also sometimes written by lay readers. Distinctive, instead, is the shape this rigor takes in lollard writings,

---

20. Ian Forrest points out this stipulation, in *Detection of Heresy*, 168.

even where it does not veer into social complaint of similarly characteristic kinds (and it often does of course, even if only in passing).

The characteristic emphases we have discovered provide us with something that the field has not yet had: a means of identifying and describing lollard writings on the basis of what their writers care about and want to convey, rather than what their opponents claim that they wanted to reject. As we continue to learn more about lollard writings, they may also give us new tools for investigating what this book has not assumed: what kinds of social groups the writers and readers formed and belonged to, and what relationships they formed over time and from place to place. When I set out to write this book I did not expect, for example, to discover a large cluster of lollard pastoral and devotional writings in what the *LALME* identifies as West Midlands dialects nor widespread close reliance on models provided by early thirteenth-century pastoral writings: these are only two examples of topics in need of more investigation. This book is far from the last word on the writings of the lollard movement. I hope to have pointed the way toward future discoveries and look forward to many more conversations.

❧ BIBLIOGRAPHY

Manuscripts

Aberystwyth, National Library of Wales, Peniarth MS 395D
Cambridge, Corpus Christi College, MS 147
Cambridge, Corpus Christi College, MS 296
Cambridge, Corpus Christi College, MS 385
Cambridge, Gonville and Caius College, MS 354/581
Cambridge, Sidney Sussex College, MS 74
Cambridge, St John's College, MS G.22
Cambridge, Trinity College, MS B.14.38
Cambridge, Trinity College, MS B.14.50
Cambridge, University Library, MS Dd.12.39
Cambridge, University Library, MS Gg.4.31
Cambridge, University Library, MS Ii.6.26
Cambridge, University Library, MS Ii.6.43
Cambridge, University Library, MS Kk.1.8
Cambridge, University Library, MS Kk.6.26
Cambridge, University Library, MS Nn.4.12
Cambridge, MA, Harvard University, MS English 738
Dublin, Trinity College, MS 72
Dublin, Trinity College, MS 75
Dublin, Trinity College, MS 115
Dublin, Trinity College, MS 155
Dublin, Trinity College, MS 241
Dublin, Trinity College, MS 244
Dublin, Trinity College, MS 245
Edinburgh, National Library of Scotland, MS Advocates 18.6.7
Edinburgh, University Library, MS 93
Glasgow, University Library, MS Hunter 520
Keio, University Library, MS 170 X 9.6
Leeds, University Library, MS Brotherton 501
Lincoln, Lincoln Cathedral, MS A.1.17 (Thornton MS)
London, British Library, Additional MS 10046
London, British Library, Additional MS 17013
London, British Library, Additional MS 22283 (Simeon MS)
London, British Library, Additional MS 30897
London, British Library, Additional MS 31044
London, British Library, MS Cotton Claudius E.2

London, British Library, MS Egerton 826
London, British Library, MS Harley 1666
London, British Library, MS Harley 2385
London, British Library, MS Harley 2398
London, British Library, MS Harley 5017
London, British Library, MS Royal 1.C.viii
London, British Library, MS Royal 1.C.ix
London, British Library, MS Royal 18.B.xxiii
London, British Library, MS Royal 18.C.xxvi
London, Lambeth Palace Library, MS 34
London, Lambeth Palace Library, MS 408
London, Westminster School, MS 3
Manchester, John Rylands Library, MS English 85
Manchester, John Rylands Library, MS English 90
Melk, Bibliothek des Benediktinerstifts, MS 1605
Norwich, Castle Museum, MS 158.926.4g.3
Oxford, Bodleian Library, MS Bodley 95
Oxford, Bodleian Library, MS Bodley 277
Oxford, Bodleian Library, MS Bodley 416
Oxford, Bodleian Library, MS Bodley 554
Oxford, Bodleian Library, MS Bodley 789
Oxford, Bodleian Library, MS Bodley 798
Oxford, Bodleian Library, MS Bodley 938
Oxford, Bodleian Library, MS Digby 102
Oxford, Bodleian Library, MS Digby 133
Oxford, Bodleian Library, MS Douce 25
Oxford, Bodleian Library, MS Douce 246
Oxford, Bodleian Library, MS Douce 274
Oxford, Bodleian Library, MS e Musaeo 180
Oxford, Bodleian Library, MS Eng. poet. a.1 (Vernon MS)
Oxford, Bodleian Library, MS Laud Misc. 23
Oxford, Bodleian Library, MS Laud Misc. 210
Oxford, Bodleian Library, MS Laud Misc. 235
Oxford, Bodleian Library, MS Laud Misc. 524
Oxford, Lincoln College, MS Latin 119
Oxford, Trinity College, MS 93
Oxford, University College, MS 96
Oxford, University College, MS 97
Oxford, University College, MS 179
Paris, Bibliothèque Ste. Geneviève, MS 3390
Princeton, NJ, Scheide Library, MS M.12
Princeton, NJ, University Library, Taylor MS 16
San Marino, CA, Huntington Library, HM 148
San Marino, CA, Huntington Library, MS HM 501
San Marino, CA, Huntington Library, MS HM 744
Shrewsbury, Shrewsbury School, MS 3
Urbana-Champaign, University of Illinois Rare Book and Manuscript Library, MS 80

Worcester, Cathedral Library, MS F.172
York, York Minster, MS XVI.L.12

Printed Editions

Aarts, F. G. A. M., ed. *Pe Pater Noster of Richard Ermyte*. The Hague: Nijhoff, 1967.

Aquinas, Thomas. *Catena aurea*. Edited and translated by J. H. Newman. 4 vols. Southampton: St. Austin Press, 1997.

Arnold, Thomas, ed. *Select English Works of Wyclif*. Vol. 3. Oxford, 1871.

Audelay, John. *Poems and Carols (Oxford, Bodleian Library MS Douce 302)*. Edited by Susanna Fein. TEAMS Middle English Texts Series. Kalamazoo, MI: Medieval Institute Publications, 2009.

Barnum, Priscilla H., ed. *Dives and Pauper*. 2 vols. (vol. 1 in 2 parts). EETS, o.s. 275, 280, 323. London: Oxford University Press, 1976–2004.

Barr, Helen, ed. *The Digby Poems: A New Edition of the Lyrics*. Exeter: University of Exeter Press, 2009.

——, ed. *The Piers Plowman Tradition*. London: Dent, 1993.

Blake, Norman, ed. *Middle English Religious Prose*. London: Arnold, 1972.

Bradley, Christopher G., ed. and trans. "The Letter of Richard Wyche: An Interrogation Narrative." *Publications of the Modern Language Association* 127 (2012): 626–42.

Brady, M. T., ed. "The Pore Caitif." PhD diss., Fordham University, 1954.

Bremmer, Rolf H., Jr., ed. *The Fyve Wyttes*. Amsterdam: Rodopi, 1987.

Capes, William W., ed. *Registrum Johannis Trefnant*. London: Canterbury and York Society, 1916.

Carruthers, Mary, and Jan M. Ziolkowski, eds. and trans. *The Medieval Craft of Memory: An Anthology of Texts and Pictures*. Philadelphia: University of Pennsylvania Press, 2002.

Chaucer, Geoffrey. *The Canterbury Tales*. Edited by Jill Mann. London: Penguin, 2005.

Cigman, Gloria, ed. *Lollard Sermons*. EETS, o.s. 294. Oxford: Oxford University Press, 1989.

Clanvowe, John. *The Boke of Cupide*. In *The Works of John Clanvowe*, edited by V. J. Scattergood, 35–53. Cambridge: Brewer, 1967.

——. *The Two Ways*. In *The Works of John Clanvowe*, edited by V. J. Scattergood, 57–80. Cambridge: Brewer, 1967.

Compston, H. F. B., ed. "The Thirty-Seven Conclusions of the Lollards." *English Historical Review* 26 (1911): 738–49.

Conlee, J. W., ed. "The *Abbey of the Holy Ghost* and the *Eight Ghostly Dwelling Places* of Huntington Library HM 744." *Medium Aevum* 44 (1975): 137–44.

Connolly, Margaret, ed. *Contemplations of the Dread and Love of God*. EETS o.s. 303. Oxford: Oxford University Press, 1993.

Consacro, D. Peter, ed. "A Critical Edition of the *Abbey of the Holy Ghost*." PhD diss., Fordham University, 1971.

Davidson, Clifford, ed. *A Tretise of Miraclis Pleyinge*. Rev. ed. Kalamazoo, MI: Medieval Institute Publications, 1993.

Diekstra, F. N. M., ed. *Book for a Simple and Devout Woman*. Groningen: Egbert Forsten, 1998.

Dove, Mary, ed. *The Earliest Advocates of the English Bible: The Texts of the Medieval Debate*. Exeter: University of Exeter Press, 2010.

Duncan, Thomas G., and Margaret Connolly, eds. *The Middle English "Mirror": Sermons from Advent to Sexagesima*. Heidelberg: Universitätsverlag, 2003.

Edmund of Abingdon. *Speculum religiosorum and Speculum ecclesie*. Edited by Helen P. Forshaw. Auctores Britannici Medii Aevi 3. Oxford: Oxford University Press, 1973.

Fanning, Clara E., ed. "The Charter of the Abbey of the Holy Ghost: A Critical Edition." PhD diss., Fordham University, 1974.

Forshall, J., ed. [*The Thirty-Seven Conclusions.*] *Remonstrance against Romish Corruptions in the Church*. London, 1851.

Forshall, J., and F. Madden, eds. *The Holy Bible, Containing the Old and New Testaments, with the Apocryphal Books, in the Earliest English Versions, made from the Latin Vulgate by John Wycliffe and His Followers*. 4 vols. Oxford, 1850; repr. New York: AMS Press, 1982.

Francis, W. Nelson. *The Book of Vices and Virtues*. EETS, o.s. 217. London: Oxford University Press, 1942.

Friedberg, Emil, ed. *Corpus iuris canonici*, vol. 2, *Decretalium collectiones*. Leipzig, 1881; repr. Graz: Akademisch Druck-u. Verlagsanstalt, 1959.

Gradon, Pamela, and Anne Hudson, eds. *English Wycliffite Sermons*. 5 vols. Oxford: Clarendon Press, 1983–96.

Grosseteste, Robert. *Dicta*. Edited by Edwin J. Westermann. *The Electronic Grosseteste*, http://www.grosseteste.com/dicta.htm.

Guibert of Nogent. *Monodies and On the Relics of Saints*. Translated and edited by Joseph McAlhany and Jay Rubenstein. London: Penguin, 2011.

Hanna, Ralph, ed. *Speculum Vitae: A Reading Edition*. 2 vols. EETS, o.s. 331–32. Oxford: Oxford University Press, 2008.

Hilton, Walter. *The Scale of Perfection, Book II*. Edited by Thomas H. Bestul. *TEAMS Middle English Texts Series* online, University of Rochester. http://www.lib.rochester.edu/camelot/teams/hilfr2.htm. Originally published in *The Scale of Perfection*, ed. Thomas H. Bestul (Kalamazoo, MI: Medieval Institute Publications, 2000).

———. *Walter Hilton's "Mixed Life" Edited from Lambeth Palace MS 472*. Edited by S. J. Ogilvie-Thomson. Salzburg: Institut für Anglistik und Amerikanistik, 1986.

Hodgson, Phyllis, ed. *The Cloud of Unknowing and Related Treatises*. Analecta Cartusiana 3. Salzburg: Institut für Anglistik und Amerikanistik, 1982.

Horner, Patrick, ed. *A Macaronic Sermon Collection from Late Medieval England, MS Bodley 649*. Studies and Texts 153. Toronto: Pontifical Institute of Mediaeval Studies, 2006.

Horstmann, C., ed. *Yorkshire Writers: Richard Rolle of Hampole, an English Father of the Church and His Followers*. 2 vols. London, 1895–96.

Hudson, Anne, ed. *Selections from English Wycliffite Writings*. Cambridge: Cambridge University Press, 1978.

———, ed. *Two Revisions of Rolle's English Psalter Commentary and the Related Canticles*. 2 vols. (of 3 projected, the last to be published as o.s. 343), EETS, o.s. 340–41 (Oxford: Oxford University Press, 2012–13).

——, ed. *Two Wycliffite Texts: The Sermon of William Taylor 1406, The Testimony of William Thorpe 1407.* EETS, o.s. 301. Oxford: Oxford University Press, 1993.

——, ed. *The Works of a Lollard Preacher.* EETS, o.s. 317. Oxford: Oxford University Press, 2001.

Hunt, Simon, ed. "An Edition of Tracts in Favour of Scriptural Translation and of Some Texts Connected with Lollard Vernacular Biblical Scholarship." 2 vols. D. Phil. thesis, University of Oxford, 1994.

Jacob, E. F. ed. *The Register of Henry Chichele, Archbishop of Canterbury, 1414–1443.* 4 vols. Oxford: Oxford University Press, 1938–47.

Jean de Condé. *La "Messe des oiseaux" et le "Dit des Jacobins et des Fremeneurs."* Edited by Jacques Ribard. Geneva: Droz, 1970.

Jefferson, Judith, ed. "An Edition of the Ten Commandments Commentary in BL Harley 2398, and the Related Version in Trinity College Dublin 245, York Minster XVI.L.12 and Harvard English 738 Together with Discussion of Related Commentaries." 2 vols. PhD diss., University of Bristol, 1995.

Kane, George, ed. *Piers Plowman: The A Version.* Rev. ed. London: Athlone, 1988.

Kane, George, and E. Talbot Donaldson, eds. *Piers Plowman: The B Version.* Rev. ed. London: Athlone, 1988.

Knighton, Henry. *Knighton's Chronicle.* Edited and translated by G. H. Martin. Oxford: Clarendon Press, 1995.

Lindberg, Conrad, ed. *The Middle English Bible: Prefatory Epistles of St. Jerome.* Oslo: Universitetsforlaget, 1978.

Love, Nicholas. *The Mirror of the Blessed Life of Jesus Christ: Full Critical Edition.* Edited by Michael G. Sargent. Exeter: University of Exeter Press, 2005.

Lydgate, John. "An Exposition of the *Pater Noster.*" In *The Minor Poems of John Lydgate,* edited by H. N. MacCracken, 60–71. EETS, e.s. 107. London: Kegan Paul, Trench, Trübner, 1911.

Mannyng, Robert. *Handlyng Synne.* Medieval and Renaissance Texts and Studies 14. Binghamton, NY: Center for Medieval and Early Renaissance Studies, 1983.

Martin, C. A., ed. "Edinburgh University Library Manuscript 93: An Annotated Edition of Selected Devotional Treatises with a Survey of Parallel Versions." 2 vols. PhD diss., University of Edinburgh, 1978.

Matthew, F. D., ed. *The English Works of Wyclif Hitherto Unprinted.* Rev. ed. EETS, o.s. 74. London: Kegan Paul, Trench, Trübner, 1902.

——, ed. "The Trial of Richard Wyche." *English Historical Review* 5 (1890): 530–44.

McCarthy, Adrian James, ed. *Book to a Mother: An Edition with Commentary.* Salzburg: Institut für Anglistik und Amerikanistik, 1981.

McSheffrey, Shannon, and Norman Tanner, eds. and trans. *Lollards of Coventry, 1486–1522.* Camden Fifth Series 23. Cambridge: Cambridge University Press, 2003.

Migne, J.-P., ed., *Patrologiae cursus completus, Series Latina,* 221 vols. Paris, 1844–91.

Millett, Bella, ed. *Ancrene Wisse.* 2 vols. EETS, o.s. 325–26. Oxford: Oxford University Press, 2005–6.

Minnis, Alastair J., A. B. Scott, and David Wallace, ed. and trans. *Medieval Literary Theory and Criticism, c. 1100–c. 1375: The Commentary Tradition.* Oxford: Clarendon Press, 1991.

Moon, Helen M., ed. *The Lyfe of Soule: An Edition with Commentary*. Salzburg: Institut für Englische Sprache und Literatur, 1978.

Nelson, Venetia, ed. *Myrour to Lewde Men and Wymmen: A Prose Version of the Speculum Vitae*. Middle English Texts. Heidelberg: Carl Winter, 1981.

Nolcken, Christina von, ed. *The Middle English Translation of the "Rosarium theologie": A Selection*. Heidenberg: Carol Winter Universitätsverlag, 1979.

Paues, Anna C., ed. *A Fourteenth Century English Biblical Version*. Cambridge: Cambridge University Press, 1904; repr. New York: AMS Press, 1974.

Pearsall, Derek, ed. *Piers Plowman: A New Annotated Edition of the C-text*. Exeter: University of Exeter Press, 2008.

Pecock, Reginald. *The Donet*. Edited by Elsie V. Hitchcock. EETS, o.s. 156. London: Oxford University Press, 1921.

———. *The Repressor of Overmuch Blaming of the Clergy*. Edited by Churchill Babington. 2 vols. London, 1860.

Perry, George G., ed. *Religious Pieces in Prose and Verse*. EETS, o.s. 26. 3rd ed. London: K. Paul, Trench, Trübner, 1914.

Reilly, Robert, ed. "A Middle English Summary of the Bible: An Edition of Trinity College (Oxon) MS 93." PhD diss., University of Washington, 1966.

Rolle, Richard. *The Psalter, or Psalms of David and Certain Canticles, with a Translation and Exposition in English by Richard Rolle of Hampole*. Edited and translated by H. R. Bramley. Oxford, 1884.

———. *Richard Rolle: Prose and Verse Edited from MS Longleat 29 and Related Manuscripts*. Ed. by S. J. Ogilvie-Thomson. EETS, o.s. 293. London: Oxford University Press, 1988.

———. *Richard Rolle: Uncollected Prose and Verse, with Related Northern Texts*. Edited by Ralph Hanna. EETS, o.s. 329. Oxford: Oxford University Press, 2007.

Ross, W. O., ed. *Middle English Sermons*. EETS, o.s. 209. London: Oxford University Press, 1960.

Shirley, W. W., ed. *Fasciculi Zizaniorum Magistri Johannis Wyclif cum Tritico*. Rolls Series 5. London, 1858.

Simmons, T. F., and H. E. Nolloth, eds. *The Lay Folks' Catechism*. EETS, o.s. 118. London: K. Paul, Trench, Trübner, 1901.

Somerset, Fiona, ed. *Four Wycliffite Dialogues*. EETS, o.s. 333. Oxford: Oxford University Press, 2009.

Staley, Lynn, ed. *The Book of Margery Kempe*. TEAMS Middle English Texts Series. Kalamazoo, MI: Medieval Institute Publications, 1996.

Swinburn, Lilian M., ed. *Lanterne of Liȝt*. EETS, o.s. 151. London: Kegan Paul, 1917.

Sylwan, Agneta, ed. *Scolastica Historia: Liber Genesis*. Corpus Christianorum: Continuatio Mediaevalis 191. Turnhout: Brepols, 2005.

Tanner, Norman, ed. and trans. *Decrees of the Ecumenical Councils*. 2 vols. London: Sheed and Ward; Washington, DC: Georgetown University Press. 1990.

———, ed. *Heresy Trials in the Diocese of Norwich, 1428–31*. Camden Fourth Series 20. London: Royal Historical Society, 1977.

Todd, J. H., ed. *Apology for Lollard Doctrines*. Camden Society. London, 1842.

Wogan-Browne, Jocelyn, et al., eds. *The Idea of the Vernacular: An Anthology of Middle English Literary Theory, 1280–1520*. University Park: Pennsylvania State University Press, 1999.

Wyclif, John. *De amore sive ad quinque quaestiones.* In Wyclif, *Opera minora,* edited by J. Loserth, Wyclif Society, 8–10. London: C. K. Paul, 1913.

——. *De blasphemia.* Edited by Michael H. Dziewicki. Wyclif Society. London: Trübner, 1893.

——. *De civili dominio.* Edited by Reginald L. Poole and Johannes Loserth. 4 vols. Wyclif Society. London: Trübner, 1885–1904.

——. *De mandatis divinis.* Edited by J. Loserth and F. D. Matthew. London: Kegan Paul, 1922.

——. *De veritate sacre scripture.* Edited by Rudolph Buddenseig. 3 vols. Wyclif Society. London: Trübner, 1905–7.

——. *Dialogus, sive Speculum ecclesie militantis.* Edited by Alfred W. Pollard. London: Trübner, 1886.

——. *Opus evangelicum.* Edited by J. Loserth. 2 vols. Wyclif Society. London: Trübner, 1895–96.

——. *Sermones.* Edited by Johann Loserth. 4 vols. Wyclif Society. London: Trübner, 1887–90.

——. *Tractatus de officio pastorali.* Edited by G. V. Lechler. Leipzig: Edelmann, 1853.

——. *Trialogus cum supplemento trialogi.* Edited by Gotthard Lechler. Oxford: Clarendon Press, 1869.

Zettersten, Arne, ed. *The English Text of the Ancrene Riwle: Edited from Magdalene College, Cambridge MS. Pepys 2498.* EETS, o.s. 274. London: Oxford University Press, 1976.

Secondary Sources

Aers, David. *Salvation and Sin: Augustine, Langland, and Fourteenth-Century Theology.* Notre Dame, IN: University of Notre Dame Press, 2009.

——. *Sanctifying Signs:Making Christian Tradition in Late Medieval England.* Notre Dame, IN: University of Notre Dame Press, 2004.

Aers, David, and Lynn Staley. *The Powers of the Holy: Religion, Politics, and Gender in Late Medieval English Culture.* University Park: Pennsylvania State University Press, 1996.

Allen, Hope Emily. "The *Speculum Vitae*: Addendum." *PMLA* 32 (1917): 133–62.

Arnold, John H. *Belief and Unbelief in Europe.* London: Hodder, 2005; repr. New York: Bloomsbury, 2010.

——. "Lollard Trials and Inquisitorial Discourse." In *Fourteenth Century England II,* edited by Chris Given-Wilson, 81–94. Woodbridge: Boydell, 2002.

——. "The Materiality of Unbelief in Late Medieval England." In *The Unorthodox Imagination in Late Medieval Britain,* edited by Sophie Page, 65–95. Manchester: Manchester University Press, 2010.

Aston, Margaret. *England's Iconoclasts.* Vol. 1, *Laws against Images.* Oxford: Clarendon Press, 1988.

——. "Were the Lollards a Sect?" In Biller and Dobson, *Medieval Church: Universities, Heresy, and the Religious Life,* 163–92.

Auerbach, Eric. "Figura." In Auerbach, *Scenes from the Drama of European Literature: Six Essays*, 11–76. New York: Meridian, 1959.

Barish, Jonas A. *The Antitheatrical Prejudice*. Berkeley: University of California Press, 1981.

Barr, Helen, and Ann M. Hutchison, eds. *Text and Controversy from Wyclif to Bale: Essays in Honour of Anne Hudson*. Turnhout: Brepols, 2005.

Bauer, Gerhard. *Claustrum animae: Untersuchungen zur Geschichte der Metapher vom Herzen als Kloster*. 2 vols. Munich: Wilhelm Fink, 1973.

Biller, Peter, and R. B. Dobson, eds. *The Medieval Church: Universities, Heresy, and the Religious Life; Studies in Honour of Gordon Leff*. Woodbridge: Boydell and Brewer, 1999.

Biller, Peter, and Anne Hudson, eds. *Heresy and Literacy, 1000–1530*. Cambridge: Cambridge University Press, 1994.

Bloomfield, Morton W., et al., eds. *Incipits of Latin Works on the Virtues and Vices, 1100–1500 AD*. Cambridge, MA: Medieval Academy, 1979.

Bose, Mishtooni, and J. Patrick Hornbeck II, eds. *Wycliffite Controversies*. Turnhout: Brepols, 2011.

Bossy, John. "Moral Arithmetic: Seven Sins into Ten Commandments." In *Conscience and Casuistry in Early Modern Europe*, edited by Edmund Leites, 214–34. Cambridge: Cambridge University Press, 1988.

Brady, Sr. M. Teresa. "Lollard Interpolations and Omissions in Manuscripts of *The Pore Caitif*." In *De Cella in Seculum: Religious and Secular Life and Devotion in Late Medieval England*, edited by Michael G. Sargent, 183–203. Woodbridge: Brewer, 1989.

Bruyne, Donatien de. *Sommaires, divisions et rubriques de la Bible latine*. Namur: Auguste Godenne, 1914.

Bryan, Jennifer. *Looking Inward: Devotional Reading and the Private Self in Late Medieval England*. Philadelphia: University of Pennsylvania Press, 2008.

Buc, Philippe. *L'ambiguïté du livre: Prince, pouvoir, et le peuple dans les commentaires de la Bible au moyen âge*. Paris: Beauchesne, 1994.

Busby, Keith. "Variance and the Politics of Textual Criticism." In *Towards a Synthesis? Essays on the New Philology*, edited by Keith Busby, 29–45. Amsterdam: Rodopi, 1993.

Camille, Michael. "Before the Gaze: The Internal Senses and Late Medieval Practices of Seeing." In *Visuality before and beyond the Renaissance: Seeing as Others Saw*, edited by Robert S. Nelson, 197–223. Cambridge: Cambridge University Press, 2000.

Campbell, Kirsty. *The Call to Read: Reginald Pecock's Books and Textual Communities*. Notre Dame, IN: University of Notre Dame Press, 2010.

Catto, J. I. "Fellows and Helpers: The Religious Identity of the Followers of Wyclif." In Biller and Dobson, *Medieval Church: Universities, Heresy, and the Religious Life*, 141–62.

———. "Shaping the Mixed Life: Thomas Arundel's Reformation." In *Image, Text, and Church, 1380–1600: Essays for Margaret Aston*, edited by Linda Clark, Maureen Jurkowski, and Colin Richmond, 94–108. Toronto: Pontifical Institute of Mediaeval Studies, 2009.

Clark, Mark. "Peter Comestor and Peter Lombard: Brothers in Deed." *Traditio* 60 (2005): 85–142.

Clarke, Peter D. *The Papal Interdict in the Thirteenth Century: A Question of Collective Guilt.* Oxford: Oxford University Press, 2007.

Clopper, Lawrence. "Is the *Tretise of Miraclis Pleyinge* a Lollard Tract against Devotional Drama?" *Viator* 34 (2003): 229–71.

———. "Miracula and the *Tretise of Miraclis Pleyinge.*" *Speculum* 65 (1990): 878–905.

Cole, Andrew. "Chaucer's English Lesson." *Speculum* 77 (2002): 1128–67.

———. *Literature and Heresy in the Age of Chaucer.* Cambridge: Cambridge University Press, 2008.

Colledge, E. "*The Recluse*: A Lollard Interpolated Version of the *Ancren Riwle.*" *Review of English Studies* 15 (1939): 1–15, 129–45.

Connolly, Margaret. "Books for the 'helpe of euery persoone þat þenkiþ to be saued': Six Devotional Anthologies from Fifteenth-Century London." *Yearbook of English Studies* 33 (2003): 170–81.

———. "Compiling the Book." In Gillespie and Wakelin, *Production of Books in England*, 129–49.

———. "The 'Eight Points of Charity' in John Rylands University Library MS English 85." In *"And gladly wolde he lerne and gladly teche": Essays on Medieval English Presented to Professor Matsuji Tajima on His Sixtieth Birthday*, edited by Y. Iyeiri and M. Connolly, 195–215. Tokyo: Kaibunsha, 2002.

———. *The Index of Middle English Prose, Handlist XIX: Manuscripts in the University Library, Cambridge (Dd–Oo).* Cambridge: Brewer, 2009.

———. "Mapping Manuscripts and Readers of *Contemplations of the Dread and Love of God.*" In *Design and Distribution of Late Medieval Manuscripts in England*, edited by Margaret Connolly and Linne R. Mooney, 261–78. York: University of York Press, 2008.

———. "Preaching by Numbers: The 'Seven Gifts of the Holy Ghost' in Late Middle English Sermons and Works of Religious Instruction." In *Preaching the Word in Manuscript and Print in Late Medieval England: Essays in Honour of Susan Powell*, edited by Martha W. Driver and Veronica O'Mara, 83–100. Turnhout: Brepols, 2013.

Constable, Giles. "Medieval Latin Metaphors." *Viator* 38 (2007): 1–20.

Copeland, Rita. *Pedagogy, Intellectuals, and Dissent in the Later Middle Ages: Lollardy and Ideas of Learning.* Cambridge: Cambridge University Press, 2001.

———. "Rhetoric and the Politics of the Literal Sense in Medieval Literary Theory: Aquinas, Wyclif, and the Lollards." In *Interpretation: Medieval and Modern*, edited by Piero Boitani and Anna Torti, 1–23. Woodbridge: Brewer, 1978.

Copeland, Rita, and Stephen Melville. "Allegory and Allegoresis, Rhetoric and Hermeneutics." *Exemplaria* 3 (1991): 159–87.

Corbellini, Sabrina. "Retelling the Bible in Medieval Italy: The Case of the Italian Gospel Harmonies." In Doležalová and Visi, *Retelling the Bible*, 213–28.

Cornelius, Roberta D. "The Figurative Castle: A Study of the Mediaeval Allegory of the Edifice with Special Reference to Religious Writings." PhD diss., Bryn Mawr College, 1930.

Craun, Edwin D. "Discarding Traditional Pastoral Ethics: Wycliffism and Slander." In Bose and Hornbeck, *Wycliffite Controversies*, 227–42.

———. *Ethics and Power in Medieval English Reformist Writing.* Cambridge: Cambridge University Press, 2010.

Cullum, P. H. "'Yf lak of charyte be not ower hynderawnce': Margery Kempe, Lynn, and the Practice of the Spiritual and Bodily Works of Mercy." In *A Companion to the Book of Margery Kempe,* edited by John H. Arnold and Katherine J. Lewis, 177–93. Cambridge: Brewer, 2004.

De Hamel, Christopher. *The Book: A History of the Bible.* London: Phaidon, 2001.

Denery, Dallas G., II. *Seeing and Being Seen in the Late Medieval World.* Cambridge: Cambridge University Press, 2005.

Diekstra, F. N. M. "The *XII Lettyngis of Prayer,* Peraldus's *Summae virtutum ac vitiorum,* and the Relation between *Þe Holy Boke Gratia Dei, Þe Pater Noster of Richard Ermyte,* and *Book for a Simple and Devout Woman.*" *English Studies* 80 (1999): 106–45.

Doležalová, Lucie. "*Biblia quasi in saculo: Summarium Biblie* and Other Medieval Bible Mnemonics." *Medium aevum quotidianum* 56 (2007): 5–35.

———, ed. *The Making of Memory in the Middle Ages.* Leiden: Brill, 2010.

Doležalová, Lucie, and Tamás Visi, eds. *Retelling the Bible: Literary, Historical, and Social Contexts.* Frankfurt am Main: Peter Lang, 2011.

Dove, Mary. *The First English Bible: The Text and Context of the Wycliffite Versions.* Cambridge: Cambridge University Press, 2007.

———. "The Lollards' Threefold Biblical Agenda." In Bose and Hornbeck, *Wycliffite Controversies,* 211–26.

———. "Wyclif and the English Bible." In Levy, *Companion to John Wyclif,* 365–406.

Duffy, Eamon. *The Stripping of the Altars: Traditional Religion in England, c. 1400–1580.* 2nd ed. New Haven, CT: Yale University Press, 2005.

Dunn, Charles W. "Romances Derived from English Legends." In Severs, *Manual of the Writings in Middle English,* 1:17–37.

Dutton, Elisabeth. "Christ the Codex: Compilation as Literary Device in *Book to a Mother.*" *Leeds Studies in English,* n.s., 35 (2004): 81–100.

Fletcher, Alan J. "A Hive of Industry or a Hornets' Nest? MS Sidney Sussex 74 and Its Scribes." In Minnis, *Late-Medieval Religious Texts and Their Transmission,* 131–55.

Fletcher, J. M. "Developments in the Faculty of Arts, 1370–1520." In *The History of the University of Oxford,* vol. 2, *Late Medieval Oxford,* edited by J. I. Catto and R. Evans, 315–45. Oxford: Clarendon Press, 1992.

Forrest, Ian. *The Detection of Heresy in Late Medieval England.* Oxford: Clarendon Press, 2005.

———. "Lollardy and Late Medieval History." In Bose and Hornbeck, *Wycliffite Controversies,* 121–34.

———. "William Swinderby and the Wycliffite Attitude to Excommunication." *Journal of Ecclesiastical History* 60 (2009): 246–69.

Fournié, Éléonore. "Les manuscrits de la *Bible historiale*: Présentation et catalogue raisonné d'une oeuvre médiévale." *L'atelier du Centre de recherches historiques* 3.2 (2009). http://acrh.revues.org/index1408.html.

Fowler, David. "Ballads." In *A Manual of the Writings in Middle English, 1050–1500,* vol. 6, edited by Albert Hartung, 1753–1808. New Haven: Connecticut Academy of Arts and Sciences, 1980.

———. "A Middle English Bible Commentary (Oxford, Trinity College MS 93)." *Manuscripta* 12 (1968): 67–78.

Gayk, Shannon. "Lollard Writings, Literary Criticism, and the Meaningfulness of Form." In Bose and Hornbeck, *Wycliffite Controversies*, 135–52.

Gelber, Hester. *It Could Have Been Otherwise: Contingency and Necessity in Dominican Theology at Oxford, 1300–1350.* Leiden: Brill, 2004.

Geltner, G. *The Making of Medieval Antifraternalism: Polemic, Violence, Deviance, and Remembrance.* Oxford: Oxford University Press, 2012.

Ghosh, Kantik. "Logic and Lollardy." *Medium Aevum* 76 (2007): 251–67.

———. "Wycliffism and Lollardy." In *The Cambridge History of Christianity*, vol. 4, *Christianity in Western Europe, c. 1100–c. 1500*, edited by Miri Rubin and Walter Simons, 433–45. Cambridge: Cambridge University Press, 2009.

———. "Wycliffite 'Affiliations': Some Intellectual-Historical Perspectives." In Bose and Hornbeck, *Wycliffite Controversies*, 13–32.

———. *The Wycliffite Heresy: Authority and the Interpretation of Texts.* Cambridge: Cambridge University Press, 2002.

Gillespie, Alexandra, and Daniel Wakelin, eds. *The Production of Books in England, 1350–1500.* Cambridge: Cambridge University Press, 2011.

Gillespie, Vincent. "Anonymous Devotional Writings." In A *Companion to Middle English Prose*, edited by A. S. G. Edwards, 127–49. Woodbridge: Boydell and Brewer, 2004.

———. "Thy Will be Done: *Piers Plowman* and the *Paternoster*." In Minnis, *Late-Medieval Religious Texts and Their Transmission*, 95–119.

Giraud, Cédric. "Introduction to Part III." In Doležalová and Visi, *Retelling the Bible*, 185–88.

Green, Richard Firth. "Jack Philpot, John of Gaunt, and a Poem of 1380." *Speculum* 66 (1991): 330–41.

Gumbert, J. Peter. "Codicological Units: Towards a Terminology for the Stratigraphy of the Non-Homogenous Codex." *Segno e testo: International Journal of Manuscripts and Their Transmission* 2 (2004): 17–42.

Gwynn, Aubrey. *English Austin Friars in the Time of Wyclif.* London: Oxford University Press, 1940.

Hanna, Ralph. "Booklets in Manuscripts: Further Considerations." In *Pursuing History: Middle English Manuscripts and Their Texts*, 21–34. Stanford, CA: Stanford University Press, 1996.

———. "English Biblical Texts before Lollardy and Their Fate." In Somerset, Havens, and Pitard, *Lollards and Their Influence*, 141–53.

———. *The English Manuscripts of Richard Rolle: A Descriptive Catalogue.* Exeter: University of Exeter Press, 2010.

———. *London Literature, 1300–1380.* Cambridge: Cambridge University Press, 2005.

———. "Verses in Sermons Again: The Case of Cambridge, Jesus College, MS Q.A.13." *Studies in Bibliography* 57 (2005–6): 63–83.

Hanna, Ralph, et al. "Latin Commentary Tradition and Vernacular Literature." In Minnis and Johnson, *Cambridge History of Literary Criticism*, 2:363–421.

Hargreaves, Henry. "Popularising Biblical Scholarship: The Role of the Wycliffite *Glossed Gospels*." In Lourdaux and Verhelst, *The Bible and Medieval Culture*, 171–89.

Harvey, Margaret. "Adam Easton and the Condemnation of John Wyclif." *English Historical Review* 113 (1998): 321–35.

Havens, Jill C. "Shading the Grey Area: Determining Heresy in Middle English Texts." In Barr and Hutchison, *Text and Controversy from Wyclif to Bale*, 337–52.

Helmholz, R. H. *The Spirit of Classical Canon Law*. Athens: University of Georgia Press, 1996.

Henry, Avril. "'The pater noster in a table ypeynted' and Some Other Presentations of Doctrine in the Vernon Manuscript." In *Studies in the Vernon Manuscript*, edited by Derek Pearsall, 89–113. Cambridge: Brewer, 1990.

Heyworth, Gregory. "Ineloquent Ends: Simplicitas, Proctolalia, and the Profane Vernacular in the *Miller's Tale*." *Speculum* 84 (2009): 956–83.

Hobbins, Daniel. *Authorship and Publicity before Print: Jean Gerson and the Transformation of Late Medieval Learning*. Philadelphia: University of Pennsylvania Press, 2009.

———. Review of *Scolastica historia: Liber Genesis*, ed. Agneta Sylwan, Corpus Christianorum: Continuatio Mediaevalis 191 (Turnhout: Brepols, 2005). *The Medieval Review*, June 4, 2005. http://quod.lib.umich.edu/t/tmr/.

Holsinger, Bruce. "Lollard Ekphrasis: Situated Aesthetics and Literary History." *Journal of Medieval and Early Modern Studies* 35 (2005): 68–89.

Hoogvliet, Margriet. "The Medieval Vernacular Bible in French as a Flexible Text: Selective and Discontinuous Reading Practices." In *Form and Function in the Medieval Bible*, edited by Eyal Poleg and Laura Light, 283–306. Leiden: Brill, 2013.

Hornbeck, J. Patrick, II. "Records of Heresy Trials." In Hornbeck, Lahey, and Somerset, *Wycliffite Spirituality*, 45–52.

———. *What Is a Lollard? Dissent and Belief in Late Medieval England*. Oxford: Oxford University Press, 2010.

———. "*Wycklyffes Wycket* and Eucharistic Theology: Cases from Sixteenth-Century Winchester." In Bose and Hornbeck, *Wycliffite Controversies*, 279–94.

———. "Wycliffite Spirituality in Heresy Trials: Personal Holiness and Spiritual Simplicity." In Hornbeck, Lahey, and Somerset, *Wycliffite Spirituality*, 24–29.

Hornbeck, J. Patrick, II, Stephen E. Lahey, and Fiona Somerset, eds. and trans. *Wycliffite Spirituality*. New York: Paulist Press, 2013.

Horobin, Simon. "Mapping the Words." In Gillespie and Wakelin, *Production of Books in England*, 59–78.

Howlett, D. R., et al. *Dictionary of Medieval Latin from British Sources*. 14 fascicles to date. London: Oxford University Press for the British Academy, 1975–.

Hudson, Anne. "A Lollard Sect Vocabulary?" Repr. in *Lollards and Their Books*, 165–80.

———. "The Examination of Lollards." Repr. in *Lollards and Their Books*, 125–40.

———. "The Expurgation of a Lollard Sermon-Cycle." Repr. in *Lollards and Their Books*, 201–15.

———. "Five Problems in Wycliffite Texts and a Suggestion." *Medium Aevum* 80 (2011): 301–24.

———. "*Laicus Litteratus*: The Paradox of Lollardy." In Biller and Hudson, *Heresy and Literacy*, 222–36.

———. "The *Lay Folk's Catechism*: A Postscript." *Viator* 18 (1988): 307–9.

———. "Lollard Book Production." In *Book Production and Publishing in Britain, 1375–1475*, edited by Jeremy Griffiths and Derek Pearsall, 125–42. Cambridge: Cambridge University Press, 1989.

———. *Lollards and Their Books*. London: Hambledon, 1985.

———. "A New Look at the *Lay Folk's Catechism*." *Viator* 16 (1985): 243–58.

———. "Middle English." In *Editing Medieval Texts: English, French, and Latin Written in England; Papers Given at the Twelfth Annual Conference on Editorial Problems, University of Toronto*, edited by A. G. Rigg, 34–57. Toronto: University of Toronto Press, 1977.

———. "Notes of an Early Fifteenth-Century Research Assistant, and the Emergence of the 267 Articles against Wyclif." *English Historical Review* 118 (2003): 685–97.

———. *The Premature Reformation: Wycliffite Texts and Lollard History*. Oxford: Oxford University Press, 1988.

———. *Studies in the Transmission of Wyclif's Writings*. Aldershot: Ashgate, 2008.

———. "Which Wyche? The Framing of the Lollard Heretic and/or Saint." In *Texts and the Repression of Medieval Heresy*, edited by Caterina Bruschi and Peter Biller, 221–37. Woodbridge: York Medieval Press, 2003.

———. "Who Is My Neighbour?" In Bose and Hornbeck, *Wycliffite Controversies*, 79–96.

Hughes, Andrew. "Defacing Becket: Damaged Books for the Office." In *Hortus Troporum: Florilegium in Honorem Gunillae Iversen*, edited by Alexandre Andrée and Erika Kihlman, 162–75. Stockholm: Stockholms Universitet, 2008.

Jolliffe, P. S. *A Check-list of Middle English Prose Writings of Spiritual Guidance*. Toronto: Pontifical Institute of Mediaeval Studies, 1974.

Jones, E. A. "Literature of Religious Instruction." In *A Companion to Medieval English Literature and Culture, c. 1350–c. 1500*, edited by Peter Brown. Malden, MA: Blackwell, 2007. *Blackwell Reference Online*. http://www.blackwellreference.com/public/book.html?id=g9780631219736_9780631219736

Jotischky, Andrew. *The Carmelites and Antiquity: Mendicants and Their Pasts in the Later Middle Ages*. Oxford: Oxford University Press, 2002.

Jurkowski, Maureen. "The Arrest of William Thorpe in Shrewsbury and the Anti-Lollard Statute of 1406." *Historical Research* 75 (2002): 273–95.

———. "Lollard Book Producers in London in 1414." In Barr and Hutchison, *Text and Controversy from Wyclif to Bale*, 201–26.

———. "Lollard Networks." In Bose and Hornbeck, *Wycliffite Controversies*, 261–78.

———. "Lollardy and Social Status in East Anglia." *Speculum* 82 (2007): 120–52.

Kantola, Ilkka. *Probability and Moral Uncertainty in Late Medieval and Early Modern Times*. Helsinki: Luther-Agricola Society, 1994.

Karnes, Michelle. *Imagination, Meditation, and Cognition in the Middle Ages*. Chicago: University of Chicago Press, 2011.

Kaster, Robert A. *Emotion, Restraint, and Community in Ancient Rome*. Oxford: Oxford University Press, 2005.

Kellogg, A. L., and Ernest W. Talbert. "The Wycliffite Pater Noster and Ten Commandments, with Special Reference to English Mss. 85 and 90 in the John Rylands Library." *Bulletin of the John Rylands Library* 42 (1960): 345–77.

Kelly, Henry Ansgar. "Literal versus Literal: The Two Versions of the Middle English Bible (fka Wycliffite Bible)." Paper presented at the International Congress on Medieval Studies, Kalamazoo, MI, May 12–15, 2011.

Kelly, Stephen, and Ryan Perry. "Devotional Cosmopolitanism in Fifteenth-Century England." In *After Arundel: Religious Writing in Fifteenth-Century England*, edited by Vincent Gillespie and Kantik Ghosh, 363–80. Turnhout: Brepols, 2012.

Kennedy, Kathleen. "Reintroducing the English Books of Hours, or 'English Primers.'" Forthcoming.

Ker, Neil R. *Medieval Manuscripts in British Libraries.* 4 vols. Oxford: Oxford University Press, 1969–92.

———. "A Middle-English Summary of the Bible." *Medium Aevum* 29 (1960): 115–18.

Kerby-Fulton, Kathryn. *Books under Suspicion: Censorship and Tolerance of Revelatory Writing in Late Medieval England.* Notre Dame, IN: University of Notre Dame Press, 2006.

———. "Eciam Lollardi." In Olson and Kerby-Fulton, *Voices in Dialogue,* 261–78.

Kerby-Fulton, Kathryn, Maidie Hilmo, and Linda Olson. *Opening Up Middle English Manuscripts: Literary and Visual Approaches.* Ithaca, NY: Cornell University Press, 2012.

Klepper, Deeana Copeland. *The Insight of Unbelievers: Nicholas of Lyra and Christian Reading of Jewish Text in the Later Middle Ages.* Philadelphia: University of Pennsylvania Press, 2007.

Knowles, Jim. "Love, Labor, Liturgy: Languages of Service in Late Medieval England." PhD diss., Duke University, 2009.

Kraebel, Andrew Brock. "The Wycliffite Bible Prologues and the Translation of Academic Discourse." Paper presented at the International Congress on Medieval Studies, Kalamazoo, MI, May 12–15, 2011.

Kuczynski, Michael P. "An Unpublished Lollard Psalms *Catena* in Huntington Library MS HM 501." *Journal of the Early Book Society* 13 (2010): 95–138.

Kuhn, Sherman M. "The Preface to a Fifteenth-Century Concordance." *Speculum* 43 (1968): 258–73.

Kumler, Aden. *Translating Truth: Ambitious Images and Religious Knowledge in Late Medieval France and England.* New Haven, CT: Yale University Press, 2011.

Kurath, Hans, Sherman M. Kuhn, and Robert E. Lewis, eds. *Middle English Dictionary.* 21 vols. Ann Arbor: University of Michigan Press, 1952–2001. Online edition at University of Michigan, http://quod.lib.umich.edu/m/med/.

Kurze, D. "Die festländischen Lollarden: Zur Geschichte der religiösen Bewegungen im ausgehenden Mittelalter." *Archiv für Kulturgeschichte* 47 (1965): 48–76.

Kwakkel, Erik. "Commercial Organization and Economic Innovation." In Gillespie and Wakelin, *Production of Books in England,* 173–91.

Lagorio, Valerie M., and Michael G. Sargent. "English Mystical Writings." In *A Manual of the Writings in Middle English, 1050–1500,* vol. 9, edited by Albert E. Hartung, 3049–3137. New Haven: Connecticut Academy of Arts and Sciences, 1993.

Lahey, Stephen E. *John Wyclif.* Oxford: Oxford University Press, 2009.

———. "John Wyclif: Spiritual and Devotional Guide?" In Hornbeck, Lahey, and Somerset, *Wycliffite Spirituality,* 30–39.

Lake, Peter. *The Boxmaker's Revenge: "Orthodoxy," "Heterodoxy," and the Politics of the Parish in Early Stuart London.* Stanford, CA: Stanford University Press, 2001.

Lake, Peter, with Michael Questier. *The Antichrist's Lewd Hat: Protestants, Papists, and Players in Post-Reformation England.* New Haven, CT: Yale University Press, 2002.

Lerner, Robert. "Afterword." In Lerner and Müller-Luckner, *Neue Richtungen in der hoch- und spätmittelalterlichen Bibelexegese,* 181–88.

——. "Ecstatic Dissent." *Speculum* 67 (1992): 33–57.

——. *The Heresy of the Free Spirit in the Later Middle Ages.* Berkeley: University of California Press, 1972.

Lerner, Robert E., and Elisabeth Müller-Luckner, eds. *Neue Richtungen in der hoch- und spätmittelalterlichen Bibelexegese.* Munich: Oldenbourg, 1996.

Levy, Ian Christopher, ed. *A Companion to John Wyclif, Late Medieval Theologian.* Leiden: Brill, 2006.

——. "A Contextualised Wyclif: *Magister Sacrae Paginae.*" In Bose and Hornbeck, *Wycliffite Controversies*, 33–57.

——. "Grace and Freedom in the Soteriology of John Wyclif." *Traditio* 60 (2005): 279–337.

——. "Holy Scripture and the Quest for Authority among Three Late Medieval Masters." *Journal of Ecclesiastical History* 61 (2010): 40–68.

——. *Holy Scripture and the Quest for Authority at the End of the Middle Ages.* Notre Dame, IN: University of Notre Dame Press, 2012.

Lewis, Anna. "Textual Borrowings, Theological Mobility, and the Lollard Pater Noster Commentary." *Philological Quarterly* 88 (2009): 1–23.

Lewis, R. E., N. F. Blake, and A. S. G. Edwards. *Index of Printed Middle English Prose.* New York: Garland, 1985.

Light, Laura. "French Bibles, c. 1200–30: A New Look at the Origin of the Paris Bible." In *The Early Medieval Bible: Its Production, Decoration, and Use,* edited by Richard Gameson, 155–76. Cambridge: Cambridge University Press, 1994.

Lourdaux, Willem, and D. Verhelst, eds. *The Bible and Medieval Culture.* Louvain: Louvain University Press, 1979.

Lubac, Henri de. *Exégèse médiévale: Les quatres sens de l'ecriture.* 2 vols. Paris: Aubier, 1959.

Lutton, Robert. *Lollardy and Orthodox Religion in Pre-Reformation England.* Woodbridge: Boydell and Brewer, 2006.

——. "Lollardy, Orthodoxy, and Cognitive Psychology." In Bose and Hornbeck, *Wycliffite Controversies*, 97–119.

——. "'Love this Name that Is IHC': Vernacular Prayers, Hymns, and Lyrics to the Holy Name of Jesus in Pre-Reformation England." In *Vernacularity in England and Wales, c. 1300–1550,* edited by Elisabeth Salter and Helen Wicker, 119–45. Turnhout: Brepols, 2011.

Malo, Robyn. "Behaving Paradoxically? Wycliffites, Shrines, and Relics." In Bose and Hornbeck, *Wycliffite Controversies*, 193–210.

McGrade, A. S. "Somersaulting Sovereignty: A Note on Reciprocal Lordship and Servitude in Wyclif." In *The Church and Sovereignty c. 590–1918: Essays in Honor of Michael Wilks,* edited by Diana Wood, 261–78. Oxford: Basil Blackwell, 1991.

McIntosh, Angus, M. L. Samuels, and Michael Benskin. *A Linguistic Atlas of Late Mediaeval English.* 4 vols. Aberdeen: Aberdeen University Press, 1985.

McNamer, Sarah. "Feeling." In *Oxford Twenty-First Century Approaches to Literature: Middle English,* edited by Paul Strohm, 241–57. Oxford: Oxford University Press, 2007.

McSheffrey, Shannon. "Heresy, Orthodoxy, and English Vernacular Religion, 1480–1525." *Past & Present* 186 (2005): 47–80.

McSparran, Frances, ed. *Middle English Compendium.* University of Michigan. Last updated February 22, 2006. http://quod.lib.umich.edu/m/mec/.

Minnis, Alastair. "Absent Glosses: A Crisis of Vernacular Commentary in Late-Medieval England?" *Essays in Medieval Studies* 20 (2003): 1–17.

———. "Affection and Imagination in *The Cloud of Unknowing* and Hilton's *Scale of Perfection.*" *Traditio* 39 (1983): 323–66.

———. "'Authorial Intention' and 'Literal Sense' in the Exegetical Theories of Richard Fitzralph and John Wyclif: An Essay in the Medieval Theories of Biblical Hermeneutics." *Proceedings of the Royal Irish Academy* 75, Section C, no. 1 (1975): 1–31.

———, ed. *Late-Medieval Religious Texts and Their Transmission: Essays in Honour of A.I. Doyle.* York Manuscripts Conferences, Proceedings 3. Woodbridge: Boydell and Brewer, 1994.

———. "Medieval Imagination and Memory." In Minnis and Johnson, *Cambridge History of Literary Criticism,* 2:239–74.

Minnis, Alastair, and Ian Johnson, eds. *The Cambridge History of Literary Criticism.* Vol. 2, *The Middle Ages.* Cambridge: Cambridge University Press, 2005.

Morey, James H. *Book and Verse: A Guide to Middle English Biblical Literature.* Urbana: University of Illinois Press, 2000.

———. "Peter Comestor, Biblical Paraphrase, and the Medieval Popular Bible." *Speculum* 68 (1993): 6–35.

Morgan, Nigel. "Books for the Liturgy and Private Prayer." In *The Cambridge History of the Book in Britain,* vol. 2, *1100–1400,* edited by Nigel Morgan and Rodney M. Thomson, 291–316. Cambridge: Cambridge University Press, 2008.

Mulchahy, M. Michèle. *"First the Bow is Bent in Study". . . Dominican Education before 1350.* Toronto: Pontifical Institute of Mediaeval Studies, 1998.

Newman, Barbara. *God and the Goddesses: Vision, Poetry, and Belief in the Middle Ages.* Philadelphia: University of Pennsylvania Press, 2003.

———. "What Did It Mean to Say 'I Saw'? The Clash between Theory and Practice in Medieval Visionary Culture." *Speculum* 80 (2005): 1–43.

Newstead, Helaine. "Arthurian Legends." In Severs, *Manual of the Writings in Middle English,* 1:38–79.

Nissé, Ruth. "Reversing Discipline: The *Tretise of Miraclis Pleyinge,* Lollard Exegesis, and the Failure of Representation." *Yearbook of Langland Studies* 11 (1997): 163–97.

Nolcken, Christina von. "Another Kind of Saint: A Lollard Perception of John Wyclif." *Studies in Church History Subsidia* 5 (1987): 429–43.

———. "The *Recluse* and Its Readers: Some Observations on a Lollard Interpolated Version of *Ancrene Wisse.*" In *A Companion to "Ancrene Wisse,"* edited by Yoko Wada, 175–96. Cambridge: Brewer, 2003.

———. "An Unremarked Group of Wycliffite Sermons in Latin." *Modern Philology* 83 (1986): 233–49.

Ocker, Christopher. *Biblical Poetics before Humanism and Reformation.* Cambridge: Cambridge University Press, 2002.

Ogilvie-Thomson, S. J. *The Index of Middle English Prose, Handlist XVI: Manuscripts in the Laudian Collection, Bodleian Library, Oxford.* Cambridge: Brewer, 2000.

Olson, Glending. "Plays as Play: A Medieval Ethical Theory of Performance and the Intellectual Context of the *Tretise of Miraclis Pleyinge.*" *Viator* 26 (1995): 195–222.

Olson, Linda, and Kathryn Kerby-Fulton, eds. *Voices in Dialogue: Reading Women in the Middle Ages.* Notre Dame, IN: University of Notre Dame Press, 2005.

Owst, G. R. *Literature and Pulpit in Medieval England.* 2nd ed. Oxford: Basil Blackwell, 1961.

Pantin, W. A. "Instructions for a Devout and Literate Layman." In *Medieval Learning and Literature: Essays Presented to Richard William Hunt,* edited by J. J. G. Alexander and M. T. Gibson, 398–422. Oxford: Clarendon Press, 1976.

Pasnau, Robert. *Theories of Cognition in the Later Middle Ages.* Cambridge: Cambridge University Press, 1997.

Patterson, Lee. *Chaucer and the Subject of History.* Madison: University of Wisconsin Press, 1991.

Pegg, Mark Gregory. *The Corruption of Angels: The Great Inquisition of 1245–1246.* Princeton, NJ: Princeton University Press, 2001.

Peikola, Matti. "'And after all, myn Aue-Maria almost to the ende': *Pierce the Ploughman's Crede* and Lollard Expositions of the Ave Maria." *English Studies* 81 (2000): 273–92.

——. "Aspects of *Mise-en-page* in Manuscripts of the *Wycliffite Bible.*" In *Medieval Texts in Context,* edited by Graham D. Caie and Denis Renevey, 28–67. Oxford: Routledge, 2008.

——. *Congregation of the Elect: Patterns of Self-Fashioning in English Lollard Writings.* Turku: University of Turku, 2000.

——. "'First is writen a clause of the bigynnynge therof': The Table of Lections in Manuscripts of the Wycliffite Bible." *Boletín Millares Carlo* 24–25 (2005–6): 343–78.

Plamper, Jan. "The History of Emotions: An Interview with William Reddy, Barbara Rosenwein, and Peter Stearns." *History and Theory* 49 (2010): 237–65.

Pouzet, Jean-Pascal. "Book Production outside Commercial Contexts." In Gillespie and Wakelin, *Production of Books in England,* 212–38.

Powell, Sue. "Pastoralia and the Lost York Plays of the Creed and Paternoster." *European Medieval Drama* 8 (2004): 35–50.

Prescott, Anne Lake. "King David as a 'Right Poet': Sidney and the Psalmist." *English Literary Renaissance* 19 (1989): 131–51.

Rand, Kari Anne. *The Index of Middle English Prose, Handlist XX: Manuscripts in the Library of Corpus Christi College, Cambridge.* Woodbridge: Boydell and Brewer, 2009.

Raschko, Mary. "Common Ground for Contrasting Ideologies: The Texts and Contexts of *A Schort Reule of Lif.*" *Viator* 40 (2009): 387–410.

Raymo, Robert. "Works of Religious and Philosophical Instruction." In *A Manual of the Writings in Middle English, 1050–1500,* vol. 7, edited by Albert E. Hartung, 2255–2378, 2467–2582. New Haven: Connecticut Academy of Arts and Sciences, 1986.

Reddy, William M. *The Navigation of Feeling: A Framework for the History of Emotions.* Cambridge: Cambridge University Press, 2001.

Rex, Richard. *The Lollards.* New York: Palgrave, 2002.

——. "Which Is Wyche? Lollardy and Sanctity in Lancastrian London." In *Martyrs and Martyrdom in England, c. 1400–1700*, edited by Thomas S. Freeman and Thomas F. Mayer, 88–106. Woodbridge: Boydell, 2007.

Rice, Nicole R. *Lay Piety and Religious Discipline in Middle English Literature*. Cambridge: Cambridge University Press, 2008.

——. "A Defensive Devotion: A Lollard *Pore Caitiff* in British Library MS Harley 2322." Paper presented at the International Congress on Medieval Studies, Kalamazoo, MI, May 13–16, 2010.

Robbins, R. H. "The 'Arma Christi' Rolls." *Modern Language Review* 34 (1939): 415–21.

——. "Levation Prayers in Middle English Verse." *Modern Philology* 40 (1942–43): 131–46.

——. "Popular Prayers in Middle English Verse." *Modern Philology* 36 (1939): 337–50.

——. "Private Prayers in Middle English Verse." *Studies in Philology* 36 (1939): 466–75.

Rosenwein, Barbara H. *Emotional Communities in the Early Middle Ages*. Ithaca, NY: Cornell University Press, 2006.

——. "Worrying about Emotions in History." *American Historical Review* 107 (2002): 821–45.

Rouse, Richard H., and Mary A. Rouse. *Preachers, Florilegia, and Sermons: Studies on the "Manipulus Florum" of Thomas of Ireland*. Toronto: Pontifical Institute of Mediaeval Studies, 1979.

Salter, Elizabeth. *Popular Reading in English, c. 1400–1600*. Manchester: Manchester University Press, 2012.

Sanok, Catherine. *Her Life Historical: Exemplarity and Female Saints' Lives in Late Medieval England*. Philadelphia: University of Pennsylvania Press, 2007.

Scase, Wendy. "'*Heu! quanta desolatio Angliae praestatur*': A Wycliffite Libel and the Naming of Heretics, Oxford 1382." In Somerset, Havens, and Pitard, *Lollards and Their Influence*, 19–36.

——. "Imagining Alternatives to the Book: The Transmission of Political Poetry in Late Medieval England." In *Imagining the Book*, edited by Stephen Kelly and John J. Thompson, 237–50. Turnhout: Brepols, 2005.

——. *Piers Plowman and the New Anti-clericalism*. Cambridge: Cambridge University Press, 1989.

Schirmer, Elizabeth. "Canon Wars and Outlier Manuscripts: Gospel Harmony in the Lollard Controversy." *Huntington Library Quarterly* 73 (2010): 1–36.

——. "Reading Lessons at Syon Abbey: The *Myroure of Oure Ladye* and the Mandates of Vernacular Theology." In Olson and Kerby-Fulton, *Voices in Dialogue*, 345–76.

——. "William Thorpe's Narrative Theology." *Studies in the Age of Chaucer* 31 (2009): 267–99.

Schüssler, Rudolf. *Moral im Zweifel*. 2 vols. Paderborn: Mentis-Verlag, 2002–6.

Severs, J. Burke, ed. A *Manual of the Writings in Middle English, 1050–1500*. Vol. 1. New Haven: Connecticut Academy of Arts and Sciences, 1967.

Simpson, James. *The Index of Middle English Prose, Handlist VII: A Handlist of Manuscripts Containing Middle English Prose in Parisian Libraries*. Cambridge: Brewer, 1989.

——. *The Oxford English Literary History*. Vol. 2, *Reform and Cultural Revolution, 1350–1547*. Oxford: Oxford University Press, 2002.

Smail, Daniel Lord. *The Consumption of Justice: Emotions, Publicity, and Legal Culture in Marseille, 1264–1423*. Ithaca, NY: Cornell University Press, 2003.

Smalley, Beryl. *The Study of the Bible in the Middle Ages*. 3rd ed. Oxford: Blackwell, 1983.

——. "Use of the 'Spiritual' Senses of Scripture in Persuasion and Argument by Scholars in the Middle Ages." *Recherches de théologie ancienne et médiévale* 52 (1985): 44–63.

Smith, Lesley. "What Was the Bible in the Twelfth and Thirteenth Centuries?" In Lerner and Müller-Luckner, *Neue Richtungen in der hoch- und spätmittelalterlichen Bibelexegese*, 1–15.

Smith, Paul. "Could the Gospel Harmony *Oon of Foure* Represent an Intermediate Version of the Wycliffite Bible?" *Studia Neophilologica* 80 (2008): 160–76.

Snape, M. G. "Some Evidence of Lollard Activity in the Diocese of Durham in the Early Fifteenth Century." *Archaeologia Aeliana*, 4th ser., 39 (1961): 355–61.

Sneddon, Clive R. "The 'Bible du XIIIe siècle': Its Medieval Public in the Light of its Manuscript Tradition." In Lourdaux and Verhelst, *The Bible and Medieval Culture*, 127–40. Louvain: Louvain University Press, 1979.

Somerset, Fiona. "Afterword." In Bose and Hornbeck, *Wycliffite Controversies*, 319–33.

——. "'As just as is a squyre': The Politics of 'Lewed Translacion' in Chaucer's *Summoner's Tale*." *Studies in the Age of Chaucer* 21 (1999): 187–207.

——. "Censorship." In Gillespie and Wakelin, *Production of Books in England*, 239–58.

——. *Clerical Discourse and Lay Audience in Late Medieval England*. Cambridge: Cambridge University Press, 1998.

——. "Emotion." In *The Cambridge Companion to Christian Mysticism*, edited by Amy Hollywood and Patricia Z. Beckman, 294–304. Cambridge: Cambridge University Press, 2012.

——. "Excitative Speech: Theories of Emotive Response from Richard Fitzralph to Margery Kempe." In *The Vernacular Spirit: Essays on Medieval Religious Literature*, edited by Renate Blumenfeld Kosinski, Duncan Robertson, and Nancy Bradley Warren, 59–79. New York: Palgrave, 2002.

——. "Here, There, and Everywhere? Wycliffite Conceptions of the Eucharist and Chaucer's 'Other' Lollard Joke." In Somerset, Havens, and Pitard, *Lollards and Their Influence*, 127–38.

——. "Lollards, Devotion, and Knowledge from an English Perspective." In *Die Devotio Moderna*, edited by Iris Kwiatkowski and Jörg Engelbrecht, 141–55. Münster: Aschendorff, 2013.

——. "'Mark him wel for he is on of þo': Training the 'Lewed' Gaze to Discern Hypocrisy." *English Literary History* 68 (2001): 315–34.

——. "Textual Transmission, Variance, and Religious Identity among Lollard Pastoralia." In *Religious Controversy in Europe, 1378–1536: Textual Transmission and Networks of Readership*, edited by Michael Van Dussen and Pavel Soukup, 71–104. Turnhout: Brepols, 2013.

——. "Wycliffite Spirituality." In Barr and Hutchison, *Text and Controversy from Wyclif to Bale*, 375–86.

Somerset, Fiona, Jill C. Havens, and Derrick G. Pitard, eds. *Lollards and Their Influence in Late Medieval England*. Woodbridge: Boydell, 2003.

Spencer, H. Leith. *English Preaching in the Late Middle Ages*. Oxford: Clarendon Press, 1993.

——. "The Fortunes of a Lollard Sermon-Cycle in the Later Fourteenth Century." *Mediaeval Studies* 48 (1986): 352–96.

Summit, Jennifer. *Memory's Library: Medieval Books in Early Modern England*. Chicago: University of Chicago Press, 2008.

Szittya, Penn R. *The Antifraternal Tradition in Medieval Literature*. Princeton, NJ: Princeton University Press, 1986.

Thompson, John, ed. *Geographies of Orthodoxy: Mapping English Pseudo-Bonaventuran Lives of Christ, 1350–1550*. 2007–10. http://www.qub.ac.uk/geographies-of-orthodoxy/.

Thomson, John A. F. *The Later Lollards, 1414–1520*. Oxford: Oxford University Press, 1965.

Thomson, W. R. *The Latin Writings of John Wyclyf: An Annotated Catalog*. Toronto: Pontifical Institute of Mediaeval Studies, 1983.

Van Dussen, Michael. *From England to Bohemia: Heresy and Communication in the Later Middle Ages*. Cambridge: Cambridge University Press, 2012.

Van Engen, John. "The Christian Middle Ages as a Historiographical Problem." *American Historical Review* 91 (1986): 519–52.

——. "Multiple Options: The World of the Fifteenth-Century Church." *Church History* 77 (2008): 257–84.

——. *Sisters and Brothers of the Common Life: The Devotio Moderna and the World of the Later Middle Ages*. Philadelphia: University of Pennsylvania Press, 2008.

——. "Studying Scripture in the Early University." In Lerner and Müller-Luckner, *Neue Richtungen in der hoch- und spätmittelalterlichen Bibelexegese*, 17–38.

Visi, Tamás. "Introduction." In Doležalová and Visi, *Retelling the Bible*, 13–43.

Wack, Mary F. *Lovesickness in the Middle Ages: The Viaticum and Its Commentaries*. Philadelphia: University of Pennsylvania Press, 1990.

Watson, Nicholas. "Fashioning the Puritan Gentry-Woman: Devotion and Dissent in *Book to a Mother*." In *Medieval Women: Texts and Contexts in Late Medieval Britain; Essays for Felicity Riddy*, edited by Jocelyn Wogan-Browne et al., 169–84. Turnhout: Brepols, 2000.

——. "Lollardy: The Anglo-Norman Heresy?" In Wogan-Browne et al., *Language and Culture in Medieval Britain*, 334–46.

——. "Middle English Versions and Audiences of Edmund of Abingdon's *Speculum Religiosorum*." In *Texts and Traditions of Medieval Pastoral Care: Essays in Honour of Bella Millett*, edited by Cate Gunn and Catherine Innes-Parker, 115–31. Woodbridge: York Medieval Press, 2009.

Watts, John. "The Pressure of the Public on Later Medieval Politics." In *Political Culture in Late Medieval Britain*, edited by Linda Clark and Christine Carpenter, 159–80. Woodbridge: Boydell, 2004.

Wenzel, Siegfried. *Latin Sermon Collections from Later Medieval England*. Cambridge: Cambridge University Press, 2005.

——. "Robert Lychlade's Oxford Sermon of 1395." *Traditio* 53 (1998): 203–30.

Whitehead, Christiania. *Castles of the Mind: A Study of Medieval Architectural Allegory*. Cardiff: University of Wales Press, 2003.

Whitman, Jon, ed. *Interpretation and Allegory, Antiquity to the Modern Period*. Leiden: Brill, 2000.

Wilks, Michael. "Wyclif and the Great Persecution." In *Wyclif: Political Ideas and Practice; Papers by Michael Wilks*, edited by Anne Hudson, 179–203. Oxford: Oxbow Books, 2000.

Williams, Raymond. *The Country and the City*. London: Chatto and Windus, 1973.

———. *Keywords: A Vocabulary of Culture and Society*. Rev. ed. London: Fontana, 1983.

———. *Marxism and Literature*. Oxford: Oxford University Press, 1977.

Winstead, Karen. *John Capgrave's Fifteenth Century*. Philadelphia: University of Pennsylvania Press, 2006.

Wogan-Browne, Jocelyn, et al., eds. *Language and Culture in Medieval Britain: The French of England, c. 1100–c. 1500*. Woodbridge: York Medieval Press, 2009.